HEDDA GABLER AND O'

HENRIK IBSEN (1828–1906) is often called 'the Father of Modern Drama'. He was born in the small Norwegian town of Skien and made his debut as a writer with the three-act play *Catilina* (1850). Between 1851 and 1864 he was artistic director and consultant for theatres in Bergen and Christiania (later spelt Kristiania; now Oslo), and contributed strongly to a renewal of Norwegian drama, writing plays such as *The Vikings at Helgeland* (1858), *Love's Comedy* (1862) and *The Pretenders* (1863). In 1864 he left Norway on a state travel stipend and went to Rome with his wife Suzannah. This marked the beginning of what would become a 27-year-long voluntary exile in Italy and Germany. Ibsen experienced a critical and commercial success with the verse drama *Brand* (1866); this was followed by his other great drama in verse, *Peer Gynt* (1867), the prose play *The League of Youth* (1869) and his colossal *Emperor and Galilean* (1873), a 'world-historical play', also in prose. The next decisive turn in Ibsen's career came with *Pillars of the Community* (1877), the beginning of the twelve-play cycle of modern prose plays. Here he turned his attention to contemporary bourgeois life, rejecting verse for good. This cycle would include *A Doll's House* (1879), *Ghosts* (1881), *An Enemy of the People* (1882), *The Wild Duck* (1884), *Rosmersholm* (1886), *The Lady from the Sea* (1888), *Hedda Gabler* (1890), *The Master Builder* (1892), *Little Eyolf* (1894), *John Gabriel Borkman* (1896) and, finally, *When We Dead Awaken* (1899). By the time Ibsen returned to Norway in 1891, he had acquired Europe-wide fame, and his plays soon entered the canons of world literature and drama. Following a series of strokes, he died at home in Kristiania at the age of seventy-eight.

DEBORAH DAWKIN originally trained and worked as an actress and theatre director for ten years. She has worked as a translator from Norwegian to English for ten years in collaboration with Erik Skuggevik and independently, translating novels, short stories, cartoons, poetry and non-fiction. Her translation of Johan Harstad's *Buzz Aldrin, What Happened to You in All the*

Confusion? (2011) was longlisted for the Best Translated Book Award, 2012. With a particular interest in translation history, Deborah currently holds a Collaborative Doctoral Award with University College London and the British Library, researching the life and work of Ibsen translator Michael Meyer.

ERIK SKUGGEVIK has a background in theatre. He has worked as a translator from Norwegian to English for fifteen years. In collaboration with Deborah Dawkin, he has translated novels by Ketil Bjørnstad and Lars Ramslie and, over many years, the cartoon strip Nemi, as well as non-fiction works by Ingar Sletten Kolloen and Petter Aaslestad. He has been a lecturer in both Translation Studies and Intercultural Communication at the University of Surrey as well as a Norwegian teacher at University College London and the University of Oslo. He currently lectures in Interpreting Studies at Oslo University College.

MARTIN PUCHNER is the Byron and Anita Wien Professor of Drama and of English and Comparative Literature at Harvard University. His prize-winning books and anthologies range from philosophy to the arts, and his best-selling *Norton Anthology of World Literature* and his HarvardX online course have brought 4,000 years of literature to students across the globe. His most recent book, *The Written World*, tells the story of literature from the invention of writing to the Internet.

TORE REM is Professor of British Literature at the Department of Literature, Area Studies and European Languages, the University of Oslo. He has published extensively on British and Scandinavian nineteenth-century literature and drama, including the books *Henry Gibson/Henrik Ibsen* (2006) and *Ibsen, Scandinavia and the Making of a World Drama* (with Narve Fulsås, 2018), as well as on life writing, the history of the book, reception studies and world literature. Rem has been Christensen Visiting Fellow at St Catherine's College, Oxford, was director of the board of the Centre for Ibsen Studies and is a member of the Norwegian Academy of Science and Letters.

HENRIK IBSEN

Hedda Gabler
and Other Plays

Translated by DEBORAH DAWKIN
and ERIK SKUGGEVIK

Introduced by MARTIN PUCHNER

General Editor TORE REM

PENGUIN BOOKS

PENGUIN CLASSICS

UK | USA | Canada | Ireland | Australia
India | New Zealand | South Africa

Penguin Books is part of the Penguin Random House group of companies
whose addresses can be found at global.penguinrandomhouse.com.

Penguin
Random House
UK

First published by Penguin Classis 2019
002

Translation copyright © Deborah Dawkin and Erik Skuggevik, 2019
Introduction copyright © Martin Puchner, 2019
Other editorial materials copyright © Tore Rem, 2019

The moral right of the translators and authors of the editorial material has been asserted

Set in 10.25/12.25 pt Sabon LT Std
Typeset by Jouve (UK), Milton Keynes
Printed and bound in Great Britain by Clays Ltd, Elcograf S.p.A.

A CIP catalogue record for this book is available from the British Library

ISBN: 978-0-141-19457-8

Contents

Chronology

1828 Henrik Johan Ibsen born to Marichen and Knud Ibsen, a retailer and timber trader, in the town of Skien, 100 km south of Oslo (then Christiania).

1833 Starts school at Skien borgerskole (*borgerskoler* were schools for the bourgeoisie of the towns).

1835 Knud Ibsen is declared bankrupt. The family's property is auctioned off, and they move to the farm Venstøp in the parish of Gjerpen, just east of Skien.

1843 Travels to the coastal town of Grimstad, about 110 km south of Skien, where he is made apprentice in an apothecary's shop.

1846 Hans Jacob Hendrichsen is born to Else Sophie Jensdatter, the apothecary's maid, on 9 October. Ibsen accepts patrimony and is required to pay maintenance for the next fourteen years.

1849 Writes *Catilina*, his first play, as well as poetry, during the winter. Has his first poem, 'I høsten' ('In Autumn'), published in a newspaper at the end of September.

1850 Leaves Grimstad on 12 April, the publication date of *Catilina*. The play is published under the pseudonym Brynjulf Bjarme. Visits his family in Skien for the last time.

Goes to the capital, Christiania, where he sits the national high school exam in the autumn, but fails in arithmetic and Greek.

His first play to be performed, *Kjæmpehøien* (*The Burial Mound*), is staged at the Christiania Theater on 26 September.

1851 Starts the journal *Manden*, later *Andhrimner*, with friends. The famous violinist Ole Bull hires Ibsen for Det norske

Theater (the Norwegian Theatre), his new venture in Bergen. Ibsen begins as an apprentice, then becomes director and resident playwright. He agrees to write and produce one new play for the theatre every year.

1852 Spends over three months in Copenhagen and Dresden studying Danish and German theatre.

1853 *Sancthansnatten* (*St John's Night*) opens on 2 January, the founding date of Det norske Theater.

1855 *Fru Inger til Østeraad* (*Lady Inger of Ostrat*) performed at Det norske Theater on 2 January.

1856 First real success with *Gildet paa Solhoug* (*The Feast at Solhoug*) at Det norske Theater; the play is subsequently performed at the Christiania Theater and published as a book.
Becomes engaged to Suzannah Daae Thoresen.

1857 *Olaf Liljekrans* premieres at Det norske Theater to a disappointing reception.
Moves to Christiania during the summer and takes up the position of artistic director at the Kristiania Norske Theater (Kristiania Norwegian Theatre) from early September.
First performance outside Norway when *The Feast at Solhoug* is staged at the Kungliga Dramatiska Teatern (Royal Dramatic Theatre) in Stockholm in November.

1858 Marries Suzannah Thoresen in Bergen on 18 June.
Hærmændene paa Helgeland (*The Vikings at Helgeland*) has its first night at the Kristiania Norske Theater on 24 November and is met with a resoundingly positive response.

1859 A son, Sigurd Ibsen, is born to Suzannah and Henrik Ibsen on 23 December.
Writes the long poem 'Paa Vidderne' ('On the Moors') as a 'New Year's Gift' to the readers of the journal *Illustreret Nyhedsblad*.

1860–61 Ibsen accumulates private debt, owes taxes and is taken to court by creditors. He drinks heavily during this period, and the family has to move a number of times. He is criticized for his choice of repertory at the Kristiania Norske Theater.
His epic poem 'Terje Vigen' appears in *Illustreret Nyhedsblad*.

1862 The theatre goes bankrupt, and Ibsen is without regular employment.

Ethnographic expedition to the West of Norway in summer, collecting fairy tales and stories.

Publishes *Kjærlighedens Komedie* (*Love's Comedy*) in *Illustreret Nyhedsblad.*

1863 Employed as 'artistic consultant' at the Christiania Theater from 1 January and made able to pay off most of his debts. The first, short Ibsen biography published by his friend Paul Botten-Hansen in *Illustreret Nyhedsblad.* Applies for a state stipend in March, but is instead awarded a travel grant of 400 *spesidaler* (in 1870 a male teacher would earn around 250 *spesidaler* a year) for a journey abroad.

Kongs-Emnerne (*The Pretenders*) published in 1,250 copies in October.

1864 *The Pretenders* performed at the Christiania Theater on 17 January. A great success.

Ibsen leaves Norway on 1 April and settles in Rome.

1865 Writes *Brand* in Ariccia.

1866 The verse drama *Brand* is published in 1,250 copies by Ibsen's new publisher Gyldendal in Copenhagen on 15 March, with three more print runs before the end of the year. The play is Ibsen's real breakthrough, helping to secure financial stability.

Given an annual stipend of 400 *spesidaler* by the Norwegian government, plus a new travel grant.

1867 Writes the verse drama *Peer Gynt* on Ischia and in Sorrento. Published in 1,250 copies on 14 November, with a second, larger print run appearing just two weeks later.

1868 At the beginning of October moves to Dresden in Germany, where he lives for the next seven years.

1869 Travels to Stockholm for a Nordic meeting for establishing a common Scandinavian orthography. Publishes *De unges Forbund* (*The League of Youth*) in 2,000 copies on 30 September; the play is performed at the Christiania Theater on 18 October.

Travels from Marseilles to Egypt in October and participates as official guest in the festivities at the opening of the Suez Canal.

1871 *Digte* (*Poems*), his first and only collection of poetry, is published in 4,000 copies on 3 May.

The Danish critic Georg Brandes, the propagator of the so-called 'Modern Breakthrough', comes to Dresden and meets Ibsen for the first time.

1872 Edmund Gosse's article 'Ibsen's New Poems' appears in *The Spectator* in March.

1873 Gosse's 'Henrik Ibsen, the Norwegian Satirist' appears in *The Fortnightly Review* in January.

Travels to Vienna in June, as a member of the jury for fine art at the World Exhibition.

Kejser og Galilæer (*Emperor and Galilean*) published in 4,000 copies on 16 October; there is a new print run of 2,000 copies in December.

Love's Comedy performed at the Christiania Theater on 24 November.

1874 Ibsen and his family in Christiania from July to the end of September, his first visit since leaving Norway in 1864.

1875 *Catilina* published in revised edition to celebrate Ibsen's twenty-fifth anniversary as a writer.

The family moves from Dresden to Munich on 13 April.

1876 *Peer Gynt* receives its first performance at the Christiania Theater, with music composed by Edvard Grieg.

Emperor and Galilean translated by Catherine Ray, Ibsen's first translation into English.

The Vikings at Helgeland premieres at Munich's Hoftheater (Court Theatre) on 10 April, making it the first Ibsen production outside Scandinavia.

1877 Is made honorary doctor at the University of Uppsala in Sweden in September.

Samfundets støtter (*Pillars of the Community*) is published in 7,000 copies on 11 October and performed at the Danish Odense Teater on 14 November.

1878 Moves to Rome in September.

1879 Travels to Amalfi with his family in July and writes most of his new play, *Et Dukkehjem* (*A Doll's House*), there. Goes on to Sorrento and then Rome in September and moves back to Munich in October.

Edmund Gosse publishes *Studies in the Literature of Northern Europe*, devoting much space to Ibsen.

A Doll's House is published in 8,000 copies on 4 December and receives its premiere at Det Kongelige Teater (the Royal Theatre) in Copenhagen on 21 December.

1880 Ibsen returns to Rome in November.

Quicksands, an adaptation by William Archer of *Pillars of the Community*, at London's Gaiety Theatre, 15 December.

1881 Goes to Sorrento in June and writes most of *Gengangere* (*Ghosts*) there; the play is published in 10,000 copies on 13 December and is met with much harsh criticism, affecting subsequent book sales.

1882 First performance of *Ghosts* takes place in Chicago on 20 May.

Miss Frances Lord translates *A Doll's House* as *Nora*.

En folkefiende (*An Enemy of the People*) published in 10,000 copies on 28 November.

1883 *An Enemy of the People* first staged at the Christiania Theater on 13 January.

1884 *Breaking a Butterfly*, Henry Arthur Jones and Henry Herman's adaptation of *A Doll's House*, premieres at the Prince's Theatre, London, on 3 March.

Vildanden (*The Wild Duck*) is published in 8,000 copies on 11 November.

1885 First performance of *The Wild Duck* at Den Nationale Scene (the National Stage) in Bergen on 9 January.

First performance of *Brand* at the Nya Teatern (New Theatre) in Stockholm on 24 March.

Henrik and Suzannah Ibsen go to Norway in early June. They travel back via Copenhagen at the end of September, and in October settle in Munich again, where they live for the six following years.

Ghosts, translated by Miss Frances Lord, serialized in Britain in the socialist journal *To-Day*.

1886 *Rosmersholm* published in 8,000 copies on 23 November.

1887 A breakthrough in Germany with the production of *Ghosts* at the Residenz-Theater (Residency Theatre) in Berlin on 9 January.

Rosmersholm staged at Den Nationale Scene in Bergen on 17 January.

1888 Ibsen turns sixty. Celebrations in Scandinavia and Germany. Henrik Jæger publishes the first biography in book form.

Fruen fra havet (*The Lady from the Sea*) published in 10,000 copies on 28 November.

Newcastle-based Walter Scott publishes *Pillars of Society, and Other Plays* (it includes *Ghosts* and *An Enemy of the People*) under the editorship of the theatre critic William Archer and with an introduction by Havelock Ellis.

1889 *The Lady from the Sea* premieres both at the Hoftheater in Weimar and at the Christiania Theater on 12 February.

The production of *A Doll's House*, with Janet Achurch as Nora, at the Novelty Theatre in London on 7 June, marks his breakthrough in Britain. This production goes on a world tour.

Pillars of the Community is produced at London's Opera Comique.

1890 André Antoine produces *Ghosts* at the Théâtre Libre (Free Theatre) in Paris, leading to a breakthrough in France.

The Lady from the Sea translated into English by Karl Marx's youngest daughter, Eleanor.

Hedda Gabler published in 10,000 copies in Copenhagen on 16 December, with translations appearing in near-synchronized editions in Berlin, London and Paris.

1891 *Hedda Gabler* receives its first performance at the Residenz-Theater (Residency Theatre) in Munich on 31 January with Ibsen present. Competing English translations by William Archer and Edmund Gosse soon follow.

Several London productions of Ibsen plays, starting with *Rosmersholm* at the Vaudeville Theatre in February. In order to avoid censorship, *Ghosts* is given a private performance by the new Independent Theatre on 13 March, leading to a big public outcry. *Hedda Gabler* is produced under the joint management of Elizabeth Robins and Marion Lea in April, with Robins in the title role, and *The Lady from the Sea* follows in May.

George Bernard Shaw publishes his *The Quintessence of*

Ibsenism, based on his lectures to the Fabian Society in the preceding year.

Henry James publishes 'On the Occasion of *Hedda Gabler*' in *The New Review* in June.

Ibsen returns to Kristiania (as it was now written after the Norwegian spelling review of 1877) on 16 July and settles there for the remainder of his life. This year he befriends the pianist Hildur Andersen, thirty-six years his junior, often considered the model for Hilde Wangel in *The Master Builder*.

1892 *The Vikings at Helgeland* is performed in Moscow on 14 January.

William and Charles Archer translate *Peer Gynt* in a prose version.

Sigurd marries the daughter of Ibsen's colleague and rival Bjørnstjerne Bjørnson.

Bygmester Solness (*The Master Builder*) is published in 10,000 copies on 12 December.

1893 *The Master Builder* is first performed at the Lessingtheater in Berlin on 19 January. It is co-translated by William Archer and Edmund Gosse into English, and premieres at London's Trafalgar Square Theatre on 20 February.

The Opera Comique in London puts on *The Master Builder*, *Hedda Gabler*, *Rosmersholm* and one act from *Brand* between 29 May and 10 June.

An Enemy of the People is produced by Herbert Beerbohm Tree at the Haymarket Theatre on 14 June. Ibsen's first commercial success on the British stage.

F. Anstey (pseudonym for Thomas Anstey Guthrie) writes a series of Ibsen parodies called *Mr Punch's Pocket Ibsen*.

1894 *The Wild Duck* at the Royalty Theatre, London, from 4 May.

Lille Eyolf (*Little Eyolf*) is published in 10,000 copies on 11 December.

Two English verse translations of *Brand*, by C. H. Herford and F. E. Garrett.

1895 *Little Eyolf* is performed at the Deutsches Theater (German Theatre) in Berlin on 12 January.

1896 *Little Eyolf* at the Avenue Theatre in London from 23 November, in a translation by William Archer.

John Gabriel Borkman is published in 12,000 copies on 15 December.

1897 World premiere of *John Gabriel Borkman* at the Svenska Teatern (Swedish Theatre) and the Suomalainen Teaatteri (Finnish Theatre) on 10 January, both in Helsinki.

1898 Gyldendal in Copenhagen publishes a People's Edition of Ibsen's collected works.

Ibsen's seventieth birthday is celebrated in Kristiania, Copenhagen and Stockholm, and he receives greetings from all over Europe and North America.

1899 *Når vi døde vågner* (*When We Dead Awaken*), his last play, is published in 12,000 copies on 22 December.

1900 *When We Dead Awaken* is performed at the Hoftheater in Stuttgart on 26 January.

C. H. Herford translates *Love's Comedy*; William Archer translates *When We Dead Awaken*.

Ibsen suffers a first stroke in March, and his health deteriorates over the next few years.

James Joyce's 'Ibsen's New Drama' appears in *The Fortnightly Review* in April.

1903 Imperial Theatre, London, produces *When We Dead Awaken* on 25 January and *The Vikings at Helgeland* on 15 April.

1906 On 23 May Henrik Ibsen dies in his home in Arbins gate 1 in Kristiania.

The Collected Works of Henrik Ibsen, translated and edited by William Archer, appears in twelve volumes over the next two years.

Introduction

In 1884, the year Henrik Ibsen published the first of the plays collected in this volume, he was happily living in Rome, the city outside Norway he knew best. He had arrived here twenty years earlier, equipped with a government travel stipend and the ambition of becoming a full-time playwright. Since then, he had lived in Dresden and Munich in addition to Italy and made good on his original ambition. He had become a well-known, if rather controversial, dramatist, at least at home.

Becoming a playwright in exile was not easy because, in leaving Norway, Ibsen had also left behind the world of the theatre that had sustained his work. At the age of twenty-three, he had started out as an acting instructor and director at Det norske Theater (The Norwegian Theatre) in Bergen, moving on to Kristiania (now Oslo) six years later. He acquired an impressive amount of experience during these years, becoming what the French would call a man of the theatre. Along the way, he had learned every aspect of the trade, working with technicians and actors, thinking about the best use of theatrical spaces, designs and styles and anticipating the preferences of his audience for future seasons. His work in the theatre also exposed him to the dominant plays of the time, which were mostly Parisian exports, with their cleverly constructed clues and revelations, impeccable sense of pacing and neat, satisfying conclusions. Norway, at the time, was a theatre culture based on translations; perhaps this experience sparked Ibsen's later goal of reaching a larger, worldwide audience. For the time being, however, it drove him to seek out themes that were specific to Scandinavia's past, to set his own dramas apart from what was being imported from elsewhere.

But then, at the very moment of his first public success on the stage, he had decided to remove himself from the Norwegian theatre community. Perhaps he felt that the practical requirements of the theatre and the tastes of audiences were constraining his work. The first plays he wrote in Roman exile, *Brand*, *Peer Gynt* and the book-length *Emperor and Galilean*, amounting to 512 pages in the first edition, were so-called closet dramas, plays meant for reading only. Ibsen's visions were too grand for the theatre, both practically and aesthetically. His new plays were dramas of ideas that grappled with the loftiest religious and philosophical problems while roaming freely across time and space. It was hard to imagine a theatre, or an audience, that would have tolerated such effusions. Ibsen was declaring his independence from theatre.

Even though Ibsen had chosen exile from Norway – and from theatre – his readership was still predominantly Scandinavian, and it was growing, despite the difficult nature of these plays.[1] The print-runs of his works were phenomenal. *Brand*, the first play he published with the Copenhagen publisher Gyldendal, brought him a new level of success with the reading public (though not on stage, since the play was not meant to be performed). There had also been indications that Ibsen was gaining followers outside Scandinavia, not least in Germany. This exiled man of the theatre was set on a new career trajectory as an author of distinctly literary plays that were addressed to readers.

But just when his future career path seemed clear once more, he made yet another turn by deciding to return to writing for the stage. This time around, however, he would seek a way of combining the two, the ambition of his literary closet dramas and the requirements of the stage. In order to achieve this goal, he would set his future plays not in the remote past but in the present, and specifically in the world of his home audience. Of all of Ibsen's twists and turns, this would prove to be the one with the most lasting importance.

Ibsen's new plays, beginning with *The League of Youth*, were set in present-day Norway, and in a particular milieu consisting of lawyers, bankers, doctors, clergymen, newspaper editors and businessmen, in short, the Norwegian bourgeoisie. Ibsen's view of this group on the whole was not favourable. The four plays he wrote between 1877 and 1882 are relentless in their attacks on middle-class characters and the institutions they inhabit. Businessmen use their power to cover up their misdeeds, as in *Pillars of the Community*, whose sarcastic title announces Ibsen's aim of showing just how rotten those pillars really were. Ibsen returned to this theme in *An Enemy of the People*, a drama exposing the corruption surrounding a spa. In *A Doll's House*, lawyers and bankers come in for special treatment, always ready to cover up a crooked deal, while in *Ghosts*, it's the clergy that is both hypocritical and misguided, hiding sordid affairs and driving people into financial ruin. Ibsen reserved his harshest treatment for the institution of marriage. The enduring force of *A Doll's House* derives from Ibsen's harsh diagnosis of just how false and one-sided the traditional bourgeois marriage really was; he saw no solution but to dissolve it altogether.

If all Ibsen had done in these plays was expose the sins of the bourgeoisie, they would not have enjoyed such lasting success. In the course of chronicling corruption, he had stumbled on a more important theme: fear of social decline. Everywhere in his plays, bourgeois characters have a reputation to keep up, and not only because of social pressure. Their professions depend on reputation; it is the most important currency of this milieu, which means that loss of reputation is its ruling nightmare. The fear of losing a reputation is the stuff from which Ibsen forged his new plays.

The fear of scandal usually depends on events that have happened in the past. Ibsen's great insight was to realize that this meant the past was continually haunting the present, and he forged a dramatic form to suit this insight. To be sure, all plays have to introduce their characters to the audience, and this usually requires glimpses into their past. But usually exposition is used to launch characters on a path of action and interaction. Ibsen reversed the emphasis and devoted more attention to the gradual uncovering of the past. (The technique was not without precedents: Sophocles' *Oedipus* had done the same, as several contemporary critics recognized.) Sometimes, this involved exposing past scandals, from crooked business deals to illegitimate children. But Ibsen went further and included events that took place in previous generations. He called this power of the past over the present inheritance. Inheritance could mean, especially for his bourgeois characters, financial inheritance, but it could also mean moral inheritance. Ibsen's characters are forever suffering from the sins of their parents, usually through some sort of medical or psychological condition that has been passed down. His doctors are very good at diagnosing these conditions, but usually the actual mechanism of inheritance remains vague, since it is not a medical condition but a technique through which Ibsen makes visible just how much the past rules over our lives.

These new plays, *A Doll's House* (1879) and *Ghosts* (1881) chief among them, made Ibsen famous – and notorious. He was immediately denounced as a rabble rouser, a reformer, a suffragist, a radical seeking to shock the bourgeoisie out of its complacency. His plays were now performed not only at home but also abroad, especially in Germany, and the print runs of his plays increased.[2] He was able to live in Rome in comfortable circumstances. What would he write next? Which new turns would his art take? Which bourgeois hypocrisy would he attack now? Ibsen would provide answers to these questions with the four plays collected in the present volume.

The Wild Duck

Ibsen called his new play, first published in Copenhagen on 11 November 1884, *The Wild Duck*, and it has all the ingredients his audience had come to expect from him. There are hints here of shady business dealings involving illegal logging, for which only one of the two business partners has been punished. Will we witness the fall of the other, as we did in *Pillars of the Community*? The play revolves around a marriage, and there are strong suggestions that this marriage is built on deceptions every bit as deep as those in *A Doll's House*. The clue? An inherited eye disease. Will we witness another confrontation in which the truth will be forced out? Gregers, the son of the surviving businessman, seems ready to do Ibsen's work for him.

But halfway through the play, it becomes clear that we won't revisit the old business deal that ruined a reputation. As for the marriage, confronting the ignorant husband with the truth turns out to be a terrible mistake.

This surprising twist could mean only one thing: Ibsen had undertaken another change in direction. Perhaps it was his increasingly scandalous reputation as a critic of the bourgeoisie that made him want to surprise his critics. Ibsen had come to be associated with Dr Stockmann in *An Enemy of the People* (1882), the outspoken central character who exposes the truth about a spa town's contaminated water supply. Now it was as if he had turned the lens on himself. If they thought they had figured out his formula, he would prove them wrong. *The Wild Duck* would show them that he had other aims than merely to ferret out his characters' past misdeeds. This time it is Gregers, the character intent on exposing everything, who turns out to be the villain, or rather, the misguided idealist who can't deal with the complexities of everyday life. Ibsen turns to another doctor – in his plays, doctors often fulfil the role of the *raisonneur*, a character removed from the main action who explains and comments on it – to explain his thinking. The problem with insisting on the truth is that people sometimes need to be fed lies that allow them to go on living. Insisting on truth in all things is a juvenile shortcoming that must be cured.

Life-lies, as the doctor calls them, the lies that make life bearable, are particularly necessary for fragile male egos, of which there are several in this play (and all across Ibsen's oeuvre). One man must sustain the illusion that he is a great inventor and provider, when in fact his wife and daughter keep things going. Another one, excess-prone, must be fed the illusion that he is 'demonic', whatever that is supposed to mean, to absolve him from responsibility for having ruined his life. It was one of Ibsen's great insights that wounded male egos were a perfect way of diagnosing the fear and trembling of the bourgeoisie.

What gives this play its title is another illusion, one that is made visible right on stage: an elaborate contraption that turns an attic space into a wilderness, complete with live rabbits and birds. It is here that father and son go a-hunting, a substitute for the real wilderness which they have lost. Apparently, the illusion is good enough for them. At least they don't have to be tricked by others into it; they have convinced themselves and are content with the result. It is here, in this artificial wilderness, that the wild duck lives, the emblem of all the other illusions that abound in this play. Ibsen's surprise message is that such illusions are good. When they are shattered, blood will be spilled.

Usually, Ibsen set his realist plays in bourgeois homes with nice pianos, roaring fireplaces and lace curtains. In *The Wild Duck*, he gave his set designers a particularly interesting challenge, namely to use the stage as a place of illusion. *The Wild Duck* is a surprising play not only because it upends what audiences had come to expect from Ibsen; it is also a play that comes closest to commenting on theatre as a space of made-up artifice, though it does so, interestingly, through photography, which was generally regarded as a technology that guaranteed a new form of realism. In this play, however, it is shown to be every bit as artificial as theatre.[3] The central metaphor of the wild duck remains ambiguous as well. Different characters interpret it in different ways, all of them wrong. One such wrong interpretation will lead to a terrible death. Perhaps this turn to meta-theatre occurred because Ibsen used this play deliberately to interrupt a successful series of plays; it may be seen as a pause, an experiment in something new and therefore an occasion to reflect on the theatre itself. In Norway, it is frequently regarded as his greatest play, after *Peer Gynt*.

Rosmersholm

A year before the publication of his next play, *Rosmersholm* (1886), Ibsen had, in 1885, moved back to Munich, where he would live for the next six years. On the face of it, *Rosmersholm* returns us to the world of political rabble rousers we know from his earlier plays. Norway at this time finds itself in the grip of a new democratic wave that threatens the status quo. Belatedly, lawyers, doctors and all the other old families are forming an alliance to turn back this democratic tide by purchasing a newspaper. The aim is to fight for decency and Christian morals, and to denounce everyone else as freethinking perverts. The political fight pits former friends against each other, and we feel that Ibsen is back in his role as a social critic. Early on in the play, it becomes clear that the conservative bourgeoisie fights dirty and that Johannes Rosmer has gone over to the democratic side, disgusted with their tactics. We are now ready for one of those political showdowns that had characterized Ibsen's earlier work.

But *Rosmersholm* isn't just a return to the old formula. Even though the political fight that divides old friends takes up a lot of room, it isn't the play's central theme. Rather, Ibsen doubles down on the technique that he had employed in most of his earlier realist plays: the power of the past. The Rosmer family has a long history and reputation to keep up and suffers for it. But the past exerts its power in more nebulous ways as well. Rosmersholm is a haunted place from the very opening scene, when we are introduced to the white horse, an apparition mysteriously connected to the death of Rosmer's wife, presumably by her own hand.

The character with the biggest secret is Rebekka West, the former live-in companion of Rosmer's wife who has insinuated herself into the household. With West, Ibsen created a type to which he would return repeatedly, the coldly scheming *femme fatale* who blithely brings destruction to those around her. As so often in Ibsen, this lethal character is explained by a dark inheritance, including suggestions of incest, a theme Ibsen had also sounded in *Ghosts*.

Rebekka West isn't just a scheming woman with a past, she is also a woman with dangerous opinions about morality, a radical who deems herself beyond good and evil. Ibsen does not present her as his own political ideal. But nor does he dismiss her ideas as merely dangerous illusions, as had been the case in *The Wild Duck*. Rebekka West is an ambivalent heroine who ultimately abandons her scheming ways as the play takes a dark and unexpected turn at the end, when this calculating schemer finds herself in the grip of wild and uncontrollable forces that lead us to the play's dramatic conclusion.

In Rebekka West Ibsen created one of several characters that have become star vehicles for female actors, along with Nora Helmer in *A Doll's House*, Hedda Tesman in *Hedda Gabler* and Hilde Wangel in *The Master Builder*. Creating grand roles for female stars was one reason for Ibsen's success and for the enduring status of his plays. But his reach would go far beyond the stage.[4] In the twentieth century, the British freethinking writer Cicely Isabel Fairfield found Rebekka West, despite her destructive actions, so compelling that she adopted her name and henceforth published under the name Rebecca West.

Both Rosmer and Rebekka West refuse to be contained either by their political ideas or by their past, much as it haunts their present life. Rather, these characters are dissatisfied with the roles life has to offer and seek to escape from them at all cost. In *A Doll's House*, Nora had fled a repressive marriage out of desperation. In *Rosmersholm*, the political debates and even the uncovering of the past merely set the stage for the great flight from bourgeois life that takes place at the end.

The Lady from the Sea

Nordic mythology had always been an interest of Ibsen's; in 1862 he had gone off to western Norway to collect Nordic fairy tales and stories. He had let this topic take over his reading drama *Peer Gynt*, where he liberally populated the landscape with trolls and other mythological figures. (He also kept troll figures on his writing desk.) But many of Ibsen's putatively realist plays, with their solid bourgeois homes, have roots in folklore and mythology as well. Even *The Wild Duck*, Ibsen's most sceptical and ironic play, evokes the Flying Dutchman, the mythic figure who is condemned to roam the seas.

In no play are these mythological roots of Ibsen's work laid bare as fully as in *The Lady from the Sea* (first published on 28 November 1888, and premiered simultaneously in Kristiania and Weimar on 12 February 1889), which takes place in the world of mermaids and mysterious sailors. At first, all this seems harmless enough, nothing but material for a minor character, a would-be sculptor with a vivid imagination, or a painting. In his later plays, Ibsen increasingly used artists working in various media to compare them to his own ambitions. Some of them work in recent crafts, such as photography in *The Wild Duck*, perhaps to help Ibsen figure out how theatre might relate to this new technology. But more often Ibsen was interested in painters and sculptors. He must have felt an affinity to them; perhaps he wanted them to represent his own profession in the midst of the bankers, doctors and businessmen that otherwise dominate his plays.

But the artistic treatment of fairy tales and mythology is just the beginning, and, as the play progresses, mythology takes on increasingly disturbing forms. At first, *The Lady from the Sea* looks like yet another haunted play. It opens with a birthday party, but there seems to be some awkwardness around the question of who is actually being celebrated. It turns out it is a dead first wife whom the husband and his two daughters commemorate in this way, to the consternation of the second wife, who keeps herself apart from the family.

In the end, it is the second wife who is most fully in the thrall of the past. There is, once again, a hint of an inherited disease when it is revealed that her mother had died mad. But for Ibsen, illness, especially inherited illness, had long ceased being a medical condition, despite the prevalence of doctors in his plays, and become part of his own mythology. This is most explicitly so in *The Lady from the Sea*. Speaking about the second wife, Mrs Wangel, one character explains her erratic behaviour medically: 'That's presumably a result of her frail state of mind.' But her husband knows better. 'It isn't just that. At its deepest level it's innate in her. Ellida belongs to the sea-people. That's the thing.'

There have been hints from the beginning that Ellida is different. She has never fitted in with the comfortable bourgeois home and its rich traditions. The water in the bay, the air, none of this is right for her; she longs for and belongs to the sea. And so she withers, another Ibsen character trapped in a false life, dreaming of escape.

Ellida's longing may be innate, but there is, as always, a backstory. It involves a strange sailor, another Flying Dutchman, who encountered Ellida ten years earlier and believes that the two are married. Not in a regular marriage, mind you. They have exchanged rings in a kind of water-ceremony, and ever since, the sailor and Ellida have shared this secret bond, even after Ellida has got married in an official, land-based ceremony to Dr Wangel. But now the sailor appears again, and Ellida must choose between the two.

Ibsen's plays contain sub-plots that cast additional light on the play's main theme, often in a lower register (something he might have learned from Shakespeare). This is the case with marriage in *The Lady from the Sea*. While we're drawn into an increasingly mythological world of the sea, minor characters, above all the wannabe sculptor, present their own idea about marriage: the wife should aid the husband and live for his art. This is a clear case of a traditional marriage that is every bit as false as Nora's in *A Doll's House*. With this marriage, at least, we know where to stand, even as the question of land versus sea in the main plot remains open to the very end. Despite all these fundamental conflicts, the play ends on a surprisingly harmonious note, perhaps because the play, or rather, its male characters, allow Ellida a choice rather than force her into taking flight.

Hedda Gabler

If it looked as if Ibsen was drifting deeper and deeper into folklore and mythology, he once again had a surprise for his audience: his next play, *Hedda Gabler*, contains no hint of them. No Flying Dutchman, no mysterious sailor, no mermaids, no white horse, or any other ghost. Perhaps Ibsen felt that he was on a track that would lead him back to *Peer Gynt*, or he feared that Nordic themes would not work as well on the Continent, where he was finding increasingly ardent followers. Be that as it may, *Hedda Gabler* is set fully and entirely in a bourgeois home, and Ibsen decided to devote all his powers to analysing its components.

Hedda Gabler premiered in Munich, on 31 January 1891. Before that, it had been printed and published in Copenhagen on 16 December 1891 for Ibsen's significant reading public. In fact, the play was available in several places at once (it was actually first published in Dano-Norwegian in London to secure English rights),[5] part of the new pattern of synchronized launches that Ibsen now enjoyed.

Ibsen begins with the setting. The drawing room is even more elaborately furnished than is usually the case in his plays (even *The Wild Duck*, which is set in a poverty-stricken attic, opens with a lavishly furnished room at another house).

A fine, spacious and tastefully furnished drawing room, decorated in dark colours. On the back wall is a wide doorway with heavy curtains that are pulled back. This doorway leads into a smaller room presented in the same style as the drawing room. On the wall to the right, there are double folding doors, which lead to the hallway. On the opposite wall, to the left, is a glass door, also with curtains pulled back. Through it can be seen a section of a roofed veranda and trees covered with autumn leaves. Towards the centre of the room is an oval table covered with a tablecloth and surrounded by chairs. Further forward, by the right-hand wall, are a wide porcelain wood stove, a tall armchair, a footstool with a cushion and two stools. In the right-hand corner, at the back, is a corner sofa and a small round table. To the front left, a little out from the wall, is a sofa. Opposite the glass door stands a piano. On either side of the doorway at the back sets of shelves contain terracotta and majolica ware. Looking into the inner room, we see a sofa, a table and a couple of chairs against the back wall. Over the sofa hangs a portrait of a handsome older gentleman in a general's uniform. Over the table hangs a ceiling lamp with an opaque, milky-white glass shade. Distributed around the drawing room are a number of bouquets of flowers arranged in china and glass vases. Other bouquets are lying on the tables. The floors in both rooms have thick carpets. Morning light. The sun shines in through the glass door.

Even for Ibsen, this is a bit much. It is almost as if he's back in his early theatre days, giving detailed instructions to carpenters, tailors and set designer before the play has even begun. At the same time, this extensive description reads like something out of a contemporary novel, perhaps a result of the fact that Ibsen knew he was addressing two audiences at once, those in the theatre and those reading his plays at home. (Extensive stage directions addressed at a reading public would soon become a hallmark of modern drama, especially at the hands of George Bernard Shaw and Eugene O'Neill.) As soon as the play opens, this elaborate stage machinery cranks into action. Hedda doesn't like direct sunlight, so the curtains have to be drawn; the piano is nice, but its style doesn't fit with the rest of the apartment, so a second piano will have to be purchased. In this home, everything has to be perfect.

The problem is money. Pretty soon we figure out that these elaborate furnishings are bought on credit. A pair of poor aunts mortgaged their annuity as surety for the loan, and Judge Brack, a somewhat shady character, helped the newly married couple to make some other, more complicated financial arrangement. Bourgeois life depends on credit, credit depends on reputation, and reputation ensures trust in future earnings. In *A Doll's House*, Nora's husband, a banker, knows this only too well; this is why he panics when his reputation is under threat. In *Hedda Gabler*, the two protagonists, the historian Tesman and his wife, Hedda, are much less financially savvy, and will suffer for it.

All this credit economy is not a problem because Tesman has been promised a professorship, and it is based on that promise that the elaborate furnishings, even the house itself, is paid for. This, after all, is how Hedda needs to live. In fact, the furnishings are just the beginning. Soon, there will be liveried servants attending to elegant guests, for Hedda intends to turn her home into the centre of the social world.

This is the beginning of the money plot, which Ibsen had used so successfully in *A Doll's House*. Inevitably, the promised professorship is suddenly less certain when a rival scholar turns up. He is a wild character – he goes on drinking rampages and ends up in shady establishments – and has consequently disgraced himself. But when the play opens, Eilert Løvborg has cleaned up his act and just come out with a bold book about the development of culture. In fact, Tesman has just picked it up from the bookstore and is amazed by its sweep. Tesman is a historian as well, of course, but of a very different sort. He has a narrowly circumscribed specialty, the domestic crafts of Brabant during the Middle Ages. Needless to say, Hedda Gabler will have nothing to do with such a topic, and is nonplussed when her husband uses their honeymoon – another big expense – for archival research (perhaps Ibsen was thinking of Casaubon, the dedicated scholar in George Eliot's novel *Middlemarch*). But we don't need to be Hedda Gabler to feel that the domestic crafts of Brabant, a region in the Low Countries, can hold little interest. Even Tesman himself doesn't seem particularly taken with his topic; in any case, he isn't making much progress with it.

The problem of money hangs over the entire play as we begin to fear that the lavishly furnished house may be taken away by creditors at any moment. But that is not all. Gradually we learn that the house was the founding myth of the marriage between Tesman and Hedda. They had talked about it when they first met, and the idea of living there in high style was what fuelled the marriage. Imagine our surprise when we learn that Hedda Gabler never even liked the house in the first place. She kept mentioning it only out of sheer boredom, for lack of anything better to say during her painful courtship with the awkward Tesman (the home crafts of Brabant not being a suitable topic of conversation).

But why did Hedda marry him? She got tired of dancing. She also had an idea that it would be fancy to be the wife of a professor (in due course, she will see the folly of this belief). As the daughter of a general, she enjoys quasi-aristocratic status, lording it over the other characters with their embroidered slippers and cheap hats. She picked Tesman based on some vague promises and, really, on a whim.

This may or may not be the entire story because Hedda Gabler is, above all, an enigma. Like Rebekka West in *Rosmersholm*, she is calculating and cold as well as wilful and capricious, playing with those around her for sheer fun. In this, she is more extreme than Rebekka West, who knew exactly what she wanted but found that it left her unsatisfied. Hedda Gabler doesn't seem to have a particular end in mind, which is why there remains something incomprehensible about her, incomprehensible but dangerous, for she is equipped with a pair of pistols, apparently her sole inheritance. She likes using them, and in any case, Ibsen knew – as any good playwright knows – that if you introduce pistols in the first act, they must go off in the last.

Ibsen didn't include any artists in this play, but his title heroine comes close: she speaks the language of beauty, perhaps because she herself is beautiful. This is why she is so particular about her furnishings and about the light. But her sense of beauty, that life must be beautiful, extends much further, and she even manages to infect others with it. Everything must be beautiful – even death.

In Hedda Gabler, Ibsen created his most enduring role. It allows actors to show off, to switch from playful bantering to steely calculation at the drop of a hat, and to dominate those around them. Above all, it allows actors to explore the hidden depth of this character, who never fully knows her own mind and who becomes increasingly bold, even brave, at the end. It is, perhaps, the single most challenging and rewarding role for an actress in all of dramatic literature, and the reason why *Hedda Gabler* has remained near the top of the Ibsen repertoire.

World Literature

The four plays collected in this volume were written during the period of Ibsen's life when he was in the process of transforming himself from a well-regarded Norwegian dramatist to a member of a much more exclusive club: world literature. For an author with a starting point in a language understood by just over four million people at the northern periphery of Europe, counting both Norway and Denmark, this was a most unlikely achievement. Ibsen, determined and always ready to try out something new, deserves much of the credit. But he was also lucky in that he was writing at a time when the idea – and the reality – of world literature was taking shape.

The term had been coined sixty years earlier by Johann Wolfgang von Goethe, on 31 January 1827, a year before the birth of Ibsen. Goethe had been talking to his secretary, Johann Peter Eckermann, reporting on his recent reading experiences.[6] Goethe was, of course, an avid reader of French literature, which dominated the literary world, including the theatre. Like Ibsen, Goethe was the manager of a theatre and therefore keenly aware of this dependence on France. In addition to French, Goethe had been an enthusiastic reader of Greek and Roman literature, which became a life-long passion that induced him to travel to Rome, a path Ibsen would later follow.

But these literatures of Europe were not enough for Goethe. Living in a provincial town in eastern Germany, far from the metropolitan centres of Europe, Goethe became increasingly unhappy with being on the receiving end of French exports and began to look for alternatives. For a time, he turned to England and adopted Shakespeare as an antidote to French literature. Another alternative to France would have been nationalism, with Goethe presenting himself as representative of a genuine German culture. Increasingly, those around him were doing just that. But Goethe chose not to pursue this path (though he was later pressed into national service). Instead, he chose world literature. World literature for him was a third way, different from both metropolitan imports and reactive nationalism.

The idea of world literature suggested itself to Goethe in part because of a changing literary marketplace. Even though he was living in a small town, numbering barely 7,000 people, at the semi-periphery of Europe, he had access to an increasingly wide range of literature hailing from the remotest times and places. Thanks to translators who profited from or were active participants in European colonialism, Goethe was able to read works of Sanskrit drama, such as Kalidasa's *Shakuntala*, as well as Persian and Arabic poetry. He was so taken with one such poet, Hafez, that he composed an entire collection of poems as a response, his *West-Eastern Divan*. He also started to read Chinese novels.[7] It was a Chinese novel that prompted him, on that fateful January afternoon in 1827, to observe to his startled secretary that the time of national literature was over, and that the era of world literature had begun.

Goethe, who was already quite old when he used the term, returned to the theme of world literature on a few subsequent occasions, but he never fully developed it. Next to pick it up was an unlikely pair of collaborators, Karl Marx and Friedrich Engels, who mention it in their Communist Manifesto, where it appears at the end of a stirring paragraph describing the creative destructions brought by bourgeois capitalism.[8] Marx and Engels emphasize that this increasingly global form of capitalism pulls the rug out from under the feet of the feudal order by creating a global market in which any hope of national autonomy is futile.

Strangely, at this point in their argument, Marx and Engels have nothing bad to say about capitalism; instead they seem to cheer it on. There is nothing better, it would seem, for this pair of radicals, than the spectacle of 'national one-sidedness' being forced into commerce with the remotest corners of the globe. It is at the stirring climax of this story that they move from material products to immaterial ones. 'The intellectual creations of individual nations become common property. National one-sidedness and narrow-mindedness become more and more impossible, and from the numerous national and local literatures there arises a world literature.'[9]

Marx and Engels's interest in world literature may be surprising, but it actually picked up on something Goethe had recognized as well: the emergence of a global market in literature. What Goethe, Marx and Engels glimpsed was finally becoming a reality towards the end of the nineteenth century, just when Ibsen was gaining prominence. Even though Ibsen was still drawing most of his royalties from Scandinavia (in part because of a lack of international copyright protections), now his plays were being translated almost immediately into other languages, especially in England, the US and Germany, with additional demand in France and Italy.[10] Ibsen was Goethe's idea of world literature come true: a peripheral author who could hold his own against

French metropolitan domination by appealing to an international market.

In achieving this status, Ibsen was aided by literary critics. The English Edmund Gosse devoted significant attention to Ibsen in a book on the literature of northern Europe; George Bernard Shaw, particularly taken with the early plays of Ibsen's realist period, hailed him as a fellow radical; William Archer, his most important translator into English, was attuned to Ibsen's poetic imagination; even Henry James spoke extremely highly of the Norwegian playwright. Equally important was the Danish critic Georg Brandes, who had taken up Goethe's mantle as promoter of world literature. He counted Ibsen among the handful of authors responsible for the 'modern breakthrough', as he called it, whose hallmark was realism. These different critics saw in Ibsen's work what they each valued most: freethinking ideas; poetic flights of fancy; psychological insight; and realism. Remarkably, they were all right. Ibsen's many surprising changes in emphasis and direction had created an oeuvre that was varied and multi-faceted, reflecting different perspectives and ideas.

Ibsen was at the forefront of what has been called the 'Scandinavian moment in world literature', which would include authors from August Strindberg to Knut Hamsun as well as the creation of the Nobel Prize in Literature, endowed by the Swedish inventor of dynamite.[11] Of the three writers, only the youngest, Hamsun, would ever receive the Nobel Prize because the Prize was initially in the hands of critics who rejected the realism associated with Ibsen and Strindberg. But the Nobel Prize itself, the fact that the Swedish Academy managed to acquire its status as the epicentre of the literary world, was connected to the confluence of forces that produced writers such as Ibsen, Strindberg and Hamsun as well as critics such as Brandes. The late nineteenth century turned out to be not only the Scandinavian moment in world literature, but also the moment when world literature, for the first time, was becoming a reality.

For Ibsen, being a world author was not an unmitigated good. The rough and tumble theatre industry didn't respect the work of this famous writer, who had to watch theatre managers butcher his work over and over again. Notoriously, a German

theatre director forced Ibsen to write an alternative ending for
A Doll's House, one in which the heroine, after her argument
with her husband, is shown her children and collapses, not
leaving.[12] Faced with the question of letting someone else write
that ending or doing the painful work himself, Ibsen chose the latter, hoping to limit the damage. Italian translations were often
worse in that they treated Ibsen's written texts as polite suggestions and took all kinds of liberties with them, seemingly
unaware that anyone might object.[13]

But despite these travails, Ibsen's work remained tied to the
theatre, the métier in which he had grown up. In time, he was
seen as the playwright who had restored a new seriousness to
an art form that many had come to associate with frivolous
plots, overwrought emotions and cheap effects. Ibsen's rise
coincided not only with the emergence of world literature, but
also with modern drama, that is, with the hope of turning
theatre into a higher art. Shunning large theatres, some play-
wrights and directors in Europe, North America and elsewhere
withdrew to smaller stages where they could experiment with
new styles ranging from naturalism, with its particular attention to setting, to symbolism, with its preference for atmosphere
and mysteries. Ibsen's plays, which had always retained a layer
of meaning that went beyond strict realism, were well suited to
all of these theatrical experiments, though they continued to
be regarded as mainstream in Norway.

And so it has lasted until today. Ibsen's great female roles
and his multi-layered plays have exhibited astonishing staying
powers. But perhaps the most important vehicle for propelling
Ibsen to the pinnacle of the dramatic world, second only to
Shakespeare, has to do with his great theme: the fears and
fantasies of the bourgeoisie. Even though he set his realist plays
in Norway, they struck home wherever a bourgeoisie existed,
and this meant, increasingly, all over the world. In chronicling
the fantasy life of the bourgeoisie, Ibsen became the great poet
of capitalism.[14]

Martin Puchner

NOTES

1. See Narve Fulsås and Tore Rem, *Ibsen, Scandinavia and the Making of a World Drama* (Cambridge: Cambridge University Press, 2018).
2. Ibid., pp. 71ff.
3. For a discussion of meta-theatre and its relation to the visual arts in Ibsen, see Toril Moi, *Henrik Ibsen and the Birth of Modernism: Art, Theater, Philosophy* (Oxford: Oxford University Press, 2006), pp. 248ff.
4. For a detailed discussion on the role of actors in the cultural transmission of Ibsen's plays, exemplified in *A Doll's House*, see Julie Holledge, Jonathan Bollen, Frode Helland and Joanne Tompkins, *A Global Doll's House: Ibsen and Distant Visions* (London: Palgrave Macmillan, 2016), pp. 26ff.
5. Fulsås and Rem, *Ibsen*, pp. 194.
6. Johann Peter Eckermann, *Gespräche mit Goethe in den letzten Jahren seines Lebens*, vols. 1 and 2 (Leipzig: Brockhaus, 1836), vol. 2, p. 325.
7. Bishop Thomas Percy, *Hau Kiou Choaan or The Pleasing History: A Translation from the Chinese Language* (London, 1761).
8. Karl Marx and Friedrich Engels, *The Communist Manifesto and Other Writings*, with an introduction and notes by Martin Puchner (New York: Barnes and Noble, 2005), pp. 10–11.
9. Ibid.
10. On Ibsen and copyright, see Fulsås and Rem, *Ibsen*, pp. 175ff.
11. On the Scandinavian moment in world literature, see Fulsås and Rem, *Ibsen*, p. 240. On the Nobel Prize, see James F. English, *The Economy of Prestige: Prizes, Awards, and the Circulation of Cultural Value* (Cambridge, Mass.: Harvard University Press, 2008).
12. Christian Janss, 'When Nora Stayed: More Light on the German Ending', *Ibsen Studies* 17, no. 1 (2017), pp. 3–27.
13. Giuliano D'Amico, *Domesticating Ibsen for Italy: Enrico and Icilio Polese's Ibsen Campaign* (Turin: Università degli Studi di Torino, 2013).
14. Franco Moretti, *The Bourgeois: Between History and Literature* (London: Verso, 2013), pp. 169ff.

Further Reading

Book Studies and Articles in English

Aarseth, Asbjørn, *Peer Gynt and Ghosts* (Basingstoke: Macmillan, 1989).

Anderman, Gunilla, *Europe on Stage: Translation and Theatre* (London: Oberon, 2005).

Binding, Paul, *With Vine-Leaves in His Hair: The Role of the Artist in Ibsen's Plays* (Norwich: Norvik Press, 2006).

Bloom, Harold (ed.), *Henrik Ibsen*, Modern Critical Views (Philadelphia: Chelsea House, 1999).

Bryan, George B., *An Ibsen Companion* (Westport, Conn.: Greenwood Press, 1984).

de Figueiredo, Ivo, *Henrik Ibsen: The Man and the Mask*, trans. Robert Ferguson (London: Yale University Press, 2019).

Durbach, Errol (ed.), *Ibsen and the Theatre* (London: Macmillan, 1980).

—— *'Ibsen the Romantic': Analogues of Paradise in the Later Plays* (London: Macmillan, 1982).

Egan, Michael (ed.), *Henrik Ibsen: The Critical Heritage* (London: Routledge, 1997 (1972)).

Ewbank, Inga-Stina et al (eds.), *Anglo-Scandinavian Cross-Currents* (Norwich: Norvik Press, 1999).

Fischer-Lichte, Erika et al. (eds.), *Global Ibsen: Performing Multiple Modernities* (London: Routledge, 2011).

Fulsås, Narve, 'Ibsen Misrepresented: Canonization, Oblivion, and the Need for History', *Ibsen Studies* 11, no. 1 (2011), pp. 3–20.

—— and Tore Rem, *Ibsen, Scandinavia and the Making of a World Drama* (Cambridge: Cambridge University Press, 2018).

Gjesdal, Kristin (ed.), *Ibsen's Hedda Gabler: Philosophical Perspectives* (Oxford: Oxford University Press, 2018).

Goldman, Michael, *Ibsen: The Dramaturgy of Fear* (New York: Columbia University Press, 1999).

Helland, Frode, *Ibsen in Practice* (London: Methuen, 2015).

Holledge, Julie, Jonathan Bollen, Frode Helland and Joanne Tompkins, *A Global Doll's House: Ibsen and Distant Visions* (London: Palgrave Macmillan, 2016).

Ibsen, Henrik, *Ibsen on Theatre*, ed. Frode Helland and Julie Holledge (London: Nick Hern Books, 2018).

Innes, Christopher (ed.), *Henrik Ibsen's Hedda Gabler: A Sourcebook* (London: Routledge, 2003).

Johnston, Brian, *The Ibsen Cycle* (University Park, Pa.: Pennsylvania University Press, 1992).

Ledger, Sally, *Henrik Ibsen*, Writers and Their Work (Tavistock: Northcote House, 2010 (1999)).

Lyons, Charles R. (ed.), *Critical Essays on Henrik Ibsen* (Boston, Mass.: G. K. Hall, 1987).

—— *Henrik Ibsen: The Divided Consciousness* (Carbondale, Ill.: Southern Illinois University Press, 1972).

McFarlane, James (ed.), *The Cambridge Companion to Ibsen* (Cambridge: Cambridge University Press, 1994).

—— *Ibsen and Meaning* (Norwich: Norvik Press, 1989).

Malone, Irina Ruppo, *Ibsen and the Irish Revival* (Basingstoke: Palgrave, 2010).

Meyer, Michael, *Henrik Ibsen* (abridged edition) (London: Cardinal, 1992 (1971)).

Moi, Toril, *Henrik Ibsen and the Birth of Modernism: Art, Theater, Philosophy* (Oxford: Oxford University Press, 2006).

Moretti, Franco, *The Bourgeois: Between History and Literature* (London: Verso, 2013).

Northam, John, *Ibsen's Dramatic Method: A Study of the Prose Dramas* (Oslo: Universitetsforlaget, 1971 (1953)).

Puchner, Martin, 'Goethe, Marx, Ibsen and the Creation of a World Literature', *Ibsen Studies* 13, no. 1 (2013), pp. 28–46.

Rem, Tore, '"The Provincial of Provincials": Ibsen's Strangeness and the Process of Canonisation', *Ibsen Studies* 4, no. 2 (2004), pp. 205–26.

Sandberg, Mark B., *Ibsen's Houses* (Cambridge: Cambridge University Press, 2015).

Shepherd-Barr, Kirsten, *Ibsen and Early Modernist Theatre, 1890–1900* (Westport, Conn.: Greenwood Press, 1997).

Templeton, Joan, *Ibsen's Women* (Cambridge: Cambridge University Press, 1997).

Törnqvist, Egil, *Ibsen: A Doll's House* (Cambridge: Cambridge University Press, 1995).

Williams, Raymond, *Drama from Ibsen to Brecht* (Harmondsworth: Penguin, 1974).

Digital and Other Resources

IbsenStage is an extremely valuable performance database: http://ibsenstage.hf.uio.no.

Ibsen.nb is a website with much useful information on Ibsen and on Ibsen productions worldwide: http://ibsen.nb.no/id/83.0.

Henrik Ibsens Skrifter is the new critical edition of Ibsen's complete works. So far only available in Norwegian: http://www.ibsen.uio.no/forside.xhtml.

Ibsen Studies is the leading Ibsen journal.

A Note on the Text

This Penguin edition is the first English-language edition based on the new historical-critical edition of Henrik Ibsen's work, *Henrik Ibsens Skrifter* (2005–10) (*HIS*). The digital edition (*HISe*) is available at http://www.ibsen.uio.no/forside.xhtml. The texts of *HIS* are based on Ibsen's first editions.

THE WILD DUCK

A Play in Five Acts

CHARACTERS

MR WERLE, *owner of the Works, etc.*
GREGERS WERLE, *his son*
OLD MR EKDAL
HJALMAR EKDAL, *Old Mr Ekdal's son,*
photographer[1]
GINA EKDAL, *Hjalmar's wife*
HEDVIG, *their daughter, fourteen years of age*[2]
MRS[3] SØRBY, *Mr Werle's housekeeper*
RELLING, *a doctor*
MOLVIK, *an ex-theologian*
GRÅBERG, *a bookkeeper*
PETTERSEN, *Mr Werle's servant*
JENSEN, *a hired servant*
A FAT PALE-FACED GENTLEMAN
A THIN-HAIRED GENTLEMAN, A NEAR-SIGHTED
GENTLEMAN, SIX OTHER GENTLEMEN,
dinner guests at Mr Werle's
OTHER HIRED SERVANTS

The first act takes place at Mr Werle's house,
the next four at Hjalmar Ekdal's home.

ACT ONE

In Mr Werle's house. An expensively and comfortably furnished study; book cabinets and upholstered furniture; writing desk covered with papers and files in the middle of the room; lamps with green shades give the room a soft light. On the back wall are open folding doors with drapes drawn back. Inside, a large, elegant living room can be seen, brightly lit with lamps and candelabras. To the front of the study on the right a small baize-covered door, which blends with the wallpaper, leads to the offices. To the front left a fireplace with glowing coals, and further back a double door to the dining room.

Mr Werle's manservant PETTERSEN, *dressed in livery, and* JENSEN, *a hired servant dressed in black, are preparing the study. In the larger living room two or three other hired servants are busy arranging and lighting candles. The hum of conversation and laughter can be heard from within the dining room; a glass is tapped with a knife; silence follows; a toast is made; shouts of bravo and then again the hum of conversation.*

PETTERSEN [*lights a lamp on the mantelpiece and places a shade over it*]: Just listen to that, Jensen! The old codger's stood at the table now, proposing a long toast to Mrs Sørby.

JENSEN [*sets out an armchair*]: Is it true, what they say, that there's something between them?

PETTERSEN: Devil knows.

JENSEN: 'Cos I reckon he was a right billy goat in his day.

PETTERSEN: Maybe.

JENSEN: They say he's holding this dinner party for his son.

PETTERSEN: Yes. His son came home yesterday.

JENSEN: I never knew Mr Werle had a son.

PETTERSEN: Oh, he's got a son all right. But he's mostly stuck up there at the Høidal Works.[4] He's not been in town all the years I've served in this house.

A MANSERVANT [*in the doorway of the adjoining room*]: Pettersen, sir, there's some old blighter here, who's –

PETTERSEN [*mumbles*]: Oh hell, is someone coming here *now*!
Old EKDAL *appears from the right of the living room. He is dressed in a threadbare coat with a high collar; woollen fingerless gloves; in his hand a stick and a fur hat; under his arm a packet wrapped in brown paper. A dirty, red-brown wig and small grey moustache.*

PETTERSEN [*walks towards him*]: Christ almighty – what are *you* doing in here?

EKDAL [*by the door*]: Urgently need to get in the office, Pettersen.

PETTERSEN: The office closed an hour ago –

EKDAL: Was told that at the gate, old chap. But Gråberg's still in there. Please, Pettersen, let me slip in *that* way. [*Points to the baize door*] I've gone in that way before.

PETTERSEN: All right, you'll have to, I s'pose. [*Opens the door*] But be sure to go out the right way after; we've got visitors.

EKDAL: I know that – hmm! Thanks, Pettersen, old friend! You're a real pal. Thanks. [*Mutters quietly*] Dunderhead!
He goes into the office; PETTERSEN *closes the door after him.*

JENSEN: Is *he* office staff too?

PETTERSEN: No, he's just someone who does a bit of extra copy work when they need it. Mind you, he was a fine chap in his time, old Ekdal.

JENSEN: Yes, he has a certain something about him.

PETTERSEN: That's right. He was a lieutenant you know.

JENSEN: Blimey – a lieutenant, was he?

PETTERSEN: He was indeed. But then he went into the timber trade or something. They say he played a dirty trick on

Mr Werle once. The two of them were together on the Høidal Works back then, you see. Oh yes, I know old Ekdal very well. We regularly share a schnapps and a bottle of stout[5] down at Madam[6] Eriksen's.

JENSEN: Don't s'pose he's got much to spend on rounds.

PETTERSEN: Christ Jensen, you must realize it's me gets the rounds. I reckon it's only right to be gracious to better folk that's taken such a fall.

JENSEN: Go bankrupt then, did he?

PETTERSEN: No, it was worse than that. He ended up in the old fortress.[7]

JENSEN: The fortress!

PETTERSEN: Or perhaps it was the county jail – [Listens] Shh, they're leaving the table now.

The door to the dining room is opened by a couple of servants from within. MRS SØRBY, *engaged in conversation with a couple of gentlemen, comes out. Gradually the entire group of diners follows, including* MR WERLE. *The last to appear are* HJALMAR EKDAL *and* GREGERS WERLE.

MRS SØRBY [*in passing, to the servant*]: Pettersen, have the coffee served in the music room.

PETTERSEN: Very well, Mrs Sørby.

She and the two gentlemen walk into the living room and then exit right. PETTERSEN *and* JENSEN *leave the same way.*

A FAT PALE-FACED GENTLEMAN [*to* A THIN-HAIRED GENTLEMAN]: Phew – that banquet – it was heavy work!

THIN-HAIRED GENTLEMAN: Oh, with a bit of goodwill one can perform wonders in three hours.

FAT GENTLEMAN: Yes, but the aftermath, the aftermath, my dear chamberlain![8]

A THIRD GENTLEMAN: I hear the mocha and the maraschino[9] are awaiting our delectation in the music room.

FAT GENTLEMAN: Hurrah! Perhaps Mrs Sørby will play us a tune.

THIN-HAIRED GENTLEMAN [*quietly*]: So long as it's not a march out of the door, eh!

FAT GENTLEMAN: Oh, no. Berta wouldn't spurn her old friends.

They laugh and go into the living room.

MR WERLE [*in a low voice, troubled*]: I don't think anyone noticed, Gregers.

GREGERS [*looks at him*]: What?

WERLE: Didn't you notice it either?

GREGERS: What should I have noticed?

WERLE: We were thirteen at table.

GREGERS: Oh? Thirteen?

WERLE [*glancing towards* HJALMAR]: We're normally twelve. [*To the others*] Please, go through, gentlemen!

He and the others in the room, except HJALMAR *and* GREGERS, *exit back right.*

HJALMAR [*who has heard the conversation*]: You shouldn't have sent me that invitation, Gregers.

GREGERS: What! The party's meant to be in *my* honour. And I shouldn't ask my best and only friend –

HJALMAR: But I don't think your father likes it. I never usually set foot in this house.

GREGERS: No, so I hear. But I had to see you and talk to you, as I'll probably be leaving again soon. – Yes, we two old school friends have certainly drifted far apart, old chap; we've not seen each other for sixteen or seventeen years.

HJALMAR: Is it that long?

GREGERS: Yes, it most certainly is. So, how are you doing, then? You're looking good. You've become quite large and portly.

HJALMAR: Hm. I'm not sure portly's the word exactly; but I do perhaps look somewhat manlier than back then.

GREGERS: You do, indeed. Your outer man hasn't suffered in the least.

HJALMAR [*in a more sombre tone*]: But the inner man, oh! Things look very different from inside, believe me! I presume you know how appallingly everything collapsed for me and mine, after the last time we saw each other.

GREGERS [*more quietly*]: Yes, how are things with your father now?

HJALMAR: Let's not talk about *that*, my friend. Naturally my poor unhappy father lives with me at home. He hasn't anybody else in the whole world. But I find all this so devastatingly sad to talk about, you understand. – Tell me instead how you've been keeping up there at the Works.

GREGERS: I've been delightfully lonely – with ample opportunity to mull over a good many things. – Come here; let's make ourselves comfortable.

He sits down in an armchair by the fireplace and gestures for HJALMAR *to sit in another next to it.*

HJALMAR [*softly*]: Anyway, Gregers, I really do want to thank you for inviting me to your father's table – I can see now that you no longer hold anything against me.

GREGERS [*puzzled*]: How could you think that I'd hold anything against you?

HJALMAR: There's no doubt you did in those first years.

GREGERS: What first years?

HJALMAR: After the catastrophe hit. And it was only natural you should. Since it was by a hair's breadth that your father wasn't dragged into all those – oh, those ghastly events!

GREGERS: And for that I'd hold something against you? Who gave you that idea?

HJALMAR: I know you did, Gregers; it was your own father who told me.

GREGERS [*surprised*]: Father? I see. Hmm. – Is that why I never heard anything from you – not one single word?

HJALMAR: Yes.

GREGERS: Even when you were starting out here as a photographer?

HJALMAR: Your father said it wasn't worth my writing to you about *anything*.

GREGERS [*stares straight ahead*]: No, no, he may have been right there. – But tell me now, Hjalmar – are you reasonably contented in your present situation?

HJALMAR [*with a slight sigh*]: Well, yes, I most certainly am; I can't really say otherwise. Initially, as you can imagine, it was a little strange for me. The circumstances in which I found myself were so completely altered. But then, everything else was so completely altered too. The utterly ruinous catastrophe with Father – the shame and the disgrace, Gregers –

GREGERS [*shaken*]: Yes, I see. I see.

HJALMAR: Naturally, I couldn't think of going on with my studies; there wasn't a penny left over; quite the contrary; there were debts; mostly to your father, I believe –

GREGERS: Hmm –

HJALMAR: Well, so I felt it best to make a clean break of it, you see – to distance myself from any old relationships and ties. It was your father in fact who advised me to do so; and when he took it upon himself to be so helpful to me –

GREGERS: Father did?

HJALMAR: Yes, surely you know that? Where would *I* have got the money to learn photography[10] and to equip a studio and set up a business? It costs a lot, you can be sure.

GREGERS: And *Father* covered those costs?

HJALMAR: Yes, my dear friend, didn't you know? I understood from him that he'd written and told you.

GREGERS: Not a word about it being *him*. He must have forgotten. We've never exchanged anything but business letters. So it was *Father* –!

HJALMAR: Yes, it certainly was. He's never wanted people to know; but, yes, it was *him*. And it was him, of course, who put me in a position to get married too. Or perhaps – you didn't know that either?

GREGERS: No, I certainly didn't know that. – [*Shakes his arm*] But, my dear Hjalmar, I can't tell you how much all this gladdens me – and troubles me. Maybe I've done my father an injustice after all – in certain respects. Yes, since this shows a generosity of heart, you see. Something like a conscience –

HJALMAR: Conscience –?

GREGERS: Yes, or whatever you want to call it. Actually, I haven't words to say how glad I am to hear this about Father. – So, you're married, Hjalmar. That's rather more than I'll ever manage. Well, I hope you have found happiness as a married man?

HJALMAR: Yes, I most certainly have. She's as clever and good a wife as any man could wish. And she's not altogether uncultured.

GREGERS [*a little puzzled*]: No, I don't suppose she is.

HJALMAR: No, life is an educator, you understand. Her daily interaction with me –; and then there are a couple of gifted people who visit us regularly. I can assure you – you wouldn't recognize Gina.

GREGERS: Gina?

HJALMAR: Yes, my friend, you don't remember that she's called Gina?

GREGERS: Who's called Gina? I've no idea –

HJALMAR: But don't you remember – she was in service here in this house for a while?

GREGERS [*looks at him*]: You mean Gina Hansen –?

HJALMAR: Yes, of course, Gina Hansen.

GREGERS: – who ran the house for us in the last year when Mother was ill?

HJALMAR: That's right. But, my dear friend, I know for certain that your father wrote and told you that I'd got married.

GREGERS [*who has got up*]: That's quite right, he did; but not that – [*Paces the floor*] Oh yes, wait now – perhaps – when I think about it. But Father's letters to me are always so brief. [*Perches on the arm of the armchair*] Listen, tell me, Hjalmar – this is all rather fun – how was it that you got to know Gina – your wife?

HJALMAR: Well, it was pretty straightforward really. Gina didn't stay in this house for long, since there was so much disruption here at the time; your mother's illness – well, Gina couldn't cope with all that, so she gave her notice and moved out. That was the year before your mother died – or maybe that same year.

GREGERS: It was in the same year. And I was up at the Works at the time. But after that?

HJALMAR: Well, Gina was living at home with her mother then, a Madam Hansen, a very clever and hard-working woman, who ran a little café. And she had a room she rented out too; a very nice, pleasant little room.

GREGERS: And you were lucky enough to come across it perhaps?

HJALMAR: Well, it was your father who put me on to it actually. And it was there – you understand – that I really got to know Gina.

GREGERS: And that resulted in your engagement?

HJALMAR: Well, yes. Young people get feelings for each other so easily – hmm –

GREGERS [*gets up and walks about a little*]: Tell me – when you got engaged – was it then that Father made it – I mean – was that when you took up photography?

HJALMAR: Absolutely. I was keen to get going and set up home as soon as possible. So your father and I both felt this photography thing was the best option. And Gina thought so too. And, there was also another reason, you see; by some lucky coincidence Gina had taken up retouching.

GREGERS: So it all fitted together miraculously well.

HJALMAR [*pleased, gets up*]: Yes, didn't it just? It fitted together miraculously well, don't you think?

GREGERS: Indeed, I must admit. It seems that Father's been almost some sort of providence for you.

HJALMAR [*moved*]: He didn't abandon his old friend's son in his hour of need.[11] Because he *does* have a heart, you see.

MRS SØRBY [*comes in, arm in arm with* MR WERLE]: Don't argue, my dearest Mr Werle; you're not to stay in there a moment longer, staring at all those lights; it's not good for you.

WERLE [*lets go of her arm and puts his hand to his eyes*]: I think you may be right.

PETTERSEN *and the hired servant* JENSEN *enter with serving trays.*

MRS SØRBY [*to the guests in the other living room*]: Help yourselves, gentlemen; if anyone wants a glass of punch they'll have to exert themselves and move in here.

FAT GENTLEMAN [*coming over to* MRS SØRBY]: But good God, is it true you've retracted our blessed freedom to smoke?

MRS SØRBY: Yes, here in Mr Werle's dominion it is outlawed, chamberlain.

THIN-HAIRED GENTLEMAN: When did you introduce these new stringent regulations in the cigar law, Mrs Sørby?

MRS SØRBY: After the last banquet, chamberlain; since certain persons allowed themselves to overstep the mark.

THIN-HAIRED GENTLEMAN: And isn't it permitted to overstep the mark just a teeny bit, Mrs Berta? Not at all?

MRS SØRBY: Under no circumstance, Chamberlain Balle.

Most of the guests have gathered in MR WERLE's *room; the servants are passing the punch glasses round.*

WERLE [*to* HJALMAR, *over by a table*]: What are *you* looking so intently at there, Ekdal?

HJALMAR: Just an album, Mr Werle.

THIN-HAIRED GENTLEMAN [*walking about*]: Aha, photographs! Yes, that's something for you all right.

FAT GENTLEMAN [*in an armchair*]: Didn't you bring any of your own?

HJALMAR: No, I didn't.

FAT GENTLEMAN: You should have; it's so good for the digestion to sit and look at pictures.

THIN-HAIRED GENTLEMAN: And it's a little contribution to the entertainment, you understand.

A NEAR-SIGHTED GENTLEMAN: And all donations are gratefully received.

MRS SØRBY: The chamberlains mean that when invited to dinner, one must labour for one's victuals, Mr Ekdal.

FAT GENTLEMAN: In a house offering such good food *that* is a pleasure.

THIN-HAIRED GENTLEMAN: And by God, when it comes to the 'struggle for existence',[12] then –

MRS SØRBY: Yes, quite!

They continue with laughter and jesting.

GREGERS [*quietly*]: You should join in, Hjalmar.

HJALMAR [*twisting with discomfort*]: What would I talk about?

FAT GENTLEMAN: Don't you think, Mr Werle, that Tokay might be considered a relatively healthy drink for the digestion?

WERLE [*by the fireplace*]: I can safely vouch for the Tokay you had today at least; it's from one of the very, very finest of vintages. But I'm sure you knew that.

FAT GENTLEMAN: Yes, it had a remarkably delicate bouquet.

HJALMAR [*unsure*]: Is there a difference between vintages?

FAT GENTLEMAN [*laughs*]: Oh, you're a fine one!

WERLE [*smiles*]: It's clearly not worth putting a noble wine in front of you.

THIN-HAIRED GENTLEMAN: It is with Tokay as with a photograph, Mr Ekdal. Sunshine is essential. Or am I mistaken?

HJALMAR: Well, the light does play a part.

MRS SØRBY: But that's exactly how it is with chamberlains; they too have an insatiable need to bask in the sunlight, they say.

THIN-HAIRED GENTLEMAN: Tut, tut, that's an old chestnut!

NEAR-SIGHTED GENTLEMAN: Madam is displaying her wit –

FAT GENTLEMAN: – and at our expense. [*Chastising*] Mrs Berta, Mrs Berta!

MRS SØRBY: Anyway, it is indisputable that different vintages can vary hugely. The oldest vintages are the finest.

NEAR-SIGHTED GENTLEMAN: Do you count *me* as an old vintage!

MRS SØRBY: Oh, far from it.

THIN-HAIRED GENTLEMAN: Oh, ho, ho! But what about *me*, my sweet Mrs Sørby –?

FAT GENTLEMAN: And me! What vintage would you count us as?

MRS SØRBY: I'd count you among the sweet vintages, my dear gentlemen.

> *She sips from a glass of punch; the chamberlains laugh and continue to joke with her.*

WERLE: Mrs Sørby always finds a way out – when she wants. But don't neglect your drinks now, gentlemen! – Pettersen, do make sure –! Gregers, I think we'll drink a glass together. [GREGERS *does not move*] Won't you join us, Ekdal? I didn't get the chance to toast you at table.

> GRÅBERG *peeps in round the baize door.*

GRÅBERG: Beg pardon, sir, but I can't get out.

WERLE: Oh. Have you been locked in again?

GRÅBERG: Yes, and Flakstad's left with the keys –

WERLE: Well, you'll just have to walk through here.

GRÅBERG: Yes, but there's someone else –

WERLE: Well, come on both of you, don't be shy.

GRÅBERG *and old* EKDAL *come out from the office.*

WERLE [*involuntarily*]: Oh no!

> *Laughter and conversation among the guests fade.* HJAL-
> MAR *starts at the sight of his father, puts his glass down
> and turns towards the fireplace.*

EKDAL [*doesn't look up, but makes short bows to each side
as he walks and mutters*]: Apologies. Came the wrong way.
Door's locked – door's locked. Apologies.

> *He and* GRÅBERG *leave in the background to the right.*

WERLE [*between his teeth*]: That infernal Gråberg.

GREGERS [*jaw dropping and eyes staring, to* HJALMAR]: But
surely that wasn't –!

FAT GENTLEMAN: What's going on? Who was that?

GREGERS: Oh, nobody. Just the bookkeeper and somebody or
other.

NEAR-SIGHTED GENTLEMAN [*to* HJALMAR]: Did *you* recognize that man?

HJALMAR: I don't know – I didn't notice –

FAT GENTLEMAN [*getting up*]: What the ruddy hell's going on
here?

> *He walks slowly over to some others, who are talking in
> lowered voices.*

MRS SØRBY [*whispers to the servant*]: Slip him a little something outside; something really nice.

PETTERSEN [*nods*]: I will. [*Leaves.*]

GREGERS [*quietly, shaken, to* HJALMAR]: So it really was him!

HJALMAR: Yes.

GREGERS: And yet you stood here and denied knowing him![13]

HJALMAR [*whispers urgently*]: But could I *really* –?

GREGERS: – acknowledge your own father?

HJALMAR [*pained*]: Oh, if you were in my place –

> *The conversations between the guests, which have been
> conducted in hushed voices, now switch to falsely loud
> voices.*

THIN-HAIRED GENTLEMAN [*approaches* HJALMAR *and*
GREGERS *amicably*]: Aha, standing here reviving old mem-
ories from our student days, are we? Eh? Don't you smoke, Mr
Ekdal? Do you want a light? Ah, that's true, we're not allowed –

HJALMAR: Thanks, not for me –

FAT GENTLEMAN: Don't you have a nice little poem you might declaim for us, Mr Ekdal? You used to do that so beautifully.

HJALMAR: I'm afraid I can't remember any.

FAT GENTLEMAN: Oh, that's a crying shame. Well, what shall we get up to now, Balle?

    Both gentlemen cross the floor out into the other living room.

HJALMAR [*sombrely*]: Gregers – I want to leave! When a man has felt the devastating blow of fate upon his head, you understand –. Say goodbye to your father for me.

GREGERS: Yes, all right. Are you going straight home?

HJALMAR: Yes. Why?

GREGERS: Well, I might come over later, then.

HJALMAR: No, please don't. Not to my place. My apartment's dismal, Gregers – especially after as brilliant a banquet as this. We can always meet somewhere in town.

MRS SØRBY [*has come closer, quietly*]: Are you leaving, Ekdal?

HJALMAR: Yes.

MRS SØRBY: Say hello to Gina.

HJALMAR: Thank you.

MRS SØRBY: And tell her I'll come up and see her some day soon.

HJALMAR: Of course, thank you. [*To* GREGERS] Stay here. I want to disappear unnoticed.

    He drifts across the room, then into the second room and leaves right.

MRS SØRBY [*quietly to the servant, who has returned*]: Well, did the old man get something to take with him?

PETTERSEN: Of course, I slipped him a bottle of cognac.

MRS SØRBY: Oh, surely you could have come up with something better.

PETTERSEN: No, no, Mrs Sørby; he likes his cognac best of all.

FAT GENTLEMAN [*in the doorway with sheet music in his hand*]: Shall we play a little something together perhaps, Mrs Sørby?

MRS SØRBY: Yes, why not? Let's do that.

THE GUESTS: Hurrah! Hurrah!

She and all the visitors walk through the living room out to the right. GREGERS *remains standing by the fireplace,* MR WERLE *looks for something on his writing desk and seems to want* GREGERS *to leave; since he doesn't move,* MR WERLE *walks towards the exit.*

GREGERS: Father, won't you wait a bit?

WERLE [*stops*]: What is it?

GREGERS: I need a word with you.

WERLE: Can't it wait until we're alone?

GREGERS: No, it can't; it's just possible that we shan't get to be alone.

WERLE [*comes closer*]: What does that mean?

During the following, distant piano music is heard from the music room.

GREGERS: How could that family be allowed to sink so miserably low?

WERLE: You mean the Ekdals, I presume.

GREGERS: Yes, I mean the Ekdals. Lieutenant Ekdal was once so close to you.

WERLE: Yes, he was far too close, unfortunately. I had to feel that and suffer the consequences of it for years. It's thanks to him that I – I too got a blot on my good name and reputation.

GREGERS [*quietly*]: Was *he* really the only guilty party?

WERLE: Who else do you have in mind?

GREGERS: Well, you were both in on that large purchase of forest –

WERLE: But wasn't it Ekdal who drew up the map of the area – that misleading map? He was the one who organized all the illegal felling on state land. He was solely responsible for the running of the business up there. I had no idea what Lieutenant Ekdal was doing.

GREGERS: I doubt Lieutenant Ekdal had much idea of what he was doing himself.

WERLE: That may be. But the fact remains that he was found guilty, and I was acquitted.

GREGERS: Yes, I know, of course, there was no proof.

WERLE: Acquittal is acquittal. Why are you raking up these disagreeable past events that made my hair grey before my

time? Is that the sort of thing you've been mulling over all
these years up there? I can assure you, Gregers – those stories are long forgotten here in town – as far as *I'm* concerned
anyway.

GREGERS: Yes, but what about the unfortunate Ekdal family?

WERLE: What exactly would you have me do for those people?
When Ekdal was freed again, he was a broken man, absolutely beyond rescue. There are people in this world who
dive to the bottom[14] if they get just a few pellets in their
body, and they never come up again. You can take my word
for it, Gregers, I have stretched myself as far as I could, short
of exposing myself to all sorts of suspicion and giving sustenance to gossip –

GREGERS: Suspicion –? I see.

WERLE: I've found Ekdal copy work from the office, and I pay
him far, far more than his work is worth –

GREGERS [*without looking at him*]: Hm; I don't doubt *that*.

WERLE: Are you laughing? Perhaps you don't think I'm telling
the truth? Admittedly, it doesn't appear on the books, since
I never record that sort of expense.

GREGERS [*smiles coldly*]: No, certain expenses are presumably best kept off the books.

WERLE [*puzzled*]: What do you mean by *that*?

GREGERS [*summoning up courage*]: Did you record what it
cost you to let Hjalmar Ekdal study photography?

WERLE: Me? How record?

GREGERS: I know now that it was you who financed it. And I
also know that it was you who were so generous in helping
him to set up business.

WERLE: Right, and I still stand accused of doing nothing for
the Ekdals? I can assure you, those people have lumbered me
with expenses aplenty.

GREGERS: Have you recorded any of those expenses?

WERLE: Why do you ask *that*?

GREGERS: Oh, there are reasons. Listen, tell me – back then,
when you were taking such a warm interest in your old
friend's son – was that when he was about to get married?

WERLE: But how the hell – how, after so many years, would I –?

GREGERS: You wrote me a letter at the time – a business letter naturally; and in a postscript it stated, quite briefly, that Hjalmar Ekdal had married a Miss Hansen.

WERLE: Well yes, that was perfectly true; that was her name.

GREGERS: But you didn't mention that this Miss Hansen was Gina Hansen – our former housemaid.

WERLE [*with a disdainful, but forced laugh*]: No, because I really didn't think you took any particular interest in our former housemaid.

GREGERS: Nor *did* I. But – [*lowers his voice*] but there were doubtless others in this house who did take a particular interest in her.

WERLE: What do you mean by *that*? [*Flares up at him*] You surely can't be referring to me?

GREGERS [*quietly but firmly*]: I am indeed referring to you.

WERLE: And you dare –! You have the audacity –! How can he – that ungrateful man – that photographer – how can he have the nerve to make such accusations!

GREGERS: Hjalmar has never even touched on the subject. I don't think he has even the slightest notion about any such thing.

WERLE: So where have you got it from? Who could say something like that?

GREGERS: My poor unhappy mother said it. And that was the last time I saw her.

WERLE: Your mother! Yes, I might have guessed! The two of you always did stick together. It was she who turned your mind against me, from the very start.

GREGERS: No, it was everything that she had to stomach and endure, until she finally buckled under and succumbed so pitifully.

WERLE: Oh, she had nothing at all to stomach and endure – no more, at least, than many! But there's no getting anywhere with sickly, neurotic people. I experienced *that* all right. And here you go harbouring such a suspicion – poking about in all sorts of old rumours and slander against your own father. Listen, Gregers, I really do think that at your age, you might apply yourself to something more useful.

GREGERS: Yes, it may well be time I did.

WERLE: Then your mind might perhaps be a little lighter than it seems to be now. Where will it lead, your sitting up there at the Works year in and year out, slaving away like a common office clerk, not collecting a penny over the standard monthly salary? It's an absolute folly on your part.

GREGERS: If only I was so sure of *that*.

WERLE: I understand, of course. You want to be independent, you don't want to be in my debt. But right now there's an opportunity for you to become independent, to be your own master in everything.

GREGERS: Really? And how –?

WERLE: When I wrote to say that you had to come to town as a matter of urgency – hm –

GREGERS: Yes, what do you really want from me? I've waited all day to find out.

WERLE: I want to propose to you that you join me in the firm.

GREGERS: Me? In your firm? As a partner?

WERLE: Yes. That wouldn't mean we'd have to be together constantly. You could take over the business here in town, and I'd move up to the Works.

GREGERS: *You* would?

WERLE: Well, you see, I haven't the capacity for work I once had. I've got to be careful with my eyes, Gregers; they've started getting rather weak.

GREGERS: But they always were.

WERLE: Not like now. Besides – circumstances might perhaps make it desirable for me to live up there – for a while at least.

GREGERS: That possibility has never occurred to me.

WERLE: Listen now, Gregers; there are so many things that divide us. But we're still father and son despite that. I think we ought to be able to come to some kind of understanding, you and I.

GREGERS: For outward appearances, you mean?

WERLE: Well, that would be something at least. Think it over, Gregers. Don't you think it could be possible? Eh?

GREGERS [*looks at him with cold eyes*]: There's something else behind all this.

WERLE: What do you mean?

GREGERS: You presumably have some use for me in mind.

WERLE: In a relationship as close as ours one person always has a use for the other.

GREGERS: Yes, so they say.

WERLE: I'd really like to have you with me at home now for a while. I am a lonely man, Gregers – have always felt lonely – throughout my life. But now more than ever, now that I'm getting on in years, I could do with having someone around.

GREGERS: But you have Mrs Sørby.

WERLE: Yes, I have indeed, and she has become, so to speak, almost indispensable to me. She's bright and even-tempered; she livens up the house – and I'm in sore need of that.

GREGERS: Well then: you've got things as you want them.

WERLE: Yes, but I'm worried that it can't last. A woman in such a relationship can easily find herself in a tricky position in the eyes of the world. Indeed, I'd almost say that a man isn't best served by it either.

GREGERS: Oh, when a man throws dinner parties like you, I'd say he can afford to take a few risks.

WERLE: Yes, but *her*, Gregers? I'm worried she won't put up with it much longer. And even if she did – if out of devotion to me she rose above the gossip and backbiting and so on –? Don't you think, Gregers – you, with your highly evolved sense of justice –

GREGERS [*interrupts him*]: Look, just tell me one thing. Are you thinking of marrying her?

WERLE: And if I were? What then?

GREGERS: I might ask the same. What then?

WERLE: Would you be absolutely unequivocally against it?

GREGERS: No, absolutely not. Not at all.

WERLE: Well, I wasn't sure if out of regard for your late mother's memory –

GREGERS: I am not neurotic.[15]

WERLE: Well, whatever you may or may not be, you've lifted a heavy stone from my heart. It's immensely precious to me that I can count on your support in this.

GREGERS [*fixing his gaze on him*]: Now I see what you want to use me for.

WERLE: Use you for? What kind of expression is that!

GREGERS: Oh, let's not quibble over a choice of words – not when we're one-to-one at least. [*Short laugh*] Yes, so that's it! That's why I had to bloody well make a personal appearance here in town. On account of Mrs Sørby there has to be some show of family life here in this house. A tableau with father and son! That'll be a first!

WERLE: How dare you take that tone!

GREGERS: When has there ever been any family life here? Never as far back as I can remember. But *now* there's need for a touch of it. Because no doubt it will look good when it can be reported that the son – carried upon the wings of piety – rushed home to his ageing father's wedding feast. Then what'll remain of all the rumours about what that poor dead woman had to suffer and endure? Not a jot. No, her son will dash them to the ground.

WERLE: Gregers – I don't think there's a man on earth who repels you as I do.

GREGERS [*quietly*]: I've seen you too close-up.

WERLE: You've seen me with your mother's eyes. [*Lowers his voice a little*] But you ought to remember that those eyes were – misted now and then.

GREGERS [*emotionally*]: I know what you're referring to. But who was to blame for mother's unfortunate weakness? You, and all those –! The last of them being this floozy[16] Hjalmar Ekdal was paired off with when you no longer – argh!

WERLE [*shrugs his shoulders*]: Word for word, like hearing your mother.

GREGERS [*without paying him any attention*]: – and now that man sits there, with his big innocent child's mind surrounded by deceit – living under the same roof with a woman like that, not knowing that what he calls his home is built on a lie! [*A step closer*] When I look back on all you've done, it's like looking out over a battlefield of shattered destinies in every direction.

WERLE: I think perhaps the gulf between us is too wide.

GREGERS [*with a controlled bow*]: I have observed that, and I will therefore take my hat and leave.

WERLE: Are you going? Leaving the house?

GREGERS: Yes, because now, at last, I see a mission to live for.

WERLE: What mission is that?

GREGERS: You would just laugh if I told you.

WERLE: A lonely man doesn't laugh so easily, Gregers.

GREGERS [*points towards the background*]: Look Father – all those old goats are playing blind man's buff with Mrs Sørby. – Goodnight and farewell.

He exits in the background to the right. Laughter and jesting are heard from the party guests, who come into view in the outer living room.

WERLE [*mutters disdainfully at* GREGERS' *back*]: Hah –! Poor boy – and he says he isn't neurotic!

ACT TWO

Hjalmar Ekdal's studio. The room, which is fairly large, is clearly in an attic. To the right there is a sloping ceiling with large skylights, half covered by a blue drape. In the corner to the right is the entrance door; in front on the same side, a door to the living room. On the wall to the left are two doors and between these an iron stove. On the back wall there is a wide double door, designed to be pushed to the sides. The studio is shabby but pleasantly arranged and furnished. Between the doors to the right, a short distance from the wall, is a sofa with a table and some chairs; on the table stands a lighted lamp with a shade; by the stove stands an old armchair. Various items of photographic equipment and instruments can be seen around the room. By the back wall, to the left of the double door, a set of shelves holding books, boxes and bottles of chemicals, various tools, equipment and other items. Photographs and small items like brushes, paper and such lie on the table.

GINA EKDAL sits on a chair at the table, sewing. HEDVIG sits on the sofa with her hands shading her eyes and her thumbs in her ears, reading a book.

GINA [*glances towards her a couple of times, as if with concealed anxiety, then says*]: Hedvig!
    HEDVIG *does not hear.*
GINA [*louder*]: Hedvig!
HEDVIG [*puts her hands down and looks up*]: Yes, Mother?
GINA: Hedvig dear, you're not to sit and read any more now.
HEDVIG: Oh, but, Mother, can't I read a bit more? Just a bit!

GINA: No, no, you must put that book down now. Your father doesn't like it; he never reads in the evenings himself.

HEDVIG [*closes the book*]: No, Father doesn't care much for reading.

GINA [*puts her sewing away and picks up a pencil and a small notepad from the table*]: Do you remember how much we paid for the butter today?

HEDVIG: It was one krone and sixty-five øre.

GINA: That's right. [*Makes a note*] It's shocking the amount of butter used in this house. And then the salami and cheese – let me see – [*writes*] – and the ham – hmm – [*Adds up*] Yes, that already tots up to –

HEDVIG: And then there's the beer.

GINA: Oh yes, that's true. [*Writes*] It all mounts up, but it can't be helped.

HEDVIG: And you and I didn't need anything hot for dinner with Father going out.

GINA: No, that was good. And I *did* make eight kroner fifty for the photographs.

HEDVIG: Goodness – *that* much!

GINA: Eight kroner fifty, exactly.

> *Silence.* GINA *resumes her sewing.* HEDVIG *takes paper and pencil and starts to draw something, with her left hand shading her eyes.*

HEDVIG: Isn't it fun to think of Father being Mr Werle's guest at a big dinner party?

GINA: You can't really say he's Mr Werle's guest. It was his son that sent for him after all. [*A short pause*] We have nothing at all to do with Mr Werle.

HEDVIG: I'm so looking forward to Father coming home. Because he promised he'd ask Mrs Sørby for some goodies for me.

GINA: Yes, there's good things aplenty in *that* house, you can be sure.

HEDVIG [*still drawing*]: And I'm kind of hungry too.

> *Old* EKDAL, *with his paper packet under his arm and another parcel in his coat pocket, comes in through the hallway door.*

GINA: Grandpa's home very late today.

EKDAL: They'd closed the office. Had to wait with Gråberg.
And I walked through – hmm.

HEDVIG: Did they give you more copy work to do, Grandpa?

EKDAL: This whole parcel. Just look at that.

GINA: Well, that's good.

HEDVIG: And you've got a parcel in your pocket too.

EKDAL: What? Oh, balderdash; that's nothing. [*Puts his walking stick in the corner*] There's hours of work here, Gina.
[*Pulls aside one of the double doors on the back wall so it is open a crack*] Shh! [*Looks for a while into the room and closes the door again quietly*] He-heh! They're all fast asleep,
the lot of them. And she's gone to bed in the basket of her own accord. He-heh.

HEDVIG: Are you certain she's not freezing cold in that basket,
Grandpa?

EKDAL: What an idea! Freezing? In all that straw? [*Walks towards the top door to the left*] There's matches in there, I take it?

GINA: The matches are on the chest of drawers.

    EKDAL *goes into his room.*

HEDVIG: It's ever so good Grandpa got all that stuff to copy.

GINA: Yes, poor old Da; then he can earn himself a bit of pocket money.

HEDVIG: And he won't be able to sit all morning down at that
horrid Madam Eriksen's establishment.[17]

GINA: Yes, that too.

    Brief silence.

HEDVIG: D'you think they're still sitting at the dinner table?

GINA: Lord only knows; they might be, I suppose.

HEDVIG: Imagine all that delicious food Father will get to eat!
I'm sure he'll be ever so happy and cheerful when he comes
back. Don't you think, Mother?

GINA: Yes; but just imagine if we could tell him we'd managed
to rent the spare room out.

HEDVIG: But there's no need for *that* tonight.

GINA: Oh, it would certainly come in useful. And it's standing
there doing nothing.

HEDVIG: No, I meant, there's no need because Father will be happy tonight anyway. It's better we keep *that* thing with the room for another time.

GINA [*looks over at her*]: Are you glad when you've something good to tell Father, when he gets home in the evening?

HEDVIG: Yes, it's more cheerful here then.

GINA [*to herself*]: Oh yes, there's something in that.

    Old EKDAL *comes back in and is heading for the door to the front left.*

GINA [*turns sideways in her chair*]: Does Grandpa want something from the kitchen, eh?

EKDAL: That was the idea. Don't get up. [*Walks out*]

GINA: He's not mucking about with the embers out there, is he? [*Waits a little*] Hedvig, go out and see what he's up to.

    Old EKDAL *comes back in with a small jug of steaming water.*

HEDVIG: You getting hot water, Grandpa?

EKDAL: Yes, I am. Need it for something. I've got to write, and my ink's turned into muddy porridge[18] – hm.

GINA: But Grandpa should eat his evening snack first. It's already in your room.

EKDAL: Forget my evening snack, Gina. I'm terribly busy, I tell you. I don't want anybody coming into my room. Nobody – hm.

    He goes into his room. GINA *and* HEDVIG *look at each other.*

GINA [*quietly*]: D'you have any idea where he got the money from?

HEDVIG: He probably got it from Gråberg.

GINA: Impossible. Gråberg always sends the money to *me*.

HEDVIG: He must have got himself a bottle on tick somewhere.

GINA: Poor old Da, I doubt anybody'll give him tick.

    HJALMAR EKDAL, *in overcoat and a grey felt hat, comes in from the right.*

GINA [*throws down her sewing and gets up*]: Oh, Ekdal,[19] are you back already?

HEDVIG [*at the same time, jumps up*]: You're back so soon, Father!

HJALMAR [*puts his hat away*]: Yes, the majority were leaving, I think.

HEDVIG: This early?

HJALMAR: Yes, well, it was a dinner party. [*Starts to take his overcoat off*]

GINA: Let me help you.

HEDVIG: Me too.

They pull his coat off him. GINA *hangs it on the back wall.*

HEDVIG: Were there many there, Father?

HJALMAR: No, not that many. There were about twelve or fourteen of us at table.

GINA: And I expect you got to talk to them all?

HJALMAR: Oh, yes, a bit, though it was Gregers who monopolized me of course.

GINA: Is Gregers as ugly as ever?

HJALMAR: Well, his looks aren't much improved. – Hasn't the old man come home?

HEDVIG: Yes, Grandpa's sitting in his room writing.

HJALMAR: Did he say anything?

GINA: No, what should he say?

HJALMAR: He didn't mention anything about –? I thought I heard that he'd been to see Gråberg. I want to go in to him for a second.

GINA: No, no, best not to –

HJALMAR: Why? Did he say he didn't want me to go in?

GINA: He doesn't really want *anyone* in there tonight –

HEDVIG [*signals*]: Hrm – hrm!

GINA [*not noticing*]: – he was out here getting hot water –

HJALMAR: Aha, is he sitting in there and –?

GINA: Yes, I think so.

HJALMAR: Oh, good Lord – my poor old white-haired father –!
Well, let him be – let him enjoy his little pleasures to the full.

Old EKDAL, *in his house coat with a lit tobacco-pipe, comes out from his room.*

EKDAL: You home? Thought it was your voice I heard.

HJALMAR: I just got here.

EKDAL: Don't suppose you saw me, eh?

HJALMAR: No, but they said you'd passed through – and so I wanted to come with you.

EKDAL: Hmm, kind of you, Hjalmar. – Who were they, all those people?

HJALMAR: Oh, various. Chamberlain Flor and Chamberlain Balle, Chamberlain Kaspersen and Chamberlain – so and so; I don't know –

EKDAL [*nods*]: You hear *that*, Gina! He's been among chamberlains, no less.

GINA: Yes, it must be very grand in that house nowadays.

HEDVIG: Did the chamberlains sing, Father? Or read aloud?

HJALMAR: No, they just talked a lot of guff. Then they wanted *me* to declaim something for them, but they didn't get me doing that.

EKDAL: Didn't get you doing that, eh?

GINA: But surely you could have?

HJALMAR: No; one oughtn't to jump to just anyone's beck and call. [*Walks about the room*] I don't at least.

EKDAL: No, Hjalmar's not a pushover.

HJALMAR: I don't know why *I* should provide the entertainment when I'm out once in a while. Let the others exert themselves. These fellows go from one fine house to the next, eating and drinking day in, day out. Let them make themselves useful for all that good food they get.

GINA: But you didn't say that, did you?

HJALMAR [*humming*]: Ho – ho – ho – I told them a thing or two.

EKDAL: Gave the chamberlains what for, eh!

HJALMAR: I might have done. [*Casually*] Later we got into a little dispute about the Tokay wine.

EKDAL: Tokay, you say? That's a very fine wine, that.

HJALMAR [*stops*]: It *can* be fine. But let me tell you, not all vintages are equally fine; it's entirely dependent on how much sun the grapes have had.

GINA: Well fancy that, you know all sorts, Ekdal.

EKDAL: And they got into a dispute about that?

HJALMAR: They wanted to have a go, but they were duly informed that the same was true of chamberlains. Not every vintage among them was equally fine – it was suggested.

GINA: Oh, the things you come up with!

EKDAL: He-heh! Got that on their dinner plates, did they?

HJALMAR: They got it right in the eye.

EKDAL: You hear that, Gina, he gave it to those chamberlains right in the eye.

GINA: Well I never, right in the eye.

HJALMAR: Yes, but I won't have any of this talked about. One doesn't go on about such things. And it was all in good humour, naturally. They were a pleasant and convivial lot; why should I hurt their feelings? No!

EKDAL: But, right in the eye –

HEDVIG [*ingratiating*]: How fun to see you in tails. You look so handsome in a tailcoat, Father!

HJALMAR: Yes, don't you think? And this one's such an impeccable fit. As though it was tailored for me – a bit tight under the arms, perhaps – help me, Hedvig. [*Pulls the tailcoat off*] I'd rather put my jacket on. Where've you put my jacket, Gina?

GINA: Here it is. [*Brings the jacket and helps him*]

HJALMAR: There we are! Remember to make sure Molvik gets his tailcoat back in the morning.

GINA [*puts it away*]: It'll be taken care of.

HJALMAR [*stretches*]: Ah, that certainly feels more kind of homely. And a loose and relaxed housecoat is more in keeping with my personality. Don't you think, Hedvig?

HEDVIG: Yes, Father!

HJALMAR: When I flick out my neckerchief into a pair of flowing ends – look here! Eh?

HEDVIG: Yes, it goes perfectly with your little handlebar moustache and big curly hair.

HJALMAR: I wouldn't quite call it curly, I'd rather say wavy.

HEDVIG: Yes, because it's *so* curly.

HJALMAR: Wavy actually.

HEDVIG [*after a short pause, pulls at his jacket*]: Father!

HJALMAR: Well, what is it?

HEDVIG: Oh, you know very well what it is.

HJALMAR: No, I most certainly don't.

HEDVIG [*laughs and pleads*]: Oh yes, Father; you're not to tease me any longer!

HJALMAR: But what *is* it then?

HEDVIG [*tugs at him*]: Oh, stupid – hand them over, Father!
You know, all those goodies you promised me.

HJALMAR: Oh no – how could I forget!

HEDVIG: No, you're just trying to trick me, Father! Shame on
you! Where have you hidden them?

HJALMAR: Oh, I really did forget. But wait a minute! I've got
something else for you, Hedvig. [*Goes to search the tailcoat
pockets*]

HEDVIG [*skips and claps her hands*]: Oh, Mother, Mother!

GINA: You see; when you're patient –

HJALMAR [*with a piece of paper*]: Look, here it is.

HEDVIG: *That?* That's just a piece of paper.

HJALMAR: It's the menu, look – the whole menu. It says 'La
Carte' – that means menu.

HEDVIG: Haven't you got anything else?

HJALMAR: I forgot the other things, I tell you. But you can
take my word for it: all those sticky sweets are a poor pleasure. Sit down at the table now and read the menu, then later
I shall describe for you how the dishes all taste. There now,
Hedvig.

HEDVIG [*fighting back her tears*]: Thank you.
    She sits down, but does not read the menu; GINA *signals
    to her;* HJALMAR *notices.*

HJALMAR [*paces about the room*]: It's beyond belief what a
family provider has to think about, and if he just forgets the
pettiest little thing – he's instantly confronted with sour faces.
Well, you get used to *that* too. [*Stops by the stove next to old
EKDAL*] Have you peeped in there this evening, Father?

EKDAL: Yes, to be sure. She's gone into her basket.

HJALMAR: Oh, she's gone into her basket! So she's starting to
get used to it.

EKDAL: Yes, just as I predicted. But, listen, there's a few other
little things –

HJALMAR: Some improvements, yes.

EKDAL: But they *must* be done, Hjalmar.

HJALMAR: Yes, let's talk a bit about those improvements,
Father. Come over here, we'll sit on the sofa.

EKDAL: Well – hmm. I think I'll fill my pipe first – ought to clean it too, perhaps. Hmm.

He goes into his room.

GINA [*smiles to* HJALMAR]: Clean his pipe, indeed.

HJALMAR: Oh well, Gina, just let him – poor shipwrecked chap. Yes, those improvements – that's something we'd best get off our hands tomorrow.

GINA: You won't have time tomorrow, Ekdal –

HEDVIG [*pleading*]: Oh, yes he will, Mother!

GINA: – remember those prints that need retouching; they've enquired after them so often now.

HJALMAR: I see; it's those prints again, is it? *They* will be finished all right. Are there any new orders maybe?

GINA: I'm afraid not; I've got nothing else tomorrow apart from those two pottrits,[20] as you know.

HJALMAR: Nothing else? Oh well, when one doesn't make the effort –

GINA: So what am I meant to do? I reckon I put as much as I can in the newspapers.

HJALMAR: Yes, the newspapers, the newspapers – you see how useful *that* is. And I don't suppose anybody's been to see the room either?

GINA: No, not yet.

HJALMAR: That was to be expected. When you don't keep your wits about you –. You really must get a grip, Gina!

HEDVIG [*walks towards him*]: Shall I perhaps bring you your flute, Father?

HJALMAR: No, no flute; *I* don't need any pleasures in this world. [*Walks about*] Oh yes, I shall work tomorrow all right – never you fear. I shall work for as long as I have strength in my body –

GINA: But Ekdal, my sweet, I didn't mean it like *that*.

HEDVIG: Father, shall I fetch a bottle of beer?

HJALMAR: Certainly not. I don't need anything. – [*Stops*] Beer? – Did you mention beer?

HEDVIG [*cheerfully*]: Yes, Father; lovely cool beer.

HJALMAR: Well – if you absolutely must, then feel free to fetch a bottle.

GINA: Yes, do that. And we'll all have a nice time.

HEDVIG *runs towards the kitchen door.*

HJALMAR [*by the stove, stops her, looks at her, suddenly takes her head in his hands and presses her to him*]: Hedvig! Hedvig!

HEDVIG [*happy and in tears*]: Oh, dear, kind Father!

HJALMAR: No, don't call me that. There was I, helping myself from the rich man's table[21] – gorging at an over-laden festive board –! And yet I managed to –!

GINA [*sits at the table*]: Oh, nonsense, nonsense, Ekdal.

HJALMAR: No, it's true! But you mustn't[22] judge me too harshly. You do know that I love you all the same.

HEDVIG [*throws her arms around him*]: And we love you very, very much, Father.

HJALMAR: And if I happen to be unreasonable once in a while, then – Lord above – remember that I'm a man besieged by a host of sorrows. Well, well! [*Dries his eyes*] No beer at a moment like this. Give me my flute.

HEDVIG *runs to the bookshelf to fetch it.*

HJALMAR: Thank you. There, now. With my flute in hand, and the two of you beside me – oh!

HEDVIG *sits down at the table with* GINA; HJALMAR *walks back and forth and resolutely starts playing a Bohemian folk dance,[23] but in a slow elegiac tempo and sensitive rendition.*

HJALMAR [*stops playing, gives* GINA *his left hand and says tenderly*]: It may be cramped and meagre under our roof, Gina. It is nonetheless home. And I say: this is a good place to be.

He resumes his playing; a moment later there is a knock at the front door.

GINA [*gets up*]: Shh, Ekdal – I think someone's coming.

HJALMAR [*puts the flute on the shelf*]: Oh, here we go again!

GINA *goes over and opens the door.*

GREGERS WERLE [*out in the hallway*]: I beg your pardon –

GINA [*steps back*]: Oh!

GREGERS: – isn't this where the photographer Mr Ekdal lives?

GINA: Yes, it is.

HJALMAR [*walks over to the door*]: Gregers! So you came after all? Well, come on in then.

GREGERS [*enters*]: I did say I'd look in on you.

HJALMAR: But tonight –? Have you left the party?

GREGERS: Both the party and the family home. – Good evening, Mrs Ekdal. I don't know whether you recognize me?

GINA: Oh, yes; young Mr Werle isn't hard to recognize.

GREGERS: No, I resemble my mother, of course – and doubtless you remember her.

HJALMAR: Have you left the house, you say?

GREGERS: Yes, I've moved into a hotel.

HJALMAR: I see. Well, since you've come, do take off your things and sit down.

GREGERS: Thanks. [*Takes his coat off. Has now changed into a plain grey suit of a rural cut*]

HJALMAR: Here on the sofa. Make yourself comfortable.

GREGERS *sits down on the sofa,* HJALMAR *at a chair by the table.*

GREGERS [*looks around*]: So this is it, Hjalmar. This is where you live, eh.

HJALMAR: This is the studio space, as you can see –

GINA: But it's roomier out here – which is why we prefer it.

HJALMAR: We had a smarter place before, but this apartment has one big advantage: it's got so many splendid additional spaces –

GINA: And we've got a room on the other side of the hallway that we can rent out.

GREGERS [*to* HJALMAR]: Oh really – so you have lodgers too.

HJALMAR: No, not yet. It's not that easy, you know; you need your wits about you. [*To* HEDVIG] How about that beer, then?

HEDVIG *nods and goes out into the kitchen.*

GREGERS: So *that's* your daughter?

HJALMAR: Yes, that's Hedvig.

GREGERS: And she's your only child?

HJALMAR: She's the only one, yes. She's our greatest joy in all the world, and – [*lowers his voice*] she's also our greatest sorrow, Gregers.

GREGERS: How do you mean?

HJALMAR: Alas; she is in grave danger of losing her sight.

GREGERS: Going blind!

HJALMAR: Yes. So far there are only the early signs, and things may be fine yet a while. But the doctor has warned us. Its progress will be inexorable.

GREGERS: What a terrible tragedy. Where could she have got it from?

HJALMAR [*sighs*]: Inherited, most probably.

GREGERS [*startled*]: Inherited?

GINA: Ekdal's mother had poor sight too.

HJALMAR: Yes, so Father says; I can't remember her, of course.

GREGERS: Poor child. And how does she take it?

HJALMAR: Well, as you can imagine, we've not had the heart to tell her. She has no suspicion of the danger. Happy and care-free and twittering like a little bird she flutters into life's eternal night. [*Overcome*] Oh, it's simply devastating for me, Gregers.

> HEDVIG *brings in a tray with beer and glasses, which she puts on the table.*

HJALMAR [*strokes her hair*]: Thank you, Hedvig, thank you.

> HEDVIG *puts her arms around his neck and whispers in his ear.*

HJALMAR: No. No bread and butter. [*Looks over*] Though, perhaps Gregers would like a slice?

GREGERS [*declining*]: No, no thank you.

HJALMAR [*still melancholy*]: Well, you could put a bit out anyway. If you've got a crust, that would be nice. And make sure there's enough butter on it.

> HEDVIG *nods contentedly and goes back out into the kitchen.*

GREGERS [*who has followed her with his gaze*]: But she looks quite good and healthy otherwise, I'd say.

GINA: Yes, there's nothing else amiss with her, thank God.

GREGERS: She'll probably resemble you in time, Mrs Ekdal. How old might she be now?

GINA: Hedvig will soon be fourteen exactly; it's her birthday the day after tomorrow.

GREGERS: Quite big for her age, then.

GINA: Yes, she's really shot up this last year.

GREGERS: It's seeing youngsters grow up that makes us realize how old we're getting ourselves. – How long have you been married now?

GINA: We've been married for – well, close on fifteen years.

GREGERS: No, really, is it that long!

GINA [*alert, looks at him*]: Yes it is, right enough.

HJALMAR: Yes, it certainly is. Fifteen years in a few months' time. [*Change of tone*] Those years up at the Works, Gregers, they must have felt very long to you.

GREGERS: They felt long when I was living them – looking back now I'm not sure where all that time went.

> Old EKDAL *comes in from his room, without his pipe, but with his old-fashioned uniform cap on his head; his gait is a little unsteady.*

EKDAL: Right you are, Hjalmar, we can sit down now and discuss those – hmm. What was it again?

HJALMAR [*goes towards him*]: Father, there's somebody here. Gregers Werle –. I don't know whether you remember him.

EKDAL [*looks at* GREGERS, *who has got up*]: Werle? That's the son, isn't it? What does he want from me?

HJALMAR: Nothing; it's me he's come to visit.

EKDAL: I see, so there's nothing wrong?

HJALMAR: No, certainly not, no.

EKDAL [*waving his arms*]: Not that it matters, you realize. I'm not scared, but –

GREGERS [*walks up to him*]: I just wanted to bring you greetings from your old hunting grounds, Lieutenant Ekdal.

EKDAL: Hunting grounds?

GREGERS: Yes, up round the Høidal Works.

EKDAL: Oh, up there. Yes, I knew that area well once.

GREGERS: Back then you were a formidable huntsman.

EKDAL: I was, yes. That's right. You're looking at my uniform. I don't ask anyone's permission to wear it in here. So long as I don't go into the street[24] with it on –

> HEDVIG *brings in a plate of buttered bread, which she puts on the table.*

HJALMAR: Sit down now, Father, and have a glass of beer. Help yourself, Gregers.

EKDAL *mutters and walks unsteadily over to the sofa.*
GREGERS *sits down on the chair closest to him,* HJALMAR
on the other side of GREGERS. GINA *sits a little fur-*
ther from the table sewing; HEDVIG *stands next to her*
father.

GREGERS: Do you remember, Lieutenant Ekdal, when Hjalmar and I came up to visit you in the summertime and at
Christmas?

EKDAL: You did? No, no, no, can't recall that. But I was a
canny hunter, if I dare say so myself. Shot some bears I did
too. Shot as many as nine.

GREGERS [*looks sympathetically at him*]: And now you never
hunt any more.

EKDAL: Oh, wouldn't say *that*, old chap. Hunt once in a while.
Well, not like *that*, of course. Because the forest, you see –
the forest, the forest –! [*Drinks*] Is the forest doing all right
up there now?

GREGERS: Not as lush as in your time. An awful lot's been
felled.

EKDAL: Felled? [*Dropping his voice, timid*] That's a dangerous business, that. Has consequences. There's revenge in the
forest.

HJALMAR [*tops up his glass*]: Here, Father – a drop more.

GREGERS: How can a man like you – a man of the great
outdoors – live in the middle of a stifling city, within these
four walls?

EKDAL [*with a little laugh, glancing over at* HJALMAR]: Oh,
it's not so bad here. Not so bad at all.

GREGERS: But everything that your whole being became
one with? The cool caressing air, a life of freedom out in
the forest and on the open moors, among the animals and
birds –?

EKDAL [*smiles*]: Hjalmar, should we show it to him?

HJALMAR [*quickly and a little embarrassed*]: Oh no, no, Father;
not tonight.

GREGERS: What does he want to show me?

HJALMAR: Oh, it's just something that – you can see it another
time.

GREGERS [*continues to old* EKDAL]: Anyway, what I meant to say was *this*, Lieutenant Ekdal, you should come up to the Works with me now; I'll be going back soon. You'd have no problem getting copy work up there too. And you don't have anything here to cheer and invigorate you.

EKDAL [*stares at him in surprise*]: *I* don't have anything to –!

GREGERS: Well, yes, you have Hjalmar, but he has his own family. And a man like you, who's always been so drawn to everything free and wild –

EKDAL [*slams the table*]: Hjalmar! He *shall* see it!

HJALMAR: But Father, is it worth it now? It's so dark –

EKDAL: Rubbish, there's the moonlight. [*Gets up*] He *shall* see it, I say. Let me through. Come and help me, Hjalmar!

HEDVIG: Oh yes, do, Father!

HJALMAR [*gets up*]: All right, then.

GREGERS [*to* GINA]: What *is* it?

GINA: Oh, you mustn't go thinking it's anything too grand.

> EKDAL *and* HJALMAR *have gone over to the back wall and they each push one half of the double doors to the side;* HEDVIG *helps old* EKDAL; GREGERS *remains standing by the sofa;* GINA *stays seated, undisturbed, sewing. Through the doorway a long, irregular attic room can be seen, with various nooks and crannies, and a couple of freestanding chimney pipes. There are skylights through which bright moonlight falls on some parts of the large room; other parts lie in deep shade.*

EKDAL [*to* GREGERS]: Please, come right over.

GREGERS [*walks over to them*]: So what *is* this then?

EKDAL: Well, have a look. Hmm.

HJALMAR [*a little embarrassed*]: All this belongs to *Father*, you understand.

GREGERS [*by the door, looking into the attic room*]: So, you keep hens, Lieutenant Ekdal!

EKDAL: I should think so – we keep hens all right, sir. They've flown up now. But you should see those hens in the daylight, oh yes!

HEDVIG: And then there's –

EKDAL: Shh, shh – not yet.

GREGERS: And you've got pigeons too, I see.

EKDAL: Oh, we do indeed have pigeons! They have their nest-ing boxes up there under the eaves, sir, because pigeons prefer to be up high, you understand.

HJALMAR: They're not all just ordinary pigeons.

EKDAL: Ordinary! No, I should think not! We've got tumblers, and a couple of pouters too. But come here! You see that pen over there by the wall?

GREGERS: Yes; what do you use that for?

EKDAL: That's where the rabbits sleep at night, sir.

GREGERS: Right; so you keep rabbits too?

EKDAL: You can be damn sure we keep rabbits! He's asking if we keep rabbits, Hjalmar! Hmm. But *now*, you see, comes the real thing! Here it comes! Move yourself, Hedvig. Stand there, sir; that's right, and now look down there. – Do you see a basket with straw in it?

GREGERS: Yes. And I can see a bird lying in the basket.

EKDAL: Hmm – 'a bird' –

GREGERS: It's a duck, isn't it?

EKDAL [*offended*]: Yes, obviously it's a duck.

HJALMAR: But what *sort* of duck, do you think?

HEDVIG: It's not any plain duck –

EKDAL: Shush!

GREGERS: And it's not a Muscovy duck either.

EKDAL: No, Mr – Werle. It's not a Muscovy duck, because it's a wild duck.

GREGERS: No, really? A wild duck?

EKDAL: Oh yes it is. That 'bird', as you called it – that's the wild duck, no less. That is our wild duck, sir.

HEDVIG: *My* wild duck. Because *I* own it.

GREGERS: And it can live up here in the attic? And it thrives here?

EKDAL: She has a trough of water to splash about in, you understand.

HJALMAR: Fresh water every other day.

GINA [*turns towards* HJALMAR]: But, Ekdal dear, it's getting so icy cold in here now.

EKDAL: Hmm, let's close up, then. It's not worth disturbing their night's rest either. Give a hand, Hedvig.

HJALMAR *and* HEDVIG *push the attic doors shut.*

EKDAL: You can see her properly another time. [*Sits down in the armchair by the stove*] Oh, they're remarkable things these wild ducks, believe me.

GREGERS: But how did you manage to catch it, Lieutenant Ekdal?

EKDAL: I didn't catch it. There's a certain man here in town whom we have to thank for it.

GREGERS [*slightly taken aback*]: That man wouldn't be my father by any chance?

EKDAL: That's right – yes. It *was* your father. Hmm.

HJALMAR: How funny you managed to guess *that*, Gregers.

GREGERS: Well, you said earlier, after all, that you were indebted to Father for a great many things, so I thought perhaps –

GINA: But we didn't get the duck from Mr Werle himself –

EKDAL: All the same, Gina, it's Håken Werle we can thank for her. [*To* GREGERS] He was out in a boat, you see, and he took a shot at her. But his eyesight's not too sharp these days, your father. Hmm – so she was only wounded.

GREGERS: I see – she got a couple of pellets in her body.

HJALMAR: Yes, she got two or three.

HEDVIG: She got them under her wing, so she couldn't fly.

GREGERS: Right, so I take it she dived to the bottom?

EKDAL [*sleepy, with a thick voice*]: Stands to reason. Wild ducks always do. Scud to the bottom – as deep as they can go, sir – clamp their beaks tight onto the plants and seaweed – and all the evil muck that's down *there*. And then they never come up again.

GREGERS: But *your* wild duck did come up again, Lieutenant Ekdal.

EKDAL: He had a quite extraordinarily canny dog, your father. – And that dog – he dived down and brought the duck up again.

GREGERS [*to* HJALMAR]: And then you got it?

HJALMAR: Not straight away; first it went home to your father's, but it wasn't thriving there, so Pettersen was told that he should finish it off –

EKDAL: [*half asleep*]: Hm – yes, Pettersen – that dunderhead –

HJALMAR [speaks more quietly]: That's how we got it, you see; because Father knows Pettersen a bit, and when he heard all this about the wild duck, he managed to get it handed over to him.

GREGERS: And it seems to be thriving perfectly, there in the attic.

HJALMAR: Yes, amazingly well. It's got quite fat. And of course it's been in there for so long now it's forgotten life in the true wild – that's what it all comes down to really.

GREGERS: You're probably right there, Hjalmar. Just don't ever let it glimpse the sea or the sky –. But I ought not to stay any longer – I think your father's asleep.

HJALMAR: Oh, that's not a problem –

GREGERS: But, while I think of it – you said you had a room for rent – a spare room?

HJALMAR: Yes; what about it? Do you perhaps know someone –?

GREGERS: May I have that room?

HJALMAR: You?

GINA: Really – you, Mr Werle –?²⁵

GREGERS: May I have the room? If so, I'll move in first thing tomorrow.

HJALMAR: Yes, with the greatest pleasure –

GINA: Really, Mr Werle, it's not a room for the likes of you.

HJALMAR: But Gina, how can you say that?

GINA: Well, the room's not big enough or light enough, and –

GREGERS: That's not so much of an issue, Mrs Ekdal.

HJALMAR: I think it's rather a nice room actually, and not at all badly furnished either.

GINA: But remember the two that live under us.

GREGERS: What two?

GINA: Oh, there's one used to be a tutor –

HJALMAR: A certain Mr Molvik.

GINA: – and there's a doctor,²⁶ called Relling.

GREGERS: Relling? I know him vaguely; he had his practice up in Høidal for a while.

GINA: They're a couple of extremely high-spirited menfolk. They often go out escapading of an evening, and then they come home dreadfully late at night, and they're not always exactly –

GREGERS: One soon gets used to that sort of thing. I hope things will turn out for me as for the wild duck –

GINA: Hmm. All the same, I think you should sleep on it first.

GREGERS: You don't seem too keen on having me in the house, Mrs Ekdal.

GINA: Lordy me, how could you think that?

HJALMAR: Yes, you are being rather peculiar, Gina. [*To* GREGERS] So you're thinking of staying on here in town for the time being?

GREGERS [*puts his coat on*]: Yes, I am thinking of staying on now.

HJALMAR: But not in your father's house? So what do you intend to do?

GREGERS: Well, if I knew *that*, old chap – I wouldn't be in such a dire state. But when I have to bear the cross of being called Gregers –. 'Gregers' – and then 'Werle' to follow; have you heard anything so hideous?

HJALMAR: Oh, I wouldn't say –.

GREGERS: Ugh! I'd want to spit on a chap with a name like that. But when one carries the cross of being Gregers – Werle in this world – as I do –

HJALMAR [*laughs*]: Ha ha. If you weren't Gregers Werle, what would you want to be?

GREGERS: If I could choose, I'd prefer to be a clever dog.

GINA: A dog?

HEDVIG [*involuntarily*]: Oh, no!

GREGERS: Yes, an extraordinarily clever dog; the kind that goes to the bottom after wild ducks when they dive under and cling hard with their beaks to the plants and seaweed down in the mud.

HJALMAR: You know what, Gregers – I have no idea what you're talking about.

GREGERS: Well, no, I don't suppose there's much sense in it either. But anyway, tomorrow morning – I shall be moving in. [*To* GINA] I won't cause you any bother; I'll do everything myself. [*To* HJALMAR] We'll talk about the rest tomorrow. – Goodnight, Mrs Ekdal. [*Nods to* HEDVIG] Goodnight!

GINA: Goodnight, Mr Werle.

HEDVIG: Goodnight.

HJALMAR [*who has lit a candle*]: Wait a minute; I must light your way. I expect it'll be dark on the stairs.

GREGERS *and* HJALMAR *walk out through the hallway door.*

GINA [*looks straight ahead, with her sewing in her lap*]: Wasn't that strange talk about him wanting to be a dog?

HEDVIG: I'll say one thing, Mother – I think he meant something else by it.

GINA: What would *that* be?

HEDVIG: I don't know, but it was as if he sort of meant something different to what he said – the whole time.

GINA: You think so? Yes, it was strange.

HJALMAR [*returning*]: The lamp was still burning. [*Blows the candle out and puts it down*] Ah, finally I can get a bite to eat. [*Starts to eat the slices of bread*] Well, you see now, Gina – when you have your wits about you –

GINA: Wits about you? How?

HJALMAR: Well, it was fortunate at least that we got that room rented out at last. And then, imagine – to someone like Gregers – a dear old friend.

GINA: Yes, I'm not sure what to say.

HEDVIG: Oh Mother, you'll see, it'll be fun!

HJALMAR: But you really are peculiar. You were so keen on getting it rented out before, and now you don't like it.

GINA: Oh yes, Ekdal, if it had only been to somebody else –. But what do you think Mr Werle Senior will say?

HJALMAR: Old Werle? It's none of his business.

GINA: But surely you realize that something's come between them again, since the son's moving out of the house. You know how it is with those two.

HJALMAR: Yes, perhaps, but –

GINA: And Mr Werle might think you're behind it –

HJALMAR: Well, just let him go on thinking that! Mr Werle has done an incredible amount for me, Lord yes – I acknowledge that. But I can't be eternally subject to him on account of that.

GINA: But, Ekdal, dear, Old Da might suffer for it. He might lose what miserable little earnings he has with Gråberg.

HJALMAR: I'd be tempted to say: I wish that were so! Isn't it humiliating for a man, like me, to have to see his grey-haired father going about like some downtrodden wretch? But the time will soon be ripe,[27] I think. [*Takes another slice of bread*] If I *have* a mission in life, I shall most surely carry it out!

HEDVIG: Oh yes, Father! Do!

GINA: Shh! Just don't wake him up!

HJALMAR [*more quietly*]: I *shall* carry it out, I say. The day will surely dawn, and then –. That's why it's good we got the room rented out, because then I'll have greater independence. And *that's* what a man who has a mission in life needs. [*Over by the armchair, emotional*] Poor old white-haired Father. Trust in your Hjalmar. He has broad shoulders, well, strong shoulders at least. – One fine day you'll wake up and –. [*To* GINA] Don't you believe me?

GINA [*gets up*]: Of course I do, but let's get him into his bed first.

HJALMAR: Yes, let's.

They gently take hold of the old man.

ACT THREE

Hjalmar Ekdal's studio; it is morning; daylight falls through the large window in the sloping roof; the curtain is drawn back.

HJALMAR sits at the table busy retouching a photograph; several other pictures lie in front of him. A little later GINA comes in through the hallway door wearing a hat and a coat; she has a basket with a lid over her arm.

HJALMAR: You back already, Gina?

GINA: Yes, can't afford to dawdle. [*Puts the basket on a chair and takes her outdoor clothes off*]

HJALMAR: Have you looked in on Gregers?

GINA: Oh yes, I have all right. It's a delightful sight in there – made it lovely the minute he arrived, he did.

HJALMAR: Really?

GINA: Yes, he said he wanted to do everything himself. And he was lighting the stove, and then he closed the flue so the whole room filled with smoke. Urgh, it made such a stink –

HJALMAR: Oh, dear.

GINA: But this is the best bit; then he goes to put it out and chucks the water from the washstand into the stove, so the floor's swimming in the worst filth ever.

HJALMAR: That's a bore.

GINA: I got the concierge up here to scrub after him, the pig. But it won't be fit to be in till later this afternoon.

HJALMAR: So where's he gone in the meantime?

GINA: He went out for a bit, he said.

HJALMAR: I popped in on him too for a moment – just after you went out.

GINA: So I heard. And you've asked him in for breakfast.[28]

HJALMAR: Just a sort of early lunchtime bite, you understand. It is his first day after all – we can't exactly avoid that. You've always got something in the house.

GINA: I'll have to try and find something.

HJALMAR: But don't go making it too stingy. Because I think Relling and Molvik will probably come up too. I just met Relling on the stairs, you see, so I had to –

GINA: We're having *those* two as well?

HJALMAR: Good God, a couple of people more or less – that's surely neither here nor there.

EKDAL [*opens his door and looks in*]: Listen here, Hjalmar – [*notices* GINA] Oh.

GINA: Does Grandpa want something?

EKDAL: No, never mind. Hmm! [*Goes back in*]

GINA [*takes her basket*]: Keep a careful watch over him, so he doesn't go out.

HJALMAR: Yes, yes, yes, I will. – Listen, Gina dear; a little herring salad would be good – I think Relling and Molvik were probably out on the booze last night.

GINA: So long as they don't land on me too soon –

HJALMAR: No, of course – you take your time.

GINA: And meanwhile you can work a bit.

HJALMAR: I *am* working! I'm working as hard as I can!

GINA: Then you'll have that off your hands at least.

She walks out into the kitchen with her basket. HJALMAR *sits for a while brushing the photograph; he works slowly and grudgingly.*

EKDAL [*peeps in, looks around the studio and says quietly*]: You busy?

HJALMAR: Yes, I'm slogging away here at these pictures –

EKDAL: Oh, God, Lord preserve us – if you're that busy, then –. Hmm! [*Goes back in; the door is left open*]

HJALMAR [*carries on a while in silence; then he puts his brush down and walks over to the door*]: Are *you* busy, Father?

EKDAL [*growling from inside*]: If *you* are busy, then *I* am busy too. Hmm!

HJALMAR: If you say so. [*Returns to his work*]

EKDAL [*shortly after, reappears in the doorway*]: Hmm. You know what, Hjalmar, I'm not really all that *terribly* busy.

HJALMAR: I thought you were writing.

EKDAL: Oh, hell! Can't that Gråberg wait a day or two? I'm sure it's not a matter of life or death.

HJALMAR: No, and you're not a slave.

EKDAL: And there's that other thing needs doing in there –

HJALMAR: You're quite right. Perhaps you want to go in there? Shall I open up for you?

EKDAL: That wouldn't be a bad idea.

HJALMAR [*gets up*]: Because then we'll have *that* off our hands.

EKDAL: Quite, yes. Needs to be ready for the morning. It is tomorrow, isn't it? Hmm?

HJALMAR: It most certainly is tomorrow.

HJALMAR *and* EKDAL *each take one of the double doors and push it back. The morning sun shines in through the skylights, some pigeons fly back and forth, others are cooing on the rafters; now and then the hens can be heard clucking further back in the attic.*

HJALMAR: Well, you'd better get a move on then, Father.

EKDAL [*goes in*]: Aren't you joining me?

HJALMAR: Well yes, you know what – I think perhaps – [*Sees* GINA *in the kitchen door*] Me? No, I don't have time, I really must work. – But now for our special mechanism –

He pulls a cord, a curtain slides down inside; its lower section made from a strip of old sailcloth, while the rest, above it, is made of a piece of stretched fishing net. The attic floor is thus no longer visible.

HJALMAR [*goes back to the table*]: There. Now perhaps I'll get a bit of peace.

GINA: Is he running amuck in there again?

HJALMAR: Would it be better if he went off down to Madam Eriksen's, perhaps? [*Sits down*] D'you want something? You *did* say –

GINA: I just wanted to ask if you think we can lay the table in *here?*

HJALMAR: Yes, there aren't any sittings booked this early, are there?

GINA: No, I'm not expecting anyone except those sweethearts who want to sit together.

HJALMAR: Oh hell, couldn't they sit together some other day!

GINA: But, Ekdal dear, I've booked them in after tea, when *you're* asleep.

HJALMAR: Right, that's good. Yes, so we'll eat in here.

GINA: Very well, but there's no rush with laying the table yet – you can go on using it a bit longer.

HJALMAR: Oh, surely you can see I'm sitting here using the table all I can!

GINA: And so then you'll be free later, won't you. [*Goes out into the kitchen again*]
   Short pause.

EKDAL [*in the attic doorway, inside the net*]: Hjalmar!

HJALMAR: What now?

EKDAL: Afraid we'll need to move the water-trough after all.

HJALMAR: Yes, that's what I've been saying all along.

EKDAL: Hm-hm-hm. [*Goes away from the door again*]
   HJALMAR *works a little, glances over towards the attic and half gets up.* HEDVIG *enters from the kitchen.*

HJALMAR [*quickly sits down again*]: What do you want?

HEDVIG: I just wanted to be with you, Father.

HJALMAR [*after a while*]: Seems to me you're going around snooping. Meant to keep watch, are you?

HEDVIG: Not at all.

HJALMAR: What's Mother up to out there now?

HEDVIG: Oh, Mother's up to her elbows in herring salad. [*Goes over to the table*] Isn't there some little way I can help you, Father?

HJALMAR: No. It's best I get on and handle all this alone – while my strength lasts. – There's no reason to worry, Hedvig, as long as your father can keep his health, then –

HEDVIG: Oh Father, you mustn't say anything so horrid.

> *She walks around a little, stops at the doorway and looks into the attic.*

HJALMAR: What's he up to now, Hedvig?

HEDVIG: It seems there's to be a new path up to the water-trough.

HJALMAR: He'll never manage *that* on his own! And *I* am sentenced to sit here –!

HEDVIG [*walks over to him*]: Let *me* have the brush, Father, I'm sure I can do it.

HJALMAR: Nonsense; you'll just ruin your eyes.

HEDVIG: No I won't. Hand me the brush.

HJALMAR [*gets up*]: Oh, all right then, it shouldn't take more than a minute or two.

HEDVIG: Oh, what harm can that do? [*Takes the brush*] There now. [*Sits down*] And here's one for me to copy from.

HJALMAR: But don't ruin your eyes! You hear? *I* don't want any responsibility. You must take full responsibility yourself, I tell you.

HEDVIG [*retouching*]: Yes, yes, I will.

HJALMAR: You're such a clever girl, Hedvig. Just a couple of minutes, you understand.

> *He sneaks past the edge of the curtain into the attic.*
> HEDVIG *sits working.* HJALMAR *and* EKDAL *are heard discussing things inside.*

HJALMAR [*appears from behind the net*]: Hedvig, pass me those pliers over there on the shelf. And the chisel, please. [*Turns to the room behind him*] Yes but, Father, look at this. Let me just show you first exactly what I'm thinking.

> HEDVIG *has fetched the tools from the shelf and hands them to him.*

HJALMAR: Thanks. Well now, Father, it's a good job I came in here. [*Disappears from the doorway; they can be heard in the attic, hammering and sawing and chatting together*]

> HEDVIG *stands watching them. After a while there is a knock on the hallway door; she doesn't notice.*

GREGERS [*without a hat*[29] *and overcoat, enters and stops for a while by the door*]: Hrm –!

HEDVIG [*turns and goes towards him*]: Good morning. Please, come right in.

GREGERS: Thank you. [*Looks towards the attic*] You[30] seem to have workmen in the house.

HEDVIG: No, it's just Father and Grandpa. I'll tell them you're here.

GREGERS: No, no, don't. I'd rather wait a bit. [*Sits down on the sofa*]

HEDVIG: It's so messy here – [*Makes as if to clear away the photographs*]

GREGERS: Oh, just leave those. Are they pictures that need finishing?

HEDVIG: Yes, it's a little something I was helping Father with.

GREGERS: Well, don't let me disturb you.

HEDVIG: No, all right.

   She moves the things closer to herself and sits back down to work; GREGERS *watches her in silence.*

GREGERS: Did the wild duck sleep well last night?

HEDVIG: Yes, thanks, I think so.

GREGERS [*turned towards the attic room*]: It looks rather different by day than it did in the moonlight yesterday.

HEDVIG: Yes, it can vary so much. It looks very different in the morning from the way it looks in the afternoon, and different when it's raining from when the weather's fine.

GREGERS: You've observed that?

HEDVIG: Well, it's plain to see.

GREGERS: Do you like being in there with the wild duck?

HEDVIG: Yes, whenever possible –

GREGERS: But you probably don't have much spare time; you go to school, I presume.

HEDVIG: No, not any more, because Father's worried I'll ruin my eyes.

GREGERS: Aha, so he gives you lessons himself then.

HEDVIG: Father promised he'd give me lessons, but he's not had the time yet.

GREGERS: But isn't there anybody else who helps you a bit then?

HEDVIG: Well, yes, there's Mr Molvik. But he's not always altogether – quite – sort of –

GREGERS: He gets drunk?

HEDVIG: Yes, most likely.

GREGERS: Well, then you've got time for all sorts of things. And in there – *there*, I imagine it must be like a world of its own?

HEDVIG: All of its own. And there are so many strange things in there.

GREGERS: Oh?

HEDVIG: Yes, there are big cabinets full of books, and in lots of the books there are pictures.

GREGERS: Aha!

HEDVIG: And there's this old writing bureau with drawers and flaps and a big clock with figurines that are supposed to pop out. But the clock's not working any more.

GREGERS: So time has stopped in there – where the wild duck is.

HEDVIG: Yes. And there are old paintboxes and the like. And all those books.

GREGERS: And you read those books?

HEDVIG: Oh, yes, whenever I can. But most of them are in English; and I don't understand that. But then I look at the pictures. – There's a really big book called *Harryson's History of London*;[31] it's probably a hundred years old, and it's got masses of pictures in it. On the cover there's an illustration of Death with an hourglass[32] and a maiden. I think it's horrid. But then there are all the other pictures with churches and castles and streets and big ships sailing on the sea.

GREGERS: But tell me, where did you get all these marvellous things from?

HEDVIG: Oh, an old sea captain lived here long ago, and he brought them home with him. They called him 'the flying Dutchman'.[33] And that's strange, because he wasn't a Dutchman at all.

GREGERS: Really?

HEDVIG: No. But in the end he disappeared and left all of it there behind him.

GREGERS: Listen, tell me – when you're sitting in there looking at those pictures, don't you ever get the urge to go out and see the big, real world for yourself?

HEDVIG: Oh, no! I want to stay here at home always, and help Father and Mother.

GREGERS: With retouching photographs?

HEDVIG: No, not only that. More than anything I want to learn how to engrave pictures like the ones in the English books.

GREGERS: Hmm, what does your father say to that?

HEDVIG: I don't think Father likes it. He's strange about that sort of thing. Imagine, he says I ought to learn to do basket-weaving and straw-plaiting![34] But I don't think *that* sounds up to much.

GREGERS: No, nor do I.

HEDVIG: But Father's right about one thing – if I'd learned to make baskets, then I could have made the wild duck's new basket.

GREGERS: You could have, yes – and you'd be the perfect person to do it.

HEDVIG: Yes, because it's *my* wild duck.

GREGERS: Indeed, it is.

HEDVIG: Oh yes! *I* own it. Though Father and Grandpa can borrow it as often as they like.

GREGERS: I see; so what do they use it for then?

HEDVIG: Oh, they tend to its needs, build things for it, that sort of thing.

GREGERS: I can imagine, because the wild duck must be the finest creature in there.

HEDVIG: Yes, she[35] is, because she is a *genuine* wild bird of course. And you have to feel sorry for her too – she has no one of her own, poor thing.

GREGERS: She has no family, unlike the rabbits –

HEDVIG: Exactly. Lots of the hens were chicks together too, but she has strayed so far from her own kind. And then there's so much mystery about the wild duck. There's nobody that knows her, and nobody that knows where she comes from.

GREGERS: And she's been to the bottom of the watery deep.

HEDVIG [*looks briefly at him, suppresses a smile and asks*]: Why do you say the watery deep?

GREGERS: What should I say?

HEDVIG: You could have said the bottom of the sea – or the seabed?

GREGERS: Oh, isn't the watery deep just as good?

HEDVIG: Yes, but it sounds so strange to me when someone else says the watery deep.

GREGERS: Why? Tell me?

HEDVIG: No, I don't want to – it's silly.

GREGERS: I doubt it. Go on, tell me why you smiled.

HEDVIG: It's because whenever it pops into my mind – without really thinking – it seems to me that – that the room and everything in it, is called 'the watery deep'. – But that's silly.

GREGERS: You shouldn't say that.

HEDVIG: Well, but it's just an attic.

GREGERS [looks fixedly at her]: Are you so certain of that?

HEDVIG [surprised]: That it's an attic?

GREGERS: Yes, do you really know that for sure?

HEDVIG is silent, looking at him open-mouthed. GINA comes in from the kitchen with the things for the table.

GREGERS [gets up]: I expect I've arrived too early for you.

GINA: Oh, you have to be somewhere; besides, it'll be ready soon. Clear the table, Hedvig.

HEDVIG clears up; she and GINA lay the table during what follows. GREGERS sits down in the armchair leafing through an album.

GREGERS: I hear you can retouch photographs, Mrs Ekdal.

GINA [with a sideways glance]: M-hm, yes I can.

GREGERS: That was a stroke of luck.

GINA: What do you mean, luck?

GREGERS: Given that Ekdal became a photographer, I mean.

HEDVIG: Mother can take photographs too.

GINA: Oh yes, I had to learn that skill for myself.

GREGERS: So perhaps it's you who runs the business?

GINA: Yes, when Ekdal hasn't the time himself, then –

GREGERS: Well, he's very occupied with his old father, I imagine.

GINA: Yes, and it's not quite the thing for a man like Ekdal to be taking pottrits of the hoi polloys.

GREGERS: I'd agree – but now that he's started out on that path –

GINA: Mr Werle, I am sure that you can understand that Ekdal is not like one of those ordinary photographers.

GREGERS: Well, no doubt! But –
   A shot is fired in the attic.

GREGERS [*jumps up*]: What's that!

GINA: Ouph, now they're shooting again.

GREGERS: They shoot too?

HEDVIG: They go hunting.

GREGERS: They what! [*Over by the attic doors*] Are you hunting, Hjalmar?

HJALMAR [*behind the net*]: Oh, you've arrived? I had no idea. I was rather occupied –. [*To* HEDVIG] And you – you didn't think to tell us, Hedvig! [*Comes into the studio*]

GREGERS: Do you go around shooting in the attic?

HJALMAR [*shows a double-barrelled pistol*]: Oh, it's just with this.

GINA: Yes, you and Old Da will have an accident with that pigstol one day.

HJALMAR [*irritated*]: I think I've told you before that a gun like this is called a pistol.

GINA: Oh, that's no better, if you ask me.

GREGERS: So, *you've* become a hunter too, Hjalmar?

HJALMAR: It's only the occasional little rabbit hunt. Mostly for Father's benefit, you understand.

GINA: Menfolk are so strange; they always need something to diversify[36] themselves with.

HJALMAR [*annoyed*]: Yes, quite; we always need something to *divert* ourselves with.

GINA: Yes, *that's* what I said.

HJALMAR: Hmm! [*To* GREGERS] Well, you see, Gregers, the attic is by lucky coincidence situated so no one can hear us when we shoot. [*Puts the pistol on the top bookshelf*] Don't touch the pistol, Hedvig! One of the barrels is loaded, just remember that.

GREGERS [*looks in through the net*]: You have a hunting rifle too, I see.

HJALMAR: That's Father's old rifle. It doesn't shoot any more; there's something wrong with the lock. But it's rather fun to have it all the same; we can take it apart and clean it once in a while and lubricate it with bone oil[37] and then screw it back together again −. Well, of course, it's Father mainly who tinkers with those things.

HEDVIG [*over by* GREGERS]: You can see the wild duck properly now.

GREGERS: Indeed, I'm looking at her at this very moment. One of her wings is trailing, I think.

HJALMAR: Well, that's no surprise; she was wounded.

GREGERS: And she drags her foot a bit. Or am I wrong?

HJALMAR: A tiny bit perhaps.

HEDVIG: Yes, 'cos *that's* the foot the dog bit.

HJALMAR: But she has no other injury or fault, and that's quite remarkable when she's had a charge of pellets in her body and been in the jaws of a dog −

GREGERS [*with a glance towards* HEDVIG]: − and been to the bottom of the watery deep − for so long.

HEDVIG [*smiles*]: Yes.

GINA [*busy at the table*]: That blessed wild duck, yes. There's been litanies aplenty over her.

HJALMAR: Hmm − is that ready soon?

GINA: Yes, any minute. Hedvig, you must come now and help me.

GINA *and* HEDVIG *go out to the kitchen.*

HJALMAR [*in a lowered voice*]: I don't think it's a good idea to stand there looking at Father. He doesn't like it.

GREGERS *moves away from the attic door.*

HJALMAR: And it's best I close up now, before the others come in. [*Frightens the animals away with his hands*] Shoo! Shoo! Off you go now! [*As he pulls the curtain up and closes the doors*] This contraption is my own invention. It's rather fun to have this sort of thing to tend to and fix when it breaks. Besides, it's totally indispensable too, you see; Gina doesn't want rabbits and hens coming in here − with this being the studio.

GREGERS: Yes of course, and it's your wife who's in charge of that perhaps?

HJALMAR: I usually entrust her with the day-to-day running of the business − then I can retreat to the living room and think about matters of greater importance.

GREGERS: And what might those be, Hjalmar?

HJALMAR: I'm surprised that you haven't asked me about *that* before. Or perhaps you've not heard talk of my new invention?

GREGERS: Invention? No.

HJALMAR: Really? You haven't? Well, up there in the forests and wilderness –

GREGERS: So you've invented something!

HJALMAR: Well, I've not quite finished it yet, but I'm working on it. I'm sure you can imagine that when I decided to sacrifice myself to photography, it wasn't in order to go around taking portraits of everyday ordinary folk.

GREGERS: No, no, your wife just said that too.

HJALMAR: I swore that if I dedicated my energies to this profession, then I would elevate it to such heights that it became both an art and a science. So I decided on making this remarkable invention.

GREGERS: And what kind of invention is it? What does it do?

HJALMAR: Well, you mustn't ask me about any such particulars yet, my friend. It takes time, you understand. And you mustn't think I am driven by vanity. I am certainly not working for my own benefit. Oh, no, it is my life's mission that guides me night and day.

GREGERS: What kind of life's mission?

HJALMAR: Are you forgetting the old man with silver hair?

GREGERS: Your poor father; yes, but what can you actually do for him?

HJALMAR: I can resurrect his self-esteem from the dead as I lift the Ekdal name to honour and glory once more.

GREGERS: So that is your life's mission.

HJALMAR: Yes. I want to rescue this shipwrecked man. His ship ran aground the instant the storm broke loose over him. He was no longer himself during the time of those frightful investigations. That pistol over there – the one we use to shoot rabbits – it has played a role in the Ekdal family tragedy.

GREGERS: The pistol! How?

HJALMAR: When judgement was passed and he knew he'd be locked up – he held that pistol in his hand –

GREGERS: He held –!

HJALMAR: Yes – but he didn't dare. He was a coward. That was how diminished, how broken his soul already was. Oh! Can you understand it? A military man, a man who'd shot nine bears, who was descended from two lieutenant colonels – well, from one after the other, of course –. Can you understand it, Gregers?

GREGERS: Yes, I can understand it perfectly.

HJALMAR: I don't. And that pistol would figure in our family history again. When he'd been put in his grey garb[38] and placed under lock and key – oh, those were dreadful times for me, believe me. I kept the blinds down at both my windows. Whenever I peeped out I saw that the sun was shining as usual. I couldn't comprehend it. I saw people walking in the street, laughing and talking about trivial things. I couldn't comprehend it. I thought all existence should stand still, as though in an eclipse.

GREGERS: That's exactly how I felt when Mother died too.

HJALMAR: It was in just such a moment Hjalmar Ekdal held this pistol to his own chest.

GREGERS: Did *you* also consider –?

HJALMAR: Yes.

GREGERS: But you didn't fire?

HJALMAR: No, at the decisive moment I won a victory over myself. I lived on. But believe me, it takes courage to choose *life* under *such* circumstances.

GREGERS: Yes, it depends on how one views it.

HJALMAR: Unquestionably, my friend. But it was for the best – since I'll have my invention ready soon, and then Dr Relling believes, as do I, that Father will be permitted to wear his uniform once more. I will demand that as my only reward.

GREGERS: So it's this thing with the uniform that he –?

HJALMAR: Yes, *that's* what he yearns for most. You can't imagine how my heart bleeds for him. Every time we celebrate a little family event – like Gina's and my wedding anniversary or whatever – in comes the old man sporting his lieutenant's uniform of happier days. But if there's as much as a knock at the door – because he doesn't dare show himself to outsiders, you see – then he scurries back into his little room as fast as his old legs will carry him. It's heart-rending for a son to witness that!

GREGERS: When approximately do you think the invention will be finished?

HJALMAR: Oh, good Lord, you really mustn't question me about particulars such as time. We are not the sole masters of something like an invention. It's largely reliant on inspiration – on the impulse of the moment – and it's almost impossible to forecast when that moment will come.

GREGERS: But it's progressing, I assume?

HJALMAR: Certainly it's progressing. Not a day passes when I don't grapple with my invention; it fills me entirely. Every afternoon, when I've eaten, I shut myself in the living room where I can mull it over in peace. But I mustn't be nagged; nothing good comes of that; Relling says so too.

GREGERS: And you don't think this business with the attic distracts you and spreads you too thin?

HJALMAR: No, no, no; on the contrary. You mustn't say that. I can't be continually poring over the same exhausting thoughts. I need something on the side to fill the waiting time. Inspiration, the sudden impulse, you see – when it comes, it comes irrespective.

GREGERS: My dear Hjalmar, it seems to me that there's something of that wild duck in you.

HJALMAR: The wild duck? How do you mean?

GREGERS: You've dived down and bitten tight onto the weeds.

HJALMAR: You refer perhaps to the near-mortal shot which hit Father in the wing – and me?

GREGERS: Not so much *that*. I wouldn't say you're maimed, but you've ended up in a poisonous swamp, Hjalmar. A disease has crept into your body, and you've gone to the bottom to die in darkness.

HJALMAR: Me? Die in darkness! No. You know what, Gregers, you really shouldn't talk like that.

GREGERS: Don't worry – I'll make certain that I get you back up. For I too have a mission in life now, you see. It came to me yesterday.

HJALMAR: Yes, that may be, but you'll leave *me* out of it. I can assure you that apart from my melancholy of course – which is eminently explainable – I feel as well as any person could wish.

GREGERS: The fact that you *do* is also caused by this poison.

HJALMAR: Really, my dear Gregers, do stop talking about diseases and poisons, I'm not at all used to such conversations. In my house nobody ever talks to me about unpleasant things.

GREGERS: Yes, *that* I can believe.

HJALMAR: No, it's not good for me. And there is no swamp-air here, as you put it. In this humble photographer's home the ceiling may be low, I'm aware – and my living standards are humble. But I am an inventor – and a family provider too. *That* lifts me above these paltry conditions. – Ah, here they come with lunch!

> GINA *and* HEDVIG *bring bottles of beer, liquor decanter, glasses etc. At the same time* RELLING *and* MOLVIK *come in from the hallway, both without hat and coat;* MOLVIK *is dressed in black.*

GINA [*puts everything on the table*]: Ah, *those* two are on the dot, of course!

RELLING: Molvik was sure he could smell herring salad and there was no holding him back. – Good morning for the second time, Ekdal.

HJALMAR: Gregers, may I present Mr Molvik and Doctor – well, you already know Relling, yes?

GREGERS: Yes, a little.

RELLING: Oh, it's Mr Werle Junior. Yes, we had a bit of a head-to-head up at the Høidal Works. So you've just moved in?

GREGERS: I moved in this morning.

RELLING: Molvik and I live below you, so you haven't far to go for a doctor and a priest, should you have use for either.

GREGERS: Thanks, that may well be required; we were thirteen at table yesterday.

HJALMAR: Oh, don't start all that unpleasantness again!

RELLING: Don't worry, Ekdal; it won't touch you.

HJALMAR: I hope so for my family's sake. But let's sit down now and eat, drink and be merry.[39]

GREGERS: Shouldn't we wait for your father?

HJALMAR: No, he wants *his* later in his room. Come on!
The men sit down to lunch, eating and drinking. GINA
and HEDVIG *go in and out serving.*

RELLING: Molvik was really swaying in his boots yesterday,
Mrs Ekdal.

GINA: Oh? Again?

RELLING: Didn't you hear him when I brought him home last
night?

GINA: No, I can't say I did.

RELLING: That's a relief – Molvik was terrible last night.

GINA: Is that true, Molvik?

MOLVIK: Let's draw a line through the night's events. These
things are not the product of my better self.

RELLING [*to* GREGERS]: An impulse comes over him, and then
I'm obliged to go out with him on the booze. Molvik is
demonic, you see.

GREGERS: Demonic?

RELLING: Molvik is demonic, yes.

GREGERS: Hmm.

RELLING: And demonic personalities aren't made to walk this
world on steady legs; they must veer off the path now and
then. – Anyway, you're still holding out up there at those
ghastly black Works?

GREGERS: I've held out until now.

RELLING: And did you ever manage to enforce that demand
you went around issuing?

GREGERS: Demand? [*Gets the point*] Oh, I see.

HJALMAR: Were *you* issuing demands, Gregers?

GREGERS: Oh nonsense.

RELLING: But he did; he used to do the rounds of all the small-
holders' cottages issuing them with something he called 'the
demand for the highest ideals'.

GREGERS: I was young then.

RELLING: You're right about that; you were very young. And
this demand for the ideal – you never got anybody to honour
it as long as *I* was up there.

GREGERS: Nor afterwards.

RELLING: Well, I presume you're wise enough now to knock the price down a bit.

GREGERS: Never when I stand before a genuine human being.

HJALMAR: Well, that seems reasonable enough to me. – A little butter, Gina.

RELLING: And a chunk of bacon for Molvik.

MOLVIK: Ugh, not bacon!

A knock at the attic door.

HJALMAR: Open up, Hedvig; Father wants to come out.

HEDVIG goes over and opens the door a crack; old EKDAL comes in with a fresh rabbit skin; she closes the door after him.

EKDAL: Morning, gentlemen! Been good hunting today. Shot a big 'un.

HJALMAR: And you've skinned it before I could come –!

EKDAL: Salted it too. It's good and tender that rabbit meat – and sweet too, tastes like sugar. Bon appétit, gentlemen! [Goes into his room]

MOLVIK [gets up]: Sorry – I can't – I must go downstairs at once –

RELLING: Drink some soda water, man!

MOLVIK [hurries]: Ugh – ugh! [Out through the hallway door]

RELLING [to HJALMAR]: Let's drink to the old huntsman.

HJALMAR [clinks glasses with him]: To the sportsman on the shores of the hereafter.

RELLING: To the grey-haired one –. [Drinks] But, tell me something – is his hair grey or white?

HJALMAR: It's pretty much halfway – though, truth be told, he's not got too many hairs left on top.

RELLING: Well, even with losses we get along in this world. Yes, all in all, you're a lucky man, Ekdal, you have this beautiful mission to strive for –

HJALMAR: And strive I do, believe me.

RELLING: And then you have your clever wife, padding in and out in her felt slippers, softly swaying her hips, looking to your every need, making you comfy.

HJALMAR: Yes, Gina – [nods at her] you're a good companion to have on life's path, my dear.

GINA: Now, now, don't sit there pontrificating[40] about me.

RELLING: And what about your Hedvig, Ekdal?

HJALMAR [*moved*]: The child, yes! The child most of all. Hedvig, come to me. [*Strokes her hair*] What day is it tomorrow, hmm?

HEDVIG [*pulls at him*]: Oh no, you mustn't say anything, Father!

HJALMAR: It's like a knife in my heart when I think how meagre it'll be; just a little celebration in the attic –

HEDVIG: Oh, but it will be lovely!

RELLING: And just wait until this remarkable invention sees the light of day, Hedvig!

HJALMAR: Yes, *then* – then you will see –! Hedvig, I've resolved to secure your future. You will want for nothing for the rest of your life. I will insist on – er – something or other for you. *That* will be this poor inventor's only reward.

HEDVIG [*whispers with her arm around his neck*]: Oh, my dear, kind father!

RELLING [*to* GREGERS]: Well now, it makes a nice change don't you think, to sit at a bountiful table in a happy family circle?

HJALMAR: Yes, I treasure these moments at the table.

GREGERS: Personally, I don't thrive in the atmosphere of a swamp.

RELLING: A swamp?

HJALMAR: Oh, don't start that again!

GINA: Pardon me, Mr Werle, there's no swamp-smell round here. For your information I air this room every single day.

GREGERS [*leaves the table*]: The stench to which *I* refer cannot be aired out.

HJALMAR: Stench!

GINA: What d'you think to that, Ekdal!

RELLING: Excuse me – it couldn't be *you* who's brought the stench in with you from those mines?

GREGERS: It's just like you to call what I bring into this house a stench.

RELLING [*crosses over to him*]: Look here, Mr Werle Junior, I strongly suspect you of still carrying an unabridged version of that 'demand for the highest ideals' in your back pocket.

GREGERS: I carry it in my breast.

RELLING: Well, wherever you ruddy well keep it, I'd advise you not to play debt collector here as long as *I* am around.

GREGERS: And if I do?

RELLING: You'll go headfirst down the stairs. Now you know.

HJALMAR [*gets up*]: No, but Relling!

GREGERS: Oh yes, just throw me out –.

GINA [*comes between them*]: You're to stop this, Relling. But I'll say *this*, Mr Werle, after you made such a foul mess in there with that stove, you've no right to come here talking to me about stench.

> *A knock on the hallway door.*

HEDVIG: Mother, there's someone knocking.

HJALMAR: Oh, here we go, more comings and goings!

GINA: Just let me –. [*Goes over to open the door, starts and shies away*] Oh! Goodness!

> MR WERLE *Senior, in a fur coat, takes a step inside.*

WERLE: Apologies, I understand my son is living here.

GINA [*gulps*]: Yes.

HJALMAR [*moves towards him*]: Mr Werle, won't you do us the honour –?

WERLE: Thanks, but I just want to speak with my son.

GREGERS: About what? Here I am.

WERLE: I wish to speak with you in your room.

GREGERS: In my room – very well – [*starts to move*]

GINA: No, that isn't in any state, Lord knows, for –

WERLE: Well, out in the hallway then. I want to talk to you in private.

HJALMAR: You can do that here, Mr Werle, sir. Come into the living room, Relling.

> HJALMAR *and* RELLING *leave to the right;* GINA *takes* HEDVIG *with her into the kitchen.*

GREGERS [*after a short pause*]: Well, we're in private now.

WERLE: You let a few comments drop last night –. And given that you've rented a room with the Ekdals, I can only assume that you've something planned against me.

GREGERS: My plan is to open Hjalmar Ekdal's eyes. He shall see his situation for what it is – that's all.

WERLE: Is *that* the life mission you spoke of yesterday?

GREGERS: Yes. *You* certainly haven't left me any other.

WERLE: So it's me who's warped your mind, Gregers?

GREGERS: You've warped my entire life. I'm not thinking about that business with Mother –. But you're the one I can thank for the fact that my conscience is hounded and plagued by guilt.

WERLE: Aha, so it's your conscience that's ailing you.

GREGERS: I should have stood up to you when the traps were laid for Lieutenant Ekdal. I should have warned him – I had a suspicion where it would lead.

WERLE: Then you should indeed have spoken out.

GREGERS: I didn't dare; that's how cowardly and scared I was. I was so unspeakably afraid of you – at that time and long afterwards.

WERLE: That fear has now passed, it appears.

GREGERS: Fortunately, yes. The crimes committed against old Ekdal, whether by myself or by – others, can never be righted, but I can free Hjalmar from all the secrets and lies in which he is presently suffocating.

WERLE: You think you'd be doing him a good turn?

GREGERS: I'm absolutely confident of it.

WERLE: You think perhaps Ekdal is the kind of man to thank you for such an act of friendship?

GREGERS: Indeed! He is that kind of man.

WERLE: Hmm – we'll see.

GREGERS: And besides – if I'm to continue living, I must find the cure for my sick conscience.

WERLE: It'll never be healed. Your conscience has been sickly since childhood. You inherited it from your mother, Gregers – it's the only legacy she left you.

GREGERS [*with a spiteful smile*]: So you still haven't swallowed the ignominy of getting your sums wrong, when you thought she'd bring you a fortune?

WERLE: Let's not get caught up in irrelevances. – You're resolved then to lead Ekdal onto what you presume to be the right path?

GREGERS: Yes, I am resolved to do so.

WERLE: Very well, I could have spared myself the walk up here. Since it's probably useless to ask you if you want to move back home with me?

GREGERS: It is.

WERLE: And you won't join the firm either?

GREGERS: No.

WERLE: Very well. But since I plan to enter a new marriage now, my estate will be divided between us.

GREGERS [*quickly*]: No. I don't want that.

WERLE: You don't?

GREGERS: No, I wouldn't dare – for the sake of my conscience.

WERLE [*after a brief pause*]: Are you travelling back up to the Works?

GREGERS: No. I consider myself as having left your service.

WERLE: But what will you do then?

GREGERS: Just fulfil my mission. Nothing else.

WERLE: And afterwards? What will you live on?

GREGERS: I've put a little of my salary aside.

WERLE: But how long will *that* last?

GREGERS: I think it'll last my time out.

WERLE: What's *that* supposed to mean?

GREGERS: I won't answer more questions.

WERLE: Goodbye then, Gregers.

GREGERS: Goodbye.

> MR WERLE *leaves.*

HJALMAR [*peeps in*]: Has he gone now?

GREGERS: Yes.

> HJALMAR *and* RELLING *come in, as do* GINA *and* HEDVIG, *from the kitchen.*

RELLING: Well, that lunch went down the drain.

GREGERS: Put on your coat, Hjalmar; you must come for a long walk with me.

HJALMAR: Yes, with pleasure. What did your father want? Was it something to do with me?

GREGERS: Just come. We must talk a little. I'll go in and fetch my coat. [*Leaves through the hallway door*]

GINA: You shouldn't go out with him, Ekdal.

RELLING: No, don't do it, old chap – stay right here.

HJALMAR [*takes his hat and outdoor coat*]: What! When a boyhood friend feels the need to open up to me in private –!

RELLING: But, damn it all – don't you see that the fellow is mad, insane, disturbed!

GINA: Yes, you hear that? His mother had the odd physical delirium too.

HJALMAR: So much greater his need for a friend's watchful eye. [*To* GINA] Do make sure dinner's ready in good time. Goodbye for now. [*Leaves through the hallway door*]

RELLING: A shame that man didn't go to hell down one of the Høidal pits.

GINA: Jesus – why do you say that?

RELLING [*muffled*]: Oh, I have my reasons.

GINA: Do you think Mr Werle Junior really is mad?

RELLING: Unfortunately not. He's no madder than most. But he certainly has one sickness in his body.

GINA: What's wrong with him, then?

RELLING: Well, I'll tell you, Mrs Ekdal. He suffers from acute righteousness-fever.

GINA: Righteousness-fever?

HEDVIG: Is that a kind of illness?

RELLING: Oh yes; it's a national illness, though it only pops up sporadically. [*Nods to* GINA] Thank you for the lunch!
    He leaves through the hallway door.

GINA [*pacing restlessly around the room*]: Ugh, that Gregers Werle – he's always been a queer fish.

HEDVIG [*stands by the table and looks at her quizzically*]: I find all this very strange.

ACT FOUR

Hjalmar Ekdal's studio. A sitting has just taken place; a camera covered with a cloth, a tripod, a couple of chairs, a console table and similar things stand around the room. Afternoon light; the sun is about to set; a little later it starts to get dark.

GINA *stands in the open hallway door with a small box and a wet glass plate*[41] *in her hand, talking to someone outside.*

GINA: Yes, definitely. When I make a promise I keep it. The first dozen will be ready on Monday. – Goodbye!
   The sound of people walking down the stairs. GINA *closes the door, slides the plate into the box and inserts it in the cloth-covered camera.*
HEDVIG [*comes in from the kitchen*]: Have they gone?
GINA [*tidying up*]: Yes, thank God, I've got rid of them at last.
HEDVIG: But have you got any idea why Father's not home yet?
GINA: Are you sure he's not downstairs with Relling?
HEDVIG: No, he isn't there. I flew down the back kitchen stairs just now and asked.
GINA: And his food's standing there getting cold too.
HEDVIG: Yes, it's odd – Father always makes sure to be home for dinner!
GINA: Oh, he'll come soon, you'll see.
HEDVIG: Oh, if only he would – I think everything's so strange here now.
GINA [*calls out*]: There he is!
   HJALMAR EKDAL *comes in through the hallway door.*
HEDVIG [*going to him*]: Father! Oh, how we've waited for you!

GINA [*glances at him*]: You *were* away an awful long time, Ekdal.

HJALMAR [*without looking at her*]: I was some time, yes.

He takes off his coat; GINA *and* HEDVIG *go to help him; he stops them.*

GINA: Have you eaten with Werle perhaps?

HJALMAR [*hangs up his coat*]: No.

GINA [*goes towards the kitchen door*]: Then I'll bring your dinner in for you.

HJALMAR: No, leave the food. I won't eat now.

HEDVIG [*goes closer*]: Aren't you well, Father?

HJALMAR: Well? Oh, yes, tolerably. Gregers and I went for an arduous walk together.

GINA: You oughtn't to go doing that, Ekdal; you're not used to it.

HJALMAR: Hmm. There are a great many things a man must get used to in this world. [*Pacing about a little*] Has anyone come while I was out?

GINA: Nobody but those two sweethearts.

HJALMAR: No new orders?

GINA: No, not today.

HEDVIG: But people will come tomorrow, you'll see, Father.

HJALMAR: Well, let's hope so – because tomorrow I plan to get down to things here in all earnest.

HEDVIG: Tomorrow! But don't you remember what day it is tomorrow?

HJALMAR: Oh, that's true –. Well, from the day after, then. From here on I want to do everything myself. I want to be left absolutely alone with all the work.

GINA: What'll be the good of *that*, Ekdal? You'll only make life miserable for yourself. I can take care of the photography, while you go on tending to your invention.

HEDVIG: And the wild duck, Father – and all the hens and rabbits and –!

HJALMAR: Don't talk to me about that silliness! From tomorrow on I shall never set foot inside that attic again.

HEDVIG: Yes, but, Father, you promised me there'd be a celebration tomorrow, and –

HJALMAR: Hmm, that's true. The day after, then. That damned wild duck, I'd like to wring its neck!

HEDVIG [*screams*]: The wild duck!

GINA: Oh, I've never heard the like!

HEDVIG [*pulls at him*]: No, but Father – it's *my* wild duck!

HJALMAR: Which is why I won't do it. I don't have the heart, Hedvig – I don't have the heart, for your sake. Though I feel very deeply that I really ought to. I shouldn't tolerate a creature under my roof that has been in *those* hands.

GINA: Oh, good Lord, just because Old Da got it from that nasty Mr Pettersen –

HJALMAR [*pacing about the room*]: There are certain demands –. What should I call them? I might say – the demands of the ideal – certain demands that a man cannot ignore, without sustaining injury to his soul.[42]

HEDVIG [*follows after him*]: Yes but, the wild duck – the poor wild duck!

HJALMAR [*stops*]: You heard me; I'll spare it – for your sake. I shan't touch one hair on its – well, as I said, I'll spare it. There are naturally far greater tasks than that to be tackled. But you should go out for a bit, as you usually do, Hedvig – the light's dim enough for you now.

HEDVIG: No, I don't much care to go out now.

HJALMAR: Yes, go on. I think you're squinting rather a lot. All these vapours in here aren't good for you. The air is dank under this roof.

HEDVIG: All right, I'll run down the kitchen stairs and walk around a bit. My hat and coat –? Oh, they're in my room. Father – you're not to do any harm to the wild duck while I'm out.

HJALMAR: Not a feather shall be plucked from its head. [*Pulls her to him*] You and I, Hedvig – we two –! Well, off you go, now.

    HEDVIG *nods to her parents and goes out through the kitchen.*

HJALMAR [*walks around without looking up*]: Gina.

GINA: Yes?

HJALMAR: From tomorrow – or let's say the day after – I'd like to do the household accounts myself.

GINA: You want to do the household accounts yourself too?

HJALMAR: Yes, or check over our income at least.

GINA: Well, God knows, *that's* quickly enough done.

HJALMAR: One wouldn't think so – it seems to me you get the money to stretch remarkably far. [*Stops to look at her*] How can that be?

GINA: That's because Hedvig and I need so little.

HJALMAR: Is it true Father gets paid very generously for that copy work at Mr Werle's?

GINA: I don't know if it's that generous. I've no idea of the going rate for such work.

HJALMAR: Well, what does he get, roughly? Tell me!

GINA: It's so up and down. I suppose it roughly covers what he costs us, with a little pocket money.

HJALMAR: What he costs us! And you've never told me that!

GINA: Well no, I couldn't – it made you so happy to think he got everything from you.

HJALMAR: So it's from Mr Werle he gets it!

GINA: Well, Mr Werle's got plenty to spare.

HJALMAR: Light the lamp!

GINA [*lights the lamp*]: And we can't be so sure it's from Mr Werle himself; it could well be Gråberg –

HJALMAR: Why are you dragging Gråberg into this?

GINA: Well, I don't know; I just thought –

HJALMAR: Hm!

GINA: Well, it wasn't me that got old Da that copy work. It was Berta, when she moved into the house.

HJALMAR: I think your voice is trembling.

GINA [*puts the shade on the lamp*]: Is it?

HJALMAR: And your hands are shaking. Or am I wrong?

GINA [*firmly*]: Tell me straight, Ekdal. What's he gone and said about me?

HJALMAR: Is it true – *can* it be true that – that there was some sort of relationship between you and Mr Werle, when you were in service in that house?

GINA: No, it isn't true. Not at that time, no. Mr Werle made advances, right enough, that he did. And his wife reckoned there was something to it – so she made a right ruckus and rumpus, and she hit me and she pulled me about – so I gave my notice.

HJALMAR: But later!

GINA: Well, I went back home. And Mother – she wasn't as moral as you thought, Ekdal; she was getting on at me about this and that the whole time – 'cos the merchant was a widower by then, of course.

HJALMAR: Right, and then!

GINA: Yes, it's probably best you know. He didn't give up till he'd had his way.

HJALMAR [*clasping his hands*]: And this, from the mother of my child! How could you hide something like that from me!

GINA: Yes, that was wrong of me. I should have told you ages ago.

HJALMAR: You should have told me straight away – then I'd have known what sort you were.

GINA: But then would you have married me?

HJALMAR: How can you even think it!

GINA: No. That's why I didn't dare tell you anything then. Because I'd grown to have feelings for you, as you know. And I couldn't go and make myself completely miserable –

HJALMAR [*walks up and down*]: And this is my Hedvig's mother! And to know now that everything I see before my eyes – [*kicks a chair*] – my entire home – I owe to some favoured predecessor! Oh, that sly seducer – that Mr Werle!

GINA: Do you regret the fourteen or fifteen years we've lived together?

HJALMAR [*standing in front of her*]: Tell me if you haven't regretted – every hour of every day – the web of secrets and lies that you – like a spider – have spun around me? Answer me that! Did you really suffer no pang of regret or remorse?

GINA: Oh, Ekdal, my sweet, I had plenty to think about with the house and the day-to-day running –.

HJALMAR: So, you never cast a probing glance at your past!

GINA: No, heavens above, I'd practically forgotten all those old intrigues.

HJALMAR: Oh, this dull, unfeeling calm! I find something so shocking about it. To think – no regret even!

GINA: But, tell me, Ekdal – what would have become of you if you hadn't got a wife like me?

HJALMAR: Like you –?

GINA: Well, I've always been a bit more sort of practical and businesslike than you. Though that's understandable, since I am a couple of years older.

HJALMAR: What would have become of me?

GINA: You'd strayed well off the path when you first met me; you can't deny that.

HJALMAR: And you call that straying? Oh, you don't understand how a man filled with grief and despair feels – especially a man of my fiery disposition.

GINA: No, you may be right. And I don't regale you one little bit for it neither – you became a good husband the instant you got a house and home. – And we've made it so nice and cosy here now; and it seemed Hedvig and I might soon be able to spend a bit extra on food and clothes for ourselves.

HJALMAR: In this swamp of lies, yes.

GINA: Urgh, to think that hideous man got free passage into this house!

HJALMAR: I also felt that our home was a good place to be. That was a delusion.[43] Where am I to find the necessary impetus now, to bring my invention into the real world? Perhaps it will die with me, and then it'll be your past conduct, Gina, that killed it.

GINA [*close to tears*]: No, you mustn't say such things, Ekdal. When I've only ever wanted to do what's best for you!

HJALMAR: What – I ask – will happen now to the dreams of the family provider? When I lay in there on the sofa, mulling over my invention – I sensed well enough then, it would drain my last drop of strength. I felt sure that the day I held the patent in my hands – that day would be my – day of departure. And my dream was that *you* would be left as the prosperous widow of the late inventor.

GINA [*dries her tears*]: No, you mustn't talk like that, Ekdal. Pray God I shall never live to see the day when I'm left a widow!

HJALMAR: Oh, that's neither here nor there. Everything is over now anyway. Everything!

GREGERS WERLE *carefully opens the hallway door and looks in.*

GREGERS: May I come in?

HJALMAR: Yes, come in.

GREGERS [*walks in with a radiant, contented face and goes to shake their hands*]: Well, my dear friends –! [*Looks from one to the other and whispers to* HJALMAR] Still not happened?

HJALMAR [*loud and clear*]: It *has* happened.

GREGERS: It has?

HJALMAR: I have experienced the bitterest moment of my life.

GREGERS: But the most elevating too, I imagine.

HJALMAR: I suppose we've got it off our hands, at least.

GINA: May God forgive you, Mr Werle.

GREGERS [*in utter amazement*]: But I don't understand.

HJALMAR: What don't you understand?

GREGERS: After such a moment of reckoning, a reckoning upon which a whole new life will be founded – a way of life, a union, in truth and without secrets –

HJALMAR: Yes, yes, I know – I do know.

GREGERS: I expected with absolute certainty that when I came through that door, I'd be bowled over by a light of transfiguration[44] from husband and wife alike. And instead I see nothing but this dull, heavy, cheerless –

GINA: Well then! [*Removes the lampshade*]

GREGERS: You don't want to understand me, Mrs Ekdal. Well, well, for you it'll probably take longer –. But what about you, Hjalmar? Surely *you* have attained a higher understanding from this great moment of reckoning.

HJALMAR: Naturally, I have. That's to say – in a way.

GREGERS: For there can be nothing in the world to compare with forgiving a wrong-doer and lifting her up to you in love.

HJALMAR: You think a man recovers so easily from the bitter cup[45] I have just drained?

GREGERS: Not an *ordinary* man, perhaps. But a man like *you* –!

HJALMAR: Yes, I do of course know that, for God's sake. But you mustn't *hound* me, Gregers. It'll take time, you understand.

GREGERS: You have a *great* deal of that wild duck in you, Hjalmar.

RELLING *has entered through the hallway door.*

RELLING: Aha; so the wild duck's in the news again?

HJALMAR: Mr Werle's wounded hunting trophy, yes.

RELLING: Mr Werle's –? You're talking about *him*, are you?

HJALMAR: About him – and – the rest of us.

RELLING [*in a lowered voice to* GREGERS]: The devil take you, sir!

HJALMAR: What are you saying?

RELLING: I am expressing a sincere wish that this quack should convey himself back home. If he stays here, he's capable of wrecking the pair of you.

GREGERS: Neither of them will be wrecked, Mr Relling. I won't speak of Hjalmar now. We know him. But even *she* certainly has something genuine, something dependable deep down.

GINA [*close to tears*]: Then you should have let me be as I *was*.

RELLING [*to* GREGERS]: Is it impertinent to ask what exactly you want in this house?

GREGERS: I want to lay the foundations for a true marriage.

RELLING: So you don't think Ekdal's marriage is good enough as it is?

GREGERS: I'm sure it is as good a marriage as most – sadly. But it isn't yet a *true* marriage.

HJALMAR: You've never had an eye for the higher ideals, have you, Relling?

RELLING: Nonsense, my boy! – With permission, Mr Werle, how many – just a rough estimate – how many true marriages have you seen in your life?

GREGERS: I barely think I've seen one.

RELLING: Nor I.

GREGERS: But I've seen countless marriages of the opposite kind. And I've had occasion to see close up what such marriages can destroy in a couple.

HJALMAR: A man's entire moral foundation can give way under his feet; *that's* what's so dreadful.

RELLING: Well, I've never actually been married myself, so I don't presume to pass judgement there. But I do know one thing – it's within a marriage that the *child* belongs. And you should both leave the child in peace.

HJALMAR: Oh – Hedvig! My poor Hedvig!

RELLING: Yes, you'd best keep Hedvig well out of it. You are two grown-up people. By all means go ahead and botch and bungle things in your own relationship, if you so desire. But the two of you will be gentle with Hedvig, I say; otherwise you might cause her injury.

HJALMAR: Cause injury?

RELLING: Yes, or she might cause an injury to herself – and maybe others too.

GINA: But how can you know that, Relling?

HJALMAR: There isn't any immediate danger to her eyes, is there?

RELLING: This has nothing to do with her eyes. But Hedvig is at a difficult age. She could get up to all sorts of mischief.

GINA: Yes, just think – she does too! She's started to muck about with the stove in the kitchen. She calls it playing fires. I often worry she'll set the house alight.

RELLING: You see, I knew it.

GREGERS [*to* RELLING]: But how do you explain that?

RELLING [*curt*]: Her voice is breaking, old man.

HJALMAR: As long as the child has *me* –! As long as *my* head is above the ground –.

There is a knock at the door.

GINA: Shh, Ekdal; there's people in the hallway. [*Calls*] Come in!

MRS SØRBY, *in her outdoor clothes, comes in.*

MRS SØRBY: Good evening!

GINA [*goes towards her*]: Oh, it's you, Berta!

MRS SØRBY: Yes, certainly it's me. But perhaps I've come at an inopportune moment?

HJALMAR: Lord help us, a messenger from *that* household –

MRS SØRBY [*to* GINA]: To be honest, I'd hoped I wouldn't find your menfolk here at this time – so I ran up to have a chat with you and say goodbye.

GINA: Oh? Are you leaving?

MRS SØRBY: Yes, first thing tomorrow – I'm going up to Høidal. Mr Werle left this afternoon. [*Casually to* GREGERS]
He sends his best wishes.

GINA: To think –!

HJALMAR: So Mr Werle has left? And you're to follow him?

MRS SØRBY: Yes, what do you say to *that*, Ekdal?

HJALMAR: I'd say, be on your guard.

GREGERS: Let me explain. My father is marrying Mrs Sørby.

HJALMAR: Is he marrying *her*!

GINA: Oh, but Berta – at last!

RELLING [*a little quake in his voice*]: This can't be true, surely?

MRS SØRBY: Yes, my dearest Relling, it certainly is true.

RELLING: Are you really getting married again?

MRS SØRBY: Well, it certainly looks that way. Mr Werle has
managed to get royal assent,[46] and then we'll celebrate the
wedding quietly up at the Works.

GREGERS: I must wish you every happiness then, as a good
stepson.

MRS SØRBY: And I must thank you, if you mean anything by
it. I do indeed hope that it'll prove a happiness for both
Werle and myself.

RELLING: You can be sure in that hope. Mr Werle never gets
drunk – as far as *I* know at least, and he doesn't seem to be
in the habit of beating his wives either, as our late horse-
doctor did.

MRS SØRBY: Oh, let Sørby rest now. Even he had his good
sides, you know.

RELLING: But I presume Mr Werle has some better sides still.

MRS SØRBY: Well, at least he's not squandered the best in himself. The man who does *that* must take the consequences.

RELLING: Tonight I'll go out with Molvik.

MRS SØRBY: You really shouldn't, Relling. Don't – for my
sake.

RELLING: There's nothing else for it. [*To* HJALMAR] If you
want to join us, then do.

GINA: No, thanks. Ekdal doesn't go in for *that* sort of dallidance.

HJALMAR [*irritated, lowered voice*]: Oh, do be quiet!

RELLING: Goodbye, Mrs – Werle. [*Leaves through the hall-way door*]

GREGERS [*to* MRS SØRBY]: It seems that you and Dr Relling know each other rather well.

MRS SØRBY: Yes, we've known each other for years. Something might have come of it between us once.

GREGERS: A good thing for you that it didn't.

MRS SØRBY: Yes, you might well say. But I've always taken care not to act on impulse. A woman really can't throw herself away.

GREGERS: Aren't you the slightest bit worried that I'll let my father get wind of this old acquaintance?

MRS SØRBY: Surely you must realize I've told him about it myself?

GREGERS: Oh?

MRS SØRBY: Your father knows every single detail that anybody in possession of the truth could find to say about me. I've told him everything; that was the first thing I did when he intimated that he had intentions.

GREGERS: Then you're more than usually candid, I think.

MRS SØRBY: Candid I have always been. We womenfolk[47] get furthest that way.

HJALMAR: What do you say to that, Gina?

GINA: Oh, we womenfolk are all very different. Some are one way and others another.

MRS SØRBY: Well, Gina, I do believe it's wisest to manage things as *I* have done. Nor has Werle kept anything hidden on his side. I'd almost say it's *that* which has created the bond between us. Now he can sit with me and talk as openly as a child. He never had the opportunity for that before. Throughout his entire youth and all his best years, that healthy, vital man heard nothing but chastising sermons. And those sermons were often about the most imaginary transgressions – from what *I've* been told.

GINA: Yes, never a truer word.

GREGERS: If the ladies wish to enter that territory, it's best I leave.

MRS SØRBY: There's no need to go on that account. I'll not say another word. I just wanted you to know that I've kept nothing secret or been underhand in any way. It might seem that I've made a very lucky strike; and, in a way, I have. But I feel nonetheless that I'm taking no more than I'm giving. I shall certainly never abandon him. And I can be of service and use to him like no one else now, since he'll soon be helpless.

HJALMAR: Soon be helpless?

GREGERS [to MRS SØRBY]: Yes, yes, don't talk about that here.

MRS SØRBY: There's no use hiding it any longer, however much he wants to. He is going blind.

HJALMAR [startled]: He's going blind? That's peculiar. Is *he* going blind too?

GINA: Oh, lots of people do.

MRS SØRBY: And you can imagine what *that* means for a businessman. Well, I shall try to use my eyes for him as best I can. But I daren't stay any longer; I'm in such a flurry right now. – Oh yes, *that's* what I meant to tell you, Ekdal: if there's any way Werle can be of service, then please do get in touch with Gråberg.

GREGERS: I think that's an offer Hjalmar Ekdal will turn down.

MRS SØRBY: Oh, really – in the past he never seemed to –

GINA: Yes but, Berta, Ekdal doesn't need anything from Mr Werle any more.

HJALMAR [slowly and weightily]: Please send my regards to your future husband and say that I intend in the near future to go to his accountant, Gråberg –

GREGERS: What! How can you want that?

HJALMAR: – go to Gråberg, I say, and demand a statement of the amount I owe his lord and master. I wish to pay this debt of honour –. Ha ha ha! Debt of honour, I might indeed call it! But enough of that. I want to repay it all, with five per cent interest.

GINA: But, Ekdal, dear, Lord alone knows we don't have the money for that.

HJALMAR: Please tell your fiancé that I am working tirelessly on my invention. Tell him that what keeps my spirits up during this arduous employment is my wish to acquit myself of this mortifying burden of debt. That is why I'm working on this invention. The entire proceeds will be used to liberate myself from the pecuniary outlay of your future spouse.

MRS SØRBY: Something must have happened in this house.

HJALMAR: It has indeed.

MRS SØRBY: Well, goodbye then. I still had a few little things to talk with you about, Gina; but they'll have to wait for another time. Goodbye.

> HJALMAR *and* GREGERS *nod farewell in silence;* GINA *walks* MRS SØRBY *to the door.*

HJALMAR: Not beyond the threshold, Gina!

> MRS SØRBY *leaves;* GINA *closes the door after her.*

HJALMAR: There you see, Gregers; I've got that burdensome debt off my hands now.

GREGERS: Soon at least.

HJALMAR: I think my stance must be seen as correct.

GREGERS: You are the man I always knew you to be.

HJALMAR: At certain moments it is impossible to disregard the demand for higher ideals. As a family provider, of course, that's something I have to tussle hard with. Since you can be sure it's no joke for a man of limited means to clear an age-old debt upon which the dust of forgetfulness, so to speak, has settled. But nevertheless – the human being in me also demands its rights.

GREGERS [*his hand on* HJALMAR's *shoulder*]: My dear Hjalmar – wasn't it good I came?

HJALMAR: Indeed.

GREGERS: That you gained full clarity in all things – wasn't that good?

HJALMAR [*slightly impatient*]: Well, yes, it was good. But there's one thing that upsets my sense of justice.

GREGERS: And what is that?

HJALMAR: It's that – oh, I'm not sure I dare talk so frankly about your father.

GREGERS: Please, don't mind me in the least.

HJALMAR: All right. Well, you see, I find something rather upsetting about the thought that it won't be *me* now, but *him*, who realizes a true marriage.

GREGERS: But how can you say such a thing!

HJALMAR: But it's true. Your father and Mrs Sørby are entering a marriage pact now, built on full confidence, built on
complete and unconditional openness on both sides; they're
sweeping nothing under the carpet; there are no secrets
underlying this relationship; they have both – if I can put it
like this – forgiven each other's trespasses.

GREGERS: Well, and what then?

HJALMAR: Yes, but it's all *there*, isn't it? It was precisely such
difficulties that you yourself said had to be overcome to
establish a true marriage.

GREGERS: But that's a completely different matter, Hjalmar.
Surely you wouldn't compare those two to either you or
her –? Well, I'm sure you understand.

HJALMAR: But I still can't escape the fact that there's something about it that wounds and offends my sense of fairness.
There appears to be no divine justice at all ruling this world.

GINA: Goodness, Ekdal! You really oughtn't to say that.

GREGERS: Hmm; let's not get into such questions.

HJALMAR: On the other hand, it's as if I see fate's corrective
finger all the same. He *is* going blind.

GINA: Oh, that may not be so certain.

HJALMAR: It is beyond doubt. We ought not to doubt it, at
least – for it is in this fact that just retribution is manifest. In
his time he blinded a naive fellow being.

GREGERS: He blinded many, sadly.

HJALMAR: And now the inexorable one, the mysterious one, is
come to demand the old merchant's own eyes.[48]

GINA: No! How dare you say something so awful! You're
frightening me.

HJALMAR: It's useful to examine life's dark side now and then.
    HEDVIG, *in hat and coat, comes in through the hallway
    door, happy and breathless.*

GINA: Back already?

HEDVIG: Yes, I didn't want to walk any more. And a good
thing too, because I just met somebody at the main gate.

HJALMAR: That was Mrs Sørby presumably.

HEDVIG: Yes.

HJALMAR [*paces up and down*]: I just hope you've seen her for the last time.

> *Silence.* HEDVIG *looks tensely from one person to the other as if to gauge the mood.*

HEDVIG [*goes up to him, coaxing*]: Father.

HJALMAR: Well – what is it, Hedvig?

HEDVIG: Mrs Sørby had something for me.

HJALMAR [*stops*]: For you?

HEDVIG: Yes. Something for tomorrow.

GINA: Berta's always had a little something for you on the day.

HJALMAR: What is it?

HEDVIG: No, you're not meant to know yet; Mother is to give it to me in bed tomorrow morning.

HJALMAR: Oh, all this collusion that I'm to be kept out of!

HEDVIG [*hurriedly*]: You can see it if you want to. It's a big letter. [*Takes the letter out of her coat pocket*]

HJALMAR: A letter too?

HEDVIG: Yes, there's *only* a letter. The rest will probably come later. But just think – a letter! I've never had a letter before. And it says 'Miss'⁴⁹ on the outside. [*Reads*] 'Miss Hedvig Ekdal.' Just imagine – that's me.

HJALMAR: Let me see the letter.

HEDVIG [*gives it to him*]: There, look.

HJALMAR: It's in Mr Werle's hand.

GINA: Are you sure, Ekdal?

HJALMAR: See for yourself.

GINA: And you think I'd know anything about that?

HJALMAR: Hedvig, may I open the letter – and read it?

HEDVIG: Yes, of course, if you want to.

GINA: No, not tonight, Ekdal; it's for tomorrow.

HEDVIG [*quietly*]: Oh, can't you just let him read it! It's probably something good, and then Father will be happy, and then it'll be nice here again.

HJALMAR: So I may open it?

HEDVIG: Yes, please do, Father. It'll be fun to know what it is.

HJALMAR: Good. [*Opens the letter, takes out a sheet, reads it through and seems confused*] But what's this –?

GINA: Well, what does it say?

HEDVIG: Oh yes, Father – tell us!

HJALMAR: Quiet, please. [*Reads it through once more; has grown pale, but says calmly*] It's a deed of gift, Hedvig.

HEDVIG: Never! What do I get then?

HJALMAR: Read it yourself.

　　HEDVIG *goes over and reads for a while by the lamp.*

HJALMAR [*in a lowered voice, clenching his fists*]: The eyes! The eyes – and now this letter!

HEDVIG [*interrupts her reading*]: Yes, but I think it's Grandpa who's to have it.

HJALMAR [*takes the letter from her*]: Gina – do you understand this?

GINA: I don't know a thing about it. Just tell me.

HJALMAR: Mr Werle writes to Hedvig that her old grandfather need no longer trouble himself with any copy work, and that hereafter he can collect a hundred kroner monthly at the office –

GREGERS: Aha!

HEDVIG: A hundred kroner, Mother! Yes, I read that.

GINA: That'll be good for Grandpa.

HJALMAR: – a hundred kroner for as long as he needs – that is to say, naturally, until he has closed his eyes.

GINA: Well, so he's provided for then, poor thing.

HJALMAR: But here it comes. You probably didn't read this, Hedvig. Afterwards, this gift will pass on to you.

HEDVIG: To me! All of it?

HJALMAR: He writes that you are guaranteed the same amount for your entire life. You hear that, Gina?

GINA: Yes, I hear it.

HEDVIG: Imagine – all the money I'll have! [*Tugs at him*] Father, Father, aren't you happy –?

HJALMAR [*avoids her*]: Happy! [*Paces the room*] Oh, what visions – what perspectives are unfolding here before me! It's Hedvig; it's towards her he's so generously mindful.

GINA: Well, Hedvig is the one with a birthday –

HEDVIG: And you'll get it all anyway, Father! You must know I'll give the money to you and Mother.

HJALMAR: To Mother, yes! There we have it.

GREGERS: Hjalmar, a trap is being set for you here.

HJALMAR: You think this is another trap?

GREGERS: When he was here this morning he said: Hjalmar Ekdal is not the man you imagine him to be.

HJALMAR: Not the man −!

GREGERS: You'll soon see, he said.

HJALMAR: You'll soon see me being fobbed off with money −!

HEDVIG: But Mother. What's going on?

GINA: Go out and take off your coat.

HEDVIG *goes out through the kitchen door, close to tears.*

GREGERS: Yes, Hjalmar − it will now be revealed which of us was right, him or me.

HJALMAR [*slowly tears the paper in half, puts both pieces on the table and says*]: Here is my answer.

GREGERS: I expected as much.

HJALMAR [*goes over to* GINA, *by the stove, and says quietly*]: And now no more secrets. If the relationship between the two of you was completely over when − when you'd grown to have feelings for me, as you put it − why did he set us up so we could get married?

GINA: He probably thought he'd get easy entrance here in this house.

HJALMAR: Just *that*? Wasn't he worried about a certain possibility?

GINA: I've no idea what you're talking about.

HJALMAR: I want to know whether − your child has the right to live under my roof.

GINA [*straightens up; eyes flashing*]: And *you* can ask that!

HJALMAR: You will answer me this one thing: Is Hedvig mine − or −? Well!

GINA [*looks at him in cold defiance*]: I don't know.

HJALMAR [*trembling slightly*]: You don't know!

GINA: How would *I* know? Being the type of woman *I* am −

HJALMAR [*quietly, turning away from her*]: Then I have nothing more to do in this house.

GREGERS: Consider this carefully, Hjalmar!

HJALMAR [*puts on his coat*]: There is nothing here to consider for a man like me.

GREGERS: Oh yes, there's a great deal to consider. The three of you must be together if you're to reach that glorious state of sacrificial forgiveness.

HJALMAR: I've no wish to reach it. Never, never! My hat! [*Takes his hat*] My home is reduced to rubble around me. [*Bursts into tears*] Gregers, I have no child!

HEDVIG [*who has opened the kitchen door*]: What are you saying! [*Goes over to him*] Father, Father!

GINA: Now look!

HJALMAR: Don't come near me, Hedvig! Go away. I can't bear the sight of you. Oh, those eyes –! Goodbye. [*Tries to get to the door*]

HEDVIG [*hangs onto him and screams loudly*]: No! No! Don't leave me!

GINA [*shouts*]: Look at the child, Ekdal! Look at the child!

HJALMAR: I don't want to! I can't! I have to get out – away from all this!

   He tears himself away from HEDVIG *and leaves through the hallway door.*

HEDVIG [*with a look of despair in her eyes*]: He's leaving us, Mother! He's leaving us! He'll never come back!

GINA: Don't cry, Hedvig. Father will be back, you'll see.

HEDVIG [*throws herself sobbing onto the sofa*]: No, no, he'll never come back to us again.

GREGERS: Do you believe I wanted everything for the best, Mrs Ekdal?

GINA: Yes, I almost think I do – but God forgive you just the same.

HEDVIG [*lying on the sofa*]: I think I'll die from all this! What have I done to him? Mother, you must get him back home!

GINA: Now, now, now; you just calm down, and I'll go out and look for him. [*Puts her outdoor clothes on*] Perhaps he's popped in on Relling. But you're not to lie there howling. You promise me?

HEDVIG [*fights to hold back the tears*]: Yes, I'll stop – if only Father comes back.

GREGERS [*to* GINA, *who is about to leave*]: Wouldn't it be better if you let him do battle with his pain first?

GINA: Oh, he'll have to do that later. First we need to quieten the child. [*Leaves through the hallway door*]

HEDVIG [*sits up and wipes her tears*]: Now you're going to tell me what's going on. Why doesn't Father want anything to do with me any more?

GREGERS: You mustn't ask about *that* until you're big and grown-up.

HEDVIG [*sobs*]: But I can't carry on being this horribly miserable till I'm big and grown-up. – I'm pretty sure I know what it is. – Perhaps I'm not Father's real child.

GREGERS [*uneasy*]: How would *that* be possible?

HEDVIG: Mother might have found me. And now perhaps Father's discovered it. I've read about things like that.

GREGERS: But then, even if that *were* true –

HEDVIG: Well, then I think he could love me just as much all the same. More perhaps. The wild duck was sent to us as a gift, and yet I love it very much.

GREGERS [*changing the subject*]: Yes, the wild duck, that's true. Let's talk a bit about the wild duck, Hedvig.

HEDVIG: The poor wild duck. He can't bear to set eyes on her any more either. Imagine, he wants to wring her neck!

GREGERS: Oh, I'm sure he doesn't.

HEDVIG: No, but he said so. And I think it was horrid of Father to say that, because I say prayers for the wild duck every evening and pray that it will be delivered from death and anything evil.[50]

GREGERS [*looks at her*]: Do you usually say evening prayers?

HEDVIG: Oh, yes.

GREGERS: Who started you doing that?

HEDVIG: Me. Because Father was so ill once and had leeches on his neck, and then he said death was close at hand.

GREGERS: Really?

HEDVIG: So I prayed for him when I went to bed. And I've kept it up ever since.

GREGERS: And now you pray for the wild duck too?

HEDVIG: I thought it best to include the wild duck, because she was so poorly at the start.

GREGERS: Do you say morning prayers too perhaps?

HEDVIG: No, not really.

GREGERS: Why not morning prayers too?

HEDVIG: In the morning it's light, and then there's not much to be scared of.

GREGERS: And this wild duck that you love so dearly – your father wanted to wring its neck?

HEDVIG: No, he said it would be best for him if he did, but he'd spare it for my sake. And that was kind of Father.

GREGERS [*a little closer*]: But what if *you* sacrificed the wild duck for *his* sake of your own free will?

HEDVIG [*gets up*]: The wild duck!

GREGERS: If you were willing to offer up the dearest thing you own in all the world?

HEDVIG: Do you think *that* would help?

GREGERS: Try it, Hedvig.

HEDVIG [*quietly, with shining eyes*]: Yes, I will try.

GREGERS: And have you got the strength of mind, do you think?

HEDVIG: I shall ask Grandpa to shoot the wild duck for me.

GREGERS: Yes, do that. But not a word to your mother about it!

HEDVIG: Why not?

GREGERS: She doesn't understand us.

HEDVIG: The wild duck. I will try tomorrow morning.

GINA *comes in through the hallway door.*

HEDVIG [*goes towards her*]: Did you find him, Mother?

GINA: No. But I heard he'd been in and got Relling to go with him.

GREGERS: Are you certain?

GINA: Yes, the concierge told me. Molvik joined them too, she said.

GREGERS: Now – when his mind so sorely needs to do battle in solitude –!

GINA [*takes her outdoor clothes off*]: Yes, menfolk are manifold. God knows where Relling's dragged him off to! I flew over to Madam Eriksen's, but they weren't there.

HEDVIG [*fighting her tears*]: Oh, what if he never ever comes home again!

GREGERS: He *will* come home again. I'll get a message to him
tomorrow; then you will see just *how* he returns. Sleep now
confident of *that*, Hedvig. Goodnight.
He leaves through the hallway door.
HEDVIG [*throws her arms around* GINA's *neck, sobbing*]:
Mother, Mother!
GINA [*pats her on her back and sighs*]: Ah, Relling was right.
That's what you get when mad folk come propagating intri-
cate demands.[51]

ACT FIVE

Hjalmar Ekdal's studio. A cold, grey morning light coming in; wet snow on the large panes in the ceiling window.

GINA, *wearing an apron, comes in with a brush and duster from the kitchen and walks towards the living-room door. At the same time* HEDVIG *runs in from the hallway.*

GINA [*stops*]: Well?

HEDVIG: Yes, Mother, I *do* think he might be down at Relling's –

GINA: You see!

HEDVIG: – because the concierge said she heard that Relling had two people with him when he came home last night.

GINA: Just as I thought.

HEDVIG: But it's no good if he doesn't want to come up to us.

GINA: But I can go down and talk to him at least.

Old EKDAL, *in a dressing gown and slippers and with a lit pipe, appears at the door to his room.*

EKDAL: Oh, Hjalmar –. Isn't Hjalmar home?

GINA: No, he must have gone out.

EKDAL: This early? And in this terrible driving snow. Well, never mind me – I can take my morning walk alone.

He pushes the attic door open; HEDVIG *helps him; he walks in; she closes the door after him.*

HEDVIG [*in a lowered voice*]: Just think, Mother, when poor Grandpa gets to hear that Father wants to leave us.

GINA: Oh, rubbish! Grandpa mustn't hear a thing about all this. It was a godsend he wasn't home last night during all the hullabaloo.

HEDVIG: Yes but –
> GREGERS *comes in through the hallway door.*

GREGERS: Well? Did you find any trace of him?

GINA: He's downstairs with Relling, they say.

GREGERS: With Relling? Has he really been out with that lot?

GINA: So it seems.

GREGERS: Yes, but he was in such desperate need to be alone and to collect himself –!

GINA: Yes, well may you say.
> RELLING *comes in from the hallway.*

HEDVIG [*moving towards him*]: Is Father downstairs with you?

GINA [*at the same time*]: Is he there?

RELLING: He certainly is.

HEDVIG: And you didn't think to tell us!

RELLING: Yes, I'm a total beastie. But first I had that other beastie to keep under control – you know, the demonic one – and then I fell asleep so heavily that –

GINA: What's Ekdal saying today?

RELLING: He's not saying a thing.

HEDVIG: He's not talking at all?

RELLING: Not a living word.

GREGERS: No. I can understand that.

GINA: So what's he up to, then?

RELLING: He's lying on the sofa snoring.

GINA: Really? Well, Ekdal's a snorer all right.

HEDVIG: He's asleep? Can he sleep?

RELLING: It appears so.

GREGERS: Understandable – with this battle that's shaken his soul –

GINA: And he's not used to roaming the night outdoors.

HEDVIG: Perhaps it's good he gets some sleep, Mother.

GINA: I think so too. So it's not worth us rousing him too soon. Thank you, Relling. Now I must get the house spick and span first, and then –. Come and help me, Hedvig.
> GINA *and* HEDVIG *go out into the living room.*

GREGERS [*turns to* RELLING]: Can you give me some insight into the spiritual stirrings that are taking place in Hjalmar Ekdal now?

RELLING: Damned if I've noticed any spiritual stirrings.

GREGERS: What? At such a turning point, when his whole life has gained a new foundation –? How can you imagine that a personality like Hjalmar –?

RELLING: Personality? Him! If he ever had even the rudiments of the kind of abnormality you call personality, then they were expertly removed, root and branch, long ago in his boyhood, I assure you.

GREGERS: *That* would be most odd – with the loving upbringing he enjoyed.

RELLING: With that pair of twisted, hysterical spinster aunts, you mean?

GREGERS: I'll have you know that those women never allowed the demand for high ideals to be forgotten – oh, yes, now you're going to make fun of me again.

RELLING: No, I'm not in the mood. Incidentally, I am well and truly informed – he's regurgitated plenty of rhetoric about his 'twin soul-mothers'. But I don't think he has much to thank them for. Ekdal's misfortune is that within his circle he's always been held up as a shining light –

GREGERS: And he *isn't* perhaps? On a deeper level, I mean?

RELLING: Well, *I've* never noticed any sign of it. That his father believed it – we'll let that pass; the old lieutenant has been an ass all his life.

GREGERS: He's been a man with a child-like spirit all his life; that's what you don't understand.

RELLING: As you please! But when our darling Hjalmar became a student of sorts, he was instantly taken to be the great light of the future among his friends too. He was handsome, of course, the lazy oaf – all peaches and cream – just what the young girls like in a fellow, and since he had such a sensitive nature and winning voice, and a knack for declaiming other people's verse and other people's ideas –

GREGERS [*indignant*]: Is it Hjalmar Ekdal you're talking about like that?

RELLING: Yes, with your permission; because that's what it looks like within the graven image before which you're lying prostrate.

GREGERS: Well now, I had no idea that I was so entirely blind.

RELLING: Oh yes, you're not far off it. Because you are a sick man too, you see.

GREGERS: You're right in that.

RELLING: Indeed. You suffer from a complicated affliction. Firstly, there's that bothersome righteousness-fever; and then, what's worse – you walk around in a haze of adulation-delirium; you have an incessant need for something outside yourself to admire.

GREGERS: Yes, it is without question outside myself that I must seek it.

RELLING: But you're woefully mistaken about the great shooting stars[52] you believe you see and hear around you. Yet again you have entered a worker's cottage and tried to enforce your demand for the ideal: here in this house there are no solvent people.

GREGERS: If you think no more highly of Hjalmar Ekdal, how can you find pleasure in spending so much time with him?

RELLING: Good God, I *am* meant to be a doctor of sorts, for what it's worth; so I have to care for the poor sick souls with whom I share a house.

GREGERS: Well, well! Is Hjalmar Ekdal sick too?

RELLING: Just about everybody is sick, sad to say.

GREGERS: And what cure do you use on Hjalmar?

RELLING: My usual. I seek to sustain the life-lie[53] within him.

GREGERS: The life-lie? I didn't quite hear –?

RELLING: Yes, I said the life-lie. The life-lie is the stimulating principle, you understand.

GREGERS: May I ask what type of life-lie Hjalmar has been infested with?

RELLING: No, you may not. I do not betray such secrets to quacks. You're capable of messing him up for me even more. But the method is tried and tested. I've applied it to Molvik too. I have made him 'demonic'. That was the remedial incision[54] I had to make in *his* neck.

GREGERS: So he's not demonic?

RELLING: What the hell does it mean to be demonic? That's

just some tosh I made up to keep him alive. If I hadn't done that, the poor swine would have gone under in self-contempt and despair years ago. And then there's the old lieutenant! Although, admittedly, he's found his own cure.

GREGERS: Lieutenant Ekdal? What about him?

RELLING: Yes, what do you make of him, the bear hunter, going about in that dark attic hunting rabbits? There isn't a happier marksman in the world than that old man, when he blusters about in there amongst all that junk. For him, the four or five dried-out Christmas trees that he's tucked away in there are the vast, refreshing Høidal forest; the cockerel and all those hens are wild game in the pine tops, and the rabbits that bumble across the attic floor are bears to tackle – that vital man of the great outdoors.

GREGERS: The unfortunate old lieutenant Ekdal, yes. He's certainly had to scale back the ideals of his youth.

RELLING: While I remember, Mr Werle Junior – don't use that foreign word: ideals. We do have the excellent Norwegian word: lies.

GREGERS: Are you saying the two are related?

RELLING: Yes, pretty much like typhoid and putrid fever.

GREGERS: Doctor Relling, I shan't give up until I've rescued Hjalmar from your claws!

RELLING: That may be the worse for *him*. Take the life-lie away from your average man, and you take his happiness with it. [*To* HEDVIG, *who comes in from the living room*] Well, little wild-duck mother, I'll go downstairs now and see if your papa is still on the sofa pondering his remarkable invention. [*Leaves through the hallway door*]

GREGERS [*going over to* HEDVIG]: I can see by your face that the deed is not done.[55]

HEDVIG: What? Oh, that business with the wild duck. No.

GREGERS: Your resolve failed you, I imagine, when you had to put it into action.

HEDVIG: No, it wasn't *that*. But when I woke up this morning and remembered what we'd talked about, I thought it was all very strange.

GREGERS: Strange?

HEDVIG: Well, I don't know –. Last night, in the moment, I thought there was something wonderful about it. But when I'd slept, and remembered it again, I didn't think much of it.

GREGERS: No, you haven't grown up here without something being lost in you, I suppose.

HEDVIG: Well, I'm not bothered about that. If only Father would come up –

GREGERS: Oh, if only your eyes had been opened to what gives life worth – if only you had the sincere, joyful and courageous will to self-sacrifice, then you'd soon see just *how* he would come to you. – But I still believe in you, Hedvig.

He walks out through the hallway door. HEDVIG *paces about the room; then decides to go into the kitchen; at that moment there is a knock from inside the attic door;* HEDVIG *goes over and opens it slightly; old* EKDAL *comes out; she pushes the door closed again.*

EKDAL: Hmm, it's no fun taking a morning walk on my own.

HEDVIG: Didn't you want to go hunting, Grandpa?

EKDAL: It's not hunting weather today. So dark; can barely see in front of you.

HEDVIG: Don't you ever want to shoot anything apart from the rabbits?

EKDAL: Aren't the rabbits good enough, perhaps?

HEDVIG: Yes, but what about the wild duck?

EKDAL: Oho; are you frightened I'll shoot your wild duck? Never in the world, my girl. I'd never do that.

HEDVIG: No, you probably *couldn't* – they say it's very difficult to shoot wild ducks.

EKDAL: Couldn't? Of course I jolly well could.

HEDVIG: How would you go about it, Grandpa – I don't mean with *my* wild duck, but others?

EKDAL: Would make sure I shot it right under the breast, you understand; that's the surest way. And they must be shot *against* the feathers, you see – not *with* the feathers.

HEDVIG: Do they die then, Grandpa?

EKDAL: Oh, they die all right – if you shoot properly. Well, I ought to go in now and spruce myself up. Hmm – that's right – hmm. [*Goes into his room*]

HEDVIG *waits a moment, glances over towards the living-room door, walks over to the bookshelf, stretches up on tiptoe, takes the double-barrelled pistol down from the shelf and looks at it.* GINA *comes in from the living room with a brush and duster.* HEDVIG *quickly puts the gun back without being noticed.*

GINA: Don't rummage about in Father's things, Hedvig.

HEDVIG [*moves away from the bookshelf*]: I just wanted to tidy up a bit.

GINA: Go out into the kitchen instead and see if the coffee's still hot. I want to take the tray when I go down to him.

HEDVIG *goes out;* GINA *starts sweeping and cleaning the studio. After a while the hallway door is opened hesitantly, and* HJALMAR EKDAL *looks in; he is wearing his coat, but no hat, he is unwashed and his hair is straggly and untidy; his eyes are tired and glazed.*

GINA [*stands with the brush in her hand looking at him*]: Oh, Ekdal – you've come after all?

HJALMAR [*steps into the room and answers in a croaky voice*]: I've come – to disappear right away.

GINA: Yes, I suppose you have. But heavens above – what *do* you look like!

HJALMAR: Look like?

GINA: And your posh winter coat and all! Well, it's got its comeuppance, I suppose.

HEDVIG [*in the kitchen door*]: Mother, shall I –? [*Sees* HJALMAR, *screams with joy and runs towards him*] Oh, Father, Father!

HJALMAR [*turns away and puts his hand out*]: Away, away! [*To* GINA] Get her away from me, I say!

GINA [*in a lowered voice*]: Go into the living room, Hedvig.
   HEDVIG *quietly does so.*

HJALMAR [*busy, pulls the desk drawer out*]: I need my books with me. Where are my books?

GINA: What books?

HJALMAR: My scientific works, naturally – the technical journals I use for my invention.

GINA [*looks in the bookshelf*]: You mean these, without any covers?

HJALMAR: Yes, they're the ones.

GINA [*puts a pile of journals on the table*]: Shouldn't I get Hedvig to cut the pages for you?

HJALMAR: I don't need any cutting done.
   Short silence.

GINA: So, you're still going to move out and leave us, Ekdal?

HJALMAR [*rummages through the books*]: Yes, that surely goes without saying.

GINA: Oh well –.

HJALMAR [*vehemently*]: Because I can't go around here, can I, and have my heart pierced through, every hour of the day!

GINA: God forgive you for thinking so ill of me.

HJALMAR: Prove –!

GINA: I think *you* should do the proving.

HJALMAR: After your past conduct? There are certain demands – I might be tempted to call them ideal demands –

GINA: But Old Da? What's going to happen to *him*, poor thing?

HJALMAR: I know my obligations – he's helpless and will move in with me. I shall go to town and make arrangements –. Hmm –. [*Hesitating*] Nobody's found my hat on the stairs, have they?

GINA: No. Have you lost your hat?

HJALMAR: Naturally I had it on when I came back last night. There's no doubt about that. But today I couldn't find it.

GINA: Oh, Lord, so where did you go with those two boozers?

HJALMAR: Oh, don't ask me about trivialities. You think I'm in the mood to remember such details?

GINA: As long as you've not caught a cold, Ekdal. [*Goes out into the kitchen*]

HJALMAR [*mutters bitterly to himself, while emptying the table drawer*]: You're a crook, Relling! – A scoundrel! – A shameful seducer! – If only I could have you assassinated!
   He puts some old letters to one side, finds the torn document from the previous day, takes it and looks at the pieces; puts it down quickly when GINA *comes in.*

GINA [*puts a full coffee tray on the table*]: Here's a drop of something warm in case you want it. And some buttered bread and salt meats to go with it.

HJALMAR [*glances at the tray*]: Salt meats? Never under this roof! Admittedly, I've not taken any solid refreshment in nearly twenty-four hours, but no matter. – My notes! The beginnings of my memoirs! Where are my diary and important papers? [*Opens the living-room door, but shrinks back*] There she is again!

GINA: Lord above, the child has to be somewhere.

HJALMAR: Get out.

    He steps aside. Terrified, HEDVIG *comes into the studio.*

HJALMAR [*with his hand on the door handle, to* GINA]: In the few last moments I spend in my former home, I wish to be spared from unwelcome intruders – [*Goes into the living room*]

HEDVIG [*dashing towards her mother, and, trembling quietly, asks*]: Is that me?

GINA: Stay in the kitchen, Hedvig – or rather – go into your own room. [*Speaks to* HJALMAR *as she goes in to him*] Wait a bit, Ekdal, don't rummage about in those drawers. *I* know where everything is.

HEDVIG [*stands motionless for a moment, anxious and indecisive, bites her lips to stop herself crying, then, clenching her fists tightly, she says quietly*]: The wild duck!

    She tiptoes across and takes the pistol from the shelf, opens the attic door a little, sneaks in and closes it after her.

    HJALMAR *and* GINA *start talking argumentatively in the living room.*

HJALMAR [*enters with some notebooks and old loose sheets, which he puts on the table*]: Oh, what good is that bag! There'll be hundreds of things I've got to lug with me.

GINA [*follows with the bag*]: So leave all your other things here for now – just take a shirt and a couple of underpants.

HJALMAR: Phew – all these arduous preparations –! [*Pulls off his coat and throws it on the sofa*]

GINA: And the coffee's getting cold too.

HJALMAR: Hmm. [*Absentmindedly takes a sip, followed by another*]

GINA [*wiping the backs of the chairs*]: The hardest thing will be to find a big attic room for all the rabbits.

HJALMAR: What! Am I meant to lug all the rabbits along with me too?

GINA: Yes, Old Da can't be without his rabbits, can he?

HJALMAR: Well, he'll just have to get used to it. *I* have to renounce far higher pleasures than rabbits.

GINA [*dusting the bookshelf*]: Shall I put your flute in the bag for you?

HJALMAR: No. No flute for me. But give me the pistol!

GINA: You want the pigstol with you?

HJALMAR: My loaded pistol. Yes.

GINA [*looks for it*]: It's gone. He must've taken it in with him.

HJALMAR: Is he in the attic?

GINA: Most probably, yes.

HJALMAR: Hmm – lonely old blighter.

He picks up a sandwich, eats it and finishes the coffee.

GINA: If we hadn't rented out the spare room, you could've moved in there.

HJALMAR: Stay under the same roof as –! Never – never!

GINA: But couldn't you settle in the living room for a day or two, at least? You'd have it all to yourself.

HJALMAR: Never within these walls!

GINA: Well, downstairs with Relling and Molvik, then?

HJALMAR: Don't mention those names! I feel my appetite fade at the mere thought of them. – No, no, I must venture out into the storm and driving snow – go from house to house and seek shelter for Father and myself.

GINA: But you haven't even got a hat, Ekdal! You've lost your hat.

HJALMAR: Oh those two scumbags, riddled with vice! A hat must be got. [*Takes another slice of bread*] Planning is required. Since I'm not of a mind to lay down my life. [*Looking for something on the tray*]

GINA: What are you looking for?

HJALMAR: Butter.

GINA: The butter's coming right away. [*Goes out into the kitchen*]

HJALMAR [*calls after her*]: Oh there's no need, I can eat dry bread.

GINA [*brings a butter dish*]: There now, I think it's freshly churned.

She pours another cup of coffee for him; he sits down on the sofa, puts more butter on his slices of bread, eats and drinks for a while in silence.

HJALMAR: Could I perhaps, without any interruption from anyone – from anyone at all – stay in the living room for a day or two?

GINA: Yes, certainly, if you wanted.

HJALMAR: Because I have no idea how I'd get all Father's things out in such a hurry.

GINA: And there's another thing – you really should tell him first that you don't want to live with the rest of us any more.

HJALMAR [*shoves the coffee cup away*]: Hmm, that too, yes. Oh, the thought of having to rake up all these complicated affairs again –. I need to think. I need breathing space. I can't carry all these burdens in one day.

GINA: Yes, and with that terrible weather out there.

HJALMAR [*touches the letter from* MR WERLE]: I see that letter's still lying around.

GINA: Well, *I* haven't touched it.

HJALMAR: Of course, that bit of paper is of no concern to me –

GINA: Well, *I* certainly have no intention of making use of it.

HJALMAR: – but it'll be a pity if it goes astray all the same – in all the upheaval when I move out, it could so easily –

GINA: I'll look after it, Ekdal.

HJALMAR: The deed of gift belongs first and foremost to Father, of course, and it'll be a matter for him if he wants to make use of it.

GINA [*sighs*]: Yes, poor Old Da –

HJALMAR: To be on the safe side –. Where can I find some glue?

GINA [*goes to the bookshelf*]: Here's the glue pot.

HJALMAR: And a brush.

GINA: Here's the brush too. [*Brings him the things*]

HJALMAR [*takes a pair of scissors*]: Just a strip of paper on the back –. [*Cuts and glues*] Far be it from me to expropriate

another man's property – far less a destitute old man's.
Well – nor somebody else's. – Right. Leave it there for now.
And when it's dry, take it away. I never want to see that
document before my eyes again. Never!

GREGERS WERLE *comes in from the hallway.*

GREGERS [*slightly surprised*]: What – are you sitting here,
Hjalmar?

HJALMAR [*gets up quickly*]: I slumped down from exhaustion.

GREGERS: You've eaten breakfast, I see.

HJALMAR: The body too imposes its demands occasionally.

GREGERS: So what have you decided?

HJALMAR: For a man like me there is but one path to walk. I
am in the process of gathering my most important posses-
sions. But it takes time, you understand.

GINA [*a little impatiently*]: Shall I prepare the living room for
you or pack your bag?

HJALMAR [*after an irritable side-glance towards* GREGERS]:
Pack – and prepare.

GINA [*takes the bag*]: Right you are, I'll pack your shirt and
your other stuff then. [*Goes into the living room and closes
the door behind her*]

GREGERS [*after a brief silence*]: I never thought this would be
how it would end. Is it really necessary for you to leave your
home?

HJALMAR [*walks about restlessly*]: So what do you suggest I
do? – I'm not cut out to be unhappy, Gregers. I need things
to be nice and secure and peaceful round me.

GREGERS: But isn't that possible? Just try at least. I feel
there's a firm foundation[56] here now to build on – and to
start out from. And remember, you have the invention to
live for.

HJALMAR: Oh, don't talk about the invention. That may be a
long way off.

GREGERS: Oh?

HJALMAR: Well, good Lord, what would you have me invent?
Others have invented most things already. It gets harder by
the day –

GREGERS: But you've put so much work into it.

HJALMAR: It was that good-for-nothing Relling who got me into it.

GREGERS: Relling?

HJALMAR: Yes, he was the one who first made me aware of my talent for some extraordinary photographic invention or other.

GREGERS: Aha – so it was Relling!

HJALMAR: Oh, I was so happy about that. Not so much the invention itself, but because Hedvig believed in it – believed in it with all her might and main as only a child can. – That's to say – I've gone around like an idiot deluding myself that she believed in it.

GREGERS: Can you really think that Hedvig could be false towards you!

HJALMAR: It makes no odds what I think now. It's Hedvig who's standing in my way. She's going to shut the sun out from my life completely.

GREGERS: Hedvig! Are you talking about Hedvig? How could *she* ever stand in your way?

HJALMAR [*without replying*]: Oh, how I have loved that child. How unspeakably happy I felt every time I came home to my humble dwelling and she flew towards me with her sweet, slightly squinting eyes. Oh what a naive fool I am! I cared for her so unspeakably much – and then I dreamed, deluded myself into believing she cared so unspeakably much for me in return.

GREGERS: Are you saying *that* was just a delusion!

HJALMAR: How can I know? I just can't get a thing out of Gina. And, of course, she lacks any sense of the ideals inherent in this complicated matter. But for you I feel a desire to open up, Gregers. It's this terrible doubt – that perhaps Hedvig never honestly loved me.

GREGERS: You might just get some testament to that. [*Listens*] What's that? I think the wild duck is screaming.

HJALMAR: The wild duck is squawking. Father's in the attic.

GREGERS: Is he! [*Lights up with joy*] I'm telling you, you might just get some testament to how much that poor misjudged Hedvig cares for you!

HJALMAR: Oh what testament can she offer me! I dare not believe in any reassurances from that side.

GREGERS: Hedvig isn't capable of betrayal.

HJALMAR: Oh Gregers, *that's* precisely what's so uncertain. Who knows what Gina and that Mrs Sørby might have sat here whispering about? And Hedvig generally has her ears open, you know. Maybe the deed of gift didn't come as such a surprise after all. I think I even sensed something of the sort.

GREGERS: But what's taken possession of you?

HJALMAR: I have had my eyes opened. Just you watch – you'll see, the deed of gift was just the start. Mrs Sørby has always had a soft spot for Hedvig, and now she's got the power to do whatever she likes for the child. They can take her away from me at any hour or moment they please.

GREGERS: Hedvig would never leave *you*.

HJALMAR: Don't you be so sure. If *they* were to stand there beckoning her with their hands full –? Oh, I – I who have loved her so unspeakably much! I would have made it my greatest joy to take her gently by the hand and lead her, as you lead a child frightened of the dark through a vast desolate space! – Now I feel a gnawing certainty – the penniless photographer up in his attic has never been enough for her. She just very slyly made sure she was on a good footing with him until the time came.

GREGERS: You don't really believe that, Hjalmar.

HJALMAR: The awful thing is that I don't know what to believe – and I'll never know. But can you really doubt the truth of what I'm saying? Hah, you have too much faith in this demand for ideals, my good Gregers! If the others turned up, hands overflowing, and called to the child: leave him – there's a life awaits you here with us –

GREGERS [*quickly*]: Yes, what then, d'you think?

HJALMAR: If I were to ask her: Hedvig, are you willing to give up that life, for my sake? [*Laughs spitefully*] Oh yes, thank you very much – you'd soon see the answer I'd get!

    A pistol shot is heard from inside the attic room.

GREGERS [*loudly, with joy*]: Hjalmar!

HJALMAR: There! Now he's off hunting again.

GINA [*enters*]: Oh, Ekdal, I think Old Da's banging about in the attic all on his own.

HJALMAR: I'll look in –

GREGERS [*excitedly, gripped*]: Wait a moment! Do you know what that was?

HJALMAR: Of course I know.

GREGERS: No, you don't. But *I* know. It was the testament!

HJALMAR: What testament?

GREGERS: It was the sacrificial act of a child. She has got your father to shoot the wild duck.

HJALMAR: Shoot the wild duck!

GINA: No, to think –!

HJALMAR: But why?

GREGERS: She wanted to sacrifice the best thing she owned in the world, for your sake – because then she thought you would have to love her again.

HJALMAR [*softly, moved*]: Oh, that child!

GINA: The things *she* comes up with!

GREGERS: She just wanted your love back, Hjalmar; she didn't feel she could live without it.

GINA [*fighting back the tears*]: There now, you can see for yourself, Ekdal.

HJALMAR: Gina, where is she?

GINA [*sniffs*]: I expect she's sitting in the kitchen, poor mite.

HJALMAR [*goes over, throws open the kitchen door and says*]: Hedvig – come! Come in here to me! [*Looks around*] No, she's not here.

GINA: Then she's in her little room.

HJALMAR [*from outside*]: No, she's not here either. [*Comes back in*] She must have gone out.

GINA: Well, you didn't want her anywhere in the house.

HJALMAR: Oh, I wish she'd just come back soon – so I can tell her properly –. Everything will be all right now, Gregers – because I really do believe now that we can start life over again.

GREGERS [*quietly*]: I knew it; through the child reparation[57] would come.

Old EKDAL *appears in the door to his room; he is in full military uniform and is busy strapping his sword around his waist.*

HJALMAR [*surprised*]: Father! Are you there!

GINA: Was he shooting in his room then?

EKDAL [*resentfully, crossing the room*]: So you're hunting alone, eh, Hjalmar?

HJALMAR [*tense, confused*]: It wasn't you shooting in the attic?

EKDAL: Me shooting? Hmm!

GREGERS [*shouts to* HJALMAR]: She's shot the wild duck herself, Ekdal!

HJALMAR: What's going on! [*Hurries to the attic door, tears it aside, looks in and screams*] Hedvig!

GINA [*runs towards the door*]: Good Lord, what is it!

HJALMAR [*walks in*]: She's lying on the floor!

GREGERS: Hedvig's –? [*Rushes in to* HJALMAR]

GINA [*at the same time*]: Hedvig! [*Rushes into the attic*] No, no, no!

EKDAL: Aha! Has *she* gone a-hunting too?

HJALMAR, GINA *and* GREGERS *are pulling* HEDVIG *into the studio; in her limp right hand the pistol is tightly clamped between her fingers.*

HJALMAR [*in distress*]: The pistol's gone off, she's shot herself. Call for help! Help!

GINA [*runs out into the hallway calling down*]: Relling! Relling! Doctor Relling; run up here quick as you can!

HJALMAR *and* GREGERS *place* HEDVIG *on the sofa.*

EKDAL [*quietly*]: The forest takes its revenge.

HJALMAR [*on his knees by her*]: She'll come round soon. Now she's coming round – yes, yes, yes.

GINA [*who has come back in*]: Where is she hit? I can't see anything –

RELLING *arrives in a hurry, followed immediately by* MOLVIK; *the latter without waistcoat and neckerchief, with his tailcoat flying open.*

RELLING: What's going on here?

GINA: They're saying Hedvig's shot herself.

HJALMAR: Come here and help!

RELLING: Shot herself!

He pulls the table aside and starts to examine her.

HJALMAR [*kneeling, looking up at him anxiously*]: It can't be anything serious, can it? Eh, Relling? She's not bleeding much. It can't be anything serious, can it?

RELLING: How did it happen?

HJALMAR: Oh, how do I know –!

GINA: She wanted to shoot the wild duck.

RELLING: The wild duck?

HJALMAR: The pistol must have gone off.

RELLING: Hm. I see.

EKDAL: The revenge of the forest. But I'm not scared anyway. [*Goes into the attic and closes the door after him*]

HJALMAR: So, Relling – why aren't you saying anything?

RELLING: The bullet has entered her chest.

HJALMAR: Yes, but she'll be all right!

RELLING: Surely you can see Hedvig isn't alive.

GINA [*bursts into tears*]: Oh my child, my child!

GREGERS [*whispers hoarsely*]: At the bottom of the watery deep.

HJALMAR [*leaps up*]: Yes, yes, but she *must* live! Oh, please God, Relling – just for one moment – just long enough for me to tell her how unspeakably much I always loved her.

RELLING: It entered the heart. Internal bleeding. She died instantly.

HJALMAR: And I, who chased her away from me like an animal! And she crept frightened into the attic and died because of her love for me. [*Sobbing*] Never to make things right again! Never to be able to tell her –! [*Clenches his fists and shouts upwards*] Oh, you up there –! If you *are* there! Why hast thou done this unto me!

GINA: Shush, shush, you mustn't usurp yourself so much. We had no right to keep her, I suppose.

MOLVIK: The child is not dead, but sleepeth.[58]

RELLING: Tosh.

HJALMAR [*goes quiet, walks over to the sofa and looks at* HEDVIG *with arms crossed over his chest*]: There she lies, so stiff and still.

RELLING [*tries to prise the pistol free*]: It's stuck fast – completely fast.

GINA: No, no, Relling, don't break her fingers; let the pigstol be.

HJALMAR: She can take it with her.

GINA: Yes, let her. But the child shan't lie on parade[59] out here. She'll go into her own room, she will. Come and help, Ekdal.

HJALMAR *and* GINA *carry* HEDVIG *between them.*

HJALMAR [*as they carry her*]: Oh, Gina, Gina, can you ever survive this!

GINA: The one must help the other. Because *now* at least she is ours half and half.

MOLVIK [*stretches his arms out and mutters*]: Praise be the Lord; to dust thou shalt return,[60] to dust thou shalt return –

RELLING [*whispers*]: Shut up, man; you're drunk.

HJALMAR *and* GINA *carry the body through the kitchen door.* RELLING *closes it after them.* MOLVIK *slinks out into the hallway.*

RELLING [*goes over to* GREGERS *and says*]: No one will fool me into thinking this was a stray shot.

GREGERS [*who has looked on in horror, shaking convulsively*]: No one can say how this dreadful thing happened.

RELLING: The powder singed the bodice of her dress. She must have pressed the gun close against her chest and fired.

GREGERS: Hedvig's death is not in vain. Did you see how the grief released something noble in him?

RELLING: Most people are noble enough when they stand grieving over a corpse. But how long do you think that splendour will last in *him*?

GREGERS: Might it not last and grow throughout his life!

RELLING: Within three-quarters of a year little Hedvig will be no more to him than a beautiful motif for a declamation.

GREGERS: And you dare say that about Hjalmar Ekdal!

RELLING: We'll talk again when the first grass has withered on her grave. Then you will hear him regurgitating the same old thing about 'the child, torn too soon from its father's bosom'; then you'll see him wallow in emotion, self-admiration and self-pity. Just you wait!

GREGERS: If *you* are right and *I* am wrong, then life is not worth living.

RELLING: Oh, life could be pretty good even so, if only we poor folk were spared the blessed debt-collectors who besiege our doors with their demand for high ideals.

GREGERS [*stares straight ahead*]: In that case I'm glad my decision is as it is.

RELLING: And what may I ask – is your decision?

GREGERS [*as he is leaving*]: To be the thirteenth man at the table.

RELLING: Huh, the devil it is.

ROSMERSHOLM

A Play in Four Acts

CHARACTERS

JOHANNES ROSMER, *owner of Rosmersholm,*
a former clergyman[1]
REBEKKA WEST, *a member of the Rosmersholm*
household
MR KROLL, *Rosmer's brother-in-law, headmaster*
ULRIK BRENDEL
PEDER MORTENSGÅRD
MRS[2] HELSETH, *housekeeper at Rosmersholm*

The action takes place at Rosmersholm, an old
manor house[3] *in the vicinity of a small fjord*
town in western Norway.

ACT ONE

The living room at Rosmersholm; spacious, old-fashioned[4] and comfortable. In the foreground, on the wall to the right, a large wood stove[5] is decorated with fresh branches of birch and wild flowers. Further back, a door. In the back wall double doors lead to the entrance hall. In the wall on the left a window, and in front of it a display stand with potted plants and flowers. Next to the stove a table, a sofa and armchairs. Hanging on all the walls are old and more recent portraits of clergymen, officers and other officials in uniform. The window is open. So are the doors that lead on to the entrance hall and the front door. Outside, an avenue of large old trees can be seen, which leads to the property. A summer evening. The sun has set.

REBEKKA WEST is sitting in an armchair by the window crocheting a large white woollen shawl, which is nearly finished. Now and then she peers out of the window, spying between the flowers. A moment later MRS HELSETH comes in from the right.

MRS HELSETH: Maybe it's best I make a start on laying the supper table, miss?[6]
REBEKKA: Yes, you do that. The pastor should be here soon.
MRS HELSETH: Isn't it awful draughty where you're sat, miss?
REBEKKA: A little. Maybe you could close the window and doors?
    MRS HELSETH goes over and closes the hall door. Then she goes to the window.

MRS HELSETH [*about to close it, looks out*]: But isn't that the pastor walking over there?

REBEKKA [*quickly*]: Where? [*Gets up*] Oh yes, it is. [*Standing behind the curtain*] Go to the side. Don't let him see us.

MRS HELSETH [*back in the room*]: Imagine, miss – he's started down the mill path again.

REBEKKA: He took the mill path the day before yesterday too. [*Peeps out between the curtain and the window frame*] But now we'll see if –

MRS HELSETH: Dare he cross over the footbridge?

REBEKKA: That's what I want to see. [*A moment later*] No. He's turning back. Taking the upper path today again. [*Comes away from the window*] Going the long way.

MRS HELSETH: Good Lord, yes. It must be awful hard for the pastor to tread upon *that* bridge. Where a thing like that has happened.

REBEKKA [*folding her work away*]: They cling to their dead for a long time here at Rosmersholm.

MRS HELSETH: I reckon, miss, it's the dead that clings a long time to Rosmersholm.

REBEKKA [*looking at her*]: The dead?

MRS HELSETH: Yes, it's almost as if they can't quite get away from them that's left behind.

REBEKKA: What gives you that idea?

MRS HELSETH: Well, I reckon the white horse[7] wouldn't come here otherwise.

REBEKKA: Yes, what is all this about the white horse, Mrs Helseth?

MRS HELSETH: Oh, it's best not to talk about it. And you don't believe in that sort of thing anyway.

REBEKKA: Do *you* believe in it?

MRS HELSETH [*goes over and closes the window*]: Oh, I don't want to give you reason to poke fun at me, miss. [*Looks out*] But look – isn't that the pastor back on the mill path again?

REBEKKA [*looking out*]: That man there? [*Goes to the window*] It's the headmaster!

MRS HELSETH: You're right, it's the headmaster.

REBEKKA: Ah, but that's wonderful! He's intending to visit us, you'll see.

MRS HELSETH: And he's walking right over the footbridge, bold as anything. Even though she was his own flesh-and-blood sister. – Well now, I'll go in and lay the supper table, miss.
She goes out to the right.
REBEKKA *stands for a moment at the window; then she waves, smiles and nods to someone outside.*
Darkness is beginning to fall.

REBEKKA [*crosses over and speaks through the door to the right*]: Oh, Mrs Helseth dear, make sure to put something extra special on the table. I'm sure you know what the head-master likes best.

MRS HELSETH [*outside*]: Yes, miss. I'll see to it.

REBEKKA [*opening the door onto the entrance hall*]: Well now, at long last –! A hearty welcome, my dear Mr Kroll!

KROLL [*in the entrance hall, putting his stick away*]: Thank you. Not causing any inconvenience, I hope?

REBEKKA: *You?* Tut, shame on you –!

KROLL [*coming in*]: Charming as ever. [*Looks around him*] Is Rosmer[8] up in his room perhaps?

REBEKKA: No, he's out walking. He's been a little longer than usual. But I'm sure he'll be back in a moment. [*Waves him towards the sofa*] Please, do take a seat for now.

KROLL [*putting his hat down*]: Thank you. [*Sits down and looks around*] Well I never, look how bright and pretty you've made this old room! Flowers just about everywhere!

REBEKKA: Mr Rosmer appreciates having fresh, living flowers around him.

KROLL: As do you, I expect.

REBEKKA: Yes. I think they have such a delightfully calming effect. We always had to deny ourselves that pleasure before.

KROLL [*nods seriously*]: Poor Beate couldn't stand their scent.

REBEKKA: Or their colours. She'd get quite bewildered –

KROLL: Yes, I seem to remember. [*In a lighter tone*] Well now, how are things out here?

REBEKKA: Oh, things take their quiet, steady course here. Each day like the last. – And with you? Your wife –?

KROLL: Oh, my dear Miss West, let's not talk about me. There's always something awry in any family. Especially in such times as we live in now.

REBEKKA [*after a brief pause, sitting down in an armchair near the sofa*]: Why haven't you come out to see us even once during the entire school holidays?

KROLL: Oh, it doesn't do to besiege people's doors –

REBEKKA: If you knew just how much we've missed you –

KROLL: – and besides, I've been travelling around, as you know –

REBEKKA: Yes, for two weeks or so. You've been attending various public meetings, I understand?

KROLL [*nods*]: And what do you say to that? Did you ever think I'd become a political agitator in my old age? Eh?

REBEKKA [*smiles*]: You've always been a bit of an agitator, Mr Kroll.

KROLL: Well, yes, for my own private amusement. But from now on it'll be in absolute earnest. – Do you read any of these radical journals?

REBEKKA: Yes, my dear Mr Kroll, I shan't deny –

KROLL: Dear Miss West, there's no fault in that. Not as far as you're concerned.

REBEKKA: No, I'd think not. I must follow events. Stay informed –

KROLL: Well, I wouldn't under any circumstance, of course, demand that you as a woman⁹ should take sides in the civic dispute – I might call it civil war – that's raging now. But I presume you've read how these 'men of the people' have taken pleasure in abusing me? The heinous insults they've felt at liberty to indulge in?

REBEKKA: Yes, but I think you've been most robust in your reply.

KROLL: I have indeed. If I say so myself. Since I've got a taste for blood now. And they'll soon discover that I'm not a man to take abuse lying down –. [*Breaks off*] No, but listen – let's not get onto that miserable and distressing subject this evening.

REBEKKA: No, let's not, my dear Mr Kroll.

KROLL: Tell me instead, how are you getting on at Rosmersholm now that you're here on your own? Now that our poor Beate –?

REBEKKA: I think I'm getting on quite well, thank you. There's a huge void left by her in many ways of course. And a sense of loss and grief too – naturally. But otherwise –

KROLL: Are you thinking of staying? Permanently, I mean?

REBEKKA: Oh, my dear Mr Kroll, I've not really given that much thought either way. And I've grown so used to this house now, that I feel I almost belong here – that *I* too belong.

KROLL: Ah, *you*. Yes, I'd most certainly have thought so.

REBEKKA: And as long as Mr Rosmer feels I can be of some comfort and use to him – then I'll no doubt stay, I expect.

KROLL [*looking at her with some emotion*]: You know – there's something rather splendid about a woman letting her entire youth pass by like that, in sacrifice for others.

REBEKKA: Oh, what else would I have had to live for?

KROLL: First you had that relentless struggle here with your unreasonable, crippled foster-father –

REBEKKA: You mustn't think that Dr West was as unreasonable up there in Finnmark.[10] It was those terrible sea voyages that broke him. But when we moved down here – well, yes, there were a couple of difficult years before his battle was over.

KROLL: Didn't things get even harder for you during the years that followed?

REBEKKA: No, how can you say such a thing! When I was so deeply fond of Beate –. And when she, poor soul, was in such dire need of care and affection.

KROLL: You have my deepest gratitude for remembering her with such forbearance.

REBEKKA [*moving a little nearer to him*]: My dear Mr Kroll, you say that so beautifully and so earnestly that I feel sure there's no ill feeling behind it.

KROLL: Ill feeling? What do you mean?

REBEKKA: Well, it would hardly be surprising if you found it painful to see me as an outsider going about doing as I please here at Rosmersholm.

KROLL: Yes, but how on earth –?

REBEKKA: But it's clear that you don't. [*Holds out her hand to him*] Thank you, thank you, my dear Mr Kroll! Thank you for that.

KROLL: But how on earth could you come up with such an idea?

REBEKKA: I started to worry because you came to see us so rarely.

KROLL: Then you really have been on the wrong track entirely, Miss West. Besides – nothing's really changed here. After all, it was you – and you alone – who already had charge of things here during poor Beate's last unhappy days.

REBEKKA: It was more of a regency in the mistress's name.

KROLL: Well, anyway –. You know something, Miss West – for my part, I'd have absolutely nothing against it if you –. But I suppose it's not appropriate to say such a thing.

REBEKKA: To say what?

KROLL: If it so happened that you took the empty place –

REBEKKA: I have the place I want, Mr Kroll.

KROLL: Yes, perhaps – in everything but name –

REBEKKA [*interrupting him, seriously*]: Shame on you, Mr Kroll! How can you sit there and jest about such a thing?

KROLL: Ah well, our good Johannes Rosmer probably feels he's had more than enough of matrimony. But nevertheless –

REBEKKA: You know – I almost have to laugh at you.

KROLL: Nonetheless –. Tell me, Miss West – if it's permitted to ask –. How old are you actually?

REBEKKA: Shame to admit, I'm already twenty-nine,[11] Mr Kroll. I'm in my thirtieth year.

KROLL: Hmm. And Rosmer – how old is he? Let me see. He's five years younger than me. So, he's a good forty-three years. I think that would be most suitable.

REBEKKA [*gets up*]: I'm sure. Very suitable, indeed. – Will you take tea with us this evening?

KROLL: Thank you – yes. I had planned to stay a while. Since there's a matter I need to discuss with our excellent friend. – And, Miss West – so you don't get any more mistaken ideas, I shall drop by as often as I can – just as in the old days.

REBEKKA: Yes, please do. [*Takes his hands in hers*] Thank you, thank you! You really are most kind.

KROLL [*growling a little*]: Really? That's rather more than I get to hear at home.

JOHANNES ROSMER *comes in through the door on the right.*

REBEKKA: Mr Rosmer[12] – do you see who's sitting here?

JOHANNES ROSMER: Mrs Helseth told me.

MR KROLL *has got to his feet.*

ROSMER [*mildly and with quiet emphasis, clasping* KROLL's *hands*]: Welcome back to this house, my dear Kroll. [*Puts his hands on his shoulders and looks into his eyes*] My dear old friend! I felt sure things between us would eventually return to the way they were.

KROLL: But my dear chap – Have you also been under the insane illusion that something was amiss?

REBEKKA [*to* ROSMER]: Yes imagine – how lovely that it was just an illusion.

ROSMER: Was it really, Kroll? So why did you withdraw from us so completely?

KROLL [*seriously and with quiet emphasis*]: Because I didn't want to come here as some living reminder of your unhappy years – and of her – of the one who met her end in the Mill Falls.

ROSMER: A gracious thought on your part. You're always so considerate. But it was quite unnecessary to stay away on that account. – Come on, let's sit on the sofa. [*They sit down*] No, it honestly doesn't cause me any pain to think about Beate. We speak of her daily. We both feel that she still belongs here in this house somehow.

KROLL: You do, really?

REBEKKA [*lighting the lamp*]: We do indeed.

ROSMER: It's just so natural. We both loved her so dearly. And both Rebekk – both Miss West[13] and I know in ourselves that we did everything within our power for that poor troubled soul. We have nothing to reproach ourselves for. – Which is why I now find a gentle comfort in thinking about Beate.

KROLL: You dear, splendid people! I shall come out to visit you every day from now on.

REBEKKA [*sitting down in an armchair*]: Well, just make sure you keep your word.

ROSMER [*with slight hesitation*]: Kroll, my friend – I do very much wish there'd not been this interruption in our getting together. You've been my first port of call for advice for as long as we've known each other. From the moment I became a student.

KROLL: Well yes, and I value that enormously. Is there perhaps something now in particular –?

ROSMER: There are so many things, so many things I'd like to discuss unreservedly with you. Matters close to my heart.

REBEKKA: Yes, Mr Rosmer, isn't that right? I think it must be so good – between old friends –

KROLL: Oh, you can be sure I've even more to discuss with you. Because I've become an active politician now, as you probably know.

ROSMER: Yes, so you have. How did that happen exactly?

KROLL: I had to, my friend. Had to, even if I didn't want to. It's impossible to remain an idle spectator any longer. Now that the Radicals have regrettably come into power – it's high time –. Which is also why I've got our little circle of friends in town to close ranks. It's high time, I say!

REBEKKA [*with a little smile*]: Well, isn't it actually rather late now?

KROLL: It would, undeniably, have been better if we'd stemmed the flow earlier. But who could possibly have foreseen what was to come? I couldn't, at least. [*Gets up and walks up and down*] Well, I've had my eyes opened now all right. Since this spirit of revolt has found its way into the school itself.

ROSMER: Into the school? Surely not into your school?

KROLL: I'm afraid so. Into my own school. What do you think of that? I've got wind of the fact that the boys in the top year – that is, some of the boys – have had a secret society for more than six months, and they've been reading Mortensgård's newspaper!

REBEKKA: Oh, *The Beacon*.

KROLL: Quite – healthy spiritual sustenance for future public servants, wouldn't you say? But what's most depressing is that it's the most gifted boys in the class who have banded

together and hatched this plot against me. It's only the sim-
pletons and idlers that have kept out of it.

REBEKKA: Do you really take that so much to heart,
headmaster?

KROLL: Do I? When I see my life's work hampered and
thwarted? [*More quietly*] Though I could almost deal with
that. The worst is yet to come. [*Looks around him*] I presume nobody's listening at the doors?

REBEKKA: No, absolutely not.

KROLL: Then let me tell you, this rebellion and discord has
entered my own home. My own peaceful home. It has disturbed the tranquillity of my family life.

ROSMER [*rising*]: What's that? Your own home –?

REBEKKA [*goes over to* KROLL]: But, my dear Mr Kroll, what's
happened?

KROLL: Can you believe that my own children –. To be brief –
Laurits is the leader of the school conspiracy. And Hilda has
embroidered a red cover in which to hide *The Beacon*.

ROSMER: I'd never have dreamed – that within your family –
in your house –

KROLL: No, who could dream of such a thing? In my house,
where obedience and order have always reigned – where
until now one single and unanimous will has presided –

REBEKKA: How does your wife take it all?

KROLL: Well, that's the most unbelievable thing of all. The
woman who has – throughout her life – in matters great
and small – shared my opinions and backed my views, even
she's taking the children's side on many issues. And now she
blames *me* for what's happened. She says I have a repressive
effect on the young. As though it somehow weren't necessary
to –. Well, that's the kind of unrest I have at home. Although
naturally I talk about it as little as possible. Such things are
best kept hushed up. [*Paces the room*] Oh, yes, yes, yes.
    He stops at the window, his hands behind his back, and
    looks out.

REBEKKA [*has gone over to* ROSMER, *and speaks in low, hur-
ried tones, unheard by* KROLL]: Do it!

ROSMER [*in the same tone*]: Not this evening.

REBEKKA [*as before*]: Yes, now.

She moves away and busies herself with the lamp.

KROLL [*going into the middle of the room*]: Well, Rosmer, now you know how the spirit of the age has cast its shadow over both my domestic and professional life.[14] And I'm not supposed to fight these corrupting, destructive, disruptive ideas with every weapon I can lay my hands on? Oh yes, my friend, I most certainly intend to. In writing and in speech – both.

ROSMER: Do you really hope to achieve anything that way?

KROLL: I want, at least, to do my duty as a citizen of the state. And I believe that every man concerned for the cause and for his fatherland is conscience-bound to do likewise. In fact – that was the main reason for my coming here to see you tonight.

ROSMER: But, my dear chap, what do you mean –? What can I –?

KROLL: You're going to help your old friends. Do as the rest of us. Lend a hand as best you can.

REBEKKA: But, Mr Kroll, you know Mr Rosmer's aversion to that sort of thing.

KROLL: That's an aversion he must now overcome. You don't follow events closely enough, Rosmer. You sit here, walled in with your historical collections. God help us – all due respect for genealogical tables and the like. But this is not the time for such pursuits – sadly. You've no idea of the situation around the country. Almost every single notion has been turned on its head. It's going to be a huge task to get all these misconceptions cleared out again.

ROSMER: I believe you're right. But that sort of work really isn't for me.

REBEKKA: Besides, I think perhaps Mr Rosmer has come to see things in life with a more open gaze than before.

KROLL [*puzzled*]: More open?

REBEKKA: Yes, or freer. Less prejudiced.

KROLL: What's this? Rosmer – surely you could never be so feeble as to allow yourself to be duped by such a chance occurrence – by some fleeting victory won by the leaders of the masses![15]

ROSMER: My dear Kroll, you know how little understanding I have of politics. But I certainly do feel there's been a greater independence of mind among people in recent years.

KROLL: Really – and you don't, for one moment, question whether that's a good thing? Besides, you're seriously mistaken, my friend. You only have to look at the opinions that are current among the radicals, both here and in town. They don't differ one jot from the wisdom that's proclaimed in *The Beacon*.

REBEKKA: Yes, Mortensgård has considerable power over many people round here.

KROLL: Yes, imagine that! A man with such a tawdry past as his! A man dismissed from his post as a schoolmaster because of an immoral relationship –! That's the sort of man who presents himself as a leader of the people! And it works! It actually works! He intends to expand his paper now, I hear. I have it from reliable sources that he's seeking a suitably competent partner.

REBEKKA: I find it strange that you and your friends don't set something up in opposition to him.

KROLL: That's precisely what we're doing now. Today we bought *The County Times*. The question of money didn't present any problems. But – [*Turns towards* ROSMER] Well, that brings me to my actual purpose in coming to see you. It's the leadership – the editorial leadership that's proving problematic, you see. Tell me, Rosmer – couldn't you, for the sake of this excellent cause, be persuaded to take it over?

ROSMER [*almost terrified*]: Me!

REBEKKA: But how could you think such a thing!

KROLL: Your horror of public meetings and reluctance to expose yourself to the uncouth behaviour at such events – is understandable. But the more discreet activity of an editor, or, to be more precise –

ROSMER: No, no, my dear friend, you mustn't ask that of me.

KROLL: I'd have liked to have a shot at something like that myself. But it would be way beyond my capacity. I'm weighed down with countless duties before I even begin –. But you, on the other hand, no longer have the pressure of any official duties. – The rest of us will obviously assist you as best we can.

ROSMER: I can't, Kroll. I'm not suited to it.

KROLL: Not suited? That's exactly what you said when your father found you a calling[16] –

ROSMER: And I was right. Which was why I left it.

KROLL: Oh, if you just make as good an editor as you were a pastor, we'll be satisfied.

ROSMER: My dear Kroll – I can tell you this once and for all – I am not doing it.

KROLL: Then surely you'll lend us your name at least.

ROSMER: My name?

KROLL: Yes, merely the name Johannes Rosmer will be an asset to our newspaper. The rest of us are already branded as party-men. I myself, so I'm told, have been denounced as a raging fanatic. Which means that we cannot, under our own names, count on the paper having any significant impact on the misguided masses. You, by contrast, have always kept out of the conflict. Your mild, honest temperament and fine intellect – your unimpeachable integrity – are known and valued by everyone in this district. And then there's the respect that your former position as a clergyman affords you. And finally your venerable family name!

ROSMER: Oh, my family name –

KROLL [pointing at the portraits]: The Rosmers of Rosmersholm – clergymen and officers. Highly respected men of service. Men of honour, one and all – a family that has occupied the highest seat in this district for nigh on two hundred years. [Places his hand on ROSMER's shoulder] Rosmer – you owe it to yourself and to your family tradition to join us and defend everything that our society has valued until now. [Turns] Well, what do you say, Miss West?

REBEKKA [with a light, quiet laugh]: My dear headmaster, this all sounds utterly ludicrous to me.

KROLL: What! Ludicrous?

REBEKKA: Yes. Since I'll tell you plainly now –

ROSMER [hurriedly]: No, no – leave it! Not now!

KROLL [*looks from one to the other*]: But, what on earth, my
dear friends –? [*Breaks off*] Ahem!

    MRS HELSETH *comes in through the door on the right.*

MRS HELSETH: There's a man at the kitchen entrance, sir. Says
he wants a word with the pastor.

ROSMER [*relieved*]: Ah, right. Well, ask him to please come in.

MRS HELSETH: Here in the living room?

ROSMER: Well, yes.

MRS HELSETH: But he don't look like the sort to be let in the
living room.

REBEKKA: So what does he look like, Mrs Helseth?

MRS HELSETH: Oh, he don't look like much, miss.

ROSMER: Didn't he give you his name?

MRS HELSETH: Yes, I think he called himself Hekman or something of the sort.

ROSMER: I don't know anyone by that name.

MRS HELSETH: And he gave the name Ulrik too.

ROSMER [*with a start*]: Ulrik Hetman! Was that it?

MRS HELSETH: That's right, Hetman.

KROLL: I'm sure I've heard that name before –

REBEKKA: Yes, I think that was the name *he* wrote under, that
strange –

ROSMER [*to* KROLL]: It's Ulrik Brendel's pseudonym.

KROLL: The prodigal[17] Ulrik Brendel. Quite right.

REBEKKA: So, he's still alive.

ROSMER: I think he was travelling with a theatre troupe.

KROLL: The last I heard, he was in the workhouse.

ROSMER: Ask him to come in, Mrs Helseth.

MRS HELSETH: All right then.

    She goes.

KROLL: Can you really bear to have this fellow in your living
room?

ROSMER: Well, he was once my tutor, as you know.

KROLL: Yes, I know that he went about stuffing your head with
rebellious ideas, and that your father chased him out of the
door with his horsewhip.

ROSMER [*with slight bitterness*]: Father was a major even in
his own home.

KROLL: Give him thanks in his grave for that, my dear Rosmer. Well now –!

MRS HELSETH *opens the door on the right for* ULRIK BRENDEL *and leaves, closing the door after her. He is an impressive figure, somewhat emaciated, but brisk and alert, with grey hair and beard. He is dressed like a common tramp. A worn-out frock coat, poor footwear, no shirt to be seen. Old black gloves which he has not taken off, a soft grubby hat clamped under his arm and a walking stick in his hand.*

ULRIK BRENDEL [*initially uncertain, then walks quickly over to* KROLL *and offers him his hand*]: Good evening, Johannes!

KROLL: Sorry, but –

BRENDEL: Did you ever expect to see me again? And within these detestable walls?

KROLL: Sorry –. [*Points to* ROSMER] Over there.

BRENDEL [*turning*]: Yes, quite right. Ah, there he is! Johannes – my boy – whom I have loved more than any –![18]

ROSMER [*reaching his hand out to him*]: My old tutor.

BRENDEL: Despite certain memories, I didn't want to pass Rosmersholm without paying a flying visit.

ROSMER: You are heartily welcome here now. Be assured of that.

BRENDEL: And this captivating lady –? [*Bows*] The lady pastor naturally.

ROSMER: Miss West.

BRENDEL: Apparently close. And yon stranger –? A brother of the cloth, I see.

ROSMER: Mr Kroll, the headmaster.

BRENDEL: Kroll? Kroll? Wait now. Did you study Philology in your younger days?

KROLL: Yes, of course.

BRENDEL: *Donnerwetter!*[19] Then naturally I knew you![20]

KROLL: Sorry –

BRENDEL: Weren't you –

KROLL: Sorry –

BRENDEL: – one of the halberdiers[21] of virtue who had me thrown out of the Debating Society?[22]

KROLL: That's possible perhaps. But I deny any closer association.

BRENDEL: Well, well! *Nach Belieben,*[23] *Herr Doktor.* It makes no odds to me. Ulrik Brendel remains the man he is, regardless.

REBEKKA: I presume you're heading in to town, Mr Brendel?

BRENDEL: The lady pastor has it in one. At intervals I am forced to strike a blow for existence. I don't do it willingly – but – *enfin*[24] – the pressing necessity –

ROSMER: Oh, my dear Mr Brendel, may I then be permitted to help you at all? In some way or other, I mean –

BRENDEL: Ah, what a suggestion! Would you wish to defile the bonds that bind us? Never, Johannes – never!

ROSMER: But then what do you intend to do in town? Trust me, you won't find it easy –

BRENDEL: Leave that to me, my boy. The die is cast.[25] Just as I stand here before you, I am embarked upon an extensive voyage. More extensive than all my earlier forays put together. [*To* KROLL] Dare I ask you, *Herr Professor – unter uns*[26] – is there any halfway respectable, decent, spacious assembly room in your esteemed town?

KROLL: The Working Men's Association Hall[27] is the biggest.

BRENDEL: And does *Herr Dozent*[28] have the requisite qualities to exert influence upon that assuredly beneficent association?

KROLL: I have nothing whatever to do with it.

REBEKKA [*to* BRENDEL]: You should apply to Peder Mortensgård.

BRENDEL: *Pardonnez-moi, madame* – what kind of idiot is he?

ROSMER: What makes you think he's an idiot?

BRENDEL: Can't I hear from the very sound of the name that its owner is a plebeian?

KROLL: That's not the answer I'd expected.

BRENDEL: But I shall overcome such qualms. There's nothing else for it. When a man – such as I – stands at a turning point in his life –. It is settled. I shall make contact with this personage – commence direct negotiations –

ROSMER: Are you seriously standing at a turning point?

BRENDEL: Doesn't my own dear boy know that wherever Ulrik Brendel stands, he is always serious? – Absolutely, my friend, I intend to put on the new man[29] now. To step out from the unassuming state of seclusion that I have hitherto observed.

ROSMER: How –?

BRENDEL: I want to seize life with an active hand. Step forward. Step up. It is the age of a storm-swept solstice[30] in which we live and breathe. – Now I wish to offer my mite upon the altar of emancipation.

KROLL: *You* too?

BRENDEL [*to them all*]: Does my public here have any deeper knowledge of my miscellaneous writings?

KROLL: No, I must confess –

REBEKKA: I've read a good many. My foster-father owned them.

BRENDEL: Fine lady of the house – then you have squandered your time. Alas, they are nothing but dross, let me tell you.

REBEKKA: Really?

BRENDEL: Those you've read, yes. My significant works are known to neither man nor woman. To nobody – except myself.

REBEKKA: How can *that* be?

BRENDEL: Because they are not written.

ROSMER: But, my dear Mr Brendel –

BRENDEL: You know, my dear Johannes, that I'm a bit of a sybarite.[31] *Ein Feinschmecker.*[32] Always have been. I love to savour things in solitude. For then, my enjoyment is double. Ten-fold double. You see – when golden dreams cascaded upon me – misted my vision – when new, expansive and dizzying thoughts were born in me – whisked me aloft upon mighty wings – then I fashioned them into poems, visions, pictures. In general terms, you understand.

ROSMER: Yes, indeed.

BRENDEL: Oh, in my time, my friend, I have savoured and drunk deep of creativity's mysterious rapture – in general terms, as I said – I have filled my hands, joyous and trembling, with the applause, the gratitude, the fame, the crown of laurels.[33] Sated myself in my private performances with an ecstasy – oh, of such a dizzying magnitude –!

KROLL: Hmm –.

ROSMER: But never written it down?

BRENDEL: Not a word. I have always felt a nauseous aversion for the dull handiwork of a scribe. Besides, why would I profane my own ideals, when I could enjoy them in their purity, and for myself? But now they shall be offered up. In truth, I feel as a mother must when she places her young daughter in the arms of a husband. But I will offer them nonetheless – offer them on the altar of emancipation. A series of well-formed lectures – across the entire land –!

REBEKKA [*animatedly*]: What a splendid gesture, Mr Brendel! You're giving the most precious thing you own.

ROSMER: The only thing.

REBEKKA [*looking meaningfully at* ROSMER]: How many are there, I wonder, who do that? Who *dare* do that?

ROSMER [*returns her glance*]: Who knows?

BRENDEL: My audience is moved. That gladdens my heart – and strengthens my will. And with that I advance into action. One thing, though –. [*To* KROLL] Could you tell me, *Herr Tutor*, whether there is a Temperance Society[34] in town? A Total Abstainers' Society? Naturally, there must be.

KROLL: Yes, at your service. I am its chairman.

BRENDEL: Didn't I know it, just by looking at you! Well, it may just be possible then, that I shall visit your home and sign myself up for a week.

KROLL: Sorry – we don't accept members on a weekly basis.

BRENDEL: *A la bonheur*,[35] Herr Pedagogue. Ulrik Brendel has never besieged the doors of such institutions. [*Turns*] But I really oughtn't to prolong my sojourn in this house, so rich in memories. I must go into town and choose a suitable lodging for myself. There must be a decent hotel, I hope?

REBEKKA: Won't you take a warming drink before you go?

BRENDEL: What sort of warming drink, dear lady?

REBEKKA: A cup of tea or –

BRENDEL: I thank the bountiful hostess of this house! But I prefer not to presume upon private hospitality. [*Waves his hand*] Prosperous lives, my good people! [*Goes towards the door, but then turns*] Oh, by the way –. Johannes – Pastor

Rosmer – will you do your former tutor a service for old friendship's sake?

ROSMER: Yes, it would be a pleasure.

BRENDEL: Good. Then lend me – just for a day or two – a newly ironed dress-shirt.

ROSMER: Nothing more?

BRENDEL: I'm travelling on foot – this time, you see. My trunk will be sent on.

ROSMER: I see. But are you sure there's nothing more?

BRENDEL: Well, you know what – perhaps you could spare an old, used summer coat?

ROSMER: Yes, yes, of course I can.

BRENDEL: And if there happened to be a pair of decent boots to go with the coat –

ROSMER: I'm sure that can be arranged. As soon as we get your address, we'll send the things on.

BRENDEL: In no way! No inconvenience on my account! I shall take these bagatelles with me.

ROSMER: Right you are. Will you come upstairs with me then?

REBEKKA: Let me go instead. Mrs Helseth and I will see to it.

BRENDEL: I could never allow this distinguished lady –!

REBEKKA: Nonsense! Come this way, Mr Brendel.

She goes out to the right.

ROSMER [*holding him back*]: Tell me – is there no other way I can be of service?

BRENDEL: I've honestly no idea what *that* might be. Although, damn it all – now that I come to think of it –! Johannes, do you happen to have eight kroner on you?

ROSMER: Let's see now. [*Opens his wallet*] I have two ten-kroner notes.[36]

BRENDEL: Oh, that's just as good. I can take those. They can always be changed in town. Thanks, for now. Remember I had two ten-kroner notes. Goodnight, my own dear boy! Goodnight to you, sir!

Goes out to the right, where ROSMER *takes his leave and shuts the door after him.*

KROLL: Merciful God – so *that* was the Ulrik Brendel who people once thought would achieve something great in this world.

ROSMER [*quietly*]: At least he's had the courage to live life in his own way. I don't think *that* is so insignificant.

KROLL: You what? A life like his? I almost believe he's capable of confusing your ideas all over again.

ROSMER: No, Kroll. I have come to my own understanding of things now.

KROLL: I wish that were so, my dear Rosmer. But you're so incredibly susceptible to outside influence.

ROSMER: Let's sit down. And then I want to talk to you.

KROLL: Yes, let's.

They sit down on the sofa.

ROSMER [*after a moment*]: It's rather nice and comfortable here now, wouldn't you say?

KROLL: Yes, very nice and comfortable – and tranquil. Yes, you've got yourself a home now all right. And I have lost mine.

ROSMER: Don't say that, my friend. That which is now rent asunder, will most surely be made whole again.

KROLL: Never. Never. The sting is embedded for ever. Things can never be as they were before.

ROSMER: Listen now, Kroll. We two have been close for many, many years now. Do you think it's conceivable that our friendship could ever be broken?

KROLL: I know of nothing on earth that could cause a breach between us. What puts that in your head?

ROSMER: It's just that you put such a decisive weight on agreement in opinions and views.

KROLL: Well, yes – but then we are generally in agreement. On the larger core questions at least.

ROSMER [*quietly*]: No. Not any longer.

KROLL [*about to leap up*]: What?

ROSMER [*holding him back*]: No, don't get up. I beg you, Kroll.

KROLL: What is this? I don't understand. Tell me straight!

ROSMER: A new summer has entered my mind. A new youthful perspective. That's why I now stand where –

KROLL: Stand where –?

ROSMER: Where your children stand.

KROLL: You? You! Impossible! *Where* do you stand now?

ROSMER: On the same side as Laurits and Hilda.

KROLL [*bows his head*]: An apostate. Johannes Rosmer an apostate.

ROSMER: I ought to have felt happy – deeply joyous about what you call my apostasy. But instead I've suffered agonies. Because I knew, of course, that it was likely to cause you such bitter sadness.

KROLL: Rosmer – Rosmer! I shall never get over this. [*Looks at him sadly*] Oh, that *you* could also want to join and lend your hand to the work of corrupting and disrupting this poor unhappy country.

ROSMER: It is the work of emancipation I wish to join.

KROLL: Yes, I'm sure. That's what it's called by the seducers and those they have led astray. But do you really think there's any emancipation to be expected from the spirit that's in the process of poisoning our entire society?

ROSMER: I don't ally myself with this prevailing spirit. Nor indeed with any of the combatants. I want to try to bring people together from all sides. As many and with as deep a conviction as I can. I want to devote my life and all my energy to this one thing – to the creation of the true democratic enlightenment of this country.

KROLL: So you don't think *we* have democracy aplenty! In my opinion the whole lot of us are well on the way to being dragged down into the mud where generally only the common folk are content.

ROSMER: That's precisely where I feel the real task of democracy lies.

KROLL: What task is that?

ROSMER: The ennoblement of all the people in this country.

KROLL: All the people –!

ROSMER: As many as possible, at least.

KROLL: By what means?

ROSMER: By emancipating minds, purifying wills, I'd say.

KROLL: You are a dreamer, Rosmer. Will *you* emancipate them? Will *you* purify them?

ROSMER: No, my friend – I seek only to awaken them. The doing of it – that is for them.

KROLL: And you think they can?

ROSMER: Yes.

KROLL: By their own power, I take it?

ROSMER: Yes, absolutely, by their own power. No other exists.

KROLL [*getting up*]: Is this talk befitting a clergyman?

ROSMER: I am no longer a clergyman.

KROLL: Yes, but – the faith you were brought up with –?

ROSMER: I no longer have it.

KROLL: You no longer –!

ROSMER [*getting up*]: I have given it up. I *had* to give it up, Kroll.

KROLL [*shaken, yet controlled*]: I see. – Well, well, well. The one presumably goes with the other. – Was that perhaps why you left the service of the Church?

ROSMER: Yes. When I felt certain in myself – when I could see it wasn't just a passing crisis of doubt, but something I neither could, nor wished to, escape – then I left.

KROLL: So this has been fermenting inside you that long. And we – your friends, have been told nothing. Rosmer, Rosmer – how could you hide this sad truth from us!

ROSMER: Because I considered it a matter of concern for myself alone. And I didn't want to cause you and our other friends unnecessary grief. I thought I could stay and live here just as before, quiet, happy and contented. I wanted to read and immerse myself in all those works, books that had been closed to me before. To allow my mind to inhabit the great world of truth and freedom which has been revealed to me now.

KROLL: An apostate. Every word proves it. But why confess your secret apostasy like this? And why now?

ROSMER: It was you who forced me to it, Kroll.

KROLL: Me? I forced you –?

ROSMER: When I heard about your violent outbursts at those public meetings – when I read about all the uncharitable speeches you'd made – your hateful attacks on those who stand on the other side – your scornful condemnation of your opponents –. Oh, Kroll – the idea that you, you – could be like that! It was then I saw it as my ineluctable duty. People are turning evil amid these hostilities. Tranquillity and happiness and reconciliation must enter their souls. *That* is why I am stepping forward now to declare myself openly for what I am. Besides, I also want to test my strength. Couldn't you – from your side – join me in this, Kroll?

KROLL: I shall never, as long as I live, ally myself with the forces of destruction in our society.

ROSMER: Well, let's fight with noble weapons at least – since it seems we *must*.

KROLL: Whosoever is not with me in life's definitive values, I no longer recognize. Nor do I owe him consideration.

ROSMER: That applies to me too?

KROLL: This breach with me is of *your* own making, Rosmer.

ROSMER: But *is* this a breach?

KROLL: This! It's a breach with everyone who has until today been close to you. Now you must take the consequences.

    REBEKKA WEST *comes in from the right and opens the door wide.*

REBEKKA: Well, well – he's on the way to his sacrificial banquet now. And we can sit down to eat. Do go in, Mr Kroll.

KROLL [*taking his hat*]: Good evening, Miss West. There's nothing more for me here.

REBEKKA [*tensely*]: What's that? [*Shuts the door and comes closer*] Have you told –?

ROSMER: He knows now.

KROLL: We shan't let go of you, Rosmer. We will force you to come back to us.

ROSMER: I'll never come back.

KROLL: We'll see. You're not the man to hold out and stand alone.

ROSMER: I won't be completely alone. – There are two of us to bear the solitude here.

KROLL: Ah –! [*A suspicion crosses his mind*] That too! Beate's words –!

ROSMER: Beate –?

KROLL [*dismisses the thought*]: No, no – that was vile –. Forgive me.

ROSMER: What? What was?

KROLL: Think no more of it. Shame! Do forgive me. Goodbye!
He goes towards the door to the entrance hall.

ROSMER [*following him*]: Kroll! It mustn't end like this between us. I'll drop by and see you tomorrow.

KROLL [*turning round in the hall*]: You shan't set foot in my house!
He takes his stick and goes.
ROSMER *stands for a moment in the open doorway; then shuts the door and goes over to the table.*

ROSMER: It's all right, Rebekka. I'm sure we'll manage to get through this. We two trusty friends. You and I.

REBEKKA: What do you think he meant by 'shame'?

ROSMER: My dear, don't bother yourself about that. He didn't believe what he was saying himself. But I'll pop in and see him tomorrow. Goodnight!

REBEKKA: Are you going up so early again – tonight? After this?

ROSMER: Tonight as always. I feel so much lighter now it's over. Look – I'm very calm, my dear Rebekka. So you should be calm too. Goodnight!

REBEKKA: Goodnight, dear friend! And sleep well!
ROSMER goes out through the door to the entrance hall; he can be heard going up the stairs.
REBEKKA goes to the wall and pulls the bell by the stove. A moment later MRS HELSETH *comes in from the right.*

REBEKKA: You may as well clear the table again, Mrs Helseth. The pastor doesn't want anything – and the headmaster's gone home.

MRS HELSETH: The headmaster's gone? So what was wrong with him?

REBEKKA [*taking up her crochet work*]: He felt sure a storm was coming –

MRS HELSETH: That's strange. There's not a fleck of cloud to be seen tonight.

REBEKKA: As long as he doesn't meet the white horse. I'm afraid we'll soon be hearing from some of these phantoms of yours.

MRS HELSETH: God forgive you, miss! Don't say such awful things.

REBEKKA: Well, well –

MRS HELSETH [*lowering her voice*]: Does miss[37] really think that someone here will pass away soon?

REBEKKA: No, of course I don't. But there are so many kinds of white horses in the world, Mrs Helseth. – Well, goodnight. I'll go to my room now.

MRS HELSETH: Goodnight, miss.

REBEKKA *takes her crochet work and goes out to the right.*

MRS HELSETH [*turns down the lamp, shakes her head and mutters to herself*]: Lord Jesus. – Lord Jesus. That Miss West. The way she talks sometimes!

ACT TWO

Rosmer's study. On the wall to the left is the entrance door. At the back of the room a doorway leading into his bedroom, a drape drawn back. To the right a window, in front of it a writing table covered with books and papers. Bookshelves and cupboards against the walls. Shabby furniture. An old-fashioned couch to the left with a table in front of it.

ROSMER, *wearing a housecoat, is sitting on a high-backed chair at the writing table. He is cutting the pages of a pamphlet and glancing through it here and there.*
A knock at the door on the left.

ROSMER [*without turning*]: Come right in.

    REBEKKA WEST *comes in, wearing a morning gown.*

REBEKKA: Good morning.

ROSMER [*turning the pages of the pamphlet*]: Good morning, dear. Was there anything you wanted?

REBEKKA: I just wanted to know if you slept well?

ROSMER: Ah, I slept very soundly. No dreams –. [*Turns*] And you?

REBEKKA: Not badly, thank you. Towards the morning hours at least –

ROSMER: I don't think my heart has felt this light in ages. Oh, it was good I said it.

REBEKKA: Yes, you shouldn't have kept quiet for so long, Johannes.[38]

ROSMER: I don't know myself how I could be such a coward.

REBEKKA: Well, it wasn't so much out of cowardice –

ROSMER: Oh, yes, yes, my dear – when I look more deeply there was some cowardice to it.

REBEKKA: All the more admirable then that you made a clean break of it. – [*Sits down next to him on a chair by the writing table*] But now I want to tell you something I've done – which you mustn't get cross about.

ROSMER: Cross? My dear, how could you think –?

REBEKKA: Because it may have been a bit presumptuous of me, but –

ROSMER: Well then, let me hear it.

REBEKKA: Yesterday evening, when that Brendel fellow was leaving – I wrote him two or three lines to take to Mortensgård.

ROSMER [*a little doubtfully*]: But, Rebekka dear –. Well, what did you write?

REBEKKA: I wrote that he'd be doing you a favour if he looked kindly on the unhappy man and helped him in whatever way he could.

ROSMER: My dear, you shouldn't have done that. You've only harmed Brendel by it. Besides, Mortensgård is a man I'd prefer to keep out of my life. You know the issues I had with him once.

REBEKKA: Don't you think it might be quite good if you got on better terms with him again?

ROSMER: Me? With Mortensgård? Why do you say that?

REBEKKA: Well, you may not be altogether safe now – given what's come between you and your friends.

ROSMER [*looking at her and shaking his head*]: Can you really believe Kroll or any of the others would want to take revenge –? That they'd be capable of –?

REBEKKA: In the first heat of the moment – my dear. Nobody can be that sure. I think – after the way the headmaster took it –

ROSMER: Oh, you should know him better than that. Kroll is an honourable man through and through. I'll go into town this afternoon and talk to him. I'll talk to them all. You'll see – it'll be fine –

MRS HELSETH *comes in through the door on the left.*

REBEKKA [*getting up*]: What is it, Mrs Helseth?

MRS HELSETH: Mr Kroll is downstairs in the hall.

ROSMER [*quickly getting up*]: Kroll!

REBEKKA: Mr Kroll! Goodness –!

MRS HELSETH: He asks if he may come up and talk to the pastor.

ROSMER [*to* REBEKKA]: What did I say! – Yes, of course he can. [*Goes to the door and shouts down the stairs*] Come on up, my dear friend! You're most welcome!

> ROSMER *stands holding the door open.* MRS HELSETH *leaves.* REBEKKA *pulls the drape over the doorway. Then she busies herself with something.*
>
> MR KROLL *comes in with his hat in his hand.*

ROSMER [*quietly, moved*]: I knew it wouldn't be the last time –

KROLL: Today I see matters in a completely different light from yesterday.

ROSMER: Yes, Kroll! You do, don't you? Now that you've thought it over –

KROLL: You misunderstand me. [*Puts his hat on the table next to the couch*] It's imperative I speak with you one to one.

ROSMER: Why shouldn't Miss West –?

REBEKKA: No, no, Mr Rosmer. I'll go.

KROLL [*looking her up and down*]: And I must apologize to the lady[39] for coming here so early in the day. For taking her by surprise before she's had a moment to –

REBEKKA [*startled*]: What do you mean? Do you find anything wrong in my going around at home in my morning gown?

KROLL: God forbid! I don't know, of course, what's regarded as usual behaviour at Rosmersholm nowadays.

ROSMER: But Kroll – you seem quite changed today!

REBEKKA: Good day to you, Mr Kroll.

> *She goes out to the left.*

KROLL: If I may –

> *He sits down on the couch.*

ROSMER: Yes, my friend, let's make ourselves comfortable and talk things over.

> *He sits down on a chair facing* MR KROLL.

KROLL: I've not had a wink of sleep since yesterday. I lay there thinking and thinking all night.

ROSMER: And so, what do you say today?

KROLL: This will take some time, Rosmer. Let me begin with an introduction of sorts. I can tell you a little about Ulrik Brendel.

ROSMER: Has he been to see you?

KROLL: No. He installed himself in a lowly tavern. In the lowest company, naturally. Drank and bought rounds for as long as he had funds. Afterwards he abused the entire company, calling them common riffraff. Which, by the by, he was right about. But then he received a thrashing and was thrown into the gutter.

ROSMER: So he's as incorrigible as ever after all.

KROLL: He'd also pawned the coat. But apparently that's been redeemed for him. Can you guess by whom?

ROSMER: By you, perhaps?

KROLL: No. By that noble Mr Mortensgård.

ROSMER: I see.

KROLL: Yes, I've been told that Mr Brendel's first visit was to that 'idiot and plebeian'.

ROSMER: Well, that was very lucky for him –.

KROLL: It was indeed. [*Leans over the table, a little closer to* ROSMER] But that leads us to a matter, which for the sake of our old – our former friendship – I feel a duty to warn you about.

ROSMER: My dear chap, what might *that* be?

KROLL: There may well be some sort of game being played in this house behind your back.

ROSMER: How can you think that? Is it Reb – Miss West you're alluding to?

KROLL: It is indeed. I can perfectly well understand it from her side. She's been accustomed to being in charge here for so long. But all the same –

ROSMER: My dear Kroll, you're completely mistaken. She and I hide absolutely nothing from each other about anything at all.

KROLL: So has she confessed to you that she has entered into correspondence with the editor of *The Beacon*?

ROSMER: Oh, you're referring to a couple of lines she sent along with Ulrik Brendel?

KROLL: So you know about that. And do you condone her taking up contact in this way with that scandalmonger who week after week seeks to put me in the stocks for both my school work and public activities?

ROSMER: My dear chap, I doubt that side of things has even occurred to her. Besides, she has complete freedom of action, just as I have.

KROLL: Oh really? Well, I suppose that's consistent with this new direction you've entered upon now. Since wherever you stand, Miss West presumably stands too?

ROSMER: She does indeed. The two of us have in faith worked forwards together.

KROLL [looking at him and shaking his head slowly]: Oh, you blind, beguiled man!

ROSMER: Me? Why do you say that?

KROLL: Because I don't dare – don't *want* to think the worst. No, no, let me finish. – You really value my friendship, Rosmer? And my respect? Don't you?

ROSMER: Surely I don't need to answer that.

KROLL: Very well, but there are other things that demand an answer – a full explanation from your side. Will you allow me perhaps to conduct a sort of cross-examination –?

ROSMER: A cross-examination?

KROLL: Yes, to question you on a few things that you might find painful to recall. You see – this apostasy of yours – or emancipation, as you call it – is wrapped up with so many other things, which, for your own sake, you must clarify for me.

ROSMER: My dear Kroll, ask me anything you like. I've nothing to hide.

KROLL: Tell me, then – what do you really believe was the deepest cause for Beate ending her own life?

ROSMER: Can you be in doubt about that? Or, to be more precise, can we ask about cause when it comes to what a sick, unhappy, mentally unstable person might do?

KROLL: Are you certain Beate was so completely unstable? The doctors weren't altogether convinced at least.

ROSMER: If the doctors had seen her the way I frequently saw her, night and day, they'd have been in no doubt.

KROLL: I didn't doubt it back then either.

ROSMER: No, it was impossible to doubt it, unfortunately. And I told you about her uncontrollable, wild passions – which she demanded I reciprocate. Oh, the fear she engendered in me! And then the totally groundless self-reproach that consumed her in those last years.

KROLL: Yes, when she'd been told she'd never have children.

ROSMER: Well, imagine for yourself –. Such agony and torment over something that wasn't her fault –! And you're suggesting she was mentally stable?

KROLL: Hmm –! Can you remember if you had any books in the house back then that dealt with the purpose of marriage[40] – according to the progressive views of our time?

ROSMER: I remember Miss West lent me a work of that sort. She'd inherited Dr West's library, as you know. But, my dear Kroll, you surely don't think we were careless enough to initiate that poor soul into such matters? I give you my solemn assurance that we're guiltless in this. It was her own disturbed mind that drove her into this maze of confusion.

KROLL: Well, I can tell you *one* thing at least. That poor, tortured, emotionally overwrought Beate ended her life so that you could live happily, live freely and – as you desired.

ROSMER [*halfway out of his chair*]: What are you trying to say?

KROLL: Listen to me calmly now, Rosmer. Because I can talk about it now. In the last year of her life she visited me twice to express her fears and despair.

ROSMER: About all this?

KROLL: No. The first time she came in and claimed you were on the path to apostasy. That you wanted to break with the faith of your forefathers.

ROSMER [*eagerly*]: What you're saying is impossible, Kroll! Absolutely impossible! You must be mistaken!

KROLL: Why?

ROSMER: Because while Beate was alive, I still had doubts, I was still in conflict with myself. It was a battle I fought alone and in absolute isolation. I don't even think Rebekka –

KROLL: Rebekka?

ROSMER: Well, yes – Miss West. I call her Rebekka because it's easier.

KROLL: So I've noticed.

ROSMER: That's why I find it incomprehensible that Beate could get hold of such an idea. And why did she never talk to me about it herself? She never did. Never a single word.

KROLL: Poor Beate – she begged and implored me to speak to you.

ROSMER: So why didn't you?

KROLL: Could I doubt for one moment, back then, that she was deranged? Such an accusation, against a man like you! – And then she came again – about a month later. She was calmer, it seemed. But, as she left, she said: 'Soon they can expect the white horse at Rosmersholm.'

ROSMER: Yes. The white horse – she often talked about that.

KROLL: And when I tried to distract her from these melancholy thoughts, she just answered: 'I don't have much time left. Since Johannes must marry[41] Rebekka immediately.'

ROSMER [*almost speechless*]: What are you saying –! I – marry –!

KROLL: That was on a Thursday afternoon. – On the Saturday evening she threw herself from the footbridge into the Mill Falls.

ROSMER: And you never warned us –!

KROLL: You know yourself how often she hinted that she was certain to die soon.

ROSMER: I know that, of course. But all the same – you *should* have warned us!

KROLL: Yes, I thought about it. But by then it was too late.

ROSMER: But why have you never before –? Why have you kept all this to yourself?

KROLL: What purpose would there be in my coming here and causing you further pain and distress? I'd taken this whole

thing to be nothing but a wild, empty fantasy. – Until yesterday evening.

ROSMER: But now you don't?

KROLL: Wasn't Beate seeing things quite clearly when she said
you would abandon your childhood faith?

ROSMER [*staring in front of him*]: Yes, I can't understand that.
It's the most incomprehensible thing in the world to me.

KROLL: Incomprehensible or not – that's how it is. And now
I ask you, Rosmer, how much truth is there in her second
accusation? In the last, I mean.

ROSMER: Accusation? But was *that* an accusation?

KROLL: Perhaps you didn't notice the exact wording? She
would soon be gone, she said –. Why? Well?

ROSMER: Well, so I could marry Rebekka –.

KROLL: That wasn't how it was worded. Beate phrased it
differently. She said: 'I don't have much time left. Since
Johannes *must* marry Rebekka *immediately*.'

ROSMER [*looks at him for a moment, then gets up*]: Now I
understand what you're saying, Kroll.

KROLL: And? What answer do you have?

ROSMER [*remains quiet, in control*]: To something so pre-
posterous –? The only fitting answer would be to point you
to the door.

KROLL [*getting up*]: Very well.

ROSMER [*standing in front of him*]: Now listen here. For over
a year – ever since Beate passed away – Rebekka West and I
have lived alone here at Rosmersholm. In all that time you
have known of Beate's accusation against us. But never for
one moment have I noticed you take any offence at the fact
that Rebekka and I were living together here.

KROLL: I had no idea until yesterday evening that it was
an apostate man and an – emancipated woman who were
cohabiting.

ROSMER: Ah –! So you don't believe that purity of mind can
be found in apostates or emancipated people? You don't
believe that they can have a natural sense of morality?

KROLL: I don't place much credit on a morality not rooted in
the faith of the Church.

ROSMER: And you'd apply that to Rebekka and myself? To my and Rebekka's relationship –?

KROLL: Much as I'd like to exempt the two of you, I can't deviate from my opinion that there's really no vast gulf between free thought and – hmm.

ROSMER: And what –?

KROLL: – and free love – since you want to know.

ROSMER [*quietly*]: And you're not ashamed to say that to me! When you've known me since my earliest youth.

KROLL: That's precisely why. I know how easily you let yourself be influenced by those you associate with. And this Rebekka of yours –. Well, this Miss West – the truth is we don't know the least thing about her. So in short, Rosmer – I'm not giving up on you. And you – well, you must seek to save yourself while there's time.

ROSMER: Save myself? How do you mean –?

MRS HELSETH *peeps in through the door on the left.*

ROSMER: What do you want?

MRS HELSETH: I was going to ask Miss West to come down.

ROSMER: Miss West isn't up here.

MRS HELSETH: Oh? [*Looks round the room*] That's odd.
She leaves.

ROSMER: You were saying –?

KROLL: Listen. Whatever's gone on here in secret while Beate was alive – and whatever is still going on – I've no wish to enquire further. You were, of course, deeply unhappy in your marriage. And in a way that must speak in your defence –

ROSMER: Oh, how little you actually know me –!

KROLL: Don't interrupt. What I want to say is – if your cohabitation with Miss West really must continue, it is absolutely crucial you hush up this about-turn – this tragic apostasy – into which she has led you. Let me speak! Let me speak! I say, if this situation must persist, think and believe whatever in God's name you like – about anything at all. But keep your opinions to yourself. This is a purely personal matter. There's no necessity for these things to be shouted across the entire land.

ROSMER: It's a necessity for me that I get out of a position that is false and ambiguous.

KROLL: But you have a duty towards the traditions of your ancestors, Rosmer! Remember that! Since time immemorial Rosmersholm has been the cornerstone of order and discipline – of respectful deference for all that is upheld and approved by the best in society. This entire region has taken its character from Rosmersholm. It will cause an unholy, an irreparable confusion if it's rumoured that *you* have broken with what I call the Rosmerian family principles.

ROSMER: My dear Kroll – I really can't share your view. I see it as my absolute duty to bring a little light and joy where the Rosmer family has created darkness and gloom for so very, very long.

KROLL [*looking severely at him*]: Oh yes, a worthy undertaking for the man with whom the ancestral line will die. Forget that, my friend. It's no task for you. You were created for the life of the quiet scholar.

ROSMER: Yes, perhaps. But now I want to join the fray of life[42] for once.

KROLL: The fray of life – do you know what that will mean for you? A life-and-death battle with all your friends.

ROSMER [*quietly*]: They can't all be as fanatical as you.

KROLL: You're a naive soul, Rosmer. An inexperienced soul. You have no idea how violently the storm will rage over you.

    MRS HELSETH *pushes the door open a crack, on the left.*

MRS HELSETH: I'm to ask from Miss West –

ROSMER: What is it?

MRS HELSETH: There's someone downstairs wants a word with the pastor.

ROSMER: Is it the man who was here yesterday afternoon perhaps?

MRS HELSETH: No, it's that Mr Mortensgård.

ROSMER: Mortensgård!

KROLL: Aha! So we've gone that far! That far already!

ROSMER: What does he want with me? Why didn't you send him away?

MRS HELSETH: Miss West said I should ask if he might come up.

ROSMER: Tell him I've got somebody here –

KROLL [*to* MRS HELSETH]: Just let him come up, Mrs Helseth.

MRS HELSETH *goes out.*

KROLL [*takes his hat*]: I quit the field – for now. But the main battle is still not fought.

ROSMER: On my life, Kroll – I have nothing whatever to do with Mortensgård.

KROLL: I no longer believe you. Not about anything. I don't believe you on any count whatsoever after this. It's war to the knife[43] now. We'll see if we can't render you harmless.

ROSMER: Oh, Kroll – how deep – how low you've sunk!

KROLL: I? And that's coming from you! Remember Beate!

ROSMER: Are you returning to *that* again!

KROLL: No. The riddle of the Mill Falls is for you to solve according to your conscience – if you still possess such a thing.

PEDER MORTENSGÅRD *comes in softly and quietly through the door on the left. He is a small, slightly built man with thin reddish hair and beard.*

KROLL [*with a look of hatred*]: Ah, *The Beacon* –. Lit here at Rosmersholm. [*Buttons up his coat*] Well, I can be in no doubt about which course to steer now.

MORTENSGÅRD [*subdued*]: *The Beacon* will always be kept alight to guide Mr Kroll home.

KROLL: Indeed, you've long displayed your goodwill. Although there *is* a commandment, of course, that says we mustn't bear false witness[44] against our neighbour –

MORTENSGÅRD: The headmaster doesn't need to teach me about the commandments.

KROLL: Not even the seventh?[45]

ROSMER: Kroll –!

MORTENSGÅRD: If that's needed, the pastor is surely the most appropriate man.

KROLL [*with hidden scorn*]: The pastor? Indeed, Pastor Rosmer is undeniably the most appropriate man in *that* area. – I wish you a profitable meeting, gentlemen!

He leaves, slamming the door after him.

ROSMER [*stands looking at the door, and says to himself*]: Oh, well – that's it, then. [*Turns*] Please tell me, Mr Mortensgård, what brings you out here to see me?

MORTENSGÅRD: It was Miss West I came to see actually. I thought I ought to thank her for the kind note I received from her yesterday.

ROSMER: I'm aware that she wrote to you. So did you get to talk to her?

MORTENSGÅRD: Yes, briefly. [*With a faint smile*] I hear that views on certain matters have changed out here at Rosmersholm.

ROSMER: My views have changed on many different matters. I might almost say – on everything.

MORTENSGÅRD: That's what Miss West said. Which is why she thought I ought to come up and talk a bit with the pastor about all this.

ROSMER: About what, Mr Mortensgård?

MORTENSGÅRD: May I be permitted to report in *The Beacon* that you've come to a different way of thinking – and that you're joining the cause for progress and freedom of thought?

ROSMER: You may indeed. In fact, I urge you to report it.

MORTENSGÅRD: It'll appear tomorrow morning then. It'll be significant news that Pastor Rosmer of Rosmersholm feels he can fight for the light in *that* sense too.

ROSMER: I don't quite understand.

MORTENSGÅRD: I'm saying that it lends strength to our party's[46] moral backbone each time we win the support of a devout Christian.

ROSMER [*rather puzzled*]: So you aren't aware –? Didn't Miss West tell you *that* too?

MORTENSGÅRD: What, pastor? It seemed Miss West was in rather a hurry. She said I ought to come upstairs and hear the rest from you.

ROSMER: In that case I must tell you that I've emancipated myself entirely. On all fronts. I have no association whatever now with the teachings of the Church. From now on these matters are immaterial to me.

MORTENSGÅRD [*looks at him in bewilderment*]: Well – if the moon dropped out of the sky, I couldn't be more –! The pastor himself has broken away –!

ROSMER: Indeed, I now stand where you have stood for years. You can share that in *The Beacon* tomorrow too.

MORTENSGÅRD: That too? No, my dear pastor –. I'm sorry – but it's best not to mention that side of things.

ROSMER: Not mention?

MORTENSGÅRD: Not straight away, I mean.

ROSMER: But I don't understand –.

MORTENSGÅRD: Well, you see, pastor –. I imagine you're not as familiar with the ins and outs of the situation as I am. But now that you've moved over to the side of free thought – and now that you – as Miss West said – want to be involved in the movement – then I take it you want to be as useful to those ideas and to the movement as you can possibly can?

ROSMER: Yes, I most certainly do.

MORTENSGÅRD: Right – but then I want to just make you aware, pastor, that if you step forward openly about this, about your leaving the Church, you'll have tied your own hands before you've even begun.

ROSMER: You think so?

MORTENSGÅRD: Indeed, you can guarantee there won't be much you can achieve in these parts then. Besides, – we already have enough freethinkers, Pastor. I'd almost say – we have too many. What the party needs are Christian elements – something everybody must respect. *That* is what we lack so badly. So the most advisable thing is for you to keep a wrap on anything like that, which isn't the public's business. That's my opinion, anyway.

ROSMER: I see. You don't dare to involve yourself with me if I openly acknowledge my apostasy?

MORTENSGÅRD [*shaking his head*]: I'd be very reluctant, pastor. Lately I've made it a rule never to support anybody or anything that wants to knock the Church.

ROSMER: So have you yourself recently turned back to the Church?

MORTENSGÅRD: That's another matter entirely.

ROSMER: I see, so that's how it is. Yes, I understand.

MORTENSGÅRD: Pastor – you have to remember that I – *I* in particular – do not have complete freedom of action.

ROSMER: So what ties *your* hands then?

MORTENSGÅRD: Being a marked man.

ROSMER: Ah – I see.

MORTENSGÅRD: A marked man, pastor. You should remember that better than anyone. Since it was first and foremost you who put that mark upon me.

ROSMER: If I'd stood then where I stand now, I'd have handled your offence more gently.

MORTENSGÅRD: No doubt. But it's too late now. You've marked me once and for all. Marked me for life. Well, you probably don't fully realize the impact of such a thing. But you may well feel its sting yourself soon, pastor.

ROSMER: I?

MORTENSGÅRD: Yes. You surely don't think Mr Kroll and his circle will forgive a breach like yours? And I hear *The County Times* will soon be out for blood. You could just find yourself a marked man too.

ROSMER: I feel myself to be unassailable in every aspect of my personal life, Mr Mortensgård. My conduct has been irreproachable.

MORTENSGÅRD [*with a warm smile*]: That's a bold statement, pastor.

ROSMER: Perhaps so. But I have the right to make it.

MORTENSGÅRD: Even if you were to scrutinize your conduct as thoroughly as you once scrutinized mine?

ROSMER: You say that so strangely. What are you alluding to? Is there something in particular?

MORTENSGÅRD: Yes, there is *one* particular thing. Just one. But just *that* could be bad enough, if malicious opponents got wind of it.

ROSMER: Please tell me then what that could be.

MORTENSGÅRD: Can't you guess, pastor?

ROSMER: No, absolutely not. I've no idea.

MORTENSGÅRD: Very well, I'd better tell you then. – I have in my custody a rather strange letter that was written here at Rosmersholm.

ROSMER: Miss West's letter, you mean? Is that so strange?

MORTENSGÅRD: No, that letter isn't strange. But some time ago I got another letter from this house.

ROSMER: Also from Miss West?

MORTENSGÅRD: No, pastor.

ROSMER: Well, from whom then? From whom?

MORTENSGÅRD: From the late mistress.

ROSMER: From my wife! *You* got a letter from my wife?

MORTENSGÅRD: Yes.

ROSMER: When?

MORTENSGÅRD: It was during the late Mrs Rosmer's final days. It must be about eighteen months ago now. And it's this letter that is so strange.

ROSMER: Surely you know that my wife was mentally ill at that time?

MORTENSGÅRD: Yes, I know many people believed that. But I don't think that's evident in the letter. When I say the letter is strange, I mean it in rather a different way.

ROSMER: What on earth did my poor wife think to write to you about?

MORTENSGÅRD: I have the letter at home. It starts more or less by saying that she's living in great fear and dread. Because there are so many evil people in these parts, she writes. And these people think only of causing you harm and injury.

ROSMER: Me?

MORTENSGÅRD: Yes, that's what she says. And then comes the strangest thing. Shall I say it, pastor?

ROSMER: Yes, of course! Tell me everything. Don't hold back.

MORTENSGÅRD: The late Mrs Rosmer begs and beseeches me to be magnanimous. She says that she knows it was you who had me dismissed from my teaching post. And so she begs me most earnestly not to take revenge.

ROSMER: How did she think you could take revenge?

MORTENSGÅRD: It says in this letter that if I should hear rumours that there were sinful goings on at Rosmersholm, I should not attach any credence to them; since it was just wicked people who were spreading them about to make you unhappy.

ROSMER: That's what the letter says?

MORTENSGÅRD: The pastor may read it himself at his convenience.

ROSMER: But I don't understand –! What did she imagine these evil rumours to be about?

MORTENSGÅRD: Firstly, pastor, that you had lapsed from the faith of your childhood. This the mistress denied vehemently – at the time. And, next – hmm –

ROSMER: Next?

MORTENSGÅRD: Well, next she writes – and this is all rather confused – that she has no knowledge of any sinful relations at Rosmersholm. That no wrong has ever been done her. And that if any such rumour should come out, she entreats me not to refer to it in *The Beacon*.

ROSMER: Is there mention of any name?

MORTENSGÅRD: No.

ROSMER: Who brought you the letter?

MORTENSGÅRD: I promised not to say. It was brought to me one evening as darkness fell.

ROSMER: If you'd asked around at the time, you'd have found out that my poor unhappy wife was mentally unstable.

MORTENSGÅRD: I did ask around, pastor. But I have to say I didn't quite get *that* impression.

ROSMER: You didn't? – But why make me aware of this old, confused letter *now*?

MORTENSGÅRD: To warn you to be extremely cautious, pastor.

ROSMER: In my personal life, you mean?

MORTENSGÅRD: Yes. You must remember that you're no longer immune from attack.

ROSMER: So you still think there's something to hide here?

MORTENSGÅRD: I can't see why an emancipated man should refrain from living life to the full. But, as I've said, just be cautious from this day on. If there's any rumour of something that challenges prejudice, you can be sure it'll reflect badly on the entire cause for freedom. – Goodbye, Pastor Rosmer.

ROSMER: Goodbye.

MORTENSGÅRD: I'll go off to the printers now and put the great news in *The Beacon*.

ROSMER: Put everything in.

MORTENSGÅRD: I shall put everything in that our good folk need to know.

He bows and leaves. ROSMER *remains at the door while* MORTENSGÅRD *goes down the stairs. The front door is heard closing.*

ROSMER [*still standing in the doorway, calls softly*]: Rebekka! Reb –. Hmm. [*Loudly*] Mrs Helseth – isn't Miss West down there?

MRS HELSETH [*from below*]: No, pastor, she's not here.

The curtain at the back of the room is drawn open. REBEKKA *comes into view in the doorway.*

REBEKKA: Rosmer!

ROSMER [*turning round*]: What! Were you in my bedroom! My dear, what were you doing in there?

REBEKKA [*goes over to him*]: I was listening.

ROSMER: But Rebekka, how could you do that?

REBEKKA: Well, I could. He was so nasty – about my morning gown –

ROSMER: Ah! So you were already in there when Kroll –?

REBEKKA: Yes. I wanted to know what he was being so secretive about.

ROSMER: I'd have told you, you know that.

REBEKKA: You'd hardly have told me everything. And certainly not in his words.

ROSMER: So did you hear everything?

REBEKKA: Most of it, I think. I had to go down for a moment when Mortensgård came.

ROSMER: And then you came back up –

REBEKKA: Don't be cross, my friend.

ROSMER: You must do whatever you feel is right. You have complete freedom. – But what do you say to all this, Rebekka –? Oh, I don't think I've ever needed you as much as I do now.

REBEKKA: You and I have both been prepared for what would come sometime.

ROSMER: No, no – not for this.

REBEKKA: Not for this?

ROSMER: I thought that sooner or later our beautiful, pure friendship might be sullied and misconstrued. But not by Kroll. I could never have believed such a thing of him. But by all those others with their crude minds and ignoble eyes. Yes, my dear – I had good reason to draw a veil so jealously over our association. It was a dangerous secret.

REBEKKA: Oh, why concern ourselves with the judgement of others? *We* know that we are without guilt.

ROSMER: Me? Without guilt? Yes, I used to think so – until today. But now – now, Rebekka –

REBEKKA: Yes, what now?

ROSMER: How do I explain Beate's horrible accusation?

REBEKKA [*vehemently*]: Oh, stop talking about Beate! Stop thinking about Beate! You'd done so well in distancing yourself from her – she's dead.

ROSMER: Now that I know all this, she seems eerily alive again.

REBEKKA: No, Rosmer – you mustn't! You mustn't!

ROSMER: Yes, I tell you. We've got to try to get to the bottom of it. How could she have strayed into this wretched misapprehension?

REBEKKA: You're surely not starting to doubt that she was close to insane?

ROSMER: Yes, dear – that's exactly what I can't be so totally certain of any longer. And besides – even if she was –

REBEKKA: If she was? Yes, what then?

ROSMER: I mean – where do we look for the likeliest cause for her sickness of mind tipping into insanity?

REBEKKA: Oh, what possible use can there be in allowing yourself to be consumed by such brooding!

ROSMER: I can't do otherwise, Rebekka. I can't let go of these nagging doubts, no matter how much I might want to.

REBEKKA: But surely there's a danger – in endlessly circling this one gloomy thought.

ROSMER [*paces about, restless and pensive*]: I must have betrayed myself in some way. She must have noticed how happy I started to feel from the moment *you* came to us.

REBEKKA: But, my dear, even if that were true –!

ROSMER: You'll see – it didn't escape her that we read the same books. That we sought each other's company and discussed all these new things together. But I can't comprehend it! I was always so careful to shield her. Looking back, it seems to me I was always at great pains to keep her away from everything to do with us. Or wasn't I, Rebekka?

REBEKKA: Yes, yes, you were indeed.

ROSMER: And you were too. And yet –! Oh, it's too awful to contemplate! So she was going around – in her sick love – silent – without saying a word – watching us – noticing everything and – misconstruing everything.

REBEKKA [*wringing her hands*]: Oh, I should never have come to Rosmersholm.

ROSMER: To think what she must have suffered in silence! All the vile things she thought to build up and piece together about us in her troubled mind. – Didn't she ever talk to you about anything that might give you some clue?

REBEKKA [*as if startled*]: To me! Do you think I'd have stayed a day longer if she had?

ROSMER: No, of course, that goes without saying. Oh, what a battle she must have fought. And fought alone, Rebekka. In despair and quite alone. – And then that final dramatic – accusatory victory – in the Mill Falls.

He throws himself into the chair at the writing table, rests his elbows on the table, and covers his face in his hands.

REBEKKA [*coming up behind him cautiously*]: Listen to me, Rosmer. If it was in your power to call Beate back – to you – to Rosmersholm – would you do it?

ROSMER: How do I know what I would or wouldn't do. I only have thoughts for this one thing – which is irrevocable.

REBEKKA: You were meant to start living now, Rosmer. You *had* begun. You had freed yourself entirely – on all fronts. You felt so happy and so light –

ROSMER: Yes, my dear – it's true, I did. But then came this crushing blow.

REBEKKA [*behind him with her arms on the back of his chair*]: How lovely it was when we used to sit downstairs in the living room as darkness fell. And helped each other plan a new way of life. You wanted to grapple with life – the living, vital life of today – as you put it. You wanted to go from house to house, a guest bringing liberation – winning the wills and minds of all – creating noble people around you in ever-widening circles. Noble people.

ROSMER: Happy noble people.

REBEKKA: Yes – happy.

ROSMER: Because it is happiness that ennobles the mind, Rebekka.

REBEKKA: Don't you think – suffering may too? Great suffering?

ROSMER: Yes – if only one could get through it. Over it. Beyond it.

REBEKKA: Then *that* is what you must do.

ROSMER [*shaking his head sadly*]: I shall never get beyond this – not completely. There'll always be a residual doubt. A question. I shall never again drink of that which makes it so wonderfully delicious to be alive.

REBEKKA [*over the back of his chair, softly*]: And what might that be, Rosmer?

ROSMER [*looking up at her*]: The joy and calm of being free from guilt.

REBEKKA [*takes a step back*]: Yes. Free from guilt.

   A short pause.

ROSMER [*with his elbows on the table, supporting his head in his hands and staring straight in front of him*]: And how skilfully she linked things up. How systematically she pieced it together. First she began harbouring a suspicion as to my orthodoxy –. How did she come up with *that* back then? But come up with it she did. And then it grew into a certainty. And then – yes, then it was very easy for her to think all these other things were plausible. [*Straightens up in his chair and runs his hands through his hair*] Oh, these wild ideas! I'll never be rid of them. I can feel it. I know it. When I least expect it, they will charge out at me and remind me of the one who is dead.

REBEKKA: Like the white horse of Rosmersholm.

ROSMER: Exactly. Racing through the dark. Through the silence.

REBEKKA: And because of these unholy figments of your mind you'll abandon that vital life you'd begun to get a hold on.

ROSMER: You're right, it's terrible. Truly terrible, Rebekka. But the choice is not mine. How can I ever get beyond this?

REBEKKA [*behind his chair*]: By forming new relationships.

ROSMER [*starts, looks up*]: New relationships!

REBEKKA: Yes, new relationships with the outside world. Live, work, be active! Don't sit here agonizing and brooding over unsolvable riddles.

ROSMER [*getting up*]: New relationships? [*Walks across the room, stops at the door and comes back*] A question occurs to me. Haven't you also asked yourself that question, Rebekka?

REBEKKA [*struggles to breathe*]: Let me – hear – what it is.

ROSMER: What form do you believe *our* relationship will take after today?

REBEKKA: I am confident our friendship will endure – whatever happens.

ROSMER: Yes, that wasn't quite what I meant. But the thing which first drew us together – which binds us so closely – our shared belief in pure cohabitation between man and woman –

REBEKKA: Yes, yes – what of it?

ROSMER: I mean such a relationship – like ours – isn't it perhaps best suited to a life in quiet, happy tranquillity –?

REBEKKA: And?

ROSMER: But now a life of strife and of unrest and emotional turmoil is opening up for me. Because I *do* want to live my life, Rebekka! I won't let myself be brought down by shadows of the unknown. I won't let my life be dictated by either the living or – anybody else.

REBEKKA: No, no, don't let that happen! Be free, Rosmer! A free man!

ROSMER: But do you know what I'm thinking? You don't? You don't see how I can best gain my freedom from all the gnawing memories – from my entire sad past?

REBEKKA: Well?

ROSMER: By setting a new and a living reality against it.

REBEKKA [*feeling for the back of the chair*]: A living –? What – is this?

ROSMER [*closer to her*]: Rebekka – what if I were to ask you – will you be my second wife?

REBEKKA [*speechless for a moment, then screams with joy*]: Your wife! Your –! Me!

ROSMER: Excellent. Let's try it. We two shall become one. There mustn't be an empty place left here by the dead any longer.

REBEKKA: Me – in Beate's place –!

ROSMER: Then she's out of the story. Completely. For ever and always.

REBEKKA [*quietly, trembling*]: You think so, Johannes?

ROSMER: It has to happen! It has to! I cannot – will not – go through life with a corpse on my back. Help me to throw it off, Rebekka. And let's stifle these memories – in freedom, joy and passion. You will be for me the only wife I ever had.

REBEKKA [*controlled*]: Don't mention this again. I will never be your wife.

ROSMER: What! Never? Don't you think that you could come to love me? Isn't there already a little hint of love in our friendship?

REBEKKA [*puts her hands over her ears as if in fear*]: Don't talk like that, Rosmer! Don't say such things!

ROSMER [*catching her by the arm*]: Yes, yes – there *is* some seed of potential in our relationship. Oh, I can see you feel the same. Don't you, Rebekka?

REBEKKA [*again calm and collected*]: Listen. I'm telling you – if you persist in this, I shall leave Rosmersholm.

ROSMER: Leave! You! You can't do that. That's impossible.

REBEKKA: It's even more impossible that I should be your wife. Never in this world can I be that.

ROSMER [*looks at her in surprise*]: You say 'never'. And you say it so strangely. Why can't you?

REBEKKA [*taking both his hands in hers*]: My dear friend – for your own sake and mine – do not ask me why. [*Lets him go*] Enough now, Johannes.

She goes towards the door on the left.

ROSMER: From this day on I will have no other question but that – why?

REBEKKA [*turns and looks at him*]: Then it's over.

ROSMER: Between you and me?

REBEKKA: Yes.

ROSMER: It'll never be over between us. You shall never leave Rosmersholm.

REBEKKA [*with her hand on the door handle*]: No, I probably shan't. But if you ever ask me again – it'll be over anyway.

ROSMER: Over anyway? What do you mean –?

REBEKKA: Because then I shall go the way Beate went. Now you know, Rosmer.

ROSMER: Rebekka –!

REBEKKA [*stops at the door and nods slowly*]: Now you know.
She leaves.

ROSMER [*stares as though lost at the closed door and says to himself*]: What – is – this?

ACT THREE

The living room at Rosmersholm. The window and hall door are open. The morning sun is seen shining outside.

REBEKKA WEST, *dressed as in the first act, is standing by the window, watering and tending to the plants. Her crochet work is lying on the armchair.* MRS HELSETH *is going around the room dusting the furniture with a feather duster.*

REBEKKA [*after a short pause*]: Strange that the pastor's staying upstairs so long today.

MRS HELSETH: Oh, he often does. He'll soon be down, I'm sure.

REBEKKA: Have you seen him at all?

MRS HELSETH: Only briefly. When I went up with his coffee, he was in his bedroom getting dressed.

REBEKKA: I'm asking because he wasn't quite himself yesterday.

MRS HELSETH: No, he didn't seem so. I wonder if there's not something amiss between him and his brother-in-law

REBEKKA: What could that be, do you think?

MRS HELSETH: I don't know. Perhaps this here Mortensgård fellow has put them up against each other.

REBEKKA: That's possible. – Do you know anything about this Peder Mortensgård?

MRS HELSETH: No, nothing. How could you even think it, miss?[47] A man like that!

REBEKKA: You mean because of that vile paper he publishes?

MRS HELSETH: Oh, not just because of *that*. – You must have heard that he had a child with a married woman whose husband had left her?

REBEKKA: I have heard talk of it. But that must have been a long time before I arrived.

MRS HELSETH: Heavens, yes, he was very young back then. And she ought to have had better sense than him. He wanted to marry her too. But of course he wasn't allowed. And they probably made him suffer for it. But Mortensgård – well, he's built himself up since, right enough. There must be plenty of folk that seek *him* out now.

REBEKKA: Most of the poorer folk prefer to turn to him when there's something afoot.

MRS HELSETH: Oh, there might just be other folk besides the poor –

REBEKKA [*secretly glances at her*]: Really?

MRS HELSETH [*by the sofa, dusting and sweeping vigorously*]: Might be some you'd least expect, miss.

REBEKKA [*arranging the flowers*]: Yes, but surely that's just something you *believe*, Mrs Helseth. After all, *you* couldn't possibly know anything like that for certain.

MRS HELSETH: So miss doesn't reckon I can know? Oh, I most certainly can. Because – since you force it out of me – I carried a letter once to Mortensgård myself.

REBEKKA [*turns*]: Really – you did!?

MRS HELSETH: Yes, I most certainly did. And that letter was written right here at Rosmersholm.

REBEKKA: Really, Mrs Helseth?

MRS HELSETH: Upon my word, it was. And it was written on quality paper. And there was a lovely red seal on the outside too.

REBEKKA: And *you* were entrusted to deliver it? Well, my dear Mrs Helseth, it's not difficult to guess who it was from.

MRS HELSETH: Oh?

REBEKKA: Naturally it was something which the poor, sick Mrs Rosmer –

MRS HELSETH: You said it, Miss West, not me.

REBEKKA: But what was in this letter? No, of course – you can't possibly know that.

MRS HELSETH: Hmm, I might just happen to know, all the same.

REBEKKA: Did she tell you what she wrote?

MRS HELSETH: Well no, not exactly. But after he – Mortensgård – had read it, he started cross-questioning me – asking me all sorts – so I got a pretty fair idea what was in it.

REBEKKA: So what do you think was in it? Oh, my dear, sweet Mrs Helseth, do tell me!

MRS HELSETH: Oh no, miss. Not for the world.

REBEKKA: Oh, surely you can tell me. We're such good friends.

MRS HELSETH: God forbid I should ever tell you *that*, miss. I can only say that it was some vile idea that they'd gone and put into the poor sick mistress's head.

REBEKKA: Who put an idea into her head?

MRS HELSETH: Evil folk, Miss West. Evil folk.

REBEKKA: Evil –?

MRS HELSETH: Yes, I say it twice over. Really evil folk, they must have been.

REBEKKA: Who are these people, do you think?

MRS HELSETH: Oh, I know what I think all right. May my lips be sealed. But there's a certain lady there in town – hmm!

REBEKKA: I can see by your face that you mean Mrs Kroll.

MRS HELSETH: Yes, she's one of a kind, she is. Always been very snooty toward me. And she's never looked upon you kindly either.

REBEKKA: Do you think Mrs Rosmer was of sound mind when she wrote that letter to Mr Mortensgård?

MRS HELSETH: Well, it's a strange thing – the mind, miss. But I don't reckon she was completely out of it.

REBEKKA: But she was rather distraught when she found out that she couldn't have children. It was *then* the madness broke out.

MRS HELSETH: Yes, she took *that* awful bad, poor lady.

REBEKKA [*takes her crochet work and sits in the chair by the window*]: Although – don't you agree that that was actually best for the pastor, Mrs Helseth?

MRS HELSETH: What was, miss?

REBEKKA: That no children came of it –? Well?

MRS HELSETH: Hmm! – I don't rightly know what to say.

REBEKKA: Oh, believe me. It was best for him. Pastor Rosmer isn't cut out for having to listen to crying babies.

MRS HELSETH: Babies don't cry at Rosmersholm, Miss West.

REBEKKA [*looking at her*]: They don't cry?

MRS HELSETH: No. In this house, little children have never been known to cry, as far back as anyone can remember.

REBEKKA: That's strange.

MRS HELSETH: Yes, *isn't* it strange? But it runs in the family. And there's something else strange. When they grow up, they never laugh. Never laugh as long as they live.

REBEKKA: But that would be most odd –

MRS HELSETH: Has miss – even once – heard or seen Mr Rosmer laugh?

REBEKKA: No, now that I think of it, I almost believe you're right. But then it doesn't seem to me that people laugh much at all in these parts.

MRS HELSETH: You're right, they don't. Folk say it started at Rosmersholm. And then I reckon it spread outwards like a sort of infection[48] – that too.

REBEKKA: You're a woman of deep insight, Mrs Helseth.

MRS HELSETH: Oh, you oughtn't to sit there and poke fun at me, miss. [*Listens*] Ssh, Ssh – the pastor's coming down. He doesn't like to see the duster in here.

She goes out through the door on the right.

JOHANNES ROSMER, *with his stick and hat in hand, comes in from the entrance hall.*

ROSMER: Good morning, Rebekka.

REBEKKA: Good morning, my dear. [*After a pause, crocheting*] Are you going out?

ROSMER: Yes.

REBEKKA: It's beautiful weather.

ROSMER: You didn't come up to see me this morning.

REBEKKA: No – I didn't. Not today.

ROSMER: Won't you from now on, perhaps?

REBEKKA: Oh, I'm not certain yet.

ROSMER: Has anything arrived for me?

REBEKKA: *The County Times* has arrived.

ROSMER: *The County Times* –!

REBEKKA: It's there on the table.

ROSMER [*putting aside his hat and stick*]: Anything in it –?

REBEKKA: Yes.

ROSMER: And you didn't send it up –

REBEKKA: You'll read it soon enough.

ROSMER: Right then. [*Picks up the newspaper and stands reading it by the table*] – What! – 'cannot warn strongly enough against spineless deserters' –. [*Looks across at her*] They're calling me a deserter, Rebekka.

REBEKKA: No names are mentioned.

ROSMER: That makes no difference. [*Reads on*] – 'secret traitors to the good cause' –. 'Judases, who brazenly admit their apostasy the instant they think the most opportune – most advantageous moment has come'. 'A reckless attack on the legacy of our forefathers'. – 'in the expectation that those who currently hold the power will not fail to offer suitable reward'. [*Puts the newspaper down on the table*] And they write these things about me. After knowing me so well and for so long. Things they don't even believe themselves. Things they know there's not one single word of truth in – but which they write anyway.

REBEKKA: There's still more.

ROSMER [*picking up the paper again*]: – 'a poor sense of judgement lends some excuse'. – 'but a corrupting influence – extending perhaps to areas which, for the time being, we shall not present for public discussion or reproof.' – [*Looks at her*] What's this?

REBEKKA: They're alluding to me, you understand.

ROSMER [*putting the paper aside*]: Rebekka – this is the doing of dishonourable men.

REBEKKA: Yes, I hardly think they can criticize Mortensgård.

ROSMER [*pacing the room*]: Something must be done to redress this. Everything that is good in people will go to ruin if this is allowed to go on any longer. But it shall not! Oh, how happy – how happy I would feel if I could bring a little light into all this ugly darkness.

REBEKKA [*getting up*]: Yes, isn't that right, Johannes? In this you have something great and magnificent to live for!

ROSMER: Imagine if I could awaken self-knowledge in them. Bring them to repent and to feel shame at themselves. Get them to come closer to one another in tolerance – in love, Rebekka.

REBEKKA: Yes, just focus all your talents on that, and you shall see – you will win.

ROSMER: I feel sure it could succeed. Oh, what a blessing it would be to live life then. No more hateful conflict. Just sporting rivalry. Every eye fixed upon the same goal. Every will, every mind rallying together – onwards – upwards – each pursuing their own natural path. Happiness for all – created by all. [*Looks out over the open landscape, then gives a start and says gloomily*] Ah! Not through me.

REBEKKA: Not –? Not through you?

ROSMER: Nor *for* me either.

REBEKKA: Oh, Rosmer, don't allow such doubts to rise up in you.

ROSMER: Happiness – my dear Rebekka – is above all that quiet, joyful, secure feeling of being free from guilt.

REBEKKA [*staring in front of her*]: Yes. This matter of guilt –.

ROSMER: Oh, you have such little knowledge of it. But I –

REBEKKA: You least!

ROSMER [*pointing out of the window*]: The Mill Falls.

REBEKKA: Oh, Johannes –!

    MRS HELSETH *looks in through the door on the right.*

MRS HELSETH: Miss!

REBEKKA: Later, later. Not now.

MRS HELSETH: Just a word, miss.

    REBEKKA *goes over to the door.* MRS HELSETH *informs her of something. They whisper together for a moment.* MRS HELSETH *nods and goes.*

ROSMER [*uneasily*]: Was that something for me?

REBEKKA: No, just a bit of housekeeping. – You should go out now in that fresh air, Johannes. Take a good long walk.

ROSMER [*takes his hat*]: Yes, come on. Let's go together.

REBEKKA: No, my dear, I can't just now. You'll have to go alone. But do shake off all these gloomy thoughts. Promise me.

ROSMER: I'm unlikely to ever shake them off – I fear.

REBEKKA: Oh, to think that anything so groundless could hold so much power over you –!

ROSMER: Sadly – it may not be so groundless. I've been lying there all night mulling it over. Perhaps Beate was right in what she saw.

REBEKKA: In what way?

ROSMER: Perhaps she was right when she believed I loved you, Rebekka.

REBEKKA: Right – in *that*?

ROSMER [*puts his hat on the table*]: I keep turning this question over in my head – whether we might have deluded ourselves all this time – in calling our relationship a friendship.

REBEKKA: Are you saying that it could just as well have been called –?

ROSMER: – love. Yes, that is what I'm saying. Even when Beate was still alive, I already gave all my thoughts to you. It was you alone I longed for. It was with you that I experienced this contented, desireless, quiet bliss. If we really think about it, Rebekka – we began our union like two children falling secretly and sweetly in love. Without demands, without dreams. Wasn't that how you felt it too? Tell me.

REBEKKA [*struggling with herself*]: Oh – I don't know what to say.

ROSMER: And it is this sense of devotion, within us, and between us, which we've taken for friendship. Oh no, Rebekka – our relationship has been a spiritual marriage – perhaps from those very first days. That's why my conscience is troubled.[49] I had no right to it – no right, for Beate's sake.

REBEKKA: No right to live in happiness? You believe that, Rosmer?

ROSMER: She looked upon our relationship through the eyes of *her* love. Judged our relationship by the nature of *her* love. Naturally. Beate could not judge otherwise than she did.

REBEKKA: But how can you blame yourself for Beate's delusions!

ROSMER: Out of love for me – in *her* way – she went into the Mill Falls. That's a solid fact, Rebekka. I can never get beyond it.

REBEKKA: Oh, think only of the great, splendid task that you've invested your life in!

ROSMER [*shaking his head*]: That can never be fulfilled, Rebekka. Not by me. Not after what I know now.

REBEKKA: Why not by you?

ROSMER: Because victory is never won for a cause that springs from a troubled conscience.

REBEKKA [*bursting out*]: Oh, this is the voice of your ancestors – their doubts – their fears – their scruples! They say here that the dead return as charging white horses. This is something similar, I think.

ROSMER: Be it what it may. How does that help when I can't get away from it? And you can believe me, Rebekka. It is as I say. Any cause that is to gain lasting victory must be carried forth by a happy and guilt-free man.

REBEKKA: Is happiness really so indispensable to *you*, Johannes?

ROSMER: Happiness? Yes – it is.

REBEKKA: For *you* – who never laugh?

ROSMER: Even for me, yes. Believe me, I have a huge capacity for happiness.

REBEKKA: You should go now, dear. Take a good long walk. You hear –? – Look, here's your hat. And your stick too.

ROSMER [*takes both*]: Thank you. And you won't come?

REBEKKA: No, no, I can't just now.

ROSMER: Oh, well. You're with me all the same.

He goes out through the hallway. A moment later REBEKKA *peeps out behind the open door. Then she goes over to the door on the right.*

REBEKKA [*opens the door; in a lowered voice*]: All right, Mrs Helseth. You can let him in now.

She crosses over to the window.

A moment later MR KROLL *comes in from the right. He bows to her silently and formally, keeping his hat in his hand.*

KROLL: He's gone then?

REBEKKA: Yes.

KROLL: Does he usually go far?

REBEKKA: Well, yes. But he's rather unpredictable today. So if you don't want to meet him –

KROLL: No, no. It's you I want to speak to. And quite alone.

REBEKKA: Then we'd better not waste any time. Do sit down, headmaster.

She sits down in an armchair by the window. KROLL
takes a chair beside her.

KROLL: Miss West – you can't imagine how deeply and painfully it cuts to my heart – this change that's taken place in
Johannes Rosmer.

REBEKKA: We expected that might be the case – to begin with.

KROLL: To begin with?

REBEKKA: Mr Rosmer felt sure that sooner or later you would
join him.

KROLL: I?

REBEKKA: You and all his other friends.

KROLL: There, you see! That's how poor his judgement is when
it comes to people and the realities of life.

REBEKKA: Well anyway – now that he clearly feels it necessary
to emancipate himself on all fronts –

KROLL: Yes, but you see – *that* is precisely what I don't believe.

REBEKKA: So what do you believe?

KROLL: I believe that *you* are behind all this.

REBEKKA: You've heard that from your wife, Mr Kroll.

KROLL: It's irrelevant where I heard it. What's certain is that I
have strong doubts – extremely strong doubts, I might say –
when I reassess and piece together your conduct since you
arrived here.

REBEKKA [*looks at him*]: I have a vague recollection that you
once had an extremely strong *faith* in me, my dear Mr Kroll.
A *warm* faith I might almost say.

KROLL [*subdued*]: Whom could you not bewitch – if you set
out to?

REBEKKA: Did I set out to –!

KROLL: Yes, you did. I'm no longer daft enough to imagine
there were any feelings at play. You simply wanted to secure
your access into Rosmersholm. To install yourself here. That
was what I was meant to help you with. I see that now.

REBEKKA: You seem to have forgotten it was Beate who
pleaded with me, begged me to move out here.

KROLL: Yes, when you'd managed to bewitch her too. Or can
it be called friendship – whatever she came to feel for you?
It turned to idolization – worship. It went as far as – what

shall I call it? – a desperate kind of infatuation. Yes, that's the right word.

REBEKKA: Be good enough to remember your sister's condition. I don't think it can be said of *me* that I am the least bit overwrought emotionally –

KROLL: No, you most certainly aren't. But that makes you all the more dangerous to those you want to gain power over. It's so easy for you to act with premeditation and total control – because you have a cold heart.

REBEKKA: Cold? Are you so sure of that?

KROLL: I'm utterly convinced of it now. Otherwise you couldn't have stayed here year after year pursuing your goal so unshakeably. Oh, yes – you've achieved what you wanted. You've got him and everything in your power. But in order to get there, you've not shrunk from making him unhappy.

REBEKKA: That isn't true. It's not me. It's *you* who has made him unhappy.

KROLL: Me!

REBEKKA: Yes, when you led him to imagine he was guilty of the terrible end that befell Beate.

KROLL: So it's affected him that deeply?

REBEKKA: That's hardly surprising. With as sensitive a mind as his –

KROLL: I thought a so-called emancipated man would be able to set himself above any scruples. – But there we have it! Yes – deep down I suppose I knew it. The man whose ancestors look down on us here – he'll never tear loose from everything that has been handed down so unerringly from generation to generation.

REBEKKA [*looking thoughtfully down in front of her*]: Johannes Rosmer has very deep roots in his ancestry. There's no doubt about that.

KROLL: Indeed, and you ought to have taken that into consideration if you had any care for him. But of course you were incapable of any such consideration. Your inherent disposition is worlds apart from his.

REBEKKA: What do you mean by that?

KROLL: I mean your predisposition. Your beginnings. Your origins – Miss West.

REBEKKA: I see. Yes, that's true – I hail from very humble circumstances. But nevertheless –

KROLL: I am not referring to rank or position. I am referring to your moral predisposition.

REBEKKA: Predisposition?

KROLL: Yes, inherent in your very birth.

REBEKKA: What are you saying?

KROLL: I'm only saying this because it explains your entire conduct.

REBEKKA: I don't understand. I want to know what you mean!

KROLL: And I was so sure you already knew. Otherwise it would seem strange that you let yourself be adopted by Dr West –

REBEKKA [*getting up*]: Ah, I see! Now I understand.

KROLL: – and take his name. Your mother's name was Gamvik.

REBEKKA [*crossing the room*]: My father's name was Gamvik, Mr Kroll.

KROLL: Your mother's occupation must have brought her into regular contact with the district physician.[50]

REBEKKA: Yes, you're right.

KROLL: And then he takes you into his home – the instant your mother dies. He treats you harshly. And yet you stay with him. You know he won't leave you a penny. All you got was a box of books. And yet you stick it out. Put up with him. Nurse him to the end.

REBEKKA [*by the table, looking at him scornfully*]: And from my doing all this – you deduce that there was something immoral – something unlawful about the circumstances of my birth!

KROLL: I attribute what you did for him to an unconscious daughterly instinct. In fact, I take your whole conduct to be a direct consequence of your origins.

REBEKKA [*vehemently*]: But there's not a word of truth in all this! And I can prove it! Dr West hadn't even come up to Finnmark when I was born.

KROLL: I'm sorry – Miss West. He went up there the year before. I've looked into it.

REBEKKA: You're mistaken, I tell you! Completely mistaken!

KROLL: You said, the day before yesterday, that you were twenty-nine. Going on for thirty.

REBEKKA: Oh? Did I say that?

KROLL: Yes, you did. And from that I can calculate –

REBEKKA: Stop! There's no point calculating. I may as well tell you straight off: I'm a year older than I pretend.

KROLL [smiling disbelievingly]: Oh, really? That's news. How did that come about?

REBEKKA: When I reached twenty-five, I thought – being un-married – that I was simply getting too old. So I decided to lie and subtract a year.

KROLL: You? An emancipated woman. *You* harbouring preju-dices in respect of marriageable age?[51]

REBEKKA: Yes, it was extremely silly – and laughable too. But something or other always clings to us that we can't free ourselves of. That's how we are.

KROLL: Well, who knows? But my calculations may be still correct. Since Dr West was up there on a flying visit the year before his appointment.

REBEKKA [bursting out]: That's not true!

KROLL: It's not?

REBEKKA: No. Because Mother never mentioned that.

KROLL: Really? She didn't?

REBEKKA: No, never. Nor Dr West. Never a word.

KROLL: Mightn't that be because they both had reason to skip a year? Just as *you* have done, Miss West. Perhaps it's a peculiarity of the family.

REBEKKA [pacing about, wringing her hands]: This is impos-sible. This is just something you'd have me believe. It isn't true. It can't be true! Never on earth –!

KROLL [gets up]: But, my dear – why in heaven's name are you getting so worked up about it? You really are scaring me! What am I to think and believe –?

REBEKKA: Nothing. You shouldn't think or believe anything.

KROLL: Then you really must explain how you can take this issue – this possibility so much to heart.

REBEKKA [*composing herself*]: It's really quite straightforward, Mr Kroll. I've no desire to be looked upon here as an illegitimate child.

KROLL: I see. Well, let's settle for that explanation – for now. Though it does seem that you've retained a certain – prejudice on this point too.

REBEKKA: Yes, I probably have.

KROLL: Well now, I suspect it's much the same with most of what you call your emancipation. You've read up on a whole heap of new ideas and opinions. You've acquired knowledge of a kind from scholarly research in various fields – research that appears to overturn much of what's been previously regarded as incontestable and irrefutable. But all of it remains theoretical for you, Miss West. Book learning. It hasn't entered your blood.

REBEKKA [*thoughtful*]: You may be right.

KROLL: Yes, look within yourself and you'll see! And if that's how it is for you, surely we can deduce how it is for Johannes Rosmer. It's sheer madness – he'll plummet straight into disaster if he steps forward and openly declares himself an apostate! Imagine – Rosmer, a man of his shy disposition! Imagine *him* ostracized – persecuted by the circle he's always belonged to. Exposed to ruthless attacks from the most respected members of our community. He's not the man to cope with that.

REBEKKA: He'll *have* to cope with it! It's too late for him to draw back now.

KROLL: It most certainly isn't too late. Not by any means. What's happened can be hushed up, or at least construed as just a passing, if regrettable, aberration. But – *one* precaution is without doubt absolutely necessary.

REBEKKA: And that is?

KROLL: You must get him to legalize the relationship, Miss West.

REBEKKA: His relationship with me?

KROLL: Yes. You must make sure he does.

REBEKKA: You really can't free yourself from the belief that our relationship needs – legalizing, as you call it?

KROLL: I've no wish to go into the specifics of the situation. But I think I'm right in observing that the area where it seems easiest to break with any so-called prejudice, is in – hmm.

REBEKKA: Is in the relationship between man and woman, you mean?

KROLL: Yes – to be honest – that's what I think.

REBEKKA [*moves across the room and looks out of the window*]: I might almost say – I wish you were right, Mr Kroll.

KROLL: What do you mean by that? You said it so strangely.

REBEKKA: Never mind! Let's not talk any more about these things. – Ah – there he is.

KROLL: Already! I'll go then.

REBEKKA [*turning to him*]: No – stay. There's something I must tell you now.

KROLL: Not right now. I don't think I can face seeing him.

REBEKKA: I beg of you – stay. Please. Or you'll regret it later. This is the last time I'll ask you for anything.

KROLL [*looks at her in surprise, and puts his hat down*]: Very well, Miss West. So be it.

> *There is a moment's silence. Then* JOHANNES ROSMER *comes in from the hall.*

ROSMER [*sees* KROLL, *stops in the doorway*]: What! Are *you* here?

REBEKKA: He'd have preferred not to meet you, Johannes.

KROLL [*involuntarily*]: Johannes!

REBEKKA: Yes, headmaster. We call each other by our first names.[52] The relationship between us has brought that about.

KROLL: Was *that* what you promised to tell me?

REBEKKA: *That* – and a little more.

ROSMER [*coming into the room*]: What is the object of your visit today?

KROLL: I wanted to try one more time to stop you and win you back.

ROSMER [*pointing to the newspaper*]: After what's written *here*?

KROLL: I didn't write it.

ROSMER: Did you take any steps to prevent it?

KROLL: That would have been indefensible with regard to the cause I serve. And besides, it wasn't in my power.

REBEKKA [*tears the newspaper into pieces, scrunches them up and throws them behind the stove*]: There! Now it's out of sight. And let it be out of mind too. There'll be nothing more of that sort, Johannes.

KROLL: Hmm, if only it was *that* easy.

REBEKKA: Come, my dear. Let's sit down. The three of us. And I shall tell you everything.

ROSMER [*sitting down involuntarily*]: What's come over you, Rebekka? This ominous calm –. What is it?

REBEKKA: The calm of decision. [*Sits down*] You too, head-master, sit down.

    MR KROLL *takes a seat on the sofa.*

ROSMER: Decision, you say. What decision?

REBEKKA: I want to give you back what you need to live your life. You shall have your guilt-free happiness back, my dear friend.

ROSMER: But what is this?

REBEKKA: I just want to tell you something. Nothing more is required.

ROSMER: So!

REBEKKA: When I came down here from Finnmark – with Dr West – I felt that a great, new, wide world had somehow opened up for me. The doctor had taught me a great variety of things. All the fragmented knowledge I had of life back then. [*Struggling and barely audible*] And then –

KROLL: And then?

ROSMER: But, Rebekka – I know all that.

REBEKKA [*collecting herself*]: Yes, yes – you're right of course. You know enough about that.

KROLL [*fixes his gaze on her*]: Perhaps it's best I leave.

REBEKKA: No, you'll sit right there, my dear Mr Kroll. [*To* ROSMER] Well, *that's* the thing, you see – I wanted to be a part of the new era[53] that was breaking through. – These new ideas. – One day Mr Kroll told me that Ulrik Brendel had had enormous power over you at one time, when you were still a boy. I thought I might be able to pick up on that again.

ROSMER: Did you come here with a hidden motive –?

REBEKKA: I wanted the two of us to walk together into freedom. Ever onwards. To the furthest limits. – But then there was that shadowy, insurmountable wall between you and complete, full emancipation.

ROSMER: Wall – what do you mean?

REBEKKA: I mean this, Johannes: you could never grow to be free unless you were in the bright sunlight. And here you were, wilting and sickening in such a dark marriage.

ROSMER: Never before today have you spoken to me of my marriage in *that* way.

REBEKKA: No, I didn't dare, I'd have frightened you.

KROLL [*nodding to* ROSMER]: You hear *that*!

REBEKKA [*continues*]: But I could see clearly where salvation lay for you, the only salvation. And so I took action.

ROSMER: What kind of action are you referring to?

KROLL: Do you mean –!

REBEKKA: Yes, Johannes –. [*Gets up*] No, don't get up. Nor you, Mr Kroll. But now it has to come out into the light of day. It wasn't you, Johannes. You are free of any guilt. It was *I* who lured – who ended up luring Beate out onto the wild, treacherous path –

ROSMER [*leaping up*]: Rebekka!

KROLL [*up from the sofa*]: – onto the treacherous path!

REBEKKA: Onto the path – that led to the Mill Falls. Now you know, both of you.

ROSMER [*as if in a daze*]: But I don't understand –. What's she standing there saying? I don't understand a single word –!

KROLL: Oh yes, my friend. I'm starting to understand.

ROSMER: But what have you done? What could you have said to her? There was nothing. Absolutely nothing!

REBEKKA: She was informed that you were working your way out of all those old-fashioned prejudices.

ROSMER: Yes, but I wasn't back then.

REBEKKA: I knew you soon would be.

KROLL [*nodding to* ROSMER]: Aha!

ROSMER: And then? What more? I want to know the rest now.

REBEKKA: Some time after – I begged and implored her to let me leave Rosmersholm.

ROSMER: Why did you want to leave – back then?

REBEKKA: I didn't want to leave. I wanted to stay here, where I was. But I told her it was probably best for us all – if I went away in time. I let her think that if I stayed any longer – then something – something might happen – who could tell what.

ROSMER: So, that's what you said and did?

REBEKKA: Yes, Johannes.

ROSMER: And *that* is what you called taking action?

REBEKKA [*in a broken voice*]: That's what I called it, yes.

ROSMER [*after a pause*]: Have you confessed everything now, Rebekka?

REBEKKA: Yes.

KROLL: Not everything.

REBEKKA [*looking fearfully at him*]: What more could there be?

KROLL: Didn't you make Beate believe in the end that it was necessary – not just best but necessary – for your and Johannes' sake, that you go elsewhere – as quickly as possible? – Well?

REBEKKA [*quietly and indistinctly*]: I may have said something of that sort too.

ROSMER [*sinking into the armchair by the window*]: And this web of lies and deceit she – that sick, unhappy soul, went around believing! Believing completely and utterly! Unshakeably! [*Looks at* REBEKKA] And she never turned to me. Never said a word! Oh, Rebekka – I can see it in your eyes – *you* advised her against it.

REBEKKA: She'd taken it into her head that she had – as a childless wife – no right to be here. And she convinced herself it was her duty to you to step aside.

ROSMER: And you – you did nothing to get her out of that delusion?

REBEKKA: No.

KROLL: You encouraged her in it perhaps? Answer! Didn't you?

REBEKKA: That was how she understood me, I imagine.

ROSMER: Yes – and she bowed to your will in everything. And so she stepped aside. [*Leaps up*] How – how could you play this appalling game?

REBEKKA: I believed there were two lives to choose between here, Johannes.

KROLL [*sternly and with authority*]: *You* had no right to make such a choice!

REBEKKA [*vehemently*]: But do you think I did all this with cold and calculated composure! I wasn't the same person at that time as the one who stands here telling you this now. And a human being has two kinds of will, I'd have thought! I wanted Beate gone. In one way or another. And yet I never thought it would actually come. With each tempting step I ventured, I felt something scream inside me: No further now! Not a step further! – And yet I *couldn't* stop! I *had* to venture just one tiny bit further. Just one. And then another – and always another. And then it *came*. – That's how such things happen.

　　Short silence.

ROSMER [*to* REBEKKA]: How do you think things will go for *you* now? After this?

REBEKKA: I must take things as they come. It's of little consequence.

KROLL: Not a word or hint of remorse! Perhaps you feel none?

REBEKKA [*coldly dismissive*]: I'm sorry, Mr Kroll – that's a matter that concerns nobody else. I must come to terms with this myself.

KROLL [*to* ROSMER]: And this is the woman you are living under the same roof with. In an intimate relationship. [*Looks round at the portraits*] Oh – those that are gone – if they could only look up now!

ROSMER: Are you going into town?

KROLL [*taking his hat*]: Yes. The sooner the better.

ROSMER [*also taking his hat*]: Then I'll come with you.

KROLL: You will? Yes, I was sure we hadn't quite lost you.

ROSMER: Come on then, Kroll! Come!

　　They both go out into the hall without looking at REBEKKA.

Shortly afterwards REBEKKA *goes cautiously to the window and looks out between the plants.*

REBEKKA [*speaking quietly to herself*]: Not across the footbridge today either. He's going round. Will never cross the Mill Falls. Never. [*Moves from the window*] Ah well!
   She goes over and rings the bell.
   Soon afterwards MRS HELSETH *comes in from the right.*

MRS HELSETH: What is it, miss?

REBEKKA: Mrs Helseth, would you perhaps be kind enough to fetch my travel case down from the loft?

MRS HELSETH: Your travel case?

REBEKKA: Yes, the brown sealskin case. You know the one.

MRS HELSETH: Yes, all right. But, Lord above – are you travelling, miss?

REBEKKA: Yes – I am going to travel, Mrs Helseth.

MRS HELSETH: Right this instant?

REBEKKA: As soon as I have packed.

MRS HELSETH: I never heard the like! But you'll be back soon, won't you, miss?

REBEKKA: I am never coming back.

MRS HELSETH: Never? But, good Lord, how will things be here at Rosmersholm when Miss West isn't here any more? Just when the poor pastor had got nice and comfortable here.

REBEKKA: Yes, but I've grown afraid today, Mrs Helseth.

MRS HELSETH: Afraid? Dear Jesus – why's that?

REBEKKA: I think I may have seen a glimpse of white horses.

MRS HELSETH: White horses! In broad daylight!

REBEKKA: Oh, they're probably out at all hours – the white horses of Rosmersholm. [*Changes tone*] Anyway – my travel bag, Mrs Helseth.

MRS HELSETH: Very good. Your travel bag.
   They both go out to the right.

ACT FOUR

The living room at Rosmersholm. It is late evening. The lamp, with a shade on it, is burning on the table.

REBEKKA WEST *stands by the table, packing some small things into a travelling bag.*

Her cloak, hat, and the white crocheted shawl are hanging on the back of the sofa.

MRS HELSETH *comes in from the right.*

MRS HELSETH [*speaks in lowered voice and seems guarded*]: Yes, all your things have been taken out now, miss. They're in the kitchen passage.
REBEKKA: Good. The driver's been sent for?
MRS HELSETH: Yes. He asks what time he should get here with the carriage.
REBEKKA: At about eleven, I think. The steamer leaves at midnight.
MRS HELSETH [*a little hesitantly*]: But the pastor? If he's not back home by that time?
REBEKKA: I'll leave anyway. If I don't see him, you can say that I'll write to him. A long letter. Say that.
MRS HELSETH: Yes, that's all very well – writing, I mean. But, my poor miss – I really do think you should try to talk to him one more time.
REBEKKA: Perhaps. Then again, perhaps not.

MRS HELSETH: Well, well – that I'd live to see this – I'd never have thought it!

REBEKKA: So what did you think, Mrs Helseth?

MRS HELSETH: Oh, I honestly thought the pastor was more of an upstanding man than that.

REBEKKA: Upstanding?

MRS HELSETH: Upon my word, I did.

REBEKKA: But, my dear Mrs Helseth, what are you saying?

MRS HELSETH: I'm only saying what's right and true, miss. He oughtn't to free himself from it like *that*, he oughtn't.

REBEKKA [*looking at her*]: But listen, Mrs Helseth. Tell me honestly – why do you think I'm leaving?

MRS HELSETH: Good Lord, likely it's necessary, miss. Well, well, well! But I really don't think the pastor's behaved too well. Mortensgård had some excuse. Her husband was still alive. So the two of them couldn't get married however much they wanted. But the pastor, well he – hmm!

REBEKKA [*with a faint smile*]: Could you really think that of myself and Pastor Rosmer?

MRS HELSETH: Never in this world. No – I mean – not until today.

REBEKKA: But today –?

MRS HELSETH: Well, after all the vile things folks say are in the papers about the pastor, then –

REBEKKA: Aha!

MRS HELSETH: Because it's my opinion, that any man who can cross over to Mortensgård's religion, well, you can believe anything of him.

REBEKKA: Yes, I suppose that's right. But what about me, then? What would you say about me?

MRS HELSETH: Lord above, miss – I don't reckon there's much to be said against you. It can't be easy for a lone woman[54] to hold out against such. We're all human after all, Miss West.

REBEKKA: Never a truer word, Mrs Helseth. We are all human. – What are you listening to?

MRS HELSETH [*quietly*]: Lord Jesus – I think that's him coming right now.

REBEKKA [*with a start*]: So he's coming, after all –! [*Resolutely*] Right. So be it.

JOHANNES ROSMER *comes in from the hall.*

ROSMER [*sees the luggage, turns to* REBEKKA *and asks*]: What does this mean?

REBEKKA: I'm leaving.

ROSMER: Straight away?

REBEKKA: Yes. [*To* MRS HELSETH] At eleven, then.

MRS HELSETH: Very well, miss.

She goes out to the right.

ROSMER [*after a brief pause*]: Where are you going, Rebekka?

REBEKKA: Up north with the steamer.

ROSMER: North? What are you going there for?

REBEKKA: Well, that's where I came from.

ROSMER: But there's nothing for you up there now.

REBEKKA: I have nothing down here either.

ROSMER: What are you thinking of doing?

REBEKKA: I don't know. I just want to put an end to this.

ROSMER: An end to it?

REBEKKA: Rosmersholm has broken me.

ROSMER [*attentive*]: Really?

REBEKKA: Shattered me entirely. I was so robust and courageous when I first arrived here. My will has been bent under an alien law. – From now on I don't think there's a thing in the world I shall dare.

ROSMER: Why not? What kind of law are you saying has –?

REBEKKA: Dearest, let's not talk about *that* now. How did it go between you and the headmaster?

ROSMER: We made our peace.

REBEKKA: I see. So that's what happened.

ROSMER: He gathered our entire circle of old friends at his place. They made me realize that the work of ennobling souls – well, it clearly isn't for me. Besides it's an utterly hopeless task anyway. – I shall let it lie.

REBEKKA: Well – perhaps that's for the best.

ROSMER: Are you saying *that* now? Are *you* of that opinion now?

REBEKKA: I've come to that opinion. Over the last couple of days.

ROSMER: You're lying, Rebekka.

REBEKKA: Lying –?

ROSMER: Yes, you're lying. You've never believed in me. You've never believed I was man enough to fight and carry the cause to victory.

REBEKKA: I believed that together the two of us might manage it somehow.

ROSMER: That isn't true. You believed *you* could do something great in life. That you could use me for what you wanted to achieve. That I could be of service to you in your purpose. *That* is what you believed.

REBEKKA: Listen, Johannes –

ROSMER [*sitting down wearily on the sofa*]: Oh, don't go on! I can see the whole thing clearly now. I was the glove, and you the hand.

REBEKKA: Listen to me, Johannes. Let's talk this over properly. It will be for the last time. [*Sits in a chair by the sofa*] I wanted to write to you about it – when I arrived up there in the north. But it's probably better you hear it now.

ROSMER: Have you even more to confess?

REBEKKA: I still have the greater part.

ROSMER: The greater part?

REBEKKA: The thing you've never suspected. The thing that brings light and shade to the rest.

ROSMER [*shaking his head*]: I don't understand.

REBEKKA: It's quite true that I did at one time spread my nets to gain entry into Rosmersholm. Because I felt I might make a success of myself here. In one way or another – you understand.

ROSMER: And you managed to drive it through – the thing you wanted.

REBEKKA: I think I could have done anything – back then. For I still had courage, my will was still free. I had no reason to be considerate. There was nothing to turn me from my path. But then it came – the thing that broke my will – filled my life with an abject fear.

ROSMER: What came? Tell me, so I can understand.

REBEKKA: It was then it came over me – this wild, uncontrollable desire –. Oh, Johannes –!

ROSMER: Desire? In you –! For what?

REBEKKA: For you.

ROSMER [*about to leap up*]: What is this!

REBEKKA [*preventing him*]: Sit still, my dear. I'll tell you more.

ROSMER: You're saying – that you loved me – in that way!

REBEKKA: I thought what I felt must be called love – back then. This was love, I thought. But it wasn't. It was as I've said. It was a wild, uncontrollable desire.

ROSMER [*speaking with difficulty*]: Rebekka – is this really you – you – sitting here telling me this?

REBEKKA: Yes – what do you say, Johannes!

ROSMER: It was this – this power which drove you to take *action*, as you put it.

REBEKKA: It came over me like a storm out at sea. Like one of those storms we get up north in the winter. It grabs you – takes you with it – as far as it will. You don't even think of resisting.

ROSMER: So it swept poor unhappy Beate into the waterfall.

REBEKKA: Yes, at the time it was as if Beate and I were battling on an upturned keel.

ROSMER: You were certainly the strongest here at Rosmersholm. Stronger than Beate and me put together.

REBEKKA: I knew you well enough to realize – there was no clear path to you until you had been set free, both in your circumstances – and in your mind.

ROSMER: I don't understand you, Rebekka. You – yourself – your actions are an unsolvable riddle to me. I am free now – both in mind and circumstance. You're now at the goal you set yourself at the start. But despite all that –!

REBEKKA: I've never stood further from my goal than now.

ROSMER: – but despite that, I say – when I asked you yesterday – when I said: be my wife – you screamed in terror, saying it could never happen.

REBEKKA: I screamed in despair, Johannes.

ROSMER: Why?

REBEKKA: Because Rosmersholm has robbed me of any power. I have had my courageous will clipped here! Mangled. The time is past when I dared risk anything at all. I've lost my capacity for action, Johannes.

ROSMER: How has this come about, tell me.

REBEKKA: It came about through living with you.

ROSMER: But how? How?

REBEKKA: When I was alone with you here – and you'd become your true self –

ROSMER: Yes?

REBEKKA: – since you were never completely yourself while Beate was alive –

ROSMER: You might be right about that, sadly.

REBEKKA: But when I started living alongside you here – in tranquillity – in solitude – when you shared all your thoughts with me unreservedly – whatever your mood – soft or tender, as the feeling took you – it was then that the great change happened. Little by little – you understand. Almost imperceptibly – but overwhelmingly in the end. Reaching to the very depths of my mind.

ROSMER: What are you saying, Rebekka?

REBEKKA: Everything else – the ugly, drunken, sensual desire – it all drew so far, so far away from me. All these agitated powers settled down calmly in silence. A sense of rest came over my mind – a stillness like that of a nesting-cliff under the midnight sun back at home.

ROSMER: Tell me more. All you can think of to tell.

REBEKKA: There isn't much more. Just *this*, that it was then that love surfaced in me. That great selfless love that finds contentment in the kind of cohabitation we two have shared.

ROSMER: Oh, if only I'd had even the tiniest suspicion of all this!

REBEKKA: It's best as it is. Yesterday – when you asked me if I would be your wife – I was jubilant –

ROSMER: Yes, you were, Rebekka, weren't you? That was how I understood it.

REBEKKA: For a moment, yes. In forgetfulness. It was my former brazen will that almost broke free again. But now it no longer has any power – no enduring power.

ROSMER: How do you explain what's happened to you?

REBEKKA: It is the ancestral Rosmerian view of life – or *your* view of life, at least – that infected my will.

ROSMER: Infected?

REBEKKA: And made it sick. Enslaved it to laws which never used to apply to me. You – life with you – has ennobled my mind –

ROSMER: Oh, if I only dared believe that!

REBEKKA: You can believe it. The Rosmerian view of life is ennobling. But – [*shakes her head*] – but – but –

ROSMER: But? Well?

REBEKKA: – but it kills joy, my friend.

ROSMER: Is that what you think, Rebekka?

REBEKKA: For me at least.

ROSMER: Yes, but are you so sure? If I asked you again now –? Begged you –

REBEKKA: Oh, my dear – don't ever mention that again! It's an impossibility –! Really it is, Johannes, since you ought to know *this* now: I have a – I have a past behind me.

ROSMER: Something more than you've told me?

REBEKKA: Yes. Something more and something other.

ROSMER [*with a faint smile*]: It's strange, isn't it, Rebekka? Imagine, I've sensed something of the sort now and then.

REBEKKA: You have? And even so –? Even then –?

ROSMER: I never actually believed it. I just toyed with it – in my head, you understand.

REBEKKA: If you so demand, I shall tell you that immediately too.

ROSMER [*dismissively*]: No, no! I don't want to hear a word. Whatever it is – I'm ready to forget it.

REBEKKA: But I'm not.

ROSMER: Oh, Rebekka –!

REBEKKA: Yes, Johannes – *that's* the terrible thing – now that all life's joys are offered to me in plenty – I've changed so much that my own past bars my way.

ROSMER: Your past is dead, Rebekka. It no longer has any hold on you – no link to you – as you *now* are.

REBEKKA: Oh my dear, those are just fine phrases. What of freedom from guilt? Where do I get *that* from?

ROSMER [*gloomily*]: Yes, yes – freedom from guilt.

REBEKKA: Freedom from guilt, yes. Therein lies joy and happiness. *That* was the knowledge you wanted to kindle in all those happy noble people of the future –

ROSMER: Ah, don't remind me. That was just a dream half done, Rebekka. A reckless flight of fancy that I no longer believe in. I don't think people can be ennobled from the outside.

REBEKKA [*quietly*]: Not through quiet love – you don't believe that?

ROSMER [*thoughtfully*]: Yes, that would be the greatest thing. The most wonderful thing in this life, I imagine. – If it were possible. [*Twists in unease*] But how shall I ever resolve that question for myself? Get to the bottom of it?

REBEKKA: Johannes, don't you believe me?

ROSMER: Ah, Rebekka – how *can* I ever fully believe in you? When you've covered up and concealed so much here! – And now you come forward with something new. If there's some motive behind this – then tell me straight out. Is there perhaps something or other you want to gain by this? I *do* most sincerely want to do everything I can for you.

REBEKKA [*wrings her hands*]: Oh, this killing doubt. Johannes – Johannes –!

ROSMER: Yes, it's terrible, isn't it? But I can do nothing about it. I'll never manage to free myself from this doubt. Never know for sure that your love for me is whole and pure.

REBEKKA: But is there really nothing deep inside you that can testify that there's been a transformation in me! And that this transformation happened *through* you – through you alone!

ROSMER: Ah, my dear, I no longer believe in my ability to transform people. I don't believe in myself any more, in any capacity. I believe in neither myself nor you.

REBEKKA [*looks darkly at him*]: How will you be able to live your life, then?

ROSMER: Yes, I don't know that myself. I've no idea. I don't think I *can* live it. And I know of nothing in this world that might be worth living for either.

REBEKKA: Oh, life – it has renewal within it. Let us hold to that, my dear. – We leave it soon enough.

ROSMER [*leaps up restlessly*]: Then give me back my faith! My belief in *you*, Rebekka! My belief in your love! Give me proof! I want proof!

REBEKKA: Proof? How can I give you proof –!

ROSMER: You *must*! [*Crosses the room*] I can't bear this desolation – this appalling emptiness – this – this –
There is a loud knock at the hall door.

REBEKKA [*jumps up from her chair*]: Ah – did you hear that? *The door opens.* ULRIK BRENDEL *comes in. He is wearing a white shirt, a black coat and good boots outside his trousers. Otherwise he is dressed as last time. He seems agitated.*

ROSMER: Ah, is it you, Mr Brendel?!

BRENDEL: Johannes, my boy – I come to greet you – farewell!

ROSMER: Where are you going, so late?

BRENDEL: Downhill.

ROSMER: What –?

BRENDEL: I am heading home, my precious one. I am homesick for the great Nothingness.

ROSMER: Something has happened to you, Mr Brendel! What is it?

BRENDEL: So, you observe the transformation? Yes – you must, I am sure. The last time I set foot in this hall – I stood before you a prosperous man, beating my breast pocket.

ROSMER: Oh? I don't quite understand –

BRENDEL: But as you see me tonight, I am a deposed king standing upon the ashes of my burned-out palace.

ROSMER: If there is anything *I* can help with –

BRENDEL: You have conserved your childlike heart, Johannes. Can you make me a loan?

ROSMER: Yes, yes, willingly!

BRENDEL: Can you spare an ideal or two?

ROSMER: What did you say?

BRENDEL: A couple of cast-off ideals. You'll be doing a good deed. Since I'm totally broke, my dear boy. Cleaned out.

REBEKKA: Didn't you manage to deliver your lecture?

BRENDEL: No, my enchanting lady. What do you think to this? Just as I'm standing there ready to empty my overflowing horn of plenty, I make a painful discovery – I am bankrupt.

REBEKKA: But what about all your unwritten works?

BRENDEL: For five and twenty years I have sat like a miser upon his locked money-chest. And then yesterday – when I opened it to take out my treasure – there was nothing. The teeth of time had ground it to dust. There was naught, *nichts*,[55] in the entire shebang.

ROSMER: But are you certain?

BRENDEL: There is no room for doubt, my darling one. Le Président[56] convinced me of that.

ROSMER: The President?

BRENDEL: Oh, well – His Excellency, then. *Ganz nach Belieben.*[57]

ROSMER: But who do you mean?

BRENDEL: Why, Peder Mortensgård, of course.

ROSMER: What!

BRENDEL [*secretively*]: Shh, shh, shh! Peder Mortensgård is lord and master of the future. Never have I been in the presence of a more impressive countenance. Peder Mortensgård possesses the gift of omnipotence. He can do anything he wants.

ROSMER: Oh, don't you believe it!

BRENDEL: Oh yes, my boy! Because Peder Mortensgård never wants to do more than he can. Peder Mortensgård is capable of living life without ideals. And *that* – you see – *that* is the secret of action and victory. That is the sum of the world's entire wisdom. *Basta!*

ROSMER [*in a low voice*]: I understand now – you are leaving poorer than when you arrived.

BRENDEL: *Bien!* Take a *Beispiel*[58] from your old tutor. Erase everything that I imprinted on you. Do not build your castle upon shifting sand.[59] And look ahead – test the ground – before you build upon the delightful creature who sweetens your life here.

REBEKKA: Do you mean me?

BRENDEL: Yes, my alluring mermaid!

REBEKKA: Why shouldn't anyone build on me?

BRENDEL [*a step closer*]: I've heard that my former apprentice has a life's mission to carry to victory.

REBEKKA: And so –?

BRENDEL: His victory is assured. But – on *one* immutable condition.

REBEKKA: What?

BRENDEL [*taking her gently by the wrist*]: That the woman who loves him will gladly go out into the kitchen and chop off her delicate, rosy-white little finger[60] – *here* – precisely *here* at the middle joint. Likewise, that the aforesaid loving woman shall – equally gladly – snip off her incomparably formed left ear. [*Lets her go, and turns to* ROSMER] Farewell, my victorious Johannes.

ROSMER: Are you leaving now? In the dark night?

BRENDEL: The dark night is best. May peace be with you both.

He leaves.

There is a moment of silence in the room.

REBEKKA [*having difficulty breathing*]: Oh, it's stifling in here! *She goes over to the window, opens it and remains standing there.*

ROSMER [*sitting in the armchair by the stove*]: There is probably nothing else for it after all, Rebekka. I see that. You *must* leave.

REBEKKA: Yes, I can see no choice.

ROSMER: Let's use this last moment. Come and sit with me here.

REBEKKA [*goes and sits on the sofa*]: What do you want, Johannes?

ROSMER: First I want to tell you *this*, that you need have no anxiety about your future.

REBEKKA [*with a smile*]: Hmm. *My* future.

ROSMER: I have prepared for all contingencies. Long ago. Whatever happens, you are provided for.

REBEKKA: That too, my dear.

ROSMER: You should have known that for yourself.

REBEKKA: I've not thought about such matters for ever and a day.

ROSMER: Well – you probably never expected that things could be other than they were between us.

REBEKKA: No, I didn't think they could.

ROSMER: Nor I. But if I were to pass away now –

REBEKKA: Oh, Johannes – you'll live longer than me.

ROSMER: Surely this miserable life is in my own power to decide over.

REBEKKA: What is this? You can't be thinking of –!

ROSMER: Do you find that so strange? After the pitiful, lamentable defeat I have suffered! When I wanted to carry my life's cause to victory –. And then fled from everything – even before the battle had really begun!

REBEKKA: Take up the fight again, Johannes! Just try – you'll see – victory will be yours. You will ennoble hundreds – thousands of minds. Just try!

ROSMER: Oh, Rebekka, when I no longer believe in my own cause?

REBEKKA: But it has already stood the test. You have ennobled *one* person, at least – me – for the rest of my life.

ROSMER: Yes – if only I dared believe that.

REBEKKA [*wringing her hands*]: But, Johannes – do you know of nothing – nothing that could make you believe it?

ROSMER [*starts, as if in fear*]: Stop! Don't even talk about it, Rebekka. Not a single word more!

REBEKKA: But that's exactly what we must talk about. Do you know of anything that would stifle your doubts? For *I* know of nothing in the world.

ROSMER: It's best for you not to know. – Best for us both.

REBEKKA: No, no, no – I won't settle for that! If you know of anything that will acquit me in your eyes, I demand as my right that you name it.

ROSMER [*as though compelled against his own will*]: Let us see, then. You say you have this great love within you. That your soul has been ennobled through me. Is that right? Have you made a careful reckoning, Rebekka? Shall we put the final balance to the test? Well?

REBEKKA: I'm prepared for that.

ROSMER: At any time?

REBEKKA: Whenever. The sooner the better.

ROSMER: Then let me see, Rebekka – if you – for my sake – this very evening. – [*Breaks off*] Oh, no, no, no!

REBEKKA: Yes, Johannes! Yes, yes! Say it, and you shall see.

ROSMER: Do you have the courage – are you willing – gladly, as Ulrik Brendel said – for my sake, this very night – gladly – to take the same path – that Beate went?

REBEKKA [*pulls herself slowly up from the sofa, and says almost voicelessly*]: Johannes –!

ROSMER: Yes, Rebekka – *that's* the question from which I will never be able to free myself – when you have left. Day and night I will return to it. Ah, I think I see you large as life before my eyes. You are standing out on the footbridge. In the very middle. Now you are leaning out over the railing! Dizzyingly pulled down towards the gushing waterfall! No. You recoil. You daren't do – what *she* dared.

REBEKKA: But if I had the courage now? And was gladly willing? What then?

ROSMER: Then I would have to believe you. Then I would have to regain belief in my cause. Faith in my capacity to ennoble people's minds. Faith in mankind's ability to be ennobled.

REBEKKA [*takes her shawl slowly, throws it over her head and says in a controlled voice*]: You shall have your belief back.

ROSMER: Have you the courage and the will – to do it, Rebekka?

REBEKKA: You must judge that tomorrow – or later – whenever they fish me up.

ROSMER [*his hand on his forehead*]: There is an alluring horror in this –!

REBEKKA: Because I'd rather not be left down there. Not longer than necessary. Arrangements must be made for me to be found.

ROSMER [*leaping up*]: But all this is – it's insane. Leave – or stay! I will believe you on your word, this time as before.

REBEKKA: Empty phrases, Johannes. No more cowardice or running away now! How can you believe me merely on my word after today?

ROSMER: But I don't want to see your defeat, Rebekka!

REBEKKA: There will be no defeat.

ROSMER: There will. You will never bring yourself to go Beate's way.

REBEKKA: You don't think so?

ROSMER: Never. You're not like Beate. You are not governed by a distorted vision of life.

REBEKKA: But I am governed by the Rosmerian vision of life – *now*. Whatever my crime – it is only right I pay the penalty.

ROSMER [*his gaze fixed on her*]: Is *that* your position?

REBEKKA: Yes.

ROSMER [*decisively*]: I see. Then, Rebekka, *I* am governed by our emancipated vision of life. There is no judge over us. So we must administer justice ourselves.

REBEKKA [*misunderstands him*]: That too. That too. My passing will save the best in you.

ROSMER: Ah, there's nothing in me left to save.

REBEKKA: Yes, there is. But me – from here on I would just be like a sea-troll[61] hanging there hampering the ship on which you sail onwards. I must go overboard. Or should I stay up here in the world, perhaps, to lug around a crippled life? And brood gloomily over the happiness that my past has made me forfeit? I must leave the game, Johannes.

ROSMER: If you go – then I go with you.

REBEKKA [*smiles, almost imperceptibly, looks at him and says quietly*]: Yes, come with me – and be witness –

ROSMER: I'll go with you, I said.

REBEKKA: As far as the footbridge – yes. You never venture out onto it.

ROSMER: You've noticed that?

REBEKKA [*broken and sad*]: Yes. – That is what made my love hopeless.

ROSMER: Rebekka – now I lay my hand upon your head.[62] [*Does as he says*] And I take you as my true wife.

REBEKKA [*taking both his hands in hers, and leaning her head on his chest*]: Thank you, Johannes. [*Lets him go*] And I shall go now – gladly.

ROSMER: Man and wife must go together.[63]

REBEKKA: Just to the bridge, Johannes.

ROSMER: Out onto it, too. As far as you go – is as far as I go with you. For now I dare to do it.

REBEKKA: Are you so absolutely certain – that this way is the best for you?

ROSMER: I know it is the only way.

REBEKKA: But what if you're deluding yourself? Suppose this were just a phantasm? One of the white horses of Rosmersholm.

ROSMER: It could well be. Since we never escape them – we, here at the manor.

REBEKKA: Then stay, Johannes!

ROSMER: The man shall follow his wife, as the wife does her husband.

REBEKKA: But, first tell me *this*. Am I following you, or you me?

ROSMER: We will never fathom that fully.

REBEKKA: Yet I should very much like to know.

ROSMER: We two follow each other, Rebekka. I you and you me.

REBEKKA: I almost think you're right.

ROSMER: Because now we two are one.

REBEKKA: Yes. Now we are one. Come! Let us go gladly.

They go out, hand in hand, through the hall, and are seen to turn to the left. The door stands open after them.

The room is empty for a little while. Then MRS HELSETH *opens the door on the right.*

MRS HELSETH: Miss, the carriage is – [*Looks round*] Not in here? Out together at this time? Well – I must say –! Hmm! [*Goes out into the hall, looks round and comes in again*] Not on the bench. Oh, well. [*Goes to the window and looks out*] Lord Jesus! What is that white thing over *there* –! – Upon my soul, if they're not both standing on the footbridge! God forgive them sinful folks! Well I never, they're throwing

their arms about each other! [*Screams loudly*] Oh – out
into – both of them! Into the waterfall! Help! Help! [*She
goes weak at the knees, holds shakily to the back of a chair
and can barely get the words out*] No. There's no help here.
The late mistress has taken them.

THE LADY
FROM THE SEA

A Play in Five Acts

CHARACTERS

DOCTOR WANGEL, *the local doctor*[1]
MRS[2] ELLIDA WANGEL, *his second wife*
BOLETTE, HILDE, *his daughters from his first marriage*
MR ARNHOLM, *a schoolmaster*[3]
MR LYNGSTRAND
MR BALLESTED
A STRANGER
YOUNG PEOPLE FROM THE TOWN
TOURISTS
SUMMER RESIDENTS

The action takes place during the summertime in a little fjord town[4] *in the northern part of Norway.*

ACT ONE

Dr Wangel's house on the left[5] with a large roofed veranda. A garden in front and all round. Below the veranda is a flagpole. On the right of the garden, an arbour with a table and chairs. A hedge with a small gate in the background. Behind the hedge is a road that follows the shoreline. Trees line the road. The fjord can be seen through the trees, and in the distance high mountain ranges and peaks. It is a warm and brilliantly clear summer morning.

BALLESTED, *a middle-aged man, dressed in an old velvet jacket and a broad-brimmed artist's hat, stands below the flagpole, sorting out the ropes. The flag is on the ground. A short distance away from him is an easel with a canvas on it. On a folding chair beside it lie brushes, a palette and a paintbox.*

BOLETTE WANGEL *comes through the open garden-room door and out onto the veranda. She is carrying a large vase of flowers, which she puts on the table.*

BOLETTE: Well, Ballested – are you getting that to go smoothly?
BALLESTED: Yes, yes, Miss[6] Bolette. Nothing to it. – Excuse my asking, but are you expecting visitors?
BOLETTE: Yes, we're expecting Mr Arnholm later this morning. He arrived in town last night.
BALLESTED: Arnholm? Wait a moment – wasn't his name Arnholm, that chap who was a tutor here some years back?
BOLETTE: Yes, that's him.
BALLESTED: I see. Returning to these parts, is he?

BOLETTE: That's why we want the flag.

BALLESTED: Well, makes sense I suppose.

> BOLETTE *goes back into the garden room.*
> *Shortly afterwards* LYNGSTRAND *comes along the road from the right, he stops out of curiosity when he sees the easel and painting materials. He is a scrawny young man, shabbily, but respectably dressed and with a delicate appearance.*

LYNGSTRAND [*outside the hedge*]: Good morning.

BALLESTED [*turns*]: Oh –! Good morning. [*Hoisting the flag*] There now – the balloon is launched. [*Fastens the ropes and busies himself at his easel*] Good morning, honoured sir. I don't think I've had the pleasure –

LYNGSTRAND: You're a painter I take it.

BALLESTED: Well yes, obviously. Shouldn't I be perhaps?

LYNGSTRAND: Well yes, I can see you are. May I venture to take a little step in?

BALLESTED: You want to come in and look maybe?

LYNGSTRAND: Yes, I'd like that very much.

BALLESTED: Oh, there's nothing significant to see yet. But feel free. Move a little closer if you like.

LYNGSTRAND: Thanks very much.

> *He comes in through the garden gate.*

BALLESTED [*painting*]: The fjord, in there between those islands, that's what I'm working on now.

LYNGSTRAND: I can see that, yes.

BALLESTED: But the figure's still missing. There's not a single model to be had here in town.

LYNGSTRAND: So there's to be a figure too?

BALLESTED: Yes. Lying by this rock in the foreground, a half-dead mermaid.

LYNGSTRAND: Why would she be half-dead?

BALLESTED: She has strayed in from the sea and can't find her way out again. And so here she lies, expiring in the brackish water, you understand.

LYNGSTRAND: Aha, I understand.

BALLESTED: It was the lady of this house who put me in mind of painting such a thing.

LYNGSTRAND: What'll you call the picture when it's finished?

BALLESTED: I propose to call it *Death of the Mermaid*.

LYNGSTRAND: Most fitting. – You might well be onto something rather good here.

BALLESTED [*looks at him*]: A member of the profession, perhaps?

LYNGSTRAND: A painter, you mean?

BALLESTED: Yes.

LYNGSTRAND: No, I am not. But I'm going to be a sculptor. My name is Hans Lyngstrand.

BALLESTED: So you're going to be a sculptor? Yes well, sculpting is also a nice, tasteful art. – I believe I've seen you in the street once or twice. Have you been with us long?

LYNGSTRAND: No, I've only been here about a fortnight. But I want to see if I can stay the whole summer.

BALLESTED: To enjoy the pleasures of the sea? Eh?

LYNGSTRAND: Yes, I've got to get my strength up a bit.

BALLESTED: Not delicate, surely?

LYNGSTRAND: Well yes, I am slightly on the delicate side. But it's nothing very serious. It's just a kind of tightness of breath in my chest.

BALLESTED: Pah – that's nothing! Although you should talk to a good doctor.

LYNGSTRAND: I thought about asking Dr Wangel, when the opportunity arises.

BALLESTED: Yes, do. [*Looks out to the left*] There's another steamboat⁷ coming. Crammed full of passengers. There's been an unparalleled boom in tourism here over the last few years.

LYNGSTRAND: Yes, there's a fair bit of traffic here, I'd say.

BALLESTED: Full of summer residents here too, it is. I often worry that our town will lose its character with all these outsiders rattling about.

LYNGSTRAND: Were you born and bred here in town?

BALLESTED: No, I wasn't. But I have accala – acclimatized. I feel attached to this place by the bonds of time and habit.

LYNGSTRAND: You've lived here a long time, then?

BALLESTED: Well, some seventeen or eighteen years. I came
   here with Skive's Theatre Troupe. But we landed in some
   financial difficulty. So the company was disbanded and scattered to the four winds.

LYNGSTRAND: But you stayed on here?

BALLESTED: I stayed on. And I've done rather well out of it.
   Back then, let me tell you, I worked in what might be
   described as stage décor.[8]

   BOLETTE *comes out carrying a rocking chair, which she
   places on the veranda.*

BOLETTE [*speaking in towards the garden room*]: Hilde – see
   if you can find the embroidered footstool for Father.

LYNGSTRAND [*walks across and, standing below the veranda,
   greets her*]: Good morning, Miss Wangel!

BOLETTE [*by the balustrade*]: Well I never, is it you, Mr
   Lyngstrand? Good morning. Excuse me a moment – I just
   have to – [*She goes into the house*]

BALLESTED: You know the family?

LYNGSTRAND: No, not exactly. I've only met with the young
   ladies at other people's houses here and there. And I talked
   briefly with Mrs Wangel last time they had music up at 'The
   Outlook'. She told me I was most welcome to come and visit
   them.

BALLESTED: Well, you know what – that's an acquaintance
   you should cultivate.

LYNGSTRAND: Yes, I have thought of visiting them. Paying a
   call,[9] as they say. If I could only find an excuse –

BALLESTED: You what – an excuse –? [*Looks to the left*] Oh,
   blast! [*Gathers his things together*] The steamship's at the
   jetty already. I must get over to the hotel. Some of the new
   arrivals may have use of me. I offer my services as a barber
   and hairdresser too, let me tell you.

LYNGSTRAND: You do seem awfully versatile.

BALLESTED: You have to know how to accala – cclimatize
   yourself to a variety of trades in a small town. Should you ever
   need anything done by way of hairdressing – a little pomade
   or the like, then just ask for the dancing master, Ballested.

LYNGSTRAND: Dancing master –?

BALLESTED: Or the chairman of the Brass Band Association,[10] if you prefer. We have a concert up at 'The Outlook' tonight. Goodbye – goodbye!

He leaves with his painting materials through the garden gate and out to the left.

HILDE *comes out with the footstool.* BOLETTE *brings more flowers.* LYNGSTRAND *greets* HILDE *from down in the garden.*

HILDE [*at the balustrade, not returning his greeting*]: Bolette said that you'd ventured right in today.

LYNGSTRAND: Yes, I took the liberty of coming in just a little way.

HILDE: So, have you been out for a morning walk?

LYNGSTRAND: Oh no – there's been no long walk today.

HILDE: Have you been bathing, then?

LYNGSTRAND: Yes, I took a brief dip in the sea. I saw your mother down there. She was going into her bathing-hut.

HILDE: Who was?

LYNGSTRAND: Your mother.

HILDE: Ah, right.

She puts the footstool in front of the rocking-chair.

BOLETTE [*as though interrupting*]: You didn't see any sign of Father's boat out on the fjord?

LYNGSTRAND: Well, I think I saw a sailboat heading in.

BOLETTE: That was probably Father. He's been out visiting patients on the islands.

She busies herself with things on the table.

LYNGSTRAND [*with one foot on the steps of the veranda*]: Well, well, it looks splendid here with those flowers –!

BOLETTE: Yes, doesn't it look nice?

LYNGSTRAND: Oh, it looks lovely. It looks as though there's some sort of celebration taking place here.

HILDE: There most certainly is.

LYNGSTRAND: Might have guessed. I assume it's your father's birthday today.

BOLETTE [*warningly to* HILDE]: Hrm – hrm!

HILDE [*taking no notice*]: No, Mother's.

LYNGSTRAND: Oh, I see – it's your mother's.

BOLETTE [*quietly, angrily*]: But, Hilde –!

HILDE [*similarly*]: Leave me alone! [*To* LYNGSTRAND] You'll be off home to get some lunch[11] now, I take it?

LYNGSTRAND [*retreating from the steps*]: Yes, I should probably go and get something inside me.

HILDE: I expect you're living quite the high life over at the hotel?

LYNGSTRAND: I'm no longer staying at the hotel. It got too expensive for me.

HILDE: Where are you staying now then?

LYNGSTRAND: I'm staying up at Mrs Jensen's house now.

HILDE: Which Mrs Jensen?

LYNGSTRAND: The midwife.

HILDE: I'm sorry, Mr Lyngstrand – but I really have better things to do, than –

LYNGSTRAND: Oh, I probably oughtn't to have said that.

HILDE: Said what?

LYNGSTRAND: What I said.

HILDE [*looks him up and down, mercilessly*]: I haven't the least idea what you mean.

LYNGSTRAND: No – no. Anyway, I'll bid you young ladies goodbye for now.

BOLETTE [*moves to the top of the steps*]: Goodbye, goodbye, Mr Lyngstrand. You really must excuse us today. – But on another occasion – when you have the time – and when you feel like it – you really must drop by and say hello to Father and – and the rest of us.

LYNGSTRAND: Oh yes, thanks very much. I'd like that immensely.
He waves and goes out through the garden gate. As he walks past on the road going to the left, he waves one more time in the direction of the veranda.

HILDE [*in a lowered voice*]: Adieu, monsieur! Now buzz off and send my regards to Old Ma Jensen![12]

BOLETTE [*quietly, shaking her by the arm*]: Hilde –! You naughty child! Are you completely mad? He could hear you easily!

HILDE: Pff – do you think I care about *that*!

BOLETTE [*looking out to the right*]: Father's coming.

DR WANGEL, *wearing travelling clothes and carrying a small bag, appears on the footpath from the right.*

WANGEL: Look, I'm back again, girls!

He comes through the gate.

BOLETTE [*goes down to meet him in the garden*]: Oh, it's wonderful that you're here.

HILDE [*also goes down to meet him*]: Are you done for the rest of the day now, Father?

WANGEL: No, I have to go down to the office a bit later. – Tell me – do you know if Arnholm has arrived?

BOLETTE: Yes, he arrived last night. We were informed by the hotel.

WANGEL: So you haven't seen him yet?

BOLETTE: No. But doubtless he'll come to see us later this morning.

WANGEL: Yes, I'm sure he will.

HILDE [*tugs at him*]: Father, please look around you.

WANGEL [*looks towards the veranda*]: Yes, I can see, children. – It's certainly very festive here.

BOLETTE: Yes, we've made it pretty, don't you think?

WANGEL: Yes, I must say you have. – Are – are we alone in the house now?

HILDE: Yes, she's gone into –

BOLETTE [*quickly interjects*]: Mother is bathing.

WANGEL [*looks affectionately at* BOLETTE *and pats her head. Then rather hesitantly he says*]: Listen now, girls – are you intending to leave it like this all day? And the flag flying all day too?

HILDE: Oh, but surely you can understand that, Father!

WANGEL: Hm – well. But, you see, girls –

BOLETTE [*winks and nods to him*]: You do realize of course that we've done all of this for Mr Arnholm. When such a good friend comes to visit you for the first time –

HILDE [*smiles and tugs at him*]: Imagine that – the man who was once Bolette's tutor, Father!

WANGEL [*with a half-smile*]: You really are a couple of schemers. Well, good heavens – I suppose it's only natural we should remember the one who is no longer with us. But nonetheless. Here, Hilde. [*Hands her his bag*] This needs to go down to my office. – No, my girls – I don't like this. Not the way it's done, you understand. The fact that every year, we –. Well – what can one say? I dare say it can't be done any other way.

HILDE [*sets off through the garden to the left with the bag, but stops, turns and points*]: Look at that gentleman coming over there. That must be the schoolmaster.

BOLETTE [*looks in that direction*]: That man *there*? [*Laughs*] Oh, you're joking! You think that middle-aged chap is Arnholm!

WANGEL: But, wait a second, children. Well, I'll be damned if it isn't him! – Yes, it is too, yes!

BOLETTE [*staring in that direction, in quiet astonishment*]: Good Lord, I think you're right –!

The schoolmaster, MR ARNHOLM, in elegant morning dress, wearing gold-rimmed spectacles and carrying a thin cane, is coming along the road from the left. He appears rather tense, looks into the garden, gives a friendly greeting and comes in through the gate.

WANGEL [*going to meet him*]: Welcome, my dear Arnholm! A hearty welcome back to your old stamping ground!

ARNHOLM: Thank you, thank you so much, Dr Wangel.

They shake hands and walk together through the garden.

ARNHOLM: And here we have the children! [*Extends his hands to them and looks at them*] I'd scarcely have recognized the two of them.

WANGEL: That I can believe.

ARNHOLM: Although – perhaps Bolette. Yes, I'd probably have recognized Bolette.

WANGEL: I'm not so sure. It must be eight or nine years since you saw her last. Yes, and so much has changed here in that time.

ARNHOLM [*looks around*]: I wouldn't say that. Apart from the fact that the trees have grown a good deal – and that an arbour's been built over *there* –

WANGEL: Well, on the surface –

ARNHOLM [*smiling*]: And, of course, that you now have two grown-up, marriageable daughters in the house.

WANGEL: Well, it's just the one who is marriageable.

HILDE [*in a lowered voice*]: Hah, listen to Father!

WANGEL: But I think we'll sit on the veranda now. It's cooler there. After you.

ARNHOLM: Thank you, my dear doctor.

> *They go up.* WANGEL *waves* ARNHOLM *over to the rocking-chair.*

WANGEL: There. Now you're just going to sit here calmly and relax. You really do look a tad strained after your journey.

ARNHOLM: Oh, it's nothing. Here in these surroundings –

BOLETTE [*to* WANGEL]: Shouldn't we take a little soda water and cordial into the garden room? It'll be too hot out here soon.

WANGEL: Yes, you do that, girls. Let's have soda water and cordial. And a little brandy perhaps.

BOLETTE: Really, brandy too?

WANGEL: Just a little drop. In case anyone wants some.

BOLETTE: If you say so. Hilde, do go down to the office with that bag.

> BOLETTE *goes into the garden room and closes the door after her.* HILDE *picks up the bag and goes through the garden behind the house to the left.*

ARNHOLM [*who has been following* BOLETTE *with his gaze*]: That's one fine – two very fine girls you have there now.

WANGEL [*sits down*]: Yes, don't you think?

ARNHOLM: Yes, it really is quite amazing with Bolette. And Hilde too. – But let's talk about you now, my dear doctor. Are you thinking of living here for the rest of your days?

WANGEL: Oh, I expect so. It's here I was born and bred, as they say. Here that I lived in total happiness with the one who left us all too soon. The woman you knew when you were here last, Arnholm.

ARNHOLM: Yes – yes.

WANGEL: And now I live here very happily with the woman I was given in her stead. Oh, I have to say fate has been good to me on the whole.

ARNHOLM: But no children from your second marriage?

WANGEL: We had a little boy two, two and a half years ago. But we didn't keep him long. He died when he was about four or five months old.

ARNHOLM: Isn't your wife at home today?

WANGEL: Yes, she should be here soon. She's down there bathing. She does so every day at this time of year. Whatever the weather.

ARNHOLM: Does she have something wrong with her?

WANGEL: Nothing wrong exactly. Although she's been strangely nervous in the last couple of years. Well, on and off, that is. I can't really work out what's the matter with her. But going into the sea, well, that seems to be her life's passion, you understand.

ARNHOLM: I remember that from before.

WANGEL [*with an almost imperceptible smile*]: Yes, of course, you know Ellida from the time you were teaching out in Skjoldviken.

ARNHOLM: Naturally. She often visited the parsonage. And I usually met her when I went out to the lighthouse to check on her father.

WANGEL: That time out there left a deep mark on her, you can be sure. People here in town have absolutely no understanding of that. They call her 'The Lady from the Sea'.

ARNHOLM: Do they, now?

WANGEL: Yes. So you see, that's why –. Do talk to her about the old days, my dear Arnholm. It will do her so much good.

ARNHOLM [*looks at him doubtfully*]: Do you have any reason to believe that?

WANGEL: I certainly have.

ELLIDA'S VOICE [*from the garden offstage to the right*]: Is that you, Wangel?

WANGEL [*gets up*]: Yes, my dearest.

    MRS ELLIDA WANGEL, *in a large, lightweight bathing wrap and wet hair loose over her shoulders, comes out from between the trees by the arbour.* MR ARNHOLM *gets up.*

WANGEL [*smiling and holding his hands out to her*]: Well, here we have our mermaid!

ELLIDA [*rushes up onto the veranda and clasps his hands*]:
Thank the Lord I can see you again! When did you get here?

WANGEL: Just now. A moment ago. [*Indicates* ARNHOLM] But
aren't you going to greet an old acquaintance –?

ELLIDA [*extends her hand to* ARNHOLM]: Ah, you've come.
Welcome! And apologies for my not being at home –

ARNHOLM: Oh, please. Don't stand on ceremony –

WANGEL: Was the water nice and fresh today?

ELLIDA: Fresh! Oh God, the water here is never fresh. Luke-
warm and sluggish. Ugh! The water is sick here in the fjords.

ARNHOLM: Sick?

ELLIDA: Yes, it's sick. And I think it makes people sick too.

WANGEL [*smiling*]: Well, that's quite a recommendation you're
giving this bathing spot.

ARNHOLM: I rather think, Mrs Wangel, that you have a unique
relationship to the sea and everything in it.

ELLIDA: Maybe. I almost think I do – yes. – But have you
noticed how festive the girls have made things for your sake?

WANGEL [*embarrassed*]: Hmm – [*Looks at his watch*] Well
now, I should –

ARNHOLM: Is it really for my sake –?

ELLIDA: But, of course. We don't make such a special effort
every day. Urgh – it's so suffocatingly hot under this roof!
[*Goes down into the garden*] Come over here! At least here
there's some sort of a breeze.

She sits down in the arbour.

ARNHOLM [*joining her*]: Actually I find the air rather fresh here.

ELLIDA: Yes, but you're used to the stuffy city air in the capital. It's dreadful there in the summer, I hear.

WANGEL [*who has also gone down into the garden*]: Hmm,
Ellida my dear, you'll probably have to entertain our good
friend on your own for a while.

ELLIDA: Have you got work to do?

WANGEL: Yes, I need to go down to the office. And then, of
course, I ought to get changed. But I won't be long –

ARNHOLM [*sits down in the arbour*]: Don't rush yourself,
my dear doctor. I'm sure your wife and I will manage to pass
the time.

WANGEL [*nods*]: Oh, yes – I'm relying on it. Right – see you later!

   He goes out through the garden to the left.

ELLIDA [*after a brief pause*]: It's rather comfortable to sit here, don't you think?

ARNHOLM: I'd say I'm sitting quite comfortably, yes.

ELLIDA: This summerhouse[13] here is called *my* summerhouse. Since I was the one who had it built. Or to be more accurate, Wangel did – for my sake.

ARNHOLM: And do you sit here often?

ELLIDA: Yes, this is where I generally sit these days.

ARNHOLM: With the girls, I assume?

ELLIDA: No, the girls – they stay on the veranda.

ARNHOLM: And Wangel?

ELLIDA: Oh, Wangel goes back and forth. One minute he's here with me, the next he's over with the children.

ARNHOLM: Is it you who wants it like that?

ELLIDA: I think all parties prefer it that way. We can speak to each other across the garden of course – on the odd occasion when we feel we have something to say.

ARNHOLM [*after a moment in thought*]: When I used to pass your way –. Out in Skjoldviken, I mean –. Hm – it's a long time ago now –.

ELLIDA: It's a good ten years since you were out there with us.

ARNHOLM: Yes, thereabouts. But when I think of you out there in the lighthouse –! The Heathen, as the old priest used to call you because your father had baptized you, according to him, with a ship's name[14] and not a name for a Christian human being –

ELLIDA: Yes, and so?

ARNHOLM: Well, the last thing I'd have believed was that I'd see you here as Mrs Wangel.

ELLIDA: Well, no, back then Wangel wasn't yet a –. Back then, the girls' first mother was still alive. Their real mother, that is –

ARNHOLM: Right. I see. But even if that hadn't been the case –. Even if he'd been as free as the wind – I'd never have expected *this* to come about.

ELLIDA: Nor I. Never on earth – not back then.

ARNHOLM: Of course, Wangel is such an excellent man. So honourable. Truly good and kind to everybody –.

ELLIDA [*warmly and sincerely*]: Yes, he is indeed!

ARNHOLM: – but he must be very different from you, I'd have thought.

ELLIDA: You're quite right. He is.

ARNHOLM: So, how did it happen then? How did it happen?

ELLIDA: Oh, my dear Mr Arnholm, you really mustn't ask me that. I could never explain these things to you. And even if I could, you'd not be able to grasp or understand it in the slightest.

ARNHOLM: Hm –. [*Lowering his voice slightly*] Have you ever confided anything about me to your husband? I'm thinking, of course, of that utterly fruitless step I took back then – when I let myself get so carried away.

ELLIDA: No. How can you think such a thing! I've not said one word to him about – about what you're referring to.

ARNHOLM: I'm happy to hear it. I was feeling rather uneasy at the thought that –

ELLIDA: You certainly don't need to be. I have simply told him – which is true – that I was very fond of you, and that you were the truest and best friend I had out there.

ARNHOLM: Thank you for that. But tell me now – why did you never write to me after I left?

ELLIDA: I thought it might cause you pain to hear from someone who – who could not respond as you'd wished. I thought it might be like opening up an old wound.

ARNHOLM: Hm –. Yes, yes, you may be right.

ELLIDA: But why didn't you ever write yourself?

ARNHOLM [*looks at her and smiles half reproachfully*]: Me? Take the initiative? And lay myself open perhaps to the suspicion of wanting to embark on something new? After a rejection like the one I'd received?

ELLIDA: No, of course, I understand. – Have you never thought of forming a new attachment since?

ARNHOLM: Never. I've remained faithful to my memories.

ELLIDA [*half jokingly*]: Oh, come on! Let these sad memories go. You should be thinking seriously instead about becoming a happily married man, I suggest.

ARNHOLM: It had better happen soon then, Mrs Wangel. Remember – I am already, shame to say, past thirty-seven.

ELLIDA: Well, all the more reason to get a move on. [*She falls silent, then continues in a serious and hushed tone*] But listen, my dear Arnholm – I want to tell you something now, which I couldn't have voiced then even if my life had depended on it.

ARNHOLM: So, what is it?

ELLIDA: At the time when you took that – that fruitless step, as you call it – I could not give you any answer other than the one I gave.

ARNHOLM: I know. You had nothing to offer me other than good friendship. I *do* know that.

ELLIDA: But what you don't know is that my entire being and all my thoughts were elsewhere back then.

ARNHOLM: Back then?

ELLIDA: Exactly.

ARNHOLM: But that's impossible! You've got the times all wrong! I doubt you even knew Wangel back then.

ELLIDA: I'm not talking about Wangel.

ARNHOLM: Not Wangel? But back then – out in Skjoldviken –. I don't remember there being one person out there to whom I could ever imagine you becoming attached.

ELLIDA: No, – that I can believe. Because the whole thing was so absolutely crazy.

ARNHOLM: But then tell me more!

ELLIDA: Oh, surely it's enough for you to know I had a prior attachment. And now you know.

ARNHOLM: But if you hadn't had a prior attachment?

ELLIDA: What then?

ARNHOLM: Would your reply to my letter have been different?

ELLIDA: How can I know? When Wangel came along the reply was indeed different.

ARNHOLM: So what's the purpose in telling me you were attached?

ELLIDA [*gets up, as if anguished and troubled*]: Because I need somebody to confide in. No, no, please just sit there.

ARNHOLM: So your husband knows nothing about this?

ELLIDA: I confessed to him at the start, that my thoughts had once been elsewhere. He has never demanded to know more. And we've never touched on it since. The whole thing was nothing short of madness anyway. And it blew over very quickly. That's to say – in a way.

ARNHOLM [*gets up*]: Only in a way? Not altogether?

ELLIDA: Well, yes, obviously! Good God, Arnholm dear, it really isn't what you're thinking. It's something so utterly incomprehensible. I don't know how I'd begin to explain it. You'd just think I was sick. Or completely mad.

ARNHOLM: My dearest Mrs Wangel – you really must and shall speak out now.

ELLIDA: All right! I'll have to try. But how could you, as a rational man, possibly understand – [*Looks out and breaks off*] Wait until later. It seems we have a visitor.

LYNGSTRAND *walks along the road from the left, and comes into the garden. He has a flower in his buttonhole and carries a large and beautiful bouquet, wrapped in paper and ribbons. He stops and hesitates for a moment near the veranda.*

ELLIDA [*at the entrance to the arbour*]: Is it the girls you're looking for, Mr Lyngstrand?

LYNGSTRAND [*turns round*]: Ah, there you are, Mrs Wangel! [*Greets her and comes closer*] No, it isn't. It isn't the young ladies. It's you, Mrs Wangel. You did give me permission to come and visit you –

ELLIDA: I did, indeed. You're always welcome here.

LYNGSTRAND: Thank you. And since by happy coincidence there's a celebration here at the house today –

ELLIDA: So, you know?

LYNGSTRAND: Oh, yes. Which is why I'd like to take the liberty of presenting you, Mrs Wangel, with this –

He bows and offers her the bouquet.

ELLIDA [*smiling*]: But, my dear Mr Lyngstrand, wouldn't it be more appropriate for you to give your splendid flowers to Mr Arnholm yourself? He is, after all, the one who –

LYNGSTRAND [*looks uncertainly at them both*]: I'm sorry – but

I don't know this gentleman. It was just –. Well, I'm here on account of the birthday, madam.

ELLIDA: Birthday? You've made a mistake, Mr Lyngstrand. There's no birthday here today.

LYNGSTRAND [*smiles knowingly*]: Oh, I know all about it! But I didn't think it was meant to be such a secret.

ELLIDA: What do you know?

LYNGSTRAND: That it's your birthday,[15] Mrs Wangel.

ELLIDA: Mine?

ARNHOLM [*looks questioningly at her*]: Today? No, that can't be right.

ELLIDA [*to* LYNGSTRAND]: What makes you think that?

LYNGSTRAND: It was Miss Hilde who let it slip. I was here for a moment, earlier today. And I asked the young ladies why they were making things so special with the flowers and flag –

ELLIDA: And?

LYNGSTRAND: – and then Miss Hilde said: Well, because today it is Mother's – birthday.

ELLIDA: Mother's –! Ah, right, I see.

ARNHOLM: Aha!

He and ELLIDA *look meaningfully at each other.*

ARNHOLM: Well, Mrs Wangel, since this young man is in the know –

ELLIDA [*to* LYNGSTRAND]: Yes, since you are in the know, then –

LYNGSTRAND [*offers the bouquet again*]: May I then be permitted to offer you my congratulations –

ELLIDA [*takes the flowers*]: Thank you very much indeed. Do sit down for a moment, Mr Lyngstrand.

ELLIDA, ARNHOLM *and* LYNGSTRAND *sit down in the arbour.*

ELLIDA: This matter – of my birthday – it was meant to be a secret, my dear schoolmaster.

ARNHOLM: Ah, I understand. It wasn't meant for the uninitiated among us.

ELLIDA [*puts the bouquet on the table*]: Precisely. Not for the uninitiated.

LYNGSTRAND: I promise not to mention it to a living soul.

ELLIDA: Oh, I didn't quite mean it like that. – But how are things with you? I think you look better than you did.

LYNGSTRAND: Yes, I do indeed believe things are looking up for me. And next year, if I manage to take a trip down to southern Europe –

ELLIDA: And you will, the girls tell me.

LYNGSTRAND: Yes, because I have a patron in Bergen who looks after me. And he's promised to help me next year.

ELLIDA: And how did you come by him?

LYNGSTRAND: Oh, it was just a great stroke of luck. I went to sea with one of his ships once.

ELLIDA: Did you now? So you were drawn to the sea?

LYNGSTRAND: No, not in the least. But after Mother died Father didn't want me hanging about at home any more. So he forced me to go to sea. Then we got shipwrecked in the English Channel on the way home. And, that was perfect for me, of course.

ELLIDA: How do you mean?

LYNGSTRAND: Well, it was because of that shipwreck I got this crick thing – here in my chest. I was in that ice-cold water for so long before they came to rescue me. Which meant, of course, I *had* to give up the sea. – Yes, it really was a great stroke of luck.

ARNHOLM: Oh? You think so?

LYNGSTRAND: Yes. Because, this crick isn't very serious, you see. And now I can become a sculptor, which I wanted so dearly to be. Imagine – being able to model that lovely clay that's so beautifully pliant between one's fingers!

ELLIDA: And what will you model? Will it be mermen and mermaids? Or ancient Vikings –?

LYNGSTRAND: No, nothing like that. As soon as I'm ready, I want to try to make a large-scale work. A group sculpture, they call it.

ELLIDA: I see – and what will this group sculpture depict?

LYNGSTRAND: Oh, it will have to be something I've experienced myself.

ARNHOLM: Yes, yes – best you keep to that.

ELLIDA: But what will it be?

LYNGSTRAND: Well, I'd thought it should be of a young sailor's wife, she's lying there asleep, strangely restless. And she's dreaming too. I think I can make her so you can see that she's dreaming.

ARNHOLM: Won't there be anything else?

LYNGSTRAND: Oh yes, there'll be one other figure. A sort of gestalt,[16] as they say. This will be her husband, who she's been unfaithful to, while he was away. And now he's been drowned at sea.

ARNHOLM: So how –?

ELLIDA: He's been drowned?

LYNGSTRAND: Yes. He's been drowned at sea. But what's strange is that he has come home nonetheless. It is the middle of the night. And he's standing there by her bed looking at her. He'll stand there streaming with water like when they drag people up from the sea.

ELLIDA [*leans back in her chair*]: That's really rather strange. [*She closes her eyes*] Oh, I can see it before me as large as life.

ARNHOLM: But good God, Mr – Mr –! You said it had to be something you'd experienced.

LYNGSTRAND: Yes, but – I *have* experienced this. In a manner of speaking.

ARNHOLM: Experienced – that a dead man –?

LYNGSTRAND: Well no, I don't mean experienced exactly. Not experienced in any material way, obviously. But nonetheless –

ELLIDA [*lively and excited*]: Tell me everything you know! I must have every detail.

ARNHOLM [*smiling*]: Yes, this must certainly be something for you. Something with an atmosphere of the sea in it.

ELLIDA: So what happened, Mr Lyngstrand?

LYNGSTRAND: Well, it was like this, when we were about to sail homewards on the brig, from a town they call Halifax, we had to leave the bosun behind in the hospital. So an American was signed on in his place. And this new bosun –

ELLIDA: The American?

LYNGSTRAND: – yes; one day he got a pile of old newspapers on loan from the captain, which he read constantly. Because he wanted to learn Norwegian, he said.

ELLIDA: Right! And then?

LYNGSTRAND: Then one evening there was a violent storm. All the men were on deck. Apart from the bosun and myself, that is. He'd sprained his foot so he couldn't walk on it. And I was poorly too, lying in my bunk. So, there he sat in the cabin reading one of those old newspapers again –

ELLIDA: I see! I see!

LYNGSTRAND: But as he's sitting there I hear a kind of roar come from him. And then when I look at him, I see that his face has gone chalky white. And then he starts to crunch and crush the paper and rip it into a thousand little pieces. But he did it really quietly, really quietly.

ELLIDA: Didn't he say anything at all? Didn't he speak?

LYNGSTRAND: Not straight away. But a little later he said as though to himself: 'Married. To another man. While I was away.'

ELLIDA [*closes her eyes and says in a low voice*]: He said that?

LYNGSTRAND: Yes. And just think – he said it in excellent Norwegian. He must have had a great gift for foreign languages, that man.

ELLIDA: And what then? What else happened?

LYNGSTRAND: Well, this strange thing happened that I'll never forget as long as I live. He continued – very quietly again: 'But mine she is, and mine she will always be. And she will come with me, even if I have to return home to fetch her, as a drowned man from the black waters of the sea.'

ELLIDA [*pours herself a glass of water. Her hand is shaking*]: Phew – it's so close here today.

LYNGSTRAND: And he said it with such force of will, I felt he'd be man enough to do it too.

ELLIDA: You don't know anything about – what became of this man?

LYNGSTRAND: Oh, Mrs Wangel, it's unlikely he's alive.

ELLIDA [*quickly*]: What makes you think that?

LYNGSTRAND: Well, we were shipwrecked in the Channel not long after that. I managed to get into the longboat with the captain and five others. The first mate went in the dinghy. Along with the American and one other man.

ELLIDA: And nobody's heard of them since?

LYNGSTRAND: No, not a thing, Mrs Wangel. My benefactor
wrote and said as much just recently. That's why I feel so
compelled to make a work of art out of it. I see the sailor's
faithless wife so lifelike before me. And then the avenger,
who is drowned but comes home from the sea nonetheless. I
can see them both so clearly.

ELLIDA: Me too. [*She gets up*] Come on – let's go inside. Or
better still, down to Wangel! I find it so suffocatingly warm
here.

She goes out of the arbour.

LYNGSTRAND [*who has also got up*]: Well, for my part I ought
to thank you and take my leave now. This really was only
meant to be a brief visit because of your birthday.

ELLIDA: As you wish. [*Holds out her hand to him*] Goodbye
and thank you for the flowers.

LYNGSTRAND *says goodbye and goes out through the
garden gate to the left.*

ARNHOLM [*gets up and goes over to* ELLIDA]: I can see that
this cut close to your heart, my dear Mrs Wangel.

ELLIDA: Yes, you might put it that way, although –

ARNHOLM: But it's really nothing more than you had to be
prepared for.

ELLIDA [*looks at him in amazement*]: Prepared!

ARNHOLM: I'd say so, yes.

ELLIDA: Prepared – for someone to return – and in such a way!

ARNHOLM: What on earth –! Is it that crazy sculptor's sea-
faring yarn –?

ELLIDA: Oh, my dear Mr Arnholm, perhaps he isn't all that
crazy.

ARNHOLM: So was it all that talk about the dead man that
shook you up like this? And there was I thinking –

ELLIDA: What were you thinking?

ARNHOLM: I thought you were just playing along to mask
your feelings. That you were sitting here in agony because
you'd found out that a family event is being secretly celebrated in the house. That your husband and his children live
a life of memories in which you are not included.

ELLIDA: Oh no, no. That can't be otherwise. I've no right to claim my husband completely and exclusively for myself.

ARNHOLM: But I think you most assuredly have.

ELLIDA: Yes. But I can't. That's the thing. I too live a separate existence – that the others are shut out from.

ARNHOLM: You? [*More quietly*] Am I right in thinking –? You – you don't really have any feelings for your husband?

ELLIDA: Oh, but I do, I do – I've grown to have the deepest feelings for him! And that's precisely why it's so terrible – so inexplicable – so altogether unthinkable –!

ARNHOLM: Now you shall confide all your sorrows to me! Won't you, Mrs Wangel?

ELLIDA: I can't, my dear friend. Not now at least. Later perhaps.

    BOLETTE *comes out onto the veranda and goes down into the garden.*

BOLETTE: Father's coming from the office now. Shouldn't we all go and sit in the garden room?

ELLIDA: Yes, let's.

    WANGEL, *wearing a change of clothes, comes with* HILDE *from behind the house on the left.*

WANGEL: Right! Here I am, free as the wind. I'm ready for a nice glass of something cool.

ELLIDA: Wait a moment!

    She fetches the bouquet from the arbour.

HILDE: Oh look! What lovely flowers! Where did you get those from?

ELLIDA: I got them from Lyngstrand, the sculptor, Hilde dear.

HILDE [*surprised*]: From Lyngstrand?

BOLETTE [*uneasy*]: Has Lyngstrand been here – again?

ELLIDA [*with a half-smile*]: Yes. He came here with these. On account of the birthday, you understand.

BOLETTE [*glancing at* HILDE]: Oh –!

HILDE [*mumbles*]: The beast!

WANGEL [*in painful embarrassment to* ELLIDA]: Hmm –. Well, you see –. Let me explain, my dearest, sweetest, darling Ellida –

ELLIDA [*interrupts*]: Come on, girls! Let's put my flowers in water together with the others.

She goes up onto the veranda.

BOLETTE [*softly to* HILDE]: You see, deep down she's nice after all.

HILDE [*her voice lowered, looking angry*]: Trickery! She's just pretending, so as to please Father.

WANGEL [*on the veranda, clasping* ELLIDA's *hand*]: Thank you – thank you! Thank you so much for this, Ellida!

ELLIDA [*arranging the flowers*]: Oh – why shouldn't I join in and make things special for – Mother's birthday?

ARNHOLM: Hmm –.

He goes up to WANGEL *and* ELLIDA. BOLETTE *and* HILDE *stay down in the garden.*

ACT TWO

Up at 'The Outlook', a high point behind the town overgrown with bushes. In the background, a cairn of stones and a weathervane. Large rocks are arranged as seating around the cairn and in the foreground. Far below in the background the outer fjord can be seen, with islands and headlands. The open sea is not visible. It is a summer's night, a soft half-light. A reddish-gold tint in the air and over the mountain peaks far in the distance. The sound of singing in four-part harmony[17] can be heard faintly from the slopes down to the right.

Young people from the town, men and women, come up in couples from the right; deep in conversation they walk past the cairn and out to the left. A few moments later BALLESTED *comes, acting as a guide for a party of foreign tourists and their ladies. He is loaded down with shawls and travel bags.*

BALLESTED [*pointing upwards with his walking stick*]: And now, *meine Damen und Herren*[18] – over *dort*[19] *ist ein*-other hill. *Das willen wir* also climb *und* then *herunter*[20] – [*He switches to English*[21] *and leads the party out to the left*]
    HILDE *comes up swiftly from the slope on the right, stops and looks back.* BOLETTE *follows a few moments later.*
BOLETTE: But, Hilde dear, why would we run away from Lyngstrand?
HILDE: Because I can't bear walking uphill so slowly. Just look – look at how he is crawling up.
BOLETTE: Oh, but you know how ill he is.
HILDE: Do you think it's really serious?

BOLETTE: Yes, I'm afraid it is.

HILDE: He went to see Father this afternoon. I wonder what Father thinks about him.

BOLETTE: Father told me it's a hardening of the lung – or something like that. He'll never reach old age, Father said.

HILDE: Really? Imagine that – that's exactly what I thought.

BOLETTE: Well, for heaven's sake, don't let it show.

HILDE: As if I would. [*Lowering her voice*] There, look – now Hans has managed to scramble up. Hans –. Don't you think you can tell just by looking at him that his name is Hans?[22]

BOLETTE [*whispers*]: Just behave yourself now! I'm warning you!

LYNGSTRAND *enters from the right, carrying a parasol.*

LYNGSTRAND: I'm awfully sorry that I couldn't keep up with you, ladies.

HILDE: Have you got yourself a parasol too, now?

LYNGSTRAND: It's your mother's. She said I should use it as a walking stick. Since I didn't bring one.

BOLETTE: Are they still down there? Father and the others?

LYNGSTRAND: Yes. Your father popped into the refreshment hall. And the others are sitting outside listening to the music. But they'll come up later, your mother said.

HILDE [*who has been watching him*]: You must be terribly tired now.

LYNGSTRAND: Yes, I believe I am perhaps just a little tired. I do indeed think I ought to sit down for a moment.

He sits down on a rock in the foreground, to the right.

HILDE [*standing in front of him*]: Did you know that there'll be dancing down by the bandstand later?

LYNGSTRAND: Yes, I heard talk of that.

HILDE: You must think that fun – dancing, I mean?

BOLETTE [*who is picking small flowers in the heather*]: Oh Hilde – do let Mr Lyngstrand catch his breath.

LYNGSTRAND [*to* HILDE]: Yes, Miss Hilde, I would love to dance – if only I could.

HILDE: Oh, I see. Have you never learned how?

LYNGSTRAND: No. I never learned how. Although *that* wasn't what I meant. I meant that I can't because of my chest.

HILDE: Because of this crick thing you say you have?

LYNGSTRAND: Yes. That's it.

HILDE: Are you very sad to have this crick thing?

LYNGSTRAND: Oh no, I can't say I am really. [*Smiles*] Because I think it's the reason people are so kind and friendly and so charitable towards me.

HILDE: Quite, and it's not at all that serious anyway.

LYNGSTRAND: No, not the least bit serious. That's what your father led me to understand too.

HILDE: And it will pass, of course, as soon as you're out on your travels.

LYNGSTRAND: Quite so. Then it will pass.

BOLETTE [*with flowers*]: Look here, Mr Lyngstrand – put these in your buttonhole.

LYNGSTRAND: Thank you very much, miss! That really is too kind of you.

HILDE [*looking down, to the right*]: There they are, down on the path.

BOLETTE [*also looking down*]: I hope they know which turn to take. No, they're going the wrong way.

LYNGSTRAND [*gets up*]: I'll run down to the bend and shout out to them.

HILDE: You'll have to shout awfully loud.

BOLETTE: No, it's not worth it. You'll just tire yourself out again.

LYNGSTRAND: Oh, it's easy going downhill.

He goes off to the right.

HILDE: Downhill, yes. [*Looks in the direction in which he has gone*] Now he's leaping about! Without a thought for the fact he has to climb back up again.

BOLETTE: Poor man –.

HILDE: If Lyngstrand asked you to marry him, would you take him?

BOLETTE: Have you gone mad?

HILDE: I mean, of course, if he didn't have this crick thing. And if he wasn't about to die. Would you take him *then*?

BOLETTE: I think it would be best if *you* took him.

HILDE: There's no way! He doesn't own a thing. He doesn't even have enough to live on himself.

BOLETTE: Then why do you always make such a fuss of him?

HILDE: Oh, I just do that on account of the crick.

BOLETTE: I've not noticed you having much sympathy for him about *that*.

HILDE: No, I haven't. But I find it so tempting.

BOLETTE: What?

HILDE: To look at him and get him to say that it's nothing serious. And that he's going to travel abroad, and that he's going to be an artist. He goes around believing it all and being so deeply pleased about the whole thing. And then it won't ever come to anything anyway. Not a chance. Because he won't get to live that long. I find that so exciting to think about.

BOLETTE: Exciting!

HILDE: Precisely, I find it exciting. I will allow myself that.

BOLETTE: Shame on you, Hilde. You really are a horrid little brat.

HILDE: And I want to be. For spite! [*Looks down the slope*] There, finally! Arnholm doesn't much like climbing uphill. [*Turns around*] Oh, by the way – do you know what I noticed about Arnholm at the dinner table?

BOLETTE: Well?

HILDE: Imagine – his hair's falling out – here, at the top of his head.

BOLETTE: Oh nonsense! I don't believe it.

HILDE: Yes. And he's got wrinkles here, next to both his eyes. My God, Bolette – how could you be so smitten by him when he was your tutor?

BOLETTE [*smiling*]: Yes, it's difficult to believe. I remember I cried brave and bitter tears once, because he said he thought Bolette was a horrible name.[23]

HILDE: Yes, imagine that! [*Looks down the slope again*] Oh no, just look down there! Now 'The Lady from the Sea' is conversing with him. Not with Father. – I wonder if the two of them have an eye for each other.

BOLETTE: You should be ashamed of yourself, really you should. How can you stand there and talk about her like that? Just when things were so good between us –

HILDE: Oh, yes – believe what you like, my girl! No, things will never be good between us and her. Because she doesn't suit us. Nor we her. God knows what Father wanted to drag her into the house for! – It wouldn't surprise me if she went mad on us one fine day.

BOLETTE: Mad! How can you think such a thing?

HILDE: Oh, that's not so strange. Her mother went mad too, of course. She died mad, I know that for a fact.

BOLETTE: Yes, God alone knows what you poke your nose into. But just don't go around talking about it. Be nice now – for Father's sake. Do you hear me, Hilde?

> WANGEL, ELLIDA, ARNHOLM *and* LYNGSTRAND *come up from the right.*

ELLIDA [*pointing towards the background*]: It's out there!

ARNHOLM: Yes, indeed. It must be in that direction.

ELLIDA: The sea lies out there.

BOLETTE [*to* ARNHOLM]: Don't you think it's splendid up here?

ARNHOLM: I think it's magnificent. An exquisite view.

WANGEL: So you've really never been up here before?

ARNHOLM: No, never. I don't even think it was accessible in my time. Not even a footpath.

WANGEL: And no amenities either. All that has come in the last few years.

BOLETTE: The view's even more splendid from 'Lodskollen',[24] over there.

WANGEL: Should we walk up there perhaps, Ellida?

ELLIDA [*sits down on a rock to the right*]: No thanks. I won't. But the rest of you can go. And in the meantime I'll sit here.

WANGEL: Well, I'll stay with you then. The girls can show Mr Arnholm round.

BOLETTE: Would you like to come with us, Mr Arnholm?

ARNHOLM: Yes, very much. Has a path been laid there too?

BOLETTE: Oh yes. There's a good wide path.

HILDE: The path's so wide that two people can easily walk arm in arm.

ARNHOLM [*joking*]: Is that so, little Miss Hilde? [*To* BOLETTE] Should the two of us put what she says to the test?

BOLETTE [*suppressing a smile*]: Absolutely. Let's do that.

They walk off, arm in arm, to the left.

HILDE [*to* LYNGSTRAND]: Shall we walk too –?

LYNGSTRAND: Arm in arm –?

HILDE: Well, why not? I don't mind.

LYNGSTRAND [*takes her arm and laughs contentedly*]: Well, this is really rather funny!

HILDE: Funny –?

LYNGSTRAND: Yes, it looks just as though we were engaged.

HILDE: You have clearly never strolled arm-in-arm with a lady before, Mr Lyngstrand.

They walk off to the left.

WANGEL [*who is standing over by the cairn*]: Dearest Ellida, we have a moment now to ourselves –

ELLIDA: Yes. Come and sit down here with me.

WANGEL [*sits down*]: It's so quiet and peaceful here. Let's talk a bit now.

ELLIDA: About what?

WANGEL: About you. And about our relationship, Ellida. I see that things can't go on as they are.

ELLIDA: What would you suggest instead?

WANGEL: Complete mutual confidence, my dear. Truly living together – just as before.

ELLIDA: Oh, if only that could be! But it's utterly impossible!

WANGEL: I think I understand you. From certain things you've let slip now and then, I think I do.

ELLIDA [*fervently*]: You don't! Don't tell me that you understand –!

WANGEL: But I do. You have an honest nature, Ellida. You have a loyal soul –

ELLIDA: Yes. I have.

WANGEL: Any relationship in which you could feel safe and happy, has to be whole and complete.

ELLIDA [*looks tensely at him*]: Well – and so?

WANGEL: You're not made to be a man's second wife.

ELLIDA: What makes you think *that* now?

WANGEL: I've often had a vague notion of it. Today it was made very clear to me. The children's memorial party –. You saw me as a sort of accomplice –. But of course – a man's

memories can't just be wiped out. Not mine at least. That's
not how I am.

ELLIDA: I know that. Oh, I know it very well.

WANGEL: But you're wrong all the same. To you it must seem
as though the children's mother was still alive. As if she was
invisibly present amongst us. You think that my mind is split
equally between you and her. That's the thought that upsets
you. You see something almost unseemly in our relationship. And that's why you no longer can – or want to live with
me as my wife.

ELLIDA [gets up]: You've seen all this, Wangel? Seen into all
this?

WANGEL: Yes, today I've finally seen into the depths of it. To
the very bottom.

ELLIDA: To the very bottom, you say. Don't you believe it.

WANGEL [gets up]: I know very well that there's still more to
all this, dearest Ellida.

ELLIDA [fearful]: You know there's more?

WANGEL: Yes. I know that the surroundings here are too much
for you to bear. The mountains weigh heavy upon your
mind. There's not enough light for you here. Not a wide
enough sky around you. Not enough strength and fullness in
the breeze.

ELLIDA: You're perfectly right. Night and day, summer and
winter it's there – this alluring pull homeward to the sea.

WANGEL: And I know it, I do, dear Ellida. [Puts his hand on
her head] And that's why this poor ailing child will be
allowed back home to what is hers.

ELLIDA: What do you mean?

WANGEL: It's quite straightforward. We're moving.

ELLIDA: Moving!

WANGEL: Yes. Out somewhere by the open sea – some place
where you can find a proper home to your own liking.

ELLIDA: Oh, dearest, don't even think about it! It's quite
impossible. You can't live happily anywhere in the world but
here.

WANGEL: We'll just have to wait and see. And besides – do you
think I could be happy here – without you?

ELLIDA: But I *am* here. And I'm going to stay here. You already have me.

WANGEL: Do I have you, Ellida?

ELLIDA: Oh, don't talk about that again. You have everything that you live and breathe for here. Your whole life's purpose is right here.

WANGEL: We'll just have to wait and see, I said. We're moving from here. Moving out there somewhere. The matter is settled, dear Ellida.

ELLIDA: But what do you think we'd stand to win by doing *that*?

WANGEL: You would win back your health and peace of mind.

ELLIDA: That's doubtful. But what about yourself! Think about yourself too. What do you stand to win?

WANGEL: I would win you, my dearest.

ELLIDA: But you can't! No, no, you can't, Wangel! That's what's so terrible – such agony to think about.

WANGEL: It'll have to be put to the test. If you're going around here with thoughts like that, there really is no other salvation for you – than to get away from here. The sooner the better. That's decided, you hear?

ELLIDA: No! Then, by God, I'd better tell you everything. Exactly as it is.

WANGEL: Yes, yes – do!

ELLIDA: You're not going to make yourself unhappy for my sake. Particularly since it can't be of any help to us, anyway.

WANGEL: So I have your word that you will tell me everything – just as it is.

ELLIDA: I will tell you it as best I can. And as I think I know it to be. – Come and sit with me.

They sit down on the rocks.

WANGEL: Well, Ellida? Go on –?

ELLIDA: The day you came out there to ask me if I could and wanted to be yours – you spoke so openly and honestly to me about your first marriage. It had been so happy, you said.

WANGEL: As indeed it was.

ELLIDA: Yes, yes, I am sure it was, dearest. That's not why I'm mentioning it now. I just want to remind you that I too, for

my part, was honest with you. I told you with absolute cand-
our that I had once held someone else dear. And that it had
come to – to a kind of engagement between us.

WANGEL: Kind of –?

ELLIDA: Yes, something of the sort. Well, it lasted such a short
time. He went away. And later I ended it. I told you all this.

WANGEL: But my dear Ellida, why are you raking all this up
again? It wasn't really anything to do with me. And I've
never so much as asked you who he was either.

ELLIDA: No, you haven't. You're always so considerate to me.

WANGEL [*smiling*]: Oh, in this case –. I could more or less
guess his name for myself.

ELLIDA: His name!

WANGEL: There weren't too many possibilities out in Skjoldviken and thereabouts. Or, to be precise, there was really
only one –

ELLIDA: I presume you think it was – Arnholm.

WANGEL: Yes, wasn't it –?

ELLIDA: No.

WANGEL: It wasn't? Well, then I have to admit my mind is a
complete blank.

ELLIDA: Can you remember when a large American ship came
into Skjoldviken late one autumn for repairs?

WANGEL: Yes, I remember it clearly. It was aboard that ship
that they found the captain murdered in his cabin one morning. I went out there myself and did a post-mortem on the
body.

ELLIDA: Yes, no doubt you did.

WANGEL: It was almost certainly the second mate who killed
him.

ELLIDA: Nobody can say that! It never came to court.

WANGEL: Even so, there can be little doubt about it. Why else
would he go off and drown himself the way he did?

ELLIDA: He didn't drown himself. He left on a northbound[25]
ship.

WANGEL [*surprised*]: How do you know that?

ELLIDA [*forces herself*]: Well, Wangel – the second mate was
the man I was – engaged to.

WANGEL [*leaping up*]: What are you saying? Can this be possible?!

ELLIDA: Yes – it is. He was the one.

WANGEL: But heavens above, Ellida –! How could you think of doing such a thing! To go and get engaged to someone like that! To a complete stranger! – What was his name?

ELLIDA: At the time he called himself Friman.[26] Later, in his letters, he signed himself Alfred Johnston.

WANGEL: And where was he from?

ELLIDA: From up in Finnmark, he said. In fact, he was born over in Finland. He probably emigrated[27] to Norway as a child – with his father, I think.

WANGEL: He's a Kven,[28] then?

ELLIDA: Yes, that's what they're called.

WANGEL: What else do you know about him?

ELLIDA: Only that he was very young when he went to sea. And that he'd gone on very long voyages.

WANGEL: Apart from that, nothing?

ELLIDA: No. We never talked much about it.

WANGEL: So what *did* you talk about?

ELLIDA: We talked about the sea mostly.

WANGEL: Ah –! About the sea of course.

ELLIDA: About stormy and calm waters. About dark nights on the sea. The sea on those sparkling sunny days. But most of all we spoke about the whales and dolphins, and the seals that like to bask on the skerries in the midday heat. And then we talked about the gulls and the eagles and all the other seabirds, you know. – Imagine – isn't it strange – when we talked about these things, it seemed to me that all the sea-beasts and sea-birds were his kin.[29]

WANGEL: And what about you –?

ELLIDA: Yes, I almost felt I became their kin too.

WANGEL: Right. And was that when you got engaged to him?

ELLIDA: Yes. He said I should.

WANGEL: Should? Had you no will of your own?

ELLIDA: Not when he was around. Oh – later it seemed quite incomprehensible to me.

WANGEL: Were you often with him?

ELLIDA: No, not very often. One day he came out to us to have a look around the lighthouse. That's how I got to know him. And after that we met once in a while. But then this business with the captain happened. And then, of course, he had to leave.

WANGEL: Well, yes, tell me a bit more about that!

ELLIDA: It was daybreak – I received a note from him. And it said I was to come out to him on Bratthammeren – you know the headland between the lighthouse and Skjoldviken.

WANGEL: Yes, of course – I know it well.

ELLIDA: I was to go there immediately, he wrote, because he wanted to talk to me.

WANGEL: And you went?

ELLIDA: Yes. I couldn't do otherwise. Anyway, then he told me that he'd stabbed the captain that same night.

WANGEL: So he said it himself! Said it straight out!

ELLIDA: Yes. But he'd only done what was right and proper, he said.

WANGEL: Right and proper? So why did he stab him?

ELLIDA: He refused to tell me. He said it wasn't fit for me to hear.

WANGEL: And you just took his word for it?

ELLIDA: Yes, it didn't occur to me to do otherwise. And he had to leave anyway. But as he was about to say goodbye –. Well, you wouldn't believe what he came up with.

WANGEL: Well? So tell me, then!

ELLIDA: He took a keychain out of his pocket and then from his finger he pulled a ring he used to wear. From me he took a little ring that I had. He put these two rings together on the keychain. And then he said that the two of us were now wedded to the sea.

WANGEL: Wedded –?

ELLIDA: Yes, that's what he said. And with that he threw the keychain and the rings with all his strength as far as he could, out into the deep.

WANGEL: And you, Ellida? You went along with this?

ELLIDA: Yes, imagine – at the time I felt as though it was meant to be. – But then, thank God – he left!

WANGEL: And when he was gone –?

ELLIDA: Oh, as you can imagine, I soon came to my senses. And began to realize how utterly misguided and meaningless the whole thing had been.

WANGEL: But you mentioned some letters earlier. So you've presumably heard from him since?

ELLIDA: Yes, I heard from him. First I got a few short lines from Archangel. He just wrote that he was going over to America. And then gave me details of where I could send a reply.

WANGEL: And did you?

ELLIDA: Immediately. Naturally I wrote that things had to be over between us. And that he shouldn't think about me any more, just as I would never think about him again.

WANGEL: But he wrote back anyway?

ELLIDA: Yes, he wrote back.

WANGEL: And what was his reply to what you'd told him?

ELLIDA: Not one word about it. It was as if I hadn't broken it off with him at all. He wrote quite calmly and deliberately saying I should wait for him. As soon as he was ready for me, he would let me know. And then I was to come to him immediately.

WANGEL: So, he wouldn't let you go?

ELLIDA: No. So I wrote again. With almost the same wording as the first time. Or even stronger.

WANGEL: And did he give up then?

ELLIDA: Oh no, don't even think it. He wrote back as calmly as before. Not a word about my having broken it off with him. So I realized, of course, it was useless. Which is why I never wrote to him again.

WANGEL: And didn't hear from him either?

ELLIDA: Oh yes, I've had three letters from him since. Once he wrote to me from California, and another time from China. The last letter I got from him was from Australia. He wrote that he was going to work in the goldmines.[30] But since then I haven't heard a word from him.

WANGEL: That man has had an extraordinary power over you, Ellida.

ELLIDA: Yes, yes. That terrible man!

WANGEL: But you mustn't think about it any more. Never! Please promise me that, my dearest, most beloved Ellida! We shall try another cure for you now. Fresher air than you find here in the fjords. The bracing, salt-laden air of the open seas! Hm? What do you say to that?

ELLIDA: Please, don't talk about it! Don't even think about it! That won't help me. I feel it so strongly – I won't be able to throw it off even out there.

WANGEL: Throw what off? My dearest – what do you mean?

ELLIDA: I mean the horror. This incomprehensible power over my mind –

WANGEL: But you *have* thrown it off. Long ago. When you broke it off with him. It was over long ago.

ELLIDA [*leaps up*]: No, that's precisely what it isn't.

WANGEL: Not over?

ELLIDA: No, Wangel – it is not over! And I'm scared it never will be over. Not in this life!

WANGEL [*his voice choked up*]: Are you saying then, that deep down you have never been able to forget this stranger?

ELLIDA: I had forgotten him. But then it was suddenly as though he came back.

WANGEL: How long ago was that?

ELLIDA: About three years ago now. Or a bit longer. – It was when I was expecting our child.

WANGEL: Ah! So it was then? Oh, Ellida – so much, so many things are starting to make sense to me.

ELLIDA: You're wrong, my dearest! This thing that's come over me –. Oh, I don't think it's ever possible to make sense of it.

WANGEL [*looks at her with a pained expression*]: To think – for three whole years you've felt love for another man. For someone else! Not for me – but for someone else!

ELLIDA: Oh, you're quite wrong. I don't feel love for anyone but you.

WANGEL [*subdued*]: Why is it then that you haven't, in all this time, wanted to live with me as my wife?

ELLIDA: It's the terror that springs from this stranger.

WANGEL: Terror –?

ELLIDA: Yes, terror. A terror so horrendous that I think only
the sea can hold it. Let me tell you now, Wangel –
*The young people from the town are coming back from the
left, they greet* ELLIDA *and* WANGEL *and go out to the
right. With them come* ARNHOLM, BOLETTE, HILDE *and*
LYNGSTRAND.

BOLETTE [*as they pass*]: Oh, are you still wandering about up
here?

ELLIDA: Yes, it's so nice and cool high up.

ARNHOLM: Well, *we're* all going down to dance.

WANGEL: Excellent, excellent. We'll soon be down too.

HILDE: Bye for now, then.

ELLIDA: Mr Lyngstrand – wait a moment.
LYNGSTRAND *stops.* ARNHOLM, BOLETTE *and* HILDE
go out to the right.

ELLIDA [*to* LYNGSTRAND]: Are you going to dance too?

LYNGSTRAND: No, Mrs Wangel, I don't think I dare.

ELLIDA: No, it's best you be careful. That thing with your
chest –. You haven't quite beaten it yet, have you?

LYNGSTRAND: Not quite altogether, no.

ELLIDA [*with some hesitation*]: How long ago would it be
since you went on that voyage –?

LYNGSTRAND: When I got my crick?

ELLIDA: Yes, the voyage you talked about this morning.

LYNGSTRAND: Oh, it must be about –. Wait a minute. Yes, it
must be a good three years ago now.

ELLIDA: So, three years.

LYNGSTRAND: Or a bit more. We set sail from America in
February. And we were shipwrecked in March. It was the
equinoctial storms that we ran into.

ELLIDA [*looks at* WANGEL]: So it was around the time –.

WANGEL: But my dear Ellida –?

ELLIDA: Well, don't let us hold you up, Mr Lyngstrand. Off
you go. But no dancing.

LYNGSTRAND: No, I'll just watch.
He goes out to the right.

WANGEL: Ellida, dear – why did you question him about that
voyage?

ELLIDA: Johnston was with him on board. I'm sure of it.

WANGEL: What brings you to that conclusion?

ELLIDA [*without answering*]: He found out on board that I'd got married to somebody else. While he was away. And it was then – at that precise moment that it came over me.

WANGEL: The terror?

ELLIDA: Yes. Without any warning, he can suddenly appear as large as life in front of me. Or rather a little to the side. He never looks *at* me. He's just there.

WANGEL: And what do you think he looks like?

ELLIDA: Exactly as when I saw him last.

WANGEL: Ten years ago?

ELLIDA: Yes. Out at Bratthammeren. What I see most clearly is his breast-pin with a big blue-white pearl in it. That pearl looks like a dead fish's eye. And it sort of stares at me.

WANGEL: Lord above –! You're more ill than I thought. More ill than you realize yourself, Ellida.

ELLIDA: Yes, yes – help me if you can! Because I feel it closing in on me, more and more.

WANGEL: And you've been going around in this state for three whole years. Carrying these secret torments without confiding in me.

ELLIDA: But I couldn't! Not before now, when it became necessary – for your sake. If I'd confided in you about all this – I'd have had to confide in you about – the unspeakable.

WANGEL: Unspeakable –?

ELLIDA [*warding him off*]: No, no, no! Don't ask! Just one last thing. Then no more. – Wangel – how do we explain – the mystery of the child's eyes –?

WANGEL: My dearest, beloved Ellida, I assure you that it was only in your imagination. The child had exactly the same eyes as other normal children.

ELLIDA: No, he did not! How could you possibly not see that? The child's eyes changed colour with the sea. If the fjord lay in sunlit calm, its eyes followed suit. In stormy weather too. – Oh, I'm sure I saw it, I know I did, even if you did not see it.

WANGEL [*yielding*]: Hmm – very well. But even if that were true? What then?

ELLIDA [*quietly, closer*]: I've seen eyes like that before.

WANGEL: When? And where –?

ELLIDA: Out on Bratthammeren. Ten years ago.

WANGEL [*steps back*]: What's that supposed to –?

ELLIDA [*whispers, trembling*]: The child had the eyes of the stranger.

WANGEL [*cries out involuntarily*]: Ellida –!

ELLIDA [*clasps her hands in lamentation above her head*]: Now surely you must understand why I never again *want* – never again *dare* to live with you as your wife!

> *She turns swiftly and runs away down the slopes to the right.*

WANGEL [*hurries after her shouting*]: Ellida – Ellida! My poor, unhappy Ellida!

ACT THREE

A secluded part of Dr Wangel's garden. The area is damp, marshy and overshadowed by large old trees. To the right, the edge of a pond can be seen, its surface slightly murky. A low, trellised fence separates the garden from the footpath and the fjord in the background. In the far distance mountain ranges and peaks beyond the fjord. It is late afternoon, almost evening.

BOLETTE *sits sewing on a stone bench to the left. On the bench lie a couple of books and a sewing basket.* HILDE *and* LYNGSTRAND, *both carrying fishing equipment, walk along the edge of the pond.*

HILDE [*makes a sign to* LYNGSTRAND]: Don't move! I can see a big one there.

LYNGSTRAND [*peering into the pond*]: Where?

HILDE [*pointing*]: Can't you see – down there. And look! Crikey, there's another one! [*Looks out through the trees*] Argh – now he's coming to scare them away from us!

BOLETTE [*looks up*]: Who's coming?

HILDE: Your schoolmaster, silly!

BOLETTE: Mine –?

HILDE: Well, he's never flipping well been mine.

    MR ARNHOLM *comes out through the trees to the right.*

ARNHOLM: Are there any fish in the pond these days?

HILDE: Yes, there are some very old carp here.

ARNHOLM: Oh, so the old carp are still alive?

HILDE: Yes. They're so tough. But we'll make sure to catch 'em now.

ARNHOLM: You might do better to try out in the fjord.

LYNGSTRAND: No, the pond is – it's somehow more mysterious.

HILDE: Yes, it's more exciting here. – Were you in the sea just now?

ARNHOLM: That's right. I've just come from the bathing-hut.

HILDE: I suppose you stayed in the enclosure then?

ARNHOLM: Yes. I'm no great swimmer.

HILDE: Can you swim on your back?

ARNHOLM: No.

HILDE: I can. [*To* LYNGSTRAND] Let's try over there on the other side.

They walk alongside the pond and exit to the right.

ARNHOLM [*moves closer to* BOLETTE]: Are you sitting here all alone, Bolette?

BOLETTE: Oh, yes. I generally do.

ARNHOLM: Isn't your mother down here in the garden?

BOLETTE: No. I think she's out walking with Father.

ARNHOLM: How is she this afternoon?

BOLETTE: I don't know exactly. I forgot to ask.

ARNHOLM: What sort of books have you got there?

BOLETTE: Oh, one of them is about botany. And the other's a geography book.

ARNHOLM: Is that your preferred kind of reading?

BOLETTE: Yes. When I can find the time –. Though, of course, I have to take care of the housekeeping first and foremost.

ARNHOLM: But doesn't your mother – your stepmother – doesn't she help you with that?

BOLETTE: No, it falls to me. I had to do it for the two years when Father was alone. And it's been that way ever since.

ARNHOLM: But you've not lost your appetite for reading.

BOLETTE: No, I read whatever I can get hold of in the way of useful books. One wants to be a little informed about the world. After all, we're so completely cut off here from everything that's going on. Well nearly, at least.

ARNHOLM: But, Bolette dear, you can't quite say that.

BOLETTE: Yes, we are. I don't think we live such very different lives from the carp in the pond down there. They've got the fjord so close, where great shoals of wild fish stream in and

out. But these poor domestic garden fish know nothing of
that. And they'll never get to join the others.

ARNHOLM: I don't think it would agree with them too well if
they were to get out.

BOLETTE: Oh, that's neither here nor there, if you ask me.

ARNHOLM: Besides, you can't really say it's completely cut off
from life here. Not in the summer anyway. I'd say this is
something of a meeting place for the world these days.
Almost a hub – in passing at least.

BOLETTE [*smiling*]: Oh yes, when you're just passing through
here yourself, it's easy for you to make fun of us.

ARNHOLM: Am I making fun –? Why would you think that?

BOLETTE: Because all this about a meeting place and a hub of
the world is just something you've heard people say in town.
They're always saying stuff like that.

ARNHOLM: Yes, if I'm honest, I have noticed.

BOLETTE: But there's not a word of truth in it really. Not for
those of us who live here all the time. What use is it to us if
the great world of outsiders passes through here on its way
up to watch the midnight sun? We don't get to join in. We
don't get to see the midnight sun. No, we just have to make
do with living life here in our carp pond.

ARNHOLM [*sits down beside her*]: Tell me this, my dear Bolette –
isn't there perhaps something, I wonder – something in
particular, I mean, that you sit here at home – longing for?

BOLETTE: Oh yes, there is indeed.

ARNHOLM: And what exactly is that? What is it you long for?

BOLETTE: Mostly, to get out of here.

ARNHOLM: That, more than anything else?

BOLETTE: Yes. And then to learn more. To get in-depth knowledge about everything.

ARNHOLM: When I was tutoring you, your father often said
you'd be allowed to study.[31]

BOLETTE: Yes, poor Father – he says so much. But when it
comes to it –. There's no real drive in Father.

ARNHOLM: No, sadly, you're right there. There isn't. But have
you ever talked to him about this? Seriously and with real
intent?

BOLETTE: No, I haven't really.

ARNHOLM: Well, you know what, you certainly should. Before it's too late, Bolette. Why don't you?

BOLETTE: Oh, I expect that's because there's no real drive in me either. No doubt that's something I've got from Father.

ARNHOLM: Hmm – aren't you perhaps doing yourself an injustice there?

BOLETTE: No, I don't think so. And Father has so little time to think about me or my future. Nor much desire to. He tends to push anything like that away from him, whenever possible. Because he is so taken up with Ellida.

ARNHOLM: With whom –? How –?

BOLETTE: I mean that he and my stepmother –. [*Breaks off*] Father and Mother have their own thing, you understand.

ARNHOLM: Well then, so much the better if you managed to get away from here.

BOLETTE: Yes, but I don't feel I have the right to that either. Not to abandon Father.

ARNHOLM: But, Bolette my dear, you'll be forced to it some day anyway. So I think the sooner you do –

BOLETTE: Yes, there's probably nothing else for it. I have to think about myself too. Try to get into some sort of employment[32] or other. When Father eventually passes away, I'll have nobody to hold on to. – But poor Father – I dread leaving him.

ARNHOLM: Dread –?

BOLETTE: Yes. For Father's own sake.

ARNHOLM: But, good Lord, what about your stepmother? She'll be here with him.

BOLETTE: Yes, of course. But she's not the least equipped for all the things Mother had such a firm hold on. There's so much this one doesn't *see*. Or perhaps doesn't *want* to – or *can't be bothered* to see. I don't know which.

ARNHOLM: Hm – I think perhaps I understand what you're saying.

BOLETTE: Poor Father – he has certain weaknesses. You may have noticed that yourself. Nor does he have enough work to fill his time. And then the fact that she's so totally incapable of giving him any support. – Although he has to take some blame for that himself.

ARNHOLM: Why is that, do you think?

BOLETTE: Oh, Father always wants to see happy faces around him. The house must always be filled with light and joy, he says. So I'm afraid he often lets her have medicines which do her no good at all in the long term.

ARNHOLM: You really believe that.

BOLETTE: Yes, I can't avoid thinking it. She's so strange at times. [*Vehemently*] But then isn't it unjust that I have to stay around here at home! It's not really any help whatsoever to Father. And I do have a duty to myself too, I think.

ARNHOLM: You know what, Bolette – you and I will talk about these things at more length.

BOLETTE: Oh, I doubt there's much point. I think I'm probably destined to stay here in the carp pond.

ARNHOLM: Not at all. That depends entirely on yourself.

BOLETTE [*animated*]: You think so?

ARNHOLM: Yes, trust me. It is completely and utterly in your own hands.

BOLETTE: Oh, I wish that were true –! Will you perhaps put in a good word for me with Father?

ARNHOLM: That too. But more importantly I want to talk open-heartedly and frankly with you, Bolette. [*Looks out to the left*] Shh! Don't let them see anything. We'll return to this later.

ELLIDA *comes from the left. She has no hat*[33] *on, only a large shawl over her head and shoulders.*

ELLIDA [*with restless animation*]: It's so nice here! It's lovely here!

ARNHOLM [*gets up*]: Have you been out for a stroll?

ELLIDA: Yes, a long, long, delightful walk on the hills with Wangel. And now we're going out sailing.

BOLETTE: Won't you sit down?

ELLIDA: No thanks. No, no sitting down.

BOLETTE [*moves along the bench*]: Because there's plenty of room.

ELLIDA [*walking around*]: No, no. No sitting. No sitting.

ARNHOLM: The walk seems to have agreed with you. You look quite exhilarated.

ELLIDA: Oh, I feel incredibly well! I feel inexpressibly happy! So safe! So safe –. [*Looks out to the left*] What's that big steamship coming in over there?

BOLETTE [*gets up and looks out*]: It must be that big English one.

ARNHOLM: It's coming alongside by the mooring buoy. Does it usually stop here?

BOLETTE: Only for half an hour. It'll travel further up into the fjord.

ELLIDA: And then out again – tomorrow. Out onto the great open sea. Right across the ocean. Imagine – being able to go with it. Oh, if only one could! If only!

ARNHOLM: Have you never been out on a proper sea voyage, Mrs Wangel?

ELLIDA: No, never. Only those little excursions up into the fjords here.

BOLETTE [*with a sigh*]: No, we shall probably have to make do with dry land.

ARNHOLM: Well, that is where we belong after all.

ELLIDA: No, I don't believe we do.

ARNHOLM: Not on dry land?

ELLIDA: No, I don't believe that. I believe that if human beings, from the very beginning, had accustomed themselves to a life at sea – in the sea[34] perhaps – then we'd have been rather more highly developed than we are. Both better and happier.

ARNHOLM: Do you really believe that?

ELLIDA: Yes, I can't help wondering if perhaps we wouldn't. I've often talked about it with Wangel –

ARNHOLM: Really, and he –?

ELLIDA: Well, he thinks there might be something in it.

ARNHOLM [*joking*]: Well, who knows. But what's done is done. We took the wrong path once and for all when we became land-creatures instead of sea-creatures. All things considered I think it's too late to rectify our error.

ELLIDA: Yes, that's the sad truth of it. And I think people suspect as much themselves. And they carry this with them like

STRANGER [*unaffected, not answering her*]: I would have liked to come to you sooner. But I couldn't. Now, I was finally able. And so, here you have me, Ellida.

ELLIDA: What do you want from me? What are you thinking of? What have you come here for?

STRANGER: You know very well that I've come to fetch you.

ELLIDA [*draws back in fear*]: Fetch me? Is *that* what you're thinking of?

STRANGER: Yes, of course.

ELLIDA: But surely you must know that I am married!

STRANGER: Yes, I know that.

ELLIDA: And yet –! Yet you come here to – to – fetch me!

STRANGER: Yes indeed, I do.

ELLIDA [*clasps her head with both hands*]: Oh this terrible –! Oh, this horror – this horror –!

STRANGER: Perhaps you don't want to?

ELLIDA [*bewildered*]: Don't look at me like that!

STRANGER: I'm asking whether you want to.

ELLIDA: No, no, no! I don't want to! Never in all eternity! I don't want to, I say! I can't and I don't want to! [*More softly*] Neither do I dare.

STRANGER [*climbs across the fence and comes into the garden*]: Well, well, Ellida – then let me tell you just one thing before I leave.

ELLIDA [*wants to run away, but can't. She is paralysed with fear and has to support herself against the trunk of a tree by the pond*]: Don't touch me! Don't come near me! No closer! Don't touch me, I say!

STRANGER [*warily, taking a few steps towards her*]: You mustn't be so frightened of me, Ellida.

ELLIDA [*throws her hands in front of her eyes*]: Don't look at me like that!

STRANGER: Just not frightened. Not frightened.

　　　DR WANGEL *comes through the garden from the left.*

WANGEL [*still in among the trees*]: Well, I suppose you've been waiting a very long time for me.

ELLIDA [*rushes to him, clings tightly to his arm and shouts*]: Oh, Wangel – save me! Save me – if you can!

WANGEL: Ellida – what in God's name –!

ELLIDA: Save me, Wangel! Can't you see him? He's standing over there!

WANGEL [*looks in the direction she is pointing*]: That man *there*? [*Goes closer*] May I ask: who *are* you? And why are you here in my garden?

STRANGER [*nods in the direction of* ELLIDA]: I want to speak to *her*.

WANGEL: I see. So then it was you –? [*To* ELLIDA] I heard there was a stranger hereabouts[38] asking for you.

STRANGER: Yes, that was me.

WANGEL: And what do you want with my wife? [*Turns*] Do you know him, Ellida?

ELLIDA [*quietly, wringing her hands*]: Do I know him? Yes, yes!

WANGEL [*quickly*]: Right!

ELLIDA: Oh, it's *him*, Wangel! It's him! The one who –!

WANGEL: What! What are you saying! [*Turns*] Are you the Johnston who once –?

STRANGER: Well – you can call me Johnston. It's all the same to me. Although that isn't my name.

WANGEL: It isn't?

STRANGER: Not any longer, no.

WANGEL: And what might you want with my wife? Because you do know, of course, that the lighthouse-keeper's daughter was married long ago. And *who* she married, you must know that too.

STRANGER: Yes, I've known that for more than three years.

ELLIDA [*tense*]: How did you find out?

STRANGER: I was on my way home to you. And I came across an old newspaper. A newspaper from these parts. *That's* where I read about the wedding.

ELLIDA [*staring into space*]: The wedding. – So *that* was what –

STRANGER: It seemed strange to me. Because what we did with those rings – that was a wedding too, Ellida.

ELLIDA [*hides her face in her hands*]: Oh –!

WANGEL: How dare you –?

STRANGER: Had you forgotten it?

ELLIDA [*feels his gaze on her and bursts out*]: Don't stand there looking at me like that!

WANGEL [*places himself in front of him*]: You'll address yourself to me and not to her.[39] So, in short – given that you now know the situation – what in fact is your purpose here? Why do you come here looking for my wife?

STRANGER: I'd promised Ellida[40] to come to her as soon as I could.

WANGEL: Ellida –! Again!

STRANGER: And Ellida made a firm promise to wait for me until I came.

WANGEL: I hear that you call my wife by her first name. That sort of familiarity is not the custom around here.

STRANGER: I know that very well. But given that she belongs first and foremost to *me* –

WANGEL: To you! You persist in –!

ELLIDA [*moves behind* WANGEL]: Oh –! He will never let me go!

WANGEL: To you! Are you saying she belongs to you!

STRANGER: Has she told you anything about two rings? My ring and Ellida's?

WANGEL: Well, yes. What of it? She ended it afterwards. You received her letters. So you know that for yourself.

STRANGER: Both Ellida and I agreed that what we did with the rings had as much power and validity as any official wedding.

ELLIDA: But I don't want to, you hear me! I don't want anything to do with you ever again! Don't look at me like that! I don't want to, I tell you!

WANGEL: You must be deranged, if you think you can come here and base any claim on such a childish game.

STRANGER: That's true. Of course, I don't have any claim – not in *your* sense of the word.

WANGEL: So what are your intentions, then? You've surely not deluded yourself into thinking you can take her from me by force! Against her own will!

STRANGER: No. What good would that be? If Ellida wants to be with me, she must leave of her own free will.

ELLIDA [*startled and bursting out*]: Free will –!

WANGEL: And you can believe such a thing –!

ELLIDA [*to herself*]: Free will –!

WANGEL: You must be deranged. Go now! We'll have nothing more to do with you.

STRANGER [*looks at his watch*]: It's nearly time for me to get back on board. [*One step closer*] Well, well, Ellida – now I have fulfilled my duty. [*Coming still closer*] I have kept my word, as I promised.

ELLIDA [*begging him, retreating*]: Ah, don't touch me!

STRANGER: And now you must think it through until tomorrow night –

WANGEL: There is nothing to think through. Now, just get out!

STRANGER [*still to* ELLIDA]: I'm going further up into the fjord with the steamer now. But tomorrow night I'll come back. And then I'll look in on you. You must wait for me here in the garden. Because I would rather settle this matter with you alone, you understand.

ELLIDA [*quietly, trembling*]: Oh, do you hear that, Wangel!

WANGEL: Just stay calm. I think we'll know well enough how to prevent this visit.

STRANGER: So, farewell for now, Ellida. Tomorrow night, then.

ELLIDA [*imploring*]: No, no – don't come tomorrow night. Don't ever come again!

STRANGER: And if by then you are of a mind to follow me over the sea –

ELLIDA: Oh, please don't look at me like that!

STRANGER: I only mean that, if so, you must be ready to travel.

WANGEL: Go up into the house, Ellida.

ELLIDA: I can't. Oh help me! Save me, Wangel!

STRANGER: Because you need to consider this – if you don't travel with me tomorrow, then it's all over.

ELLIDA [*looks at him, trembling*]: Then it's all over? For good –?

STRANGER [*nods*]: It can never be reversed, Ellida. I will never come to this country again. You'll never see me again. Never hear from me either. Then I'll be dead and gone from you for good.

ELLIDA [*breathes anxiously*]: Oh –!

STRANGER: So think carefully about what you do. Farewell. [*Turns, climbs over the fence, stops and says*] Yes, Ellida – be ready to travel tomorrow night. Because I will come here to fetch you then.

    He walks slowly and calmly down the path and out to the right.

ELLIDA [*following him with her gaze for a moment*]: My own free will, he said! Imagine – he said I should travel with him of my own free will.

WANGEL: Just stay calm. He's gone now. And you will never see him again.

ELLIDA: Oh, how can you say that? He's coming back again tomorrow night.

WANGEL: Let him come. It most certainly won't be you he meets.

ELLIDA [*shakes her head*]: Oh, Wangel, don't go thinking you can stop him.

WANGEL: But I can, my dear – just put your trust in me.

ELLIDA [*lost in thought, not hearing him*]: When he's been here – tomorrow night –? And when he's travelled across the sea with the steamship –?

WANGEL: Yes, what then?

ELLIDA: I wonder, will he really never – never come back again?

WANGEL: He won't, dear Ellida, you can rest assured. What would he do here after this? He has heard it from your own lips now, that you want nothing to do with him. So the matter is closed.

ELLIDA [*to herself*]: Tomorrow then. Or never.

WANGEL: And if he ever considered coming back –

ELLIDA [*tense*]: Then what –?

WANGEL: It is in our power to render him harmless.

ELLIDA: Don't be so sure.

WANGEL: It is in our power, I tell you! If there's no other way to get him to leave you in peace, he'll be made to answer for the murder of the captain.

ELLIDA [*vehemently*]: No, no! Not that! We don't know anything about the murder of the captain! Absolutely nothing!

WANGEL: We don't? He confessed it to you himself!

ELLIDA: No, nothing about that! If you say anything, I'll deny it. Don't lock him up! He belongs out on the open sea! Out there, that's where he belongs.

WANGEL [*looks at her and says slowly*]: Oh, Ellida – Ellida!

ELLIDA [*clings to him passionately*]: Oh, my dearest – deliver me from that man!

WANGEL [*frees himself gently*]: Come! Come with me!

LYNGSTRAND *and* HILDE, *both carrying fishing equipment, appear from the right by the pond.*

LYNGSTRAND [*hurries towards* ELLIDA]: Oh, Mrs Wangel, there's something peculiar you must hear!

WANGEL: What is it?

LYNGSTRAND: Imagine – we've seen the American!

WANGEL: The American?

HILDE: Yes, I saw him too.

LYNGSTRAND: He went up behind the garden and then aboard the big English steamer.

WANGEL: Where do you know that man from?

LYNGSTRAND: I was on the seas with him once. I was so certain he'd drowned. But he's very much alive.

WANGEL: Do you know anything more about him?

LYNGSTRAND: No. But it seems he's come to take revenge on his faithless sailor-wife.

WANGEL: What are you saying?

HILDE: Lyngstrand wants to make an artwork out of him.

WANGEL: I don't understand a word –

ELLIDA: You'll hear about it all later.

ARNHOLM *and* BOLETTE *arrive from the left on the footpath beyond the garden fence.*

BOLETTE [*to the people in the garden*]: Come and look! The English steamship's going up the fjord.

A large steamship glides slowly past in the distance.

LYNGSTRAND [*to* HILDE, *by the fence*]: Tonight he is sure to come to haunt her.

HILDE [*nodding*]: To haunt the faithless sailor-wife – yes.

LYNGSTRAND: Imagine – round about midnight.

HILDE: I think it'll be so exciting.

ELLIDA [*follows the ship with her gaze*]: Tomorrow then –

WANGEL: And then never again.

ELLIDA [*quietly and trembling*]: Oh Wangel – save me from myself!

WANGEL [*looks at her anxiously*]: Ellida! I sense it – there's something behind all this.

ELLIDA: The pull – is behind it.

WANGEL: The pull –?

ELLIDA: That man is like the sea.

> *She walks slowly, deep in thought, through the garden and out to the left.*
>
> WANGEL *walks uneasily beside her, watching her closely.*

ACT FOUR

Dr Wangel's garden room. Doors to the right and left. In the background, between the two windows, a glass door is open onto the veranda. Below it, we can see part of the garden. A sofa with a table in front of it to the left. To the right a piano, and further back a large flower arrangement. In the middle of the room, a round table with chairs around it. On the table, a flowering rosebush surrounded by other pot plants. It is late morning.

Inside the room, next to the table on the left, BOLETTE *is sitting on the sofa busy with some embroidery.* LYNGSTRAND *is sitting on a chair at the top end of the table. Down in the garden* BALLESTED *is sitting painting.* HILDE *stands beside him, watching.*

LYNGSTRAND [*with his arms on the table, sitting for a while in silence, watching* BOLETTE *work*]: It must be awfully difficult to embroider a border like that, Miss Wangel.

BOLETTE: Oh no. It's not that difficult. So long as you make sure to count properly –

LYNGSTRAND: Count? Do you have to count as well?

BOLETTE: Yes, the stitches. Look.

LYNGSTRAND: Right, yes! Imagine that! It's almost a kind of art. Can you draw too?

BOLETTE: Yes, when I have a template to go by.

LYNGSTRAND: Not otherwise?

BOLETTE: No, not otherwise.

LYNGSTRAND: So it isn't a real art, after all.

BOLETTE: No, it's more of a – a craft.

LYNGSTRAND: But I do believe you could *learn* to make art.

BOLETTE: When I don't have any talent?

LYNGSTRAND: Even then. If you could be with a real genuine artist all the time.

BOLETTE: You believe I could learn from him?

LYNGSTRAND: Not exactly learn in the ordinary way. But I do believe it might come to you bit by bit. Almost as if by some sort of miracle, Miss Wangel.

BOLETTE: How very odd.

LYNGSTRAND [*after a pause*]: Have you given much thought to –? I mean – have you ever thought deeply and seriously about marriage, Miss Wangel?

BOLETTE [*flashes a glance at him*]: About –? No.

LYNGSTRAND: I have.

BOLETTE: Really? Have you now.

LYNGSTRAND: Oh yes – I think about such things very often. Mostly about marriage. And I've read about it in various books, too. I believe marriage can be regarded as a kind of miracle. The way a woman is transformed and gradually shifts over to her husband to become like him.

BOLETTE: Taking on his interests, you mean?

LYNGSTRAND: Precisely, yes!

BOLETTE: I see, but his abilities? And his talents and skills?

LYNGSTRAND: Hm, yes – I do wonder if those don't also –

BOLETTE: But then perhaps you also believe that whatever a man has learned from reading – or his own reasoning – *that* could also somehow be transferred to his wife?

LYNGSTRAND: That too, yes. Bit by bit. As though by a miracle. But I know, of course, this can only happen in a marriage that is faithful and loving and really happy.

BOLETTE: Has it never occurred to you that a man might equally well be pulled towards his wife? Become like her, I mean.

LYNGSTRAND: A man? No, I've not thought that.

BOLETTE: But why not one as well as the other?

LYNGSTRAND: No, because a man has a vocation[41] to live for. And *that* is what makes a man so strong and steadfast, Miss Wangel. He has a vocation in his life, you see.

BOLETTE: Every man?

LYNGSTRAND: Well, no. I am thinking more of the artist.

BOLETTE: Do you think it's right for an artist to go off and get married?

LYNGSTRAND: Yes, I do indeed. If he can find someone he has real feelings for –

BOLETTE: Even so. I think he'd do better to live for his art alone.

LYNGSTRAND: And so he should. But he can do that just as well if he gets married.

BOLETTE: All right, but what about her?

LYNGSTRAND: Her? What do you mean –?

BOLETTE: The woman he marries. What should she live for?

LYNGSTRAND: She should live for his art too. My feeling is that a woman ought to feel deeply happy with *that*.

BOLETTE: Hm – I'm not so sure –

LYNGSTRAND: Oh yes, Miss Wangel, believe me. It's not just the honour and respect that she enjoys on his account –. To me that's almost the least important thing. But the fact that she can help him to create – that she can ease his workload by being near him and being a comfort to him and looking after him, making his life truly pleasurable. I think that would be quite delightful for a woman.

BOLETTE: Oh, you have no idea how selfish you are!

LYNGSTRAND: Am *I* selfish?! Great heavens –! Oh, if only you knew me a bit better – [*Leans closer in to her*] Miss Wangel – when I am gone – and I shall be soon –

BOLETTE [*looks at him with sympathy*]: Now, now, you're not to start believing anything so sad.

LYNGSTRAND: I don't think it's really that sad.

BOLETTE: How do you mean?

LYNGSTRAND: Well, in a month I'll be leaving on my travels. First from here. And then I'll be heading down to the south of Europe.[42]

BOLETTE: Oh, in that way! I see.

LYNGSTRAND: Would you think about me once in a while, Miss Wangel?

BOLETTE: Yes, I'd be glad to.

LYNGSTRAND [*happy*]: No, you must promise me!

BOLETTE: Yes, I promise you.

LYNGSTRAND: By all that is most sacred, Miss Bolette?

BOLETTE: By all that is most sacred. [*Her mood changes*] Oh, but what's the point of all this? It doesn't lead anywhere at all.

LYNGSTRAND: How can you say that! It would be delightful for me to know that you were going around here at home thinking about me.

BOLETTE: Yes, but what then?

LYNGSTRAND: Well, I don't quite know what then –

BOLETTE: Nor I. There's such a lot standing in the way. Everything imaginable is in the way, if you ask me.

LYNGSTRAND: Oh, some miracle or other might happen. A happy intervention of providence – or something of the sort. I do believe I have luck on my side.

BOLETTE [*animatedly*]: Yes, indeed! You do believe that, surely?

LYNGSTRAND: Oh yes, I believe it absolutely. And then – in a few years – when I get back home as a celebrated sculptor, comfortably off and bursting with health –

BOLETTE: Yes, indeed. We very much hope you do.

LYNGSTRAND: You can be secure in that hope. As long as you think of me faithfully and warmly while I am away in the south. And I have your word on that now.

BOLETTE: You have. [*Shakes her head*] But it still doesn't lead anywhere.

LYNGSTRAND: Yes, Miss Bolette, it will at least lead to my working much more easily and speedily on my artwork.

BOLETTE: You truly believe that?

LYNGSTRAND: Yes, I feel it within me. And I can't help thinking it would be exhilarating for you too – here in this backwater – to know that you somehow helped me to create something.

BOLETTE [*looks at him*]: I see – but you, from your side?

LYNGSTRAND: Me –?

BOLETTE [*looks out into the garden*]: Ssh! Let's talk about something else. Here comes the schoolmaster.

MR ARNHOLM *is seen arriving down in the garden from the left.*

He stops and speaks to BALLESTED *and* HILDE.

LYNGSTRAND: Are you fond of your old tutor, Miss Bolette?

BOLETTE: Am I fond of him?

LYNGSTRAND: Yes, I mean, do you really like him?

BOLETTE: Yes, I do. He's very good to have as a friend and adviser. – And he's always so helpful, whenever he can be.

LYNGSTRAND: But isn't it odd that he's never got married?

BOLETTE: Do you think that's so odd?

LYNGSTRAND: Yes. Since he's a well-to-do man, they say.

BOLETTE: He probably is. But I don't suppose it's been that easy for him to find someone who'd want him.

LYNGSTRAND: Why not?

BOLETTE: Well, he's been a tutor to nearly all the young girls he knows. He says so himself.

LYNGSTRAND: Yes, what does *that* matter?

BOLETTE: But, good God, you don't marry a man who's been your tutor!

LYNGSTRAND: Don't you think a young girl could love her tutor?

BOLETTE: Not after she's properly grown up.

LYNGSTRAND: Well, I never!

BOLETTE [*warning*]: Hush – hush!

Meanwhile BALLESTED *has been gathering his things together and now carries them out to the right of the garden.* HILDE *is helping him.* ARNHOLM *walks up onto the veranda and comes into the garden room.*

ARNHOLM: Good morning, my dear Bolette. Good morning, Mr – Mr – hmm!

He looks displeased and nods coldly to LYNGSTRAND, *who gets up and bows.*

BOLETTE [*gets up and goes to meet* ARNHOLM]: Good morning, Mr Arnholm.

ARNHOLM: How are things here today?

BOLETTE: Fine, thank you.

ARNHOLM: Is your stepmother out bathing today again?

BOLETTE: No, she's up in her room.

ARNHOLM: Not feeling too bright?

BOLETTE: I don't know. She's locked herself in.

ARNHOLM: Hmm – has she now?

LYNGSTRAND: I think Mrs Wangel got rather agitated about that American yesterday.

ARNHOLM: What do *you* know about that?

LYNGSTRAND: I told her I'd seen him alive and walking about behind the garden.

ARNHOLM: Oh, I see.

BOLETTE [*to* ARNHOLM]: You and Father must have sat up late last night.

ARNHOLM: Yes, rather late. We got talking about something very serious.

BOLETTE: Did you manage to talk to him a little about me too?

ARNHOLM: No, my dear Bolette. I didn't get that far. He was so preoccupied with something else.

BOLETTE [*sighing*]: Yes, well – he always is.

ARNHOLM [*looks at her meaningfully*]: But later today you and I will talk further about these matters. – Where is your father now? Not home, maybe?

BOLETTE: Yes, he is. He must be down in the office. I'll go and fetch him.

ARNHOLM: No thanks. Don't do that. I'd prefer to go down to him.

BOLETTE [*listening out to the left*]: Wait a minute, Mr Arnholm. I think that's Father coming down the stairs. Yes. He must have gone up there to look in on her.

WANGEL *comes in through the door on the left.*

WANGEL [*extends his hand to* ARNHOLM]: Well, my dear friend, are you here already? It was kind of you to come so early. I'd like to talk further with you.

BOLETTE [*to* LYNGSTRAND]: Shall we join Hilde down in the garden for a while?

LYNGSTRAND: Yes, with pleasure, Miss Wangel.

He and BOLETTE *go down into the garden and out through the trees in the background.*

ARNHOLM [*who has followed them with his gaze, turns to* WANGEL]: Do you know much about that young man?

WANGEL: No, nothing at all.

ARNHOLM: Do you approve of him hanging around with the girls so much?

WANGEL: Does he? I hadn't really noticed.

ARNHOLM: You really should keep an eye on these things, you know.

WANGEL: Yes, you're probably right. But, good Lord, what's a poor man to do? The girls have got so used to looking after themselves. They refuse to be told anything, either by me or by Ellida.

ARNHOLM: Not her either?

WANGEL: No. Besides I can hardly expect her to get involved in that kind of thing. It's not her strong point. [*Breaking off*] But *that* wasn't what we were going to discuss. Tell me – have you had any more thoughts about the matter? About everything I told you?

ARNHOLM: I've thought of nothing else since we parted last night.

WANGEL: And what do you think ought to be done?

ARNHOLM: My dear Wangel, I think as a doctor you must know better than I.

WANGEL: Oh, if you only knew how difficult it is for a doctor to make sound judgements about a patient for whom he has such deep feelings! And then, of course, this isn't any ordinary illness. No ordinary doctor can help here – and no ordinary medicine.

ARNHOLM: How is she today?

WANGEL: I was up with her just now, and she appeared to be quite calm. But behind all her moods there's something hidden, that I can't get any proper hold on. And she's so erratic of course – so unpredictable – she can change so suddenly.

ARNHOLM: That's presumably a result of her frail state of mind.

WANGEL: It isn't just that. At its deepest level it's innate in her. Ellida belongs to the sea-people. That's the thing.

ARNHOLM: What do you mean by that, doctor?

WANGEL: Have you never noticed that the people out there by the open sea are a kind of race unto themselves? It's almost as if they lived the life of the ocean itself. There's a singing of waves – and an ebb and flow too – both in their thinking and in their sensibilities. And they can never be transplanted.

Oh, I should have considered *that* before. It was an absolute sin against Ellida to take her from out there and move her in here!

ARNHOLM: Have you come to that opinion now?

WANGEL: Increasingly, yes. But I should have said all this to myself beforehand. Oh, deep down I knew it, of course. But I didn't want to admit it. Because I was so in love with her, you see! So I thought first and foremost about myself. That is how irresponsibly selfish I was back then.

ARNHOLM: Hm – no doubt every man is slightly selfish in these situations. Besides, I've never noticed such a fault in you, Dr Wangel.

WANGEL [*paces restlessly back and forth*]: Oh, but I was! And I have continued to be so ever since. I am so much, much older than her. I ought to have been like a father to her – and a guide. Ought to have done my best to develop her mind, bring clarity to her thinking. But unfortunately that's never happened. I've not really had the drive to do it, you see! Because I wanted her just as she was. But then things got worse and worse with her. And I really didn't know what to do. [*More quietly*] That was why, in my anguish, I wrote to you and asked you to come and visit us.

ARNHOLM [*looks at him in surprise*]: What? Was that why you wrote to me?

WANGEL: Yes. But please forget about that.

ARNHOLM: But for heaven's sake, my dear Wangel – what good did you actually think I could do? I don't understand.

WANGEL: No, that's hardly surprising. Because I was on the wrong track. I believed Ellida's heart had been fixed on you once. That it was secretly still a little fixed on you. That it might perhaps do her good to able to see you again and get to talk to you about her home and about the old days.

ARNHOLM: So it was your wife you were referring to in your letter, when you said there was somebody here who was waiting – and perhaps longing for me!

WANGEL: Yes. Who else?

ARNHOLM [*quickly*]: No, of course, you're right. – But I didn't understand.

WANGEL: That's unsurprising, as I said. I was, of course, on the wrong track entirely.

ARNHOLM: And *you* say you are selfish?

WANGEL: Oh, but I had so much guilt to atone for. I didn't feel I could ignore any method, if it might perhaps ease her mind a little.

ARNHOLM: So how do you explain the power that this stranger wields over her?

WANGEL: Hmm, my dear friend – there may well be aspects of this case that don't *allow* for explanation.

ARNHOLM: Something that is in and of itself beyond explanation, you mean? Beyond all explanation?

WANGEL: Beyond explanation for now, at least.

ARNHOLM: Do you believe in such things?

WANGEL: I neither believe in them nor deny them. I simply don't know. So I leave it at that.

ARNHOLM: Yes, but tell me one thing now. Her strange and disturbing assertion that the child's eyes –?

WANGEL [*eagerly*]: The thing about the eyes – I don't believe that at all! I don't *want* to believe in such a thing. It must be a pure figment of the imagination on her part. Nothing else.

ARNHOLM: Did you notice the man's eyes when you saw him yesterday?

WANGEL: I did indeed.

ARNHOLM: And you found no kind of resemblance?

WANGEL [*evasively*]: Hmm – heavens above, what should I say? There wasn't much light, of course, when I saw him. Besides, Ellida had talked so much about the resemblance beforehand –. I simply don't know if I was in any state to see him objectively.

ARNHOLM: No, no, that's quite possible. But what about this other thing? That all this anxiety and restlessness came over her at precisely the time when this stranger appears to have been on his voyage home.

WANGEL: Well, you see – that's something else she must have invented and dreamed up over the last two days. It certainly didn't come over her as suddenly – all at once – as she now claims. But after she'd heard from this young Mr Lyngstrand that Johnston – or Friman – or whatever his name is – that he was making his way here three years ago – in March – she clearly believes now that this mental unrest gripped her in that self-same month.

ARNHOLM: But it didn't?

WANGEL: Absolutely not. There were clues and signs that pointed to it long before then. – Admittedly she had – coincidentally – a rather violent attack in that March three years ago –

ARNHOLM: So maybe –!

WANGEL: Yes, but *that* can be explained very simply by her condition – the situation – she found herself in at that time.

ARNHOLM: So, sign versus sign.

WANGEL [*wringing his hands*]: And then not to be able to help her! Not to see any way out! Not to see any remedy at all –!

ARNHOLM: What if you could decide perhaps to change location? Move elsewhere? So that she could live in an environment where she'd feel more at home?

WANGEL: Oh, my friend – don't you think I've offered her *that* too! I've suggested that we should move to Skjoldviken. But she won't.

ARNHOLM: Not even that?

WANGEL: No. Because she doesn't think any good would come of it. And she may well be right there, of course.

ARNHOLM: Hmm – really?

WANGEL: Yes. And besides – when I think about it more closely – I don't actually know how I could put it into action. I'm not really sure I can justify moving to such a remote place as far as the girls are concerned. After all, they need to live in a place where there's at least *some* prospect of their being provided for one day.

ARNHOLM: Provided for? So you're already thinking about *that*?

WANGEL: Good Lord, yes – I have to think about that too! But then again – on the other hand – consideration for my poor sick Ellida –! Oh my dear Arnholm – I really do stand – in many ways – between fire and water!

ARNHOLM: When it comes to Bolette perhaps you don't need to be so very worried – [*Breaks off*] I wonder where she's – where they've got to?

He goes to the open door and looks out.

WANGEL [*moving over to the piano*]: Oh, I'd gladly make any sacrifice it took – for all three of them. – If I just knew what.

ELLIDA *comes in through the door on the left.*

ELLIDA [*quickly to* WANGEL]: Please don't go out this morning!

WANGEL: No, no, of course. I'll stay at home with you. [*Gestures towards* ARNHOLM, *who comes closer*] But won't you say good morning to our friend?

ELLIDA [*turns*]: Oh, it's you, Mr Arnholm. [*Holds out her hand to him*] Good morning.

ARNHOLM: Good morning, Mrs Wangel. So, not taking your usual dip today?

ELLIDA: No, no! That's out of the question today. But perhaps you'd like to sit down for a bit?

ARNHOLM: Thanks awfully – but not now. [*Looks at* WANGEL] I promised the girls I'd join them down in the garden.

ELLIDA: Well, heaven knows whether you'll find them in the garden. I'm never too clear about their movements.

WANGEL: Oh yes, I'm pretty sure they're busy down by the pond.

ARNHOLM: Well, I'm sure I'll track them down.

He nods and crosses the veranda and goes out into the garden to the right.

ELLIDA: What time is it, Wangel?

WANGEL [*looks at his watch*]: It's a little after eleven.

ELLIDA: A little after. And at eleven o'clock – or towards midnight tonight, the steamship will come. Oh, if only this were over!

WANGEL [*comes closer to her*]: Ellida, dearest – there's something I'd like to ask you.

ELLIDA: What is it?

WANGEL: The night before last – up at 'The Outlook' – you said that in the last three years you'd often seen him before you, large as life.

ELLIDA: And so I have. You must believe me.

WANGEL: Right, but how did you see him?

ELLIDA: How did I see him?

WANGEL: I mean – how did he look to you, when you thought you saw him?

ELLIDA: But Wangel, dear – you know for yourself now what he looks like.

WANGEL: And he looked like that in your imagination?

ELLIDA: Yes, he did.

WANGEL: Exactly as you saw him yesterday evening in reality?

ELLIDA: Yes, exactly like that.

WANGEL: But then, how was it that you didn't recognize him straight away?

ELLIDA [*startled*]: Didn't I?

WANGEL: No. You said yourself afterwards that you had no idea who the stranger was at first.

ELLIDA [*struck*]: Yes, I believe you're right! Don't you think that's peculiar, Wangel? Imagine that – I didn't recognize him at once!

WANGEL: It was only by his eyes, you said –

ELLIDA: Oh yes – the eyes! The eyes!

WANGEL: Right – but up at 'The Outlook' you said that he always appeared to you, just as he was when you parted. Out there, ten years ago.

ELLIDA: Did I say that?

WANGEL: Yes.

ELLIDA: Then he must have looked almost the same then as now.

WANGEL: No. You gave a rather different description of him the day before yesterday, on the way home. Ten years ago he didn't have a beard, you said. He was quite differently dressed too. And the breast-pin with the pearl in it –? This man certainly didn't have one.

ELLIDA: No, he didn't.

WANGEL [*looks searchingly at her*]: Think about it a bit, my dear Ellida. Or – perhaps you can no longer remember what he looked like when he stood with you on Bratthammeren?

ELLIDA [*reflecting, closing her eyes for a few moments*]: Not very clearly. No – today I can't remember at all. Isn't that peculiar?

WANGEL: Not so peculiar actually. A new and real image stepped out before you. And now *that* overshadows the old one – so you can no longer see it.

ELLIDA: Do you think so, Wangel?

WANGEL: Yes. And it overshadows your sick imaginings too. So it's a good thing the reality came.

ELLIDA: Good! Are you saying it was good?

WANGEL: Yes. The fact that it came – that may perhaps be your cure.

ELLIDA [*sits down on the sofa*]: Wangel – come and sit here with me. I must tell you everything I am thinking.

WANGEL: Yes, do, my dearest Ellida.

He sits down on a chair on the other side of the table.

ELLIDA: The fact is, it was an utter disaster – for both of us – that you and I got together.

WANGEL [*startled*]: What are you saying?

ELLIDA: Yes. It was. And it makes absolute sense too. It couldn't be anything but a disaster. Not after the way you and I got together.

WANGEL: What was wrong with the way –?

ELLIDA: Listen, Wangel – there's no longer any point in us going around lying to ourselves – and to each other.

WANGEL: Is that what we're doing! We're lying, you say?

ELLIDA: Yes we are. Or – we're disguising the truth at least. Because the truth – the absolute, plain truth – is *this* – that you came out there – and bought me.

WANGEL: Bought –? – Did you say – bought!

ELLIDA: Oh, I wasn't one bit better than you. I agreed to the deal. I sold myself to you.

WANGEL [*looks at her full of pain*]: Ellida – do you really have the heart to call it that?

ELLIDA: But is there another name for it!? You couldn't bear the emptiness in your house any more. You were looking around for a new wife –

WANGEL: And for a new mother for the children, Ellida.

ELLIDA: That too, perhaps – along the way. Although – you had no idea whether I was up to the task. After all, you'd only seen me – and talked to me briefly a couple of times. You took a fancy to me, and so –

WANGEL: Oh yes, call it whatever you like.

ELLIDA: And I, for my part –. I just stood there helpless, clueless and completely alone. Of course, it seemed reasonable

for me to take the deal – when you came and offered to provide for me for the rest of my life.

WANGEL: I certainly did not see it just in terms of providing for
you, Ellida dear. I asked you honestly if you wanted to share
with myself and the children the little I could call my own.

ELLIDA: Yes, you did. But I should not have accepted it nonetheless. I should never have done so. Not at any price! Not
sold myself! Better to do the most menial work – better to
live in the poorest conditions – but of my own free will – and
of my own choice.

WANGEL [*gets up*]: So have the five or six years we've lived
together been utterly worthless to you?

ELLIDA: Oh, please don't think that, Wangel! My time with
you has been as good as anyone could wish. But I did not
walk into your home of my own free will. That is the point.

WANGEL [*looks at her*]: Not of your own – free will!

ELLIDA: No. It was not with a free will that I came with you.

WANGEL [*subdued*]: Ah – I remember – the phrase from
yesterday.

ELLIDA: Everything lies in that phrase. It has shed a light on
things for me. That's why I can see it now.

WANGEL: See what?

ELLIDA: I see that the life the two of us live with each other –
is not really a marriage.

WANGEL [*bitterly*]: That's true enough. The life we live *now* is
not a marriage.

ELLIDA: Nor was it before. Never. Not from the outset. [*She
looks into space*] The first – *that* could have been an absolute and true marriage.

WANGEL: The first? What first do you mean?

ELLIDA: Mine – with *him*.

WANGEL [*looks at her stunned*]: I really do not understand you!

ELLIDA: Oh, my dear Wangel – let's not lie to each other. Or
to ourselves.

WANGEL: Very well! So what now?

ELLIDA: Well, you see – we can never get away from the fact –
that a promise given of one's free will is just as binding as
any marriage ceremony.

WANGEL: But what on earth –!

ELLIDA [*gets up with forceful determination*]: Give me permission to leave you, Wangel!

WANGEL: Ellida –! Ellida –!

ELLIDA: Yes, yes – just give me permission to do it! Believe me – there is no other possible outcome anyway. Not after the way we came together.

WANGEL [*in controlled pain*]: So, it's come to this between us.

ELLIDA: It had to come to this. It couldn't be otherwise.

WANGEL [*looks sadly at her*]: So I've not even managed to win you through our life together. Never – never wholly possessed you.

ELLIDA: Oh, Wangel – if only I could feel for you as deeply as I wanted. And as you deserve! But I know for sure – it will never happen.

WANGEL: Divorce, then? It's a divorce – a formal, legal divorce – that you want?

ELLIDA: My dear, you understand me so little. It really isn't the form it takes that I care about. Because, for me, it doesn't depend on any outer things. What I want is that you and I should agree, of our own free will, to release each other.

WANGEL [*bitterly, nods slowly*]: Reverse the deal – I see.

ELLIDA [*lively*]: Exactly that! Reverse the deal!

WANGEL: And what then, Ellida? Afterwards? Have you thought how things will look for us both? How life will turn out for you and for me?

ELLIDA: That's neither here nor there. Afterwards it must take whatever shape it takes. What I'm asking and pleading with you for, Wangel – is the most important thing! Just set me free. Give me my absolute freedom again!

WANGEL: Ellida – this is a terrible demand you are making of me. At least give me time to collect myself and come to a decision. Let's talk it through properly with each other. And give yourself time too, to think over what you are doing!

ELLIDA: But there is no time now to waste on that! I need my freedom back today!

WANGEL: Why today?

ELLIDA: Because – it is tonight that he is coming.

WANGEL [*startled*]: Coming! Him! What has this stranger to do with this?

ELLIDA: I want to stand before him in complete freedom.

WANGEL: And then – what are you intending to do then?

ELLIDA: I don't want to hide behind the fact that I am another man's wife. I don't want to hide behind not having a choice. Then there would be no decision in it.

WANGEL: You're talking about choice! Choice, Ellida! Choice in this matter!

ELLIDA: Yes, I must have choice. A choice either way. To let him leave alone –. Or then again – to go with him.

WANGEL: Do you understand what you're saying? Go with him! Put your entire fate in his hands!

ELLIDA: Didn't I put my entire fate in *your* hands? And – without much thought.

WANGEL: That may be so. But him! Him! A complete stranger! A person you know so little about!

ELLIDA: Oh, but I knew *you* even less perhaps. And yet I still came with you.

WANGEL: At least back then you knew roughly what kind of life you were going to. But now? In this? Please consider! What do you know here? You know nothing at all. Not even who he is – or what he is.

ELLIDA [*looking straight in front of her*]: That's true. And *that* is the horror of it.

WANGEL: Yes, it is indeed horrifying –

ELLIDA: And that's why I feel that I *must* face this.

WANGEL [*looks at her*]: Because it seems to you a horror?

ELLIDA: Yes. That's precisely why.

WANGEL [*closer to her*]: Ellida, listen – what do you actually mean by the word 'horror'?

ELLIDA [*reflecting on it*]: The horror – it's the thing which both frightens and pulls me.

WANGEL: Pulls too?

ELLIDA: Mainly pulls – I think.

WANGEL [*slowly*]: You are kin with the sea.

ELLIDA: That too is the horror.

WANGEL: And the horror about *you* as well. You both frighten and pull.

ELLIDA: Do you think so, Wangel?

WANGEL: I have probably never really known you after all. Not in depth. I'm beginning to realize that now.

ELLIDA: That's why you must set me free! Release me from all bonds with you and yours! I am not the one you took me for. You can see that for yourself now. Now we can part with understanding – and free will.

WANGEL [*heavy hearted*]: It might perhaps be best for us both – if we parted. – But still I *can't*! – For me *you* represent the horror, Ellida. The thing that pulls – that's what is strongest in you.

ELLIDA: You think so?

WANGEL: Let's try to get through this day with composure. With absolute calm of mind. I *dare* not release you and let you go today. I'm not permitted to do that. For your sake, I'm not permitted, Ellida. I assert my right and duty to protect you.

ELLIDA: Protect? What is there to protect me from here? There is absolutely no external violence or power that threatens me. The horror lies deeper, Wangel. The horror – it is the pull I feel within my own mind. And what can you do about that?

WANGEL: I can strengthen and support you in resisting it.

ELLIDA: Yes – if I *wanted* to resist.

WANGEL: Don't you want to?

ELLIDA: Oh, that's precisely what I don't know myself!

WANGEL: Tonight everything will be decided, my dear Ellida –

ELLIDA [*bursts out*]: Yes, just think! The decision is near! A decision for life!

WANGEL: – and then tomorrow –

ELLIDA: Yes, tomorrow! Maybe my rightful future will be forfeited then!

WANGEL: Your rightful –?

ELLIDA: A complete and full life in freedom forfeited – forfeited for me! And perhaps – for him too.

WANGEL [*quietly, grasping her wrists*]: Ellida, do you love this stranger?

ELLIDA: Do I –? Oh, what do I know? I just know that for me he is the horror and that –

WANGEL: – and that?

ELLIDA [*tears herself loose*]: – and that it is with him I feel I belong.

WANGEL [*bows his head*]: I think I begin to understand.

ELLIDA: And what help can you give against this? What advice do you have for me?

WANGEL [*looks sadly at her*]: Tomorrow – he will have gone. This disaster will be banished from your mind. And then I will be willing to release you and let you go. We'll reverse the deal, Ellida.

ELLIDA: Oh Wangel –! Tomorrow – then it will be too late –!

WANGEL [*looks out towards the garden*]: The children! The children –! Let us at least spare them – for now.

   ARNHOLM, BOLETTE, HILDE *and* LYNGSTRAND *come to the foreground in the garden.* LYNGSTRAND *says good-bye and goes out to the left. The rest come into the garden room.*

ARNHOLM: Wait till you hear the plans we've been busy making –

HILDE: Yes, we're going out on the fjord this evening and –

BOLETTE: No, don't say anything!

WANGEL: We've been busy making plans too.

ARNHOLM: Ah – really?

WANGEL: Ellida's leaving for Skjoldviken tomorrow – for a while.

BOLETTE: Leaving –?

ARNHOLM: Well, that's very sensible, Mrs Wangel.

WANGEL: Ellida wants to go back home. Home to the sea.

HILDE [*leaping towards* ELLIDA]: Are you leaving?! Are you leaving us?!

ELLIDA [*taken aback*]: But, Hilde! What's got into you?

HILDE [*pulls herself together*]: Oh, it's nothing. [*Turns away from her, in a lowered voice*] Just leave!

BOLETTE [*worried*]: Father – I can see it in your face – *you're* leaving too – for Skjoldviken!

WANGEL: Absolutely not, no. I'll pop out there now and then perhaps –

BOLETTE: And in to us –?

WANGEL: I'll pop in here too –

BOLETTE: – now and then, yes!

WANGEL: My dear children, that's how it *has* to be.

He paces the room.

ARNHOLM [*whispers*]: We'll talk later, Bolette.

He goes over to WANGEL. *They talk quietly near the door.*

ELLIDA [*quietly to* BOLETTE]: What's the matter with Hilde? She seemed quite agitated.

BOLETTE: Have you never noticed what Hilde's been thirsting for, day in and day out?

ELLIDA: Thirsted for?

BOLETTE: Ever since *you* came into this house.

ELLIDA: No, no – what?

BOLETTE: One single loving word from you.

ELLIDA: Ah –! Might there be a task for me here?

She clasps her hands to her head and stares ahead of her, motionless, as though besieged by conflicting thoughts and feelings.

WANGEL *and* ARNHOLM *cross the room, deep in whispered conversation.*

BOLETTE *goes and looks into the side room to the right. Then she flings the door open.*

BOLETTE: Well, Father dear – food's on the table – in case you –

WANGEL [*with forced calm*]: Is it, my child? That's good. You first, schoolmaster! Let's go in now and drain a farewell goblet with – with 'The Lady from the Sea'.

They move towards the door, right.

ACT FIVE

The corner of Dr Wangel's garden near the carp pond. The twilight of the summer night is deepening.

ARNHOLM, BOLETTE, LYNGSTRAND and HILDE in a boat, punting from the left along the edge of the fjord.

HILDE: Look, we can easily jump ashore here!

ARNHOLM: No, no, don't do that!

LYNGSTRAND: I can't jump, Miss Hilde.

HILDE: And you, Mr Arnholm, can't you jump either?

ARNHOLM: I'd rather not.

BOLETTE: Then let's bring her in by the bathing-hut steps.
They continue punting out to the right.
At the same time BALLESTED *comes along the footpath from the right, carrying sheet music and a French horn. He waves to the people in the boat, turns and talks to them. Their replies are heard moving further and further into the distance.*

BALLESTED: What did you say? – Certainly it's on account of the English steamer. Because it's the last time she'll be here this year. But if you want to enjoy the music, you mustn't linger too long. [*Shouts*] What? [*Shakes his head*] Can't hear what you're saying!
ELLIDA, with her shawl over her head, enters from the left, followed by WANGEL.

WANGEL: But, Ellida dear – I assure you – there's still plenty of time.

ELLIDA: No, no – there isn't. He could come any moment.

BALLESTED [*outside the garden fence*]: Why, good evening, Doctor Wangel. Good evening, Mrs Wangel.

WANGEL [*becomes aware of him*]: Ah, you're here? Is there going to be music again tonight?

BALLESTED: Yes. The Brass Band Association are intending to play. There's no shortage of opportunity for festivity at this time of year. Tonight it'll be in honour of the Englander.

ELLIDA: The Englander! Is she already in sight?

BALLESTED: Not yet. But she's coming in all right – between the islands. Before you know it our visitor will be upon us.

ELLIDA: Indeed – that's just it.

WANGEL [*half turned to* ELLIDA]: Tonight will be the final visit. Then, gone for good.

BALLESTED: A melancholy thought, doctor sir. But that's why, as I said, we want to do the honours now. Ah me! The happy summer season is drawing to an end. 'Soon shall each and every strait be closed',[43] as it says in the tragedy.

ELLIDA: Every strait closed – yes.

BALLESTED: Sad to think of. We've been summer's happy children for many weeks and months now. It'll be hard to adjust to the dark winter season again. Well, at first, I mean. For human beings *can* accal-ac-limatize, Mrs Wangel. Indeed they can.

He waves and goes out to the left.

ELLIDA [*looks out over the fjord*]: Oh, this agonizing suspense! This last torturous half-hour before the decision.

WANGEL: So it still stands firm that you want to speak to him yourself?

ELLIDA: I *must* speak to him myself. It is of my own free will that I must make my choice.

WANGEL: You have no choice, Ellida. You are not permitted to choose. Not permitted by me.

ELLIDA: You can never prevent my choice. Neither you nor anyone. You can forbid me to travel with him – to follow him – if that's what I choose. You can hold me here by force. Against my will. That, you can do. But if I choose – choose in my deepest mind – choose him and not you – if that is what I want or have to choose – you cannot prevent it.

WANGEL: No, you're right. That, I cannot prevent.

ELLIDA: And I have nothing to fight back with either! There's nothing in the world here at home that pulls me or binds me. I am utterly rootless in your house, Wangel. I don't own the children. I don't own their hearts, I mean. I never have. – When I leave – that is, *if* I leave – either with him tonight – or out to Skjoldviken tomorrow, I have no keys[44] to hand over – no little instructions to leave about this or that. That's how utterly rootless I am in your house. How utterly outside everything I've been from the very first moment.

WANGEL: You wanted it like that yourself.

ELLIDA: No, I didn't. I've neither wanted nor *not* wanted it. I simply let everything stay as I found it on the day I arrived. It is you – and nobody else – who have wanted it like that.

WANGEL: I thought I was doing what was best for you.

ELLIDA: Yes, Wangel, I know, really I do! But there's a payback in this. Something taking its revenge. Because now there's no power to bind me here – no support for me here – no help – nothing to pull me in towards the very thing that should have been our innermost joint possession.

WANGEL: Of course, I see that, Ellida. Which is why, from tomorrow, you shall have your freedom back. From now on you shall live your own life.

ELLIDA: And you call *that* my own life! Oh no, my own, rightful life went off track when I came to live with you. [*She clenches her hands in fear and unease*] And now – tonight – in half an hour – the man whose trust I betrayed will come – the man to whom I should have held fast, just as he held fast to me! Now he is coming to offer me the chance – for the last and only time – to live life over again – to live my own rightful life – the life that frightens and pulls me – and which I *cannot* let go of. Not of my own free will!

WANGEL: That's exactly why you need your husband – and your doctor – to take the power from you – and to act on your behalf.

ELLIDA: Yes, Wangel, I do understand. Oh, you mustn't believe there aren't times when I think there'd be peace and salvation in taking refuge with you – when I try to defy all the powers that pull and frighten me. But I simply can't. No, no – I can't!

WANGEL: Come, Ellida – let's walk up and down a bit together.

ELLIDA: I would really like to. But I daren't. Because he said I should wait for him here.

WANGEL: Just come. You still have time.

ELLIDA: Are you sure?

WANGEL: There's ample time, I tell you.

ELLIDA: Let's walk a little then.

They go out in the foreground to the right.

Meanwhile ARNHOLM *and* BOLETTE *appear at the upper edge of the pond.*

BOLETTE [*noticing* WANGEL *and* ELLIDA *walking away*]: Look there –!

ARNHOLM [*quietly*]: Ssh – let them go.

BOLETTE: Can you work out what's been going on between them this last day or two?

ARNHOLM: Have you noticed something?

BOLETTE: *Have* I –!

ARNHOLM: Anything particular?

BOLETTE: Oh, yes. Various things. Haven't *you*?

ARNHOLM: Oh, I'm not really sure –

BOLETTE: Oh, yes you have. You just don't want to say.

ARNHOLM: I think it'll be good for your stepmother to take that little trip.

BOLETTE: You think so?

ARNHOLM: I wonder if it wouldn't be good for all parties if she got out there for a bit, now and then.

BOLETTE: If she moves back home to Skjoldviken tomorrow, she'll never come back to us.

ARNHOLM: But my dear Bolette, where do you get that idea?

BOLETTE: Oh, I'm absolutely certain of it. Just you watch! You'll see – she won't come back. Not as long as Hilde and I are in the house, at least.

ARNHOLM: Hilde too?

BOLETTE: Well, it might just be all right with Hilde. She's still not much more than a child. And deep down, I think she

worships Ellida. But it's different with me, you see. A stepmother who isn't that much older than yourself –

ARNHOLM: Bolette dear – it may not be too long before you're
able to get out.

BOLETTE [*eagerly*]: Really? Have you spoken to Father about
it then?

ARNHOLM: Yes, that too.

BOLETTE: Well – and what did he say?

ARNHOLM: Hmm – your father is, of course, preoccupied
with other thoughts these days –

BOLETTE: Yes, that's what I said before.

ARNHOLM: But I did get this much out of him, that you probably shouldn't count on any help from him.

BOLETTE: None –?

ARNHOLM: He explained his situation to me very clearly. Felt
such a thing was an outright impossibility for him.

BOLETTE [*reproachfully*]: And you had the heart to stand
there and make fun of me.

ARNHOLM: That wasn't my meaning, Bolette dear. It rests with
you wholly and completely – whether or not you get away.

BOLETTE: What rests with me did you say?

ARNHOLM: Whether you'll get out into the world. Get to learn
about all the things you most want to know about. Take
part in that life you go around thirsting for here at home.
Live your life in brighter circumstances, Bolette. What do
you say to that?

BOLETTE [*claps her hands*]: Oh, how heavenly –! Yes, but it's
all totally impossible. If Father won't or can't, then –. Well,
I've nobody else in the whole world I can turn to.

ARNHOLM: You couldn't perhaps bring yourself to accept a
helping hand from your old – your former tutor?

BOLETTE: From you, Mr Arnholm? Would you be willing to –?

ARNHOLM: To stand by you? I'd be most glad to. In word and
in deed. You can rely on it. – Can we make it a deal? Well?
Will you accept?

BOLETTE: Will I accept?! The chance to get out – to see the
world – to study properly! All the things that have seemed
such a glorious impossibility –!

ARNHOLM: Yes, it can all be a reality for you now. If you only want it.

BOLETTE: And you want to help me attain this unutterable joy! Oh – but tell me – *can* I really accept such a sacrifice from a stranger?

ARNHOLM: From me you can most certainly accept it, Bolette. From me you can accept anything and everything.

BOLETTE [*grasps his hands*]: Yes, I almost believe I can too! I don't know how it is; but – [*Bursts out*] Oh, I could laugh and cry with joy! With elation! Oh – I'm going to be allowed to live for real after all! I began to be so frightened that life would pass me by.

ARNHOLM: You need have no fear of that, my dear Bolette. But now you must tell me absolutely frankly – whether there is anything – anything that binds you here?

BOLETTE: Binds me? No, nothing.

ARNHOLM: Nothing at all?

BOLETTE: No, nothing at all. That is – I feel bound to Father in a way of course. And Hilde too. But –

ARNHOLM: Well – you'll have to leave your father sooner or later anyway. And Hilde will at some point make her own way in life. So it's only a question of time. Nothing more. But apart from that, there's nothing else that binds you here? No relationship of any kind?

BOLETTE: No, none whatsoever. As far as that goes I can go absolutely anywhere.

ARNHOLM: Well, in that case, my dear Bolette – you shall come with me.

BOLETTE [*claps her hands*]: Oh, God in heaven, what a joy to think of!

ARNHOLM: Because I hope that you have complete confidence in me?

BOLETTE: Yes, I most certainly have!

ARNHOLM: And you feel you can place yourself and your future safely in my hands, Bolette? Isn't that right? You do, don't you?

BOLETTE: Yes, absolutely. Why wouldn't I? Can you doubt it! You're my old tutor – my tutor from the *old* days, I mean.

ARNHOLM: Not just because of that. I'm really not concerned with that side of things. But –. Well – so you are free, Bolette. There's no relationship that binds you. And so I am asking you then – if you might want – might consider an attachment – to me – for life?

BOLETTE [*steps back in terror*]: Oh – what are you saying?

ARNHOLM: For life, Bolette. If you will be my wife.

BOLETTE [*beside herself*]: No, no, no! This is impossible! Absolutely impossible!

ARNHOLM: Would it really be so completely impossible for you to –?

BOLETTE: But you can't possibly mean what you're saying, Mr Arnholm! [*Looks at him*] Or –. Perhaps –. Was that what you meant – when you offered to do so much for me?

ARNHOLM: Now listen to me for a moment, Bolette. I seem to have given you rather a shock.

BOLETTE: How could something like that – coming from you – how could it do anything – but come as a shock!

ARNHOLM: Yes, you're probably right. You didn't know, of course – couldn't know, that it was for your sake I made this journey here.

BOLETTE: You came here for – for my sake?

ARNHOLM: Yes, indeed I did, Bolette. In the spring I got a letter from your father. And there was a phrase in it which caused me to believe – hmm – that you held your former tutor in – in more than friendly remembrance.

BOLETTE: How could Father write such a thing!

ARNHOLM: It wasn't what he meant at all. But nonetheless I entertained the illusion that there was a young girl here longing for my return. – No, please don't interrupt me now, my dear Bolette! And – you can surely see – when a man, like myself, is no longer in the flush of youth, such a belief – or illusion – can make an extremely strong impression. There grew in me a living – thankful inclination towards you. I felt I had to come to you. To see you again. And to tell you that I shared the feelings which I had convinced myself you had for me.

BOLETTE: But now you know that it wasn't like that! That it was a misunderstanding!

ARNHOLM: That doesn't help, Bolette. The image of you – such as I carry inside me – will always be coloured and shaped by the feelings that this misapprehension created in me. You can't understand this perhaps. But that's how it is.

BOLETTE: I never thought it possible that anything like this could happen.

ARNHOLM: But now that it's been shown that it could after all? What do you say, Bolette? Couldn't you decide – well, to be my wife?

BOLETTE: Oh, but I think that's quite impossible, Mr Arnholm. You were my tutor after all! I can't imagine having any other sort of relationship to you.

ARNHOLM: Well, well – since you don't think you can –. Then our relationship will of course remain unchanged, Bolette.

BOLETTE: What do you mean?

ARNHOLM: Of course, I stand by my offer anyway. I will ensure that you get out from here to see the world. Get a chance to study something you really want to. Have security and independence in your life. I will assure your future too, Bolette. In me you will always have a good, loyal and dependable friend. I want you to know that!

BOLETTE: For God's sake, Mr Arnholm – this is all utterly impossible now.

ARNHOLM: Is this impossible, too?

BOLETTE: Yes, you must be able to see that! After everything you've told me – and after the answer I've given you. – Oh, you must be able to understand that I can't possibly accept so much from you! I can't accept anything whatever from you. Not after this!

ARNHOLM: So you'd prefer to sit here at home and let life pass you by?

BOLETTE: Oh, that's incredibly painful to contemplate!

ARNHOLM: Are you going to renounce the chance of seeing the outside world? To renounce taking part in all the things you are, as you said yourself, thirsting for? Knowing that there is infinitely more out there – and yet never really finding anything out about it? Think it through, Bolette.

BOLETTE: Yes, yes – you're quite right, Mr Arnholm.

ARNHOLM: And then – one day when your father is no longer here – you'll be left standing helpless and alone in the world. Or having to give yourself to another man – towards whom – perhaps – you may not feel any warmth either.

BOLETTE: Yes – I can see it's true – everything you're saying. But still –! Or, then again, perhaps –?

ARNHOLM [*quickly*]: Yes?

BOLETTE [*looks at him as if in two minds*]: Perhaps it's not so completely impossible after all –.

ARNHOLM: What, Bolette?

BOLETTE: That it could work – if I agreed – to it – to what you said.

ARNHOLM: You mean you might be willing to –? That you'd allow me at least the pleasure of helping you as a loyal friend?

BOLETTE: No, no! Never that! *That* would be utterly impossible now. – No – Mr Arnholm – better that you take me.

ARNHOLM: Bolette! Will you, after all?

BOLETTE: Yes – I believe – I will.

ARNHOLM: Will you really be my wife!

BOLETTE: Yes. If you still think you – you should take me.

ARNHOLM: If I still think –! [*Clasps her hand*] Oh thank you – thank you, Bolette! As to what you said earlier – your doubts – they don't discourage me. If your heart is not completely mine now, I'm sure I'll manage to win it. Oh, Bolette, I shall carry you[45] safely in my arms!

BOLETTE: And I'll get to see the world. Get to live as part of it. You've promised me that.

ARNHOLM: And I stand by that.

BOLETTE: And be allowed to study whatever I want.

ARNHOLM: I'll be your teacher myself. As before, Bolette. Remember that last school year –.

BOLETTE [*quiet and deep in her own thoughts*]: Imagine – to know that you're free – and to journey out into the unknown. And not to have to go fretting about the future. Not to go worrying over earning some stupid livelihood –.

ARNHOLM: No, you'll never have to waste a moment's thought on such things. And *that* – don't you agree, Bolette dear – is a pretty good thing? Is it not?

BOLETTE: Yes. It certainly is. That's the truth.

ARNHOLM [*puts his arm around her waist*]: Oh, you'll see how nice and snug you and I will make things together! And how safe and sound, and trusting, the companionship between us will be, Bolette!

BOLETTE: Yes, I'm also beginning to – I actually do believe – that this has a chance of working. [*Looks out to the right and quickly frees herself*] Ah! You mustn't say anything!

ARNHOLM: What is it, my dear?

BOLETTE: Oh, it's that poor –. [*Points*] Look over there.

ARNHOLM: Is it your father –?

BOLETTE: No, it's that young sculptor. He's walking over there with Hilde.

ARNHOLM: Ah, Lyngstrand. What's wrong with him?

BOLETTE: Oh, you know how weak and ill he is.

ARNHOLM: Yes, if it's not just in his imagination.

BOLETTE: Oh no, it's real enough. He won't last long. But perhaps that's best for him.

ARNHOLM: My dear, why would *that* be best for him?

BOLETTE: Well, because – because nothing will ever come of his art anyway. – Let's go before they get here.

ARNHOLM: Most gladly, my dearest Bolette.

HILDE *and* LYNGSTRAND *appear by the pond.*

HILDE: Hey – hey! Won't the lord and his lady wait for us?

ARNHOLM: Bolette and I would rather walk ahead a little.

He and BOLETTE *go out to the left.*

LYNGSTRAND [*with a quiet laugh*]: It's terribly fun round here today. Everybody out walking in pairs. Always two-by-two.

HILDE [*looks in their direction*]: I could almost swear he's busy proposing to her.

LYNGSTRAND: Really? Have you noticed anything like that?

HILDE: Well yes. It's not hard – if you have your eyes about you.

LYNGSTRAND: But Miss Bolette won't take him. I'm certain of it.

HILDE: No. Because she thinks he's got so old-looking. And she reckons he'll soon be bald too.

LYNGSTRAND: Well, *that's* not all. She wouldn't take him anyway.

HILDE: How can you know that?

LYNGSTRAND: Because there's someone else she's promised to think about.

HILDE: Just to think about?

LYNGSTRAND: While he's away, yes.

HILDE: Oh, then I suppose it must be *you* she's going to think about!

LYNGSTRAND: It just might be.

HILDE: Did she promise you to do that?

LYNGSTRAND: Yes, indeed – she promised! But please don't tell her that you know.

HILDE: My lips are sealed. I am as silent as the grave.

LYNGSTRAND: I think it's very kind of her.

HILDE: And when you get back home – will you get engaged to her then? And marry her too?

LYNGSTRAND: No, that wouldn't do at all. I couldn't possibly think about such things in the first few years. And when I do get that far, I expect she'll have got a bit too old for me.

HILDE: But you still want her to go about thinking of you?

LYNGSTRAND: Well, yes, because it's so very useful to me. To me as an artist, you understand. And after all, she can do it easily, not having any proper vocation[46] of her own. – But it is nonetheless kind of her.

HILDE: Do you think you can work faster on your sculpture knowing that Bolette is here thinking of you?

LYNGSTRAND: Yes, I imagine so. This thing, you see, of knowing that somewhere in the world there's a young, fine, silent woman, who's quietly dreaming about one –. I feel that must be something very – very –. Well, I don't quite know what the word is.

HILDE: Do you mean perhaps – exciting?

LYNGSTRAND: Exciting? Yes. Exciting, that's what I mean. Or something similar. [*Looks at her for a few moments*] You're so astute, Miss Hilde. You really are very astute. When I come back home again, you'll be about the same age as your sister is now. You might even look like your sister looks now. And perhaps you'll be of the same disposition too, as she is now. So that you'll have become, in a way, both yourself and her – in a single gestalt, so to speak.

HILDE: Would you like that?

LYNGSTRAND: I'm not sure. Yes, I almost think I would. But, now – this summer – I prefer you to be only like yourself. And exactly as you are.

HILDE: Do you like me best this way?

LYNGSTRAND: Yes, I like you a great deal this way.

HILDE: Hm – tell me – as an artist – do you approve of the fact I always wear light-coloured summer dresses?

LYNGSTRAND: Yes, I approve of it greatly.

HILDE: So do you think light colours suit me?

LYNGSTRAND: Yes, light colours suit you beautifully, to my taste.

HILDE: But tell me – as an artist – how do you think I'd look in black?

LYNGSTRAND: In black, Miss Hilde?

HILDE: Yes, all in black. Do you think I'd look good like that?

LYNGSTRAND: Black isn't really a colour for the summer. Although you'd certainly look splendid in black too. Particularly with your looks.

HILDE [*looking straight ahead*]: In black right up to my neck. – Black frills all around. – Black gloves. – And a long black veil at the back.

LYNGSTRAND: If you were dressed like that, Miss Hilde, I'd wish I was a painter – and I'd paint a young, lovely, grieving widow.

HILDE: Or a young, grieving bride.

LYNGSTRAND: Yes, that would suit you even better. But surely you wouldn't want to dress like that?

HILDE: I don't really know. But I think it's exciting.

LYNGSTRAND: Exciting?

HILDE: Exciting to think about, yes. [*Suddenly points to the left*] Oh, look at *that*!

LYNGSTRAND [*looks*]: The big English steamship. And right by the jetty!

WANGEL *and* ELLIDA *appear near the pond.*

WANGEL: No, I assure you, my dear Ellida – you're wrong! [*Sees*

the others] Oh, are you here? Aren't I right, Mr Lyngstrand –
she hasn't come into view yet?

LYNGSTRAND: The big Englander?

WANGEL: Yes!

LYNGSTRAND [*points*]: She's lying out there already, doctor.

ELLIDA: Ah –! I knew it.

WANGEL: Arrived!

LYNGSTRAND: Like a thief in the night,⁴⁷ one might say. Quite
soundlessly –

WANGEL: You must accompany Hilde to the jetty. Hurry up!
She probably wants to hear the music.

LYNGSTRAND: Yes, doctor, we were just leaving.

WANGEL: The rest of us will come later perhaps. We'll come in
a bit.

HILDE [*whispers to* LYNGSTRAND]: They're *also* going two by
two.
    She and LYNGSTRAND *go out through the garden to the
    left. Horn music is heard far out on the fjord during the
    rest of the scene.*

ELLIDA: Arrived! He's here! Yes, yes – I feel it.

WANGEL: You should go inside, Ellida. Let me speak to him
alone.

ELLIDA: Oh – that's impossible! Impossible, I say! [*Cries out*]
Ah – do you see him, Wangel?
    The STRANGER *comes from the left and stops on the path
    outside the garden fence.*

STRANGER [*greets* ELLIDA]: Good evening. So, here I am again,
Ellida.

ELLIDA: Yes, yes – the hour has come.⁴⁸

STRANGER: Are you ready to travel? Or aren't you?

WANGEL: You can see for yourself that she is not.

STRANGER: It isn't about travelling clothes or the like, that I'm
asking. Or packed suitcases. Everything she needs for the journey I have brought with me on board. I've arranged a cabin for
her too. [*To* ELLIDA] So I'm asking you if you are ready to
come with me – to come with me of your own free will?

ELLIDA [*imploring*]: Oh, don't ask me! Don't tempt me like
that!

A steamship's bell is heard in the distance.

STRANGER: Now the first bell[49] is ringing on board. Now you must say yes or no.

ELLIDA [*wringing her hands*]: Decision! Decision for my whole life! Never to be able to reverse it!

STRANGER: Never. In half an hour it will be too late.

ELLIDA [*looks at him, timidly and searchingly*]: Why do you hold to me so resolutely?

STRANGER: Don't you feel, as I do, that the two of us belong together?

ELLIDA: You mean because of the promise?

STRANGER: Promises bind no one. Neither man nor woman. When I hold so resolutely to you, it is because I *cannot* do otherwise.

ELLIDA [*quietly trembling*]: Why didn't you come sooner?

WANGEL: Ellida!

ELLIDA [*bursts out*]: Oh, this thing which pulls and tempts and seduces – into the unknown! The entire power of the sea is gathered within it.

The STRANGER *steps across the garden fence.*

ELLIDA [*retreats behind* WANGEL]: What is it? What do you want?

STRANGER: I see it – and I hear it in you, Ellida – it will be *me* you choose in the end.

WANGEL [*moves towards him*]: My wife has no choice here. I am the one who will both choose for her and – protect her. Yes, protect! If you do not remove yourself from this place – out of this country – never to come back – are you fully aware of what you'll be exposing yourself to then?

ELLIDA: No, no, Wangel! Not that!

STRANGER: What will you do to me?

WANGEL: I will have you arrested – as a criminal! Immediately! Before you can get on board! Because I am fully informed about the murder out at Skjoldviken.

ELLIDA: Oh, Wangel – how can you –!

STRANGER: I was prepared for this. Which is why – [*he takes a revolver from his breast pocket*] – which is why I also came equipped with this.

ELLIDA [*throws herself in front of* WANGEL]: No, no – don't
   kill him! Kill me instead!

STRANGER: Neither you, nor him. Relax. This is for my own
   use. I will live and die a free man.

ELLIDA [*with increasing emotion*]: Wangel! Let me say this to
   you – say it so he hears it! Of course you can hold me back!
   You have the power and the means to do so! And that's what
   you intend. But my very being – all my thoughts – all the long-
   ings and desires that pull me – *those* you cannot bind! They
   will yearn, they will chase – out into the unknown – into that
   which I was created for – and which you have closed for me!

WANGEL [*in quiet pain*]: Yes, I see it, of course, Ellida! Step by
   step you are slipping from me. The craving for the boundless
   and infinite – the unattainable – it'll drive you into the darkness of the night in the end.

ELLIDA: Oh, yes, yes – I feel it – like black soundless wings
   over me!

WANGEL: It will not come to that. There is no other salvation
   for you. I can at least see no other. So that is why – why I
   allow – the deal to be reversed as of this moment. Now you
   can choose your path – in absolute – absolute freedom.

ELLIDA [*stares at him for a few moments, speechless*]: Is it
   true – true – what you're saying? Do you mean it – from the
   depths of your heart?

WANGEL: Yes – from the depths of my whole, anguished heart,
   I mean it.

ELLIDA: And you *can* really do this? You can actually let it
   happen!

WANGEL: Yes I can. I can – because I love you so much.

ELLIDA [*quietly trembling*]: So I have come that close – touched
   you that deeply –.

WANGEL: The years and a life shared have made it so.

ELLIDA: And I – who failed to see it!

WANGEL: Your thoughts took other paths. But now – now you
   are fully released from me, from whatever is mine, and from
   my children. Now your rightful life can – return to – to its
   true path once more. Because now you have freedom to
   choose. The responsibility is your own, Ellida.

ELLIDA [*clasps her head and stares unseeingly at* WANGEL]:
Freedom and – and responsibility! Responsibility too? –
There's – transformation in this!
   The steamship's bell rings again.

STRANGER: Do you hear, Ellida? The last bell is ringing now!
Come!

ELLIDA [*turns to him, looks at him steadily and says with
force in her voice*]: I shall never come with you after this.

STRANGER: You won't come!

ELLIDA [*clinging to* WANGEL]: Oh – I'll never leave you after this!

WANGEL: Ellida – Ellida!

STRANGER: It is over then?

ELLIDA: Yes! It is over for all time!

STRANGER: I see that, yes. There is something here that is
stronger than my will.

ELLIDA: Your will no longer has one jot of power over me. To
me you are a dead man – who has come home from the sea.
And who will return to it again. But I no longer fear you.
And I no longer feel any pull towards you.

STRANGER: Farewell, Mrs Wangel! [*He swings himself over
the garden fence*] From now on you[50] are nothing but – a
shipwreck in my life that I survived.
   He goes out to the left.

WANGEL [*looks at* ELLIDA *for a moment*]: Ellida – your mind
is like the sea. It ebbs and it flows. From where did this
transformation come?

ELLIDA: Oh, don't you realize that the transformation came –
that the transformation *had* to come – when I could choose
freely.

WANGEL: And the unknown – it no longer pulls on you?

ELLIDA: It neither pulls nor frightens me. I've been allowed to
face it – to go into it – if I so wanted, at least. I could choose
it now. And so I could also renounce it.

WANGEL: I'm beginning to understand you – little by little.
You think and feel in pictures – in visual images. Your
yearning and craving for the sea – your pull towards him –
towards that stranger – it has been the expression of your
awakening and growing demand for freedom. Nothing more.

ELLIDA: Oh, I don't know what to say to that. But you have been a good doctor to me. You *found* – and you dared to *use* the right medicine – the *only* medicine that could help me.

WANGEL: Yes, in moments of crisis and danger we doctors take huge risks. – But does this mean you're coming back to me now, Ellida?

ELLIDA: Yes, my dear, faithful Wangel – now I am coming back to you. Now I can. Because now I am coming to you freely – of my own free will – and on my own responsibility.

WANGEL [*looks at her lovingly*]: Ellida! Ellida! Oh – to think that we can now live completely for each other –

ELLIDA: – and with shared life memories. Yours – as well as mine.

WANGEL: That's right, my dearest Ellida!

ELLIDA: – and for our two children, Wangel.

WANGEL: *Ours*, did you say?

ELLIDA: Children that I don't own – but whom I think I might win.

WANGEL: Ours –! [*He quickly kisses her hands in joy*] Oh – thank you for that word!

HILDE, BALLESTED, LYNGSTRAND, ARNHOLM *and* BOLETTE *come through the garden, from the left.* *Simultaneously many of the town's young people and summer residents appear on the path outside.*

HILDE [*quietly to* LYNGSTRAND]: Oh, look – she and Father look just like a newly engaged couple!

BALLESTED [*who has overheard*]: It's summertime, little miss.

ARNHOLM [*looks towards* WANGEL *and* ELLIDA]: *Now* the Englander is sailing.

BOLETTE [*going to the fence*]: You can see her best from here.

LYNGSTRAND: The last voyage[51] this year.

BALLESTED: 'Soon shall each and every strait be closed', as the poet says. It's sad, Mrs Wangel! And now we're losing you too for a time. I hear you're moving out to Skjoldviken tomorrow.

WANGEL: No – that's not happening. Because tonight we two have reversed our decision.

ARNHOLM [*looks from one to the other*]: Ah – really!

BOLETTE [*coming towards them*]: Father – is that true?!

HILDE [*to* ELLIDA]: Will you stay with us after all!

ELLIDA: Yes, my dear Hilde – if you want me, that is.

HILDE [*between tears and joy*]: Oh – to think! If – if I want –?!

ARNHOLM [*to* ELLIDA]: This certainly comes as a surprise –!

ELLIDA [*with a serious smile*]: Well, you see, Mr Arnholm –.
Do you remember – what we talked about yesterday? Once
we've become land-creatures – then we can't find the way
back again – out to the sea. Nor to the life of the sea.

BALLESTED: But that's exactly how it is with my mermaid.

ELLIDA: Yes, more or less.

BALLESTED: With only this difference that the *mermaid –
she dies as a result*. Human beings, in contrast – they can
aclaim-acclim-atize themselves. Oh yes, I assure you, Mrs
Wangel – they *can* acc-cli-matize themselves!

ELLIDA: Yes, with freedom they can, Mr Ballested.

WANGEL: And responsibility, dearest Ellida.

ELLIDA [*quickly, giving him her hand*]: That's it precisely.
The large steamship glides silently out over the fjord.
The music is heard closer to land.

HEDDA GABLER

A Play in Four Acts

CHARACTERS

JØRGEN TESMAN, *scholar*[1] *of cultural history*
MRS[2] HEDDA TESMAN, *his wife*
MISS[3] JULIANE TESMAN, *his aunt*
MRS ELVSTED
JUDGE[4] BRACK
EILERT[5] LØVBORG
BERTA,[6] *the Tesmans' maid*

The action takes place in Tesman's villa,
on the west side[7] *of town.*

ACT ONE

A fine, spacious and tastefully furnished drawing room, deco-
rated in dark colours. On the back wall is a wide doorway
with heavy curtains that are pulled back. This doorway leads
into a smaller room presented in the same style as the drawing
room. On the wall to the right, there are double folding doors,
which lead to the hallway. On the opposite wall, to the left, is
a glass door, also with curtains pulled back. Through it can
be seen a section of a roofed veranda and trees covered with
autumn leaves. Towards the centre of the room is an oval table
covered with a tablecloth and surrounded by chairs. Further
forward, by the right-hand wall, are a wide porcelain wood
stove,[8] *a tall armchair, a footstool with a cushion and two*
stools. In the right-hand corner, at the back, is a corner sofa
and a small round table. To the front left, a little out from the
wall, is a sofa. Opposite the glass door stands a piano. On
either side of the doorway at the back sets of shelves contain
terracotta and majolica ware. Looking into the inner room,
we see a sofa, a table and a couple of chairs against the back
wall. Over the sofa hangs a portrait of a handsome older gen-
tleman in a general's uniform. Over the table hangs a ceiling
lamp with an opaque, milky-white glass shade. Distributed
around the drawing room are a number of bouquets of flowers
arranged in china and glass vases. Other bouquets are lying
on the tables. The floors in both rooms have thick carpets.
Morning light. The sun shines in through the glass door.

MISS JULIANE TESMAN, *with a hat and parasol, enters from*
the hallway, followed by BERTA, *who is carrying a bouquet of*

flowers wrapped in paper. MISS TESMAN *is a handsome and kindly-looking woman of about sixty-five years. Primly, but simply dressed in grey walking attire.*⁹ BERTA *is a maid, middle-aged, with a plain, somewhat rural appearance.*

MISS TESMAN [*stops inside the door, listens and says in a low voice*]: Well, I never! I don't think they're even up yet!

BERTA [*also in a low voice*]: That's just what I said, miss. Just think – with the steamboat coming so late last night. And then afterwards! Heavens – all them things the young mistress insisted on having unpacked before she'd settle.

MISS TESMAN: Yes, well – just let them have a good rest. But they'll definitely need some fresh morning air in here, when they come.

She walks over to the glass door and flings it wide open.

BERTA [*by the table, puzzling over what to do with the bouquet in her hand*]: I'll be blessed if there's even one suitable space left now. I think I'll have to put them here, miss. [*Displays the bouquet on the front of the piano*]

MISS TESMAN: So, you've got yourself a new master and mistress now, Berta my dear. Lord alone knows how terribly hard it's been for me to let you go.

BERTA [*close to tears*]: And for me too, miss! What can I say? After spending so many of our Lord's years in the mistresses' service.

MISS TESMAN: We must take things as they come, Berta. There's honestly nothing else for it. Jørgen *must* have you with him here in the house, you understand. He *must*. After all, you've been so used to looking after him ever since he was a little boy.

BERTA: Yes but, miss, I do think an awful lot about *her* that's lying there at home. Poor thing, so completely helpless. And then that new girl! *She'll* never, not for all the world, learn how to do things proper for that poor ailing soul.

MISS TESMAN: Oh, I'm sure I'll get her trained up. And I do take most of it upon myself, you know. You needn't be uneasy on my poor sister's account, Berta dear.

BERTA: Yes, but then there's something else too, miss. I'm ever so worried I won't do everything to the young mistress's satisfaction.

MISS TESMAN: Oh, heavens – there may perhaps be the occasional thing at the start –

BERTA: Since she's probably very particular.

MISS TESMAN: You can be sure of that. General Gabler's[10] daughter. The way she was used to things when the general was alive. Can you remember when she rode along the road with her father? In that long black habit? And with a feather in her hat?

BERTA: Ooh, yes – I should think I do! – But I'd never have believed back then that she and the young master[11] would make a match of it.

MISS TESMAN: Nor I. – But just one thing – Berta – while I remember: from now on you mustn't call Jørgen just *Master* Jørgen. You must say Doctor.

BERTA: Yes, the young mistress talked about that too – last night – the minute they came in the door. So is it *really* true, miss?

MISS TESMAN: It most certainly is. Just imagine, Berta – they made him a doctor abroad. Just recently, on his travels you understand. I'd not heard a word about it – before he told me down at the steamship pier.

BERTA: Well, I reckon he could be anything at all, that one. He's that clever. But I never thought he'd take up curing folk too.

MISS TESMAN: Well no, he's not become that sort of doctor. – [*Nods importantly*] By the way, you may soon have to start calling him something even grander.

BERTA: Never! What would that be, miss?

MISS TESMAN [*smiles*]: Hm – wouldn't you like to know! – [*Emotional*] Oh, Lord – if only our dearest departed Jochum could look up from his grave and see what's become of his little boy! [*Looks around*] But listen, Berta – why have you done *that*? – Taken all the dust sheets off the furniture?

BERTA: The mistress said I should. She can't abide dust sheets on chairs, she said.

MISS TESMAN: Are they going to be in here then – on a daily basis?

BERTA: Yes, it seemed that way. According to the mistress that is. Because he – the doctor – he said nothing.

JØRGEN TESMAN *comes humming from the right*[12] *inside the rear room, carrying an open, empty suitcase. He is a youthful man of thirty-three, of medium height, a little overweight, with an open, round and contented face, blond hair and beard. He wears glasses and wears a comfortable, slightly shabby housecoat.*

MISS TESMAN: Good morning, good morning, Jørgen!

TESMAN [*in the doorway*]: Auntie Ju![13] Dear Auntie Ju! [*He goes over to shake her hand*] All the way out here – and so early in the day! What?

MISS TESMAN: Well, I had to check in on you both, you know.

TESMAN: And when you've not even had a proper night's rest!

MISS TESMAN: Oh, it's no trouble.

TESMAN: But you got home all right from the pier? What?

MISS TESMAN: Yes, I did indeed – thank heavens. The judge was kind enough to walk me right to my door.

TESMAN: We were terribly upset not to be able to take you in the carriage. But you saw for yourself –. Hedda had so many boxes that had to come with us.

MISS TESMAN: Yes, she certainly did have a rather large number of boxes.

BERTA [*to* TESMAN]: Should I go in perhaps and ask the mistress if there's anything I can help her with?

TESMAN: No, thanks, Berta – it's best you don't. She said, if she wants you for anything she'll ring.

BERTA [*towards the right*]: Yes, I see.

TESMAN: But, look here, Berta dear – take this case with you.

BERTA [*takes it*]: I'll put it up in the attic.

She goes out through the hallway door.

TESMAN: Just think, Auntie dearest – that entire case was stuffed to the brim with nothing but transcripts. It's absolutely incredible you know, what I've managed to collect together from all those archives. Remarkable old things that nobody even knew existed –

MISS TESMAN: Yes, well, you clearly didn't waste your time on your honeymoon, Jørgen.

TESMAN: No, I venture to say that I didn't. But do take off your hat, Auntie. Here now! Let me untie the ribbon. What?

MISS TESMAN [*as he does so*]: Oh, goodness me – this feels just as though you were still at home with us.

TESMAN [*turns the hat in his hands*]: Well, I never – what a fine and magnificent hat you've invested in!

MISS TESMAN: I bought it for Hedda's sake.

TESMAN: For Hedda's sake? Eh?

MISS TESMAN: Yes, so Hedda won't be ashamed of me if we're out in the street together.

TESMAN [*pats her on the cheek*]: You really do think of everything, dear Auntie Ju! [*Puts the hat on a chair by the table*] And now – look – we'll sit down here on the sofa. Have ourselves a little chat before Hedda comes.

> *They sit down. She puts her parasol in the corner by the sofa.*

MISS TESMAN [*takes both his hands and looks at him*]: What a blessing it is to have you back large as life before my eyes, Jørgen! My dear Jørgen – our dearly beloved Jochum's very own boy!

TESMAN: And for me! To see you again, Auntie Ju! You, who have been both father and mother to me.

MISS TESMAN: Yes, I know you'll always hold your old aunts close in your affections.

TESMAN: So, there's no improvement at all in Auntie Rina.

MISS TESMAN: Sadly, no – I don't think there's any improvement to be expected in her, poor thing. She's lying there just as she has all these years. But, pray God I get to keep her a while longer! Otherwise I'll be lost for what to do with my life, Jørgen. Especially now, you see, when I no longer have you to look after.

TESMAN [*pats her on her back*]: There, there now –!

MISS TESMAN [*suddenly switches*]: Oh, but to think *you* are a married man now, Jørgen! – And that it was *you* who went off with Hedda Gabler! The lovely Hedda Gabler. To think! The one who was surrounded by so many admirers!

TESMAN [*hums a little and smiles with satisfaction*]: Yes, I do believe I've a few good friends around here in town who are rather envious of me. What?

MISS TESMAN: And that you were able to go on such a long honeymoon! More than five – almost six months –

TESMAN: Well – it has been a sort of study trip for me too, of course. All those archives that I had to investigate. Not to mention the immense number of books I had to read through!

MISS TESMAN: Yes, that's right, I'm sure. [*More confidentially and quietly*] But listen now, Jørgen – haven't you got something – something special to tell me?

TESMAN: From the trip?

MISS TESMAN: Yes.

TESMAN: No, I know of nothing other than what I wrote in my letters. And that I got my doctorate down there – but I told you that yesterday.

MISS TESMAN: Oh yes, that sort of thing, yes. But I mean – if you might – how shall I say – have any kind of – prospects of –?

TESMAN: Prospects?

MISS TESMAN: Good Lord, Jørgen. I am your old auntie, aren't I?

TESMAN: Well, yes, I do indeed have prospects.

MISS TESMAN: And?

TESMAN: I have the very best prospects of becoming a professor one of these days.

MISS TESMAN: Yes, a professor, yes –

TESMAN: Or in fact – I might even say that I am certain I shall. But sweet Auntie Ju – you already know that yourself!

MISS TESMAN [*laughing a little*]: Yes, of course I do. You're quite right. [*Changes tack*] – But we were discussing your trip. – It must have cost an awful lot of money, Jørgen?

TESMAN: Goodness, yes – although that big grant helped a good way towards it.

MISS TESMAN: But I simply cannot imagine how you managed to make it stretch for two.

TESMAN: Well, no, I don't suppose it's so easy to imagine? What?

MISS TESMAN: And especially when travelling with a lady. Because then, from what I have heard, it can get inordinately more costly.

TESMAN: Indeed, that goes without saying – it does get a tad more costly. But Hedda *had* to have that trip, Auntie! She really *had* to. Nothing else would do.

MISS TESMAN: Well, no, I don't suppose it would. A honeymoon seems to be a must nowadays. – But, tell me – have you taken a proper look around the apartment now?

TESMAN: Oh yes, believe me. I've been up and about since daybreak.

MISS TESMAN: And what do you think of it all?

TESMAN: Splendid! Absolutely splendid! It's just that I can't understand what we'll do with the two empty rooms between the rear room there and Hedda's bedroom.

MISS TESMAN [*chuckling*]: Oh, Jørgen my dear, I'm sure there'll be a use for them – in due course.

TESMAN: Yes, you're absolutely right, Auntie Ju! As I expand my book collection, then –. Eh?

MISS TESMAN: Quite, my dear boy. It was your book collection I was thinking of.

TESMAN: More than anything, I'm pleased on Hedda's account. She said so often before our engagement that the Right Honourable[14] Mrs Falk's villa was the only place she would ever really want to live.

MISS TESMAN: Yes, to think – and that it happened to come up for sale like that. Just when the two of you had left for your trip.

TESMAN: Yes, Auntie Ju, luck was certainly on our side. Eh?

MISS TESMAN: But costly, my dear Jørgen! It'll be costly for you – all this.

TESMAN [*looks at her a little crestfallen*]: Yes, I suppose it might be, Auntie?

MISS TESMAN: Oh, Lord above!

TESMAN: How much do you think? Round about? What?

MISS TESMAN: Well, I can't possibly know that until all the bills arrive.

TESMAN: Well, luckily Judge Brack secured very favourable terms for me. He wrote to tell Hedda that himself.

MISS TESMAN: Yes, my boy, never you worry about that. – And I've offered security for the furniture and all the carpets too.

TESMAN: Security? You? Dear Auntie Ju – what kind of security could *you* give?

MISS TESMAN: I've set up a mortgage against our annuity.

TESMAN [*leaps to his feet*]: What? Against your – and Auntie Rina's annuity!

MISS TESMAN: Yes, I saw no other way, you understand.

TESMAN [*stops in front of her*]: But have you gone completely mad, Auntie! That interest money – it's all you and Rina have to live on.

MISS TESMAN: Now, now – don't get so worked up about it. The whole thing is just a formality, you understand. That's what Judge Brack said too. It was he who was kind enough to arrange it all for me. Just a formality, he said.

TESMAN: Yes, that may be. But still –

MISS TESMAN: After all, you'll have your own salary to draw on now. And, good gracious, what if we did have to fork out a little –? Chip in a bit at the start –? For us that's just something of a joy.

TESMAN: Oh, Auntie – will you never tire of making sacrifices for me!

MISS TESMAN [*stands up and puts her hands on his shoulders*]: Do I have any other pleasure in this world but to smooth your path, my dearest boy? You, who had neither father nor mother to cling to. And we are close to our goal now! Things may have looked dark at times. But, praise be, you've come out on top, Jørgen!

TESMAN: Yes, it's quite extraordinary how everything's fallen into place.

MISS TESMAN: Yes – and those who opposed you – who wanted to bar your way – they are beneath you now. They are fallen, Jørgen! And the man who posed the greatest danger – he has taken the hardest fall. – And now he lies – poor misguided creature – in a bed of his own making.

TESMAN: Have you heard anything about Eilert? Since I went away, I mean?

MISS TESMAN: Only that he's apparently brought out a new book.

TESMAN: What's that? Eilert Løvborg? Just recently? What?

MISS TESMAN: Yes, so they say. Lord alone knows if it can be of any merit, my dear? No, when *your* new book comes out – that'll be something altogether different, Jørgen! What's it going to be about?

TESMAN: It'll be about Brabantine[15] domestic crafts in the Middle Ages.

MISS TESMAN: Never! To think you can write about something like that!

TESMAN: Although it may still be some time before the book comes out. I've got these extensive collections, of course, that must be sorted first.

MISS TESMAN: Yes, sorting and collecting – you're so very good at that too. It isn't for nothing that you are our dearly beloved Jochum's son.

TESMAN: And I'm so looking forward to getting down to it. Especially now that I have my own lovely house and home to work in.

MISS TESMAN: And first and foremost now that you have the woman of your heart's desire, my dear Jørgen.

TESMAN [*embraces her*]: Oh yes, yes, Auntie Ju! Hedda – that is the very loveliest thing of all! [*Looks to the doorway*] I believe she's coming now. What?

    HEDDA *comes in from the left through the back room. She is a woman of twenty-nine years. Face and appearance noble and dignified. Her complexion has a matte pallor. Eyes are steely grey and express a cold, clear calm. Her hair is a beautiful mid-brown, but not particularly abundant. She is dressed in a tasteful, somewhat loose-fitting morning gown.*

MISS TESMAN [*goes to meet* HEDDA]: Good morning, dear Hedda! A very good morning!

HEDDA [*reaches her hand out*]: Good morning, dear Miss Tesman! Visiting so early? How sweet of you.

MISS TESMAN [*seems a little awkward*]: So – has the young mistress slept well in her new home?

HEDDA: Oh yes, thank you! Tolerably.

TESMAN [*laughs*]: Tolerably? That's a good one, Hedda! You were sleeping like a log when I got up.

HEDDA: Fortunately. Anyway, we must accustom ourselves to all things new, Miss Tesman. Little by little. [*Looks to the left*] Ugh, look – the maid has opened the veranda door. There's a veritable ocean of sun pouring in here.

MISS TESMAN [*moves towards the door*]: Well, we'll close it then.

HEDDA: No, no, don't. Tesman darling,[16] draw the curtains. It gives a softer light.

TESMAN [*by the door*]: Yes, of course – of course. – There you are, Hedda – now you have both shade and fresh air.

HEDDA: Yes, fresh air certainly wouldn't come amiss in here. All these blessed flowers –. But, my dear Miss Tesman – won't you take a seat?

MISS TESMAN: No, thank you! Now that I know everything's all right here – thanks be to God! I'd better think about getting back home. To that poor soul who's lying there waiting in such dire need.

TESMAN: Do please send her lots and lots of love. And tell her I'll come in to see her later today.

MISS TESMAN: Yes, yes, I certainly will. Oh, by the way, Jørgen – [*rummages in her dress pocket*] I'd almost forgotten. I've got something for you here.

TESMAN: Whatever is it, Auntie?

MISS TESMAN [*pulls out a flat parcel in newspaper and hands it to him*]: There you are, my boy.

TESMAN [*opens it*]: Well, good Lord – have you looked after them for me, Auntie Ju?! Hedda! Isn't that just so touching? What?

HEDDA [*by the shelves on the right*]: Yes, darling, but what is it?

TESMAN: My old morning shoes! Slippers,[17] Hedda!

HEDDA: Oh, right. I remember you often talked about them on our trip.

TESMAN: Yes, I missed them so awfully. [*Walks over to her*] Here you are, look, Hedda.

HEDDA [*goes towards the wood stove*]: No thanks, I'm really not interested.

TESMAN [*walks after her*]: Yes, but just think – Auntie Rina lay there embroidering these for me. Ill as she was. Oh, you'd never believe how many memories are attached to them.

HEDDA [*by the table*]: Not for me exactly.

MISS TESMAN: Hedda may have a point there, Jørgen.

TESMAN: Yes, but I think that now she's part of the family –

HEDDA [*interrupting him*]: That maid, Tesman – it's clear we'll never get on with her.

MISS TESMAN: Not get on with Berta?

TESMAN: Darling – whatever makes you think *that*? What?

HEDDA [*points*]: Look at that! She's left her old hat on the chair.

TESMAN [*horrified, drops the slippers on the floor*]: But Hedda –!

HEDDA: Just think – if anyone came and saw that.

TESMAN: No, but Hedda – that's Auntie Ju's hat!

HEDDA: Really?

MISS TESMAN [*takes the hat*]: Yes, it is indeed mine. And it is certainly not old either, little Hedda.

HEDDA: I really didn't look at it too closely, Miss Tesman.

MISS TESMAN [*ties the hat on*]: It's the first time I've worn it actually. Yes, as our good Lord can vouch.

TESMAN: And magnificent it is too. Absolutely splendid.

MISS TESMAN: Oh, no need to exaggerate, Jørgen dear. [*Looks around*] My parasol –? Oh, there. [*Takes it*] After all, that is mine too. [*Mutters*] Not Berta's.

TESMAN: New hat and new parasol! Just think, Hedda!

HEDDA: Very elegant and charming.

TESMAN: Yes, aren't they? What? But, Auntie, do take a good look at Hedda before you go! Look, how elegant and charming *she* is!

MISS TESMAN: Oh, my dear, *that's* nothing new. Hedda has of course always been lovely.

She nods and moves to the right.

TESMAN [*follows her*]: Yes, but have you noticed how plump and buxom she's got? How she's filled out during the trip.

HEDDA [*walks across the floor*]: Oh, drop it –!

MISS TESMAN [*has stopped and turned*]: Filled out?

TESMAN: Yes, Auntie Ju, you can't see it that well when she's wearing that dress. But *I*, who have occasion to –

HEDDA [*by the glass door, impatiently*]: Oh, you have occasion to nothing!

TESMAN: It must be the mountain air in the Tyrol –

HEDDA [*curtly, interrupting*]: I'm precisely the same as when I left.

TESMAN: Yes, so you insist. But there's no way you are. Don't you agree, Auntie?

MISS TESMAN [*has folded her hands and stares at her*]: Lovely – lovely – lovely Hedda. [*Goes over to* HEDDA *and takes her head in both hands, bends forward and kisses her on the hair*] May the Lord God bless and protect Hedda Tesman. For Jørgen's sake.

HEDDA [*frees herself gently*]: Oh –! Do let me go.

MISS TESMAN [*quietly moved*]: I shall come in every single day to see the two of you.

TESMAN: Oh yes, please do, Auntie! What?

MISS TESMAN: Goodbye – goodbye!

> *She leaves through the hallway door.* TESMAN *follows her out. The door remains half open.* TESMAN *can be heard repeating his message for Aunt Rina and saying thank you for the slippers.*
>
> *Meanwhile,* HEDDA *walks across the floor, raises her arms, clenching her fists as in a rage. Pulls the curtains away from the glass door, remains standing there looking out.*
>
> *Shortly after,* TESMAN *comes back in and closes the door after him.*

TESMAN [*picks the slippers up from the floor*]: What are you standing there looking at, Hedda?

HEDDA [*again calm and controlled*]: I'm just standing here looking at the leaves. Everything's so yellow. And so withered.

TESMAN [*wraps his shoes up and puts them on the table*]: Yes – but then we are into September now.

HEDDA [*again uneasy*]: Yes, to think – we're already into – into September.

TESMAN: Don't you think Auntie Ju was rather strange, darling? Practically in a state of rapture? Do you have any idea what got into her? What?

HEDDA: Well, I barely know her, of course. Isn't she often like that?

TESMAN: No, not like she was today.

HEDDA [*walks away from the glass door*]: Do you think she was offended by that business with the hat?

TESMAN: Oh, not at all. Perhaps a tiny bit, in the moment –

HEDDA: But what kind of behaviour is it to fling off your hat in the drawing room? It's not the done thing.

TESMAN: Well, you can be sure Auntie Ju won't ever do it again.

HEDDA: Anyway, I'm sure I can smooth things out with her.

TESMAN: Yes, dear, kind Hedda, if you would!

HEDDA: When you go in to them later, you can invite her to come out and visit us this evening.

TESMAN: Yes, I most certainly shall. And then there's one thing you could do that would make her immensely happy.

HEDDA: Well?

TESMAN: If you could just bring yourself to call her Auntie Ju.[18] For my sake, Hedda? What?

HEDDA: No, no, Tesman – dear God, you really mustn't ask that of me. I've told you once before. I'll try to call her Aunt. And that will have to do.

TESMAN: All right then. But I just think, now that you're part of the family, then –

HEDDA: Hm – I'm not so sure –

She walks across the room towards the doorway.

TESMAN [*close behind*]: Is there something wrong, Hedda? What?

HEDDA: I'm just looking at my old piano. It doesn't quite fit in with everything else.

TESMAN: As soon as I draw my first salary, we'll make sure to get it changed.

HEDDA: No, no – not changed. I don't want to get rid of it. We could put it in the back room instead. And then we can get another one here in its place. When the occasion allows, I mean.

TESMAN [*a little unsure*]: Yes – I suppose we could do that.

HEDDA [*picks up the bouquet on the piano*]: These flowers weren't here last night when we arrived.

TESMAN: Auntie Ju must have brought them for you.

HEDDA [*looks in amongst the flowers*]: A visiting card. [*Picks it out and reads*] 'Will return later today.' Can you guess who it's from?

TESMAN: No. Well, who then?

HEDDA: It says 'Mrs Elvsted'.[19]

TESMAN: No, really? Mrs Elvsted! Miss Rysing as she was. Eh?

HEDDA: Yes, exactly. The one with that irritating hair that always brought her so much attention. Your old flame, I've heard.

TESMAN [*laughs*]: Well, that didn't last long. And it was also before I knew you, Hedda. But to think – she's back in town.

HEDDA: Strange she should pay us a visit.[20] After all, I only know her from our time at the high school[21] together.

TESMAN: No, I've not seen her either for – Lord knows how long. Unbelievable that she can stick it out up there in such a backwater. What?

HEDDA [*thinks about it for a moment, then exclaims*]: But, Tesman – isn't it up there somewhere that he – that man – Eilert Løvborg is staying?

TESMAN: Yes, it is indeed.

BERTA *enters the door to the hallway.*

BERTA: Ma'am, she's here again, the lady who came and left flowers a while since. [*Points*] The ones Ma'am is holding.

HEDDA: Ah, is she now? Good, would you let her in then.

BERTA *opens the door for* MRS ELVSTED *and then leaves.* MRS ELVSTED *is of slight build, with beautiful, soft facial features. Her eyes are light blue, large, round and somewhat protruding, with an anxious, questioning expression. Her hair is strikingly blonde, almost yellowish-white, and exceptionally rich and wavy. She is a couple of years younger than* HEDDA. *She is dressed in a dark visiting costume, tasteful but not quite according to the latest fashion.*

HEDDA [*she goes to greet her warmly*]: Good morning, my dear Mrs Elvsted. What terrific fun it is to see you once more.

MRS ELVSTED [*nervously, trying to control herself*]: Yes, it's a very long time since we met.

TESMAN [*extends his hand to her*]: As it is for the two of us. What?

HEDDA: Thank you for your lovely flowers –

MRS ELVSTED: Oh, it's nothing –. I'd have come straight away yesterday afternoon. But then I heard you were off travelling –

TESMAN: You've just arrived in town then? What?

MRS ELVSTED: I arrived here yesterday at about midday. Oh, I was in total despair when I heard you weren't at home.

HEDDA: Despair? Why?

TESMAN: But my dear Mrs Rysing – Mrs Elvsted I mean –

HEDDA: Nothing wrong, is there?

MRS ELVSTED: Indeed, there is. And I don't know another living soul in town to whom I could turn.

HEDDA [*puts the bouquet on the table*]: Come, we'll sit here on the sofa –

MRS ELVSTED: Oh, I'm far too restless and jittery to sit down.

HEDDA: Surely not. Come on now.

> She pulls MRS ELVSTED *down onto the sofa and sits beside her.*

TESMAN: Well? And so –?

HEDDA: Has anything in particular happened up at your place?

MRS ELVSTED: Well – it both has and has not. Oh – I do so earnestly hope that you won't misunderstand me –

HEDDA: But then you'd do best to speak straight out, Mrs Elvsted.

TESMAN: After all, that's presumably why you're here. What?

MRS ELVSTED: Yes, yes – it is indeed. And so I must tell you – if you don't already know – that Eilert Løvborg is also in town.

HEDDA: Is Løvborg –?

TESMAN: Never! Is Eilert Løvborg back? Just think, Hedda!

HEDDA: Good God, I *can* hear!

MRS ELVSTED: He's been here for about a week already. Just think – a whole week! In this dangerous city. Alone! With all the bad company that's to be found here.

HEDDA: But, my dear Mrs Elvsted – what has *he* to do with you?

MRS ELVSTED [*looks at her with trepidation and says quickly*]: He's been tutoring the children.

HEDDA: Your children?

MRS ELVSTED: My husband's. I don't have any.

HEDDA: Your stepchildren then.

MRS ELVSTED: Yes.

TESMAN [*faltering*]: Was he sufficiently – I don't know how I should put it – sufficiently – ordered in his life and habits to be charged with such a task? What?

MRS ELVSTED: In the last couple of years there's not been a thing to be said against him.

TESMAN: Really? Just think, Hedda!

HEDDA: I can hear.

MRS ELVSTED: Not the slightest thing, I assure you. Not in any respect. But still –. Now that I know he's here – in this big city –. And with all that money in his hands. I'm deadly afraid for him.

TESMAN: But why didn't he stay up there then, where he was? With you and your husband?

MRS ELVSTED: After his book had come out, he became restless and fidgety up at our place.

TESMAN: Oh, yes – Auntie Ju said he'd brought out a new book.

MRS ELVSTED: Yes, a great new book, dealing with cultural development[22] – a sort of overview. That was a fortnight ago now. And when it was bought and read so widely – and attracted so much attention –

TESMAN: So it did, did it? Then it must be something he's had lying around from his better days.

MRS ELVSTED: From before, you mean?

TESMAN: Well, yes.

MRS ELVSTED: No, he wrote the entire thing up there with us. Just now – in the past year.

TESMAN: Well, that's very gratifying to hear, isn't it, Hedda! Just think, darling!

MRS ELVSTED: Ah, yes, if it lasts, that is.

HEDDA: Have you seen him here in town?

MRS ELVSTED: No, not yet. I had such trouble tracking down his address. But I finally got it this morning.

HEDDA [*looks inquisitively at her*]: I must say, I find it a little strange that your husband – hmm –

MRS ELVSTED [*shrinks nervously*]: That my husband? What?

HEDDA: That he'd send *you* to town on such an errand. That he doesn't come here himself to care for his friend.

MRS ELVSTED: Oh no, no – my husband hasn't time for that. And then there was – some shopping I needed to do.

HEDDA [*with a little smile*]: Well, that's another matter of course.

MRS ELVSTED [*rises quickly and in agitation*]: And now I beg you earnestly, Mr Tesman – make Eilert Løvborg welcome, if he comes to you! And he will, most certainly. Good Lord – you've been such good friends in the past. And then, of course, you're both working in the exact same fields of study. The same area of scholarship – as far as I understand.

TESMAN: Well yes, in the past at least.

MRS ELVSTED: Yes, so I do most urgently beg that you – you too – will keep a watchful eye over him. You will, won't you, Mr Tesman – you promise me?

TESMAN: Yes, with pleasure, Mrs Rysing.

HEDDA: Elvsted.

TESMAN: I shall of course do everything for Eilert that is in my power. You can rely on it.

MRS ELVSTED: Oh, how incredibly kind of you! [*Shakes his hand*] Thank you, thank you, thank you! [*Alarmed*] Yes, because my husband is so very fond of him!

HEDDA [*gets up*]: You should write to him, Tesman. After all, he may not come to you just like that, of his own accord.

TESMAN: Yes, I dare say that would be the right thing, Hedda? What?

HEDDA: Do it sooner rather than later. Straight away, I'd say.

MRS ELVSTED [*pleading*]: Oh yes, if you could!

TESMAN: I'll write this instant. Do you have his address, Mrs – Mrs Elvsted?

MRS ELVSTED: Yes. [*Takes a slip of paper out of her pocket and gives it to him*] Here it is.

TESMAN: Good, good. Then I'll go in – [*Looks around*] Oh, I almost forgot – my slippers? Ah, there. [*Takes the parcel and is about to leave*]

HEDDA: Be sure to make it a warm, friendly letter. And of a good length too.

TESMAN: Yes, I'll do that.

MRS ELVSTED: But please, not a word about my asking you on his behalf!

TESMAN: No, that of course goes without saying. What?
He leaves through the back room to the right.

HEDDA [*goes over to* MRS ELVSTED, *smiles and says quietly*]: There now! We just killed two birds with one stone.

MRS ELVSTED: What do you mean?

HEDDA: Didn't you realize I wanted him to go?

MRS ELVSTED: Yes, to write the letter –

HEDDA: And so as to be able to talk to you alone.

MRS ELVSTED [*confused*]: About this?

HEDDA: Yes, absolutely.

MRS ELVSTED [*anxiously*]: But there's *nothing* more to it, Mrs Tesman! Really, nothing more!

HEDDA: Oh, but I think there is. There's a great deal more. That much I understand. Come here – we'll sit down and have a proper heart-to-heart.
She forces MRS ELVSTED *down into the armchair by the stove and sits down herself on one of the stools.*

MRS ELVSTED [*worried, looks at her watch*]: But my dear, kind Mrs Tesman –. I was thinking of going now actually.

HEDDA: Oh, there's no hurry, surely. – Well? Tell me a bit about how things are for you at home.

MRS ELVSTED: Oh, that's *precisely* what I'd rather not touch on.

HEDDA: But to me, my dear –? Good Lord, we were at school together.

MRS ELVSTED: Yes, but you were a class above me. Oh, how dreadfully frightened I was of you back then.

HEDDA: Were you frightened of me?

MRS ELVSTED: Yes, dreadfully frightened. Because whenever we met on the stairs you always used to scruff up my hair.

HEDDA: No, did I do *that*?

MRS ELVSTED: Yes, and once you said you were going to burn it all off.

HEDDA: Oh, that was just talk, you know that.

MRS ELVSTED: Yes, but I was so stupid back then. – And since then at least – we've gone such separate ways – so far from each other. Our circles were, of course, so completely different.

HEDDA: Well, we shall have to get closer again then. Listen! At school we always called each other by our first names –[23]

MRS ELVSTED: No, you're mistaken, surely.

HEDDA: I certainly am not! I remember it very clearly. And that's why we must confide in each other now, just like in the old days. [*Moves closer on the stool*] There now! [*Kisses her on the cheek*] You must drop all formality now and call me Hedda.[24]

MRS ELVSTED [*squeezes and pats her hands*]: Ah, what goodness and kindness –! That's something I'm really not accustomed to.

HEDDA: Come, come, come! And I shall, just as in the old days, call you my dearest Thora.

MRS ELVSTED: My name is Thea.

HEDDA: Yes, that's right. Of course. I meant Thea. [*Looks at her with sympathy*] So, you're unaccustomed to goodness and kindness, Thea, my friend? In your own home?

MRS ELVSTED: Oh, if only I had a home! But I don't. Never did.

HEDDA [*looks at her a while*]: I suspected it must be something of the sort.

MRS ELVSTED [*stares helplessly in front of her*]: Yes – yes – yes.

HEDDA: I can't quite remember now. But wasn't it as a housekeeper that you first went up there to the chief bailiff's place?

MRS ELVSTED: Well, it was actually meant to be as a governess. But his wife – as she was then – she was poorly – and bedridden most of the time. So I had to take care of the house too.

HEDDA: But then – in the end – you became mistress of the house.

MRS ELVSTED [*heavily*]: Yes, I did indeed.

HEDDA: Let me see –. Roughly how long ago was that?

MRS ELVSTED: That I got married?

HEDDA: Yes.

MRS ELVSTED: It's about five years ago now.

HEDDA: Yes, that's right; it must be.

MRS ELVSTED: Oh, these five years –! Or most of all the last two or three. Oh, if you could only imagine, Mrs –²⁵

HEDDA [*gives her a light slap on the back of her hand*]: Mrs –? Naughty, Thea!

MRS ELVSTED: Oh, I'm sorry, I'll try. – Yes, Hedda, if you could only – if you had any idea –

HEDDA [*casually*]: Eilert Løvborg has been up there for three years, I believe.

MRS ELVSTED [*looks at her uncertainly*]: Eilert Løvborg? Yes – he has.

HEDDA: Did you already know him from here in town?

MRS ELVSTED: Scarcely at all. Well, that is – by name of course.

HEDDA: But then – then he entered your household up there?

MRS ELVSTED: He came over to us every day. He was teaching the children, you see. Because I couldn't manage it all on my own in the end.

HEDDA: No, that's quite understandable. – And your husband –? He's often away presumably?

MRS ELVSTED: Yes, Mrs – Hedda – you can imagine, as chief bailiff he has to travel around the district regularly.

HEDDA [*leans on the arm of the chair*]: Thea – my poor, sweet Thea – you're to tell me everything now – just as it is.

MRS ELVSTED: All right, ask me then.

HEDDA: What is your husband *really* like, Thea dear? I mean – you know – when you're with him. Is he good to you?

MRS ELVSTED [*evasively*]: Doubtless he believes he does everything for the best.

HEDDA: I just think he must be much too old for you. Probably over twenty years older?

MRS ELVSTED [*irritably*]: That too. That and other things. Everything about him is objectionable to me! We don't have a single idea in common. Nothing at all – he and I.

HEDDA: But isn't he fond of you at least? In his own way?

MRS ELVSTED: Oh, I don't know what he is. I'm probably just useful to him. And it doesn't cost much to keep me. I'm cheap.

HEDDA: That's stupid of you.

MRS ELVSTED [*shakes her head*]: It can't be otherwise. Not with him. He doesn't really seem to have much fondness for anyone but himself. And a little for the children perhaps.

HEDDA: And for Eilert Løvborg, Thea.

MRS ELVSTED [*looks over at her*]: Eilert Løvborg! What makes you think that?

HEDDA: But my dear – I'd presume that if he sends you all the way into town after him – [*Smiles almost imperceptibly*] Besides, you said it yourself to Tesman.

MRS ELVSTED [*with a nervous twitch*]: Really? Yes, I suppose I did. [*Exclaims quietly*] Very well – I may as well tell you sooner rather than later! Since it's bound to come to light anyway.

HEDDA: But, my dear Thea –?

MRS ELVSTED: Well, to be brief! My husband knew absolutely nothing of my travelling here.

HEDDA: What's that? Your husband knew nothing of it?

MRS ELVSTED: No, of course not. And besides, he wasn't at home. He was away travelling too. Oh, I couldn't stick it out any longer, Hedda! Totally impossible! To be as alone as I would have been up there from now on.

HEDDA: Well? And so?

MRS ELVSTED: So I packed some of my things together, you see. The essentials. On the quiet. And then I left the house.

HEDDA: Just like that?

MRS ELVSTED: Yes. And took the train straight here into town.

HEDDA: But my dear, good Thea – you dared to do that!

MRS ELVSTED [*gets up and walks across the floor*]: Well, what on earth else could I do!

HEDDA: But what do you think your husband will say when you go back home?

MRS ELVSTED [*by the table, looks over at her*]: Up there to *him*?

HEDDA: Well yes – yes?

MRS ELVSTED: I'll never go back to him.

HEDDA [*gets up and goes closer*]: So you have – in all serious-ness – left the whole lot behind?

MRS ELVSTED: Yes. I didn't feel there was anything else I could do.

HEDDA: And then – to leave so openly.

MRS ELVSTED: Oh, you can't conceal a thing like that anyway.

HEDDA: But what do you think people will say about you, Thea?

MRS ELVSTED: Oh, for God's sake, they'll have to say whatever they like. [*She sits down on the sofa, heavy with weariness*] I've done nothing but what I *had* to do.

HEDDA [*after a short silence*]: What do you plan to do now? What will you do with yourself?

MRS ELVSTED: I don't know yet. All I know is that I *must* live here where Eilert Løvborg lives. – If I *am* to live, that is.

HEDDA [*moves a chair closer from the table, sits beside her and strokes her hands*]: Thea, dear Thea – how did it come about – this friendship – between you and Eilert Løvborg?

MRS ELVSTED: Oh, it happened little by little. I almost got a sort of power over him.

HEDDA: And?

MRS ELVSTED: He set aside his old habits. Not because I asked him to. I never dared do that. But he probably noticed that I objected to them. And so he gave them up.

HEDDA [*concealing an involuntary, scornful smile*]: So, you've restored him²⁶ – as they say – you, my little Thea.

MRS ELVSTED: Well, that's what he says, at least. And he – for his part – has made a sort of real human being of me. Taught me to think – and to understand so many things.

HEDDA: So did he give *you* lessons too?

MRS ELVSTED: Not lessons exactly. But he talked to me. Talked about such a wide variety of things. And then came that lovely, joyous moment when I came to share in his work! Was allowed to help him!

HEDDA: You were, were you?

MRS ELVSTED: Yes! Whenever he wrote something, we both had to be in on it.

HEDDA: Like two good comrades, you mean?

MRS ELVSTED [*full of life*]: Comrades! Yes, to think, Hedda – that's what *he* called it too! – Oh, I should feel deeply happy, of course. But I can't, not really. Because I don't know if it will last in the long term.

HEDDA: Are you no surer of him than that?

MRS ELVSTED [*heavily*]: The shadow of a woman stands between Eilert Løvborg and myself.

HEDDA [*with a look of suspense*]: Who could *that* be?

MRS ELVSTED: Don't know. Someone or other from – from his past. Someone he seems never to have forgotten.

HEDDA: What has he said – about that?

MRS ELVSTED: He has only once – just vaguely – hinted at it.

HEDDA: Ah! And what did he say?

MRS ELVSTED: He said that when they parted she threatened to shoot him with a pistol.

HEDDA [*cold, composed*]: Oh, really! Nobody uses such a thing round here.

MRS ELVSTED: No. Which is why I think it must be the red-haired singer he once –

HEDDA: Yes, quite possibly.

MRS ELVSTED: Because I remember it being said that she carried a loaded weapon.

HEDDA: Well – it's obviously her, then.

MRS ELVSTED [*wrings her hands*]: Yes, but imagine, Hedda – I've heard that this singer – she's in town again! Oh – I'm in total despair –

HEDDA [*glances towards the back room*]: Shh! Tesman's coming. [*Gets up and whispers*] Thea – all this must stay between you and me.

MRS ELVSTED [*jumps up*]: Oh yes – yes! For heaven's sake –!
     JØRGEN TESMAN, *with a letter in his hand, comes from the right through the back room.*

TESMAN: There – the epistle is ready and done.

HEDDA: That's good. But I think Mrs Elvsted wants to leave. Wait here. I'll go with her to the garden gate.

TESMAN: Hedda, dear – could Berta perhaps take care of this?

HEDDA [*takes the letter*]: I'll tell her.
     BERTA *comes in from the hallway.*

BERTA: Judge Brack is here and asks if he might pop in and see the master and mistress.

HEDDA: Yes, tell the judge to come right in. And then – listen –
throw this letter in the postbox.

BERTA [*takes the letter*]: Very well, ma'am.

She opens the door for JUDGE BRACK, *and then goes out.*
The judge is a man of forty-five years. He is short but well
built, supple in his movements. He has a roundish face
with a noble profile. His hair is cut short,[27] *mostly still*
black and carefully styled. His eyes are lively, playful.
Thick eyebrows and a handlebar moustache, with short
clipped ends. He wears an elegant walking suit, although
it is a little too youthful for his age. He uses a lorgnette,
which he occasionally lets fall.

BRACK [*with his hat in his hand, bows*]: May one dare to come
by this early in the day?

HEDDA: One most certainly may.

TESMAN [*takes his hand*]: You're always welcome. [*Making*
the introductions] Judge Brack – Miss Rysing –

HEDDA: Oh –!

BRACK [*bows*]: Ah – an absolute pleasure –

HEDDA [*looks at him and laughs*]: It's rather fun to be able to
scrutinize you in the daylight, Mr Brack.

BRACK: Transformed – you find, perhaps?

HEDDA: Yes, a tad younger, I'd say.

BRACK: Thanking you most humbly.

TESMAN: But what do you say about Hedda! Doesn't she look
buxom? What? She's veritably –

HEDDA: Oh, do leave me out of it. Thank the judge instead for
all the inconvenience he's gone to –

BRACK: Oh, nonsense – it was my pleasure –

HEDDA: Yes, you're a loyal soul. But my friend here is simply
burning to be on her way. *Au revoir*, judge. I'll be back in a
tick.

Mutual farewells. MRS ELVSTED *and* HEDDA *leave through*
the hallway door.

BRACK: So – is your wife tolerably pleased –?

TESMAN: Yes, we can't thank you enough. That is – things
will have to be moved around here and there, I'm told. And

there are still one or two things lacking, of course. We may have to procure a few more little items.

BRACK: Oh? Really?

TESMAN: But you shan't trouble yourself over those. Hedda said that she'll see to whatever's lacking herself. – Shouldn't we sit down? What?

BRACK: Thanks, for a moment. [*Sits down by the table*] There's something I wish to discuss with you, my dear Tesman.

TESMAN: Really? Ah, I understand! [*Sits down*] The more serious phase of the party is about to start. What?

BRACK: Oh, there's no great rush with the finances yet. Although, when it comes to that, I might have wished we'd been a little more frugal.

TESMAN: But that would never do! Think of Hedda, old chap. You – who know her so well! I could hardly present her with petit bourgeois[28] surroundings!

BRACK: No, no – there's the rub.

TESMAN: And then – luckily – it can't be long before I get my appointment.

BRACK: Well, you know, these things can often drag out rather.

TESMAN: Have you perhaps heard something? What?

BRACK: Nothing specific –. [*Breaking off*] Though, of course – there is one piece of news I can tell you.

TESMAN: Well?

BRACK: Your old friend, Eilert Løvborg, is back in town.

TESMAN: I know that already.

BRACK: Oh? Where did you hear it?

TESMAN: She told us, that woman who just went out with Hedda.

BRACK: I see. What was her name again? I didn't quite hear –

TESMAN: Mrs Elvsted.

BRACK: Ah – the chief bailiff's wife. Yes – he's been staying up there with them apparently.

TESMAN: And imagine – I hear to my great pleasure that he's become an altogether decent human being again!

BRACK: Yes, so they claim.

TESMAN: And he seems to have brought out a new book. What?

BRACK: Lord, yes!

TESMAN: And it's aroused some attention too, I hear!

BRACK: A truly extraordinary level of attention.

TESMAN: Just think – isn't that gratifying to hear? A man with his unusual talents –. I was sadly convinced that he'd run aground for good.

BRACK: And that was doubtless the general opinion of him.

TESMAN: But I simply cannot understand what he'll do with himself now! What on earth is he going to make his living from? Eh?

HEDDA *has come in through the hallway door during the last remark.*

HEDDA [*to* BRACK, *laughs rather spitefully*]: Tesman's constantly going around worrying about how one will make a living.

TESMAN: Oh heavens – we're sitting here talking about that poor Eilert Løvborg.

HEDDA [*glances at him quickly*]: Oh, really? [*Sits down in the armchair by the stove and asks indifferently*] So what's the matter with *him*?

TESMAN: Well – he probably squandered his inheritance ages ago. And he can't write a new book every year. Eh? So, I really do ask, what is to become of him?

BRACK: I might just be able to tell you a bit about that.

TESMAN: Well?

BRACK: You must remember he has relatives with more than a little influence.

TESMAN: Unfortunately – those relatives have completely washed their hands of him.

BRACK: They used to call him the hope of the family.

TESMAN: Used to, yes! But he scuppered that himself.

HEDDA: Who knows? [*Smiles faintly*] Up at the Elvsteds' they seem to have restored him –

BRACK: And with this book coming out –

TESMAN: Well, well, God grant they'll offer him help in some way or another. I've just written to him. And, Hedda, I invited him to come over this evening.

BRACK: But, my dear friend, you're coming to my bachelor party tonight. You promised on the pier last night.

HEDDA: Had you forgotten, Tesman?

TESMAN: Yes, I had indeed.

BRACK: Anyway, you can rest assured he won't turn up.

TESMAN: Why do you think that? Eh?

BRACK [*a little hesitant, gets up and rests his hands on the back of the chair*]: My dear Tesman –. And you too, Mrs Tesman –. I can't in all conscience allow you to remain ignorant of something that – that –

TESMAN: Something that concerns Eilert –?

BRACK: Both you and him.

TESMAN: But my dear judge, say it then!

BRACK: You ought to prepare yourself for the possibility that your appointment may not come as quickly as you either wish or expect.

TESMAN [*jumps uneasily to his feet*]: Has something come in the way? What?

BRACK: Election to the post may now perhaps be dependent on a competition –

TESMAN: A competition! Just think, Hedda!

HEDDA [*leans further back in the chair*]: Oh, really – really!

TESMAN: But with whom? It can't be with –?

BRACK: Yes, indeed. With Eilert Løvborg.

TESMAN [*clasping his hands together*]: No, no – this is quite unthinkable! Utterly impossible! What?

BRACK: Hmm – we may nonetheless see it happen.

TESMAN: But, Judge Brack – that would show a most unbelievable lack of consideration towards me. [*Waves his arms*] After all – just think – I am a married man! We were married on the basis of these prospects, Hedda and I. We've taken on a massive debt. And borrowed money from Auntie Ju as well. Good God – I was as good as promised that position. Wasn't I?

BRACK: Now, now, now – you'll almost certainly get the position anyway. But after a preliminary contest.

HEDDA [*unmoving in the armchair*]: Just think, Tesman – it'll almost be like a kind of sport.[29]

TESMAN: But, Hedda darling, how can you take this with such indifference!

HEDDA [*as before*]: I most certainly don't. I'm truly excited about the outcome.

BRACK: Whatever the case, Mrs Tesman, it's best you know how things stand. I mean – before you go ahead with all those little purchases I hear you're threatening to make.

HEDDA: This can't change a thing.

BRACK: Really? That's a different matter. Farewell! [*To* TESMAN] I'll drop by and fetch you when I take my afternoon walk.

TESMAN: Yes, yes – I really don't know which way up I am.

HEDDA [*lying down, stretches her hand out*]: Goodbye, judge. Until later.

BRACK: Thank you. Goodbye, goodbye.

TESMAN [*follows him to the door*]: Goodbye, Brack! Please do forgive me –

JUDGE BRACK *leaves through the hallway door.*

TESMAN [*walks across the floor*]: Oh, Hedda – one should never venture into the land of fairy tales. What?

HEDDA [*looks at him and smiles*]: And *you* do that, do you?

TESMAN: Yes, my darling – it can't be denied – it was a fairy tale to go and get married and set up home based on mere prospects.

HEDDA: You may be right.

TESMAN: Well – Hedda, at least we have our comfortable home! Imagine – the home that we both spent our time dreaming of. Fantasized over, I might almost say. What?

HEDDA [*gets up slowly and wearily*]: The agreement was that we'd have a social life. And a house run accordingly.

TESMAN: Yes, good God – I was so looking forward to that! Just think – seeing you as hostess to a select circle! What? Well, well, well – we shall just have to stick together in solitude for now, Hedda. Just have Auntie Ju over now and then. – Oh, for you it should all have been so very – very different –!

HEDDA: So I won't have my liveried servant right away.

TESMAN: Oh no – I'm afraid not. Keeping servants – that's quite out of the question, you understand.

HEDDA: And the horse I was supposed to have –

TESMAN [*shocked*]: Horse!

HEDDA: – I daren't even contemplate that now.

TESMAN: No, God preserve me – that goes without saying!

HEDDA [*walks across the floor*]: Ah well – I do have *one* thing at least to amuse myself with in the meantime.

TESMAN [*joyfully*]: Oh, thank the good Lord for that! And what might that be, Hedda? Eh?

HEDDA [*by the doorway, looks at him with concealed scorn*]: My pistols – Jørgen.

TESMAN [*anxious*]: The pistols!

HEDDA [*with cold eyes*]: General Gabler's pistols.

  She walks through the back room to the left side.

TESMAN [*runs over to the doorway and calls after her*]: No, God bless you, my darling Hedda – don't touch those dangerous things! For my sake, Hedda! What?

ACT TWO

The room at Tesman's as in Act One, except that the piano has been removed and an elegant little writing desk with bookshelves put in its place. By the sofa to the left a smallish table is placed. Most of the flowers have been removed. Mrs Elvsted's bouquet stands on the larger table towards the front. – It is afternoon.

HEDDA, dressed in a tea gown, is alone in the room. She stands by the open glass door, loading a revolver. A matching one lies in an open revolver case on the writing desk.

HEDDA [*looks down into the garden and shouts*]: Good day again, judge!

BRACK [*heard from below in the distance*]: Likewise, Mrs Tesman!

HEDDA [*raises her gun and aims*]: Now I'm going to shoot you, Judge Brack!

BRACK [*shouts from below*]: No-no-no! Don't stand like that aiming at me!

HEDDA: That's what comes of taking the back way!
She shoots.

BRACK [*closer*]: Are you completely mad –!

HEDDA: Oh, good God – did I hit you perhaps?

BRACK [*still outside*]: Do stop these silly pranks!

HEDDA: Come on in then, judge.

JUDGE BRACK, dressed now as though for a gentleman's party, comes in through the glass door. He carries a light overcoat on his arm.

BRACK: Bloody hell – are you still persisting with that sport? What do you shoot at?

HEDDA: I just stand like this and shoot into thin air.

BRACK [*carefully takes the gun out of her hand*]: Allow me, madam. [*Looks at it*] Ah, it's this one – I know it well. [*Looks around*] Do we have the case? Yes, here it is. [*Lays the pistol in it and closes it*] We'll have no more of that little game for today.

HEDDA: Well, what in God's name do you want me to do with myself?

BRACK: Haven't you had any visitors?

HEDDA [*closes the glass door*]: Not one. All my intimate acquaintances are presumably still in the country.

BRACK: And Tesman's not at home either?

HEDDA [*by the writing desk, shutting the revolver case in the drawer*]: No. The minute he'd eaten he ran over to his aunties. As he didn't expect you so early.

BRACK: Hmm – I didn't think of that. That was stupid of me.

HEDDA [*turns her head and looks at him*]: Why stupid?

BRACK: Well, if I had, I would have come over a little – earlier.

HEDDA [*walks across the floor*]: Then you'd have found absolutely nobody here. Since I've been inside changing my clothes after lunch.[30]

BRACK: And there isn't any sort of little crack in the door one could negotiate through?

HEDDA: No, you've forgotten to arrange one of those.

BRACK: That was *also* stupid of me.

HEDDA: Well, we shall just have to sit here together, then. And wait. Because Tesman isn't likely to be home any time soon.

BRACK: No, good Lord, I shall be patient.

HEDDA *sits down in the corner of the sofa.* BRACK *puts his overcoat over the back of the nearest chair and sits down, but keeps his hat in his hands. Short pause. They look at each other.*

HEDDA: Well?

BRACK [*in the same tone*]: Well?

HEDDA: I was the first to ask.

BRACK [*leans slightly forward*]: Yes, let's have ourselves a nice little chat, Mrs Hedda.

HEDDA [*leans further back in the sofa*]: Doesn't it feel like an eternity to you since we spoke last? – Well, the trifling exchanges of last night and this morning – I'd hardly count that as anything.

BRACK: But like this – between ourselves? As a twosome, you mean?

HEDDA: Quite. More or less.

BRACK: I've spent every single day here wishing you were safely back home.

HEDDA: And I've spent the entire time wishing the exact same.

BRACK: You? Really, Mrs Hedda? And there was I thinking you were having such fun on your travels!

HEDDA: Oh, believe that if you can!

BRACK: But that's what Tesman said in all his letters.

HEDDA: Yes, *he* would! Since for him, the loveliest thing he knows is to go rummaging about in book collections. And then to sit and copy out old parchments – or whatever they are.

BRACK [*with slight malice*]: Well, that, of course, is his calling[31] in the world. In part, at least.

HEDDA: Yes, it is indeed. And then I dare say –. But for me! Oh no, my dear judge – I have been excruciatingly bored.

BRACK [*sympathetically*]: You really mean that? In all seriousness?

HEDDA: Yes, surely you can imagine that for yourself –! A full six months, like that, never meeting a single individual who knew the least thing about our circle. And with whom one might talk of things that are of interest to us.

BRACK: Yes, yes – I'd feel the absence of that too.

HEDDA: And then what's most insufferable –

BRACK: Yes?

HEDDA: – having to spend all your time – all eternity – with just one person.

BRACK [*nods in agreement*]: From morning to night – yes. Imagine – every hour of the day.

HEDDA: I said: all eternity.

BRACK: Quite. Although I'd have thought with our excellent Tesman one might surely manage to –

HEDDA: Tesman is – an academic, my dear.

BRACK: Indubitably.

HEDDA: And academics are not at all fun to go travelling with. Not for too long at least.

BRACK: Not even – the academic one *loves*?

HEDDA: Ugh – don't use that sickly word!

BRACK [*startled*]: But, Mrs Hedda!

HEDDA [*half laughing, half annoyed*]: Well, you should just try it! Listening to cultural history from morning till night –

BRACK: For all eternity –

HEDDA: Yes-yes-yes! And then this stuff about domestic crafts in the Middle Ages –! That really is the ghastliest thing of all!

BRACK [*looks quizzically at her*]: But, tell me – how am I then to understand –? Hmm –

HEDDA: That I and Jørgen Tesman made a match of it, you mean?

BRACK: Well, yes, let's put it that way.

HEDDA: Good God, do you really find it so strange?

BRACK: Both yes and no – Mrs Hedda.

HEDDA: I was wearied of dancing, my dear judge. My time was over – [*Gives a little shudder*] Ugh, no – I don't want to say that really. Nor think it!

BRACK: You certainly have no reason to either.

HEDDA: Oh – reason –. [*Looks searchingly at him*] And Jørgen Tesman – one must admit he's a very correct sort of person in every respect.

BRACK: Both correct and reliable. Good Lord, yes.

HEDDA: And I can't find anything specifically absurd about him. – Can *you*?

BRACK: Absurd? N-no – I can't exactly say –

HEDDA: Well. Anyway, he's an extremely industrious collector at least! – It may be that he'll even get quite far with it in time.

BRACK [*looks rather uncertainly at her*]: I thought you felt, like everyone else, that he'd be a man of some prominence.

HEDDA [*with a weary expression*]: Yes, I did. And when he came along in full battle mode determined to be allowed to provide for me –. I can't think why I wouldn't accept?

BRACK: No-no. Seen from *that* perspective –

HEDDA: It was certainly more than my other gallant friends were willing to offer, my dear judge.

BRACK [*laughing*]: Well, I can't reliably answer for the others. But for my part, I'm sure you know I've always cherished a – a certain respect for the bonds of marriage. Generally speaking, Mrs Hedda.

HEDDA [*jokingly*]: Oh, I certainly never had any hopes as regards *you*.

BRACK: My only desire is this, to have a good, trusting circle of acquaintances, where I can be of service in word and deed, and be allowed to come and go as – as a tried and tested friend –

HEDDA: Of the man of the house, you mean?

BRACK [*leans over*]: To be honest – of the wife preferably. Followed closely by the husband too, naturally. You know what – one of those – let me say, three-way relationships – can in fact be hugely agreeable to all parties.

HEDDA: Yes, many a time I missed a third party on my travels. Ugh – sitting in a railway carriage, just the two of us –!

BRACK: Luckily your nuptial journey is over now –

HEDDA [*shakes her head*]: The journey might be long – very long still. I've merely reached a stop on the line.

BRACK: Well, then, one jumps out. Takes a little stretch, Mrs Hedda.

HEDDA: I never jump out.

BRACK: Really – never?

HEDDA: No. There's always somebody around who –

BRACK [*laughing*]: – who looks at your ankles,[32] you mean?

HEDDA: Precisely.

BRACK: Yes but, good Lord –

HEDDA [*with a dismissive gesture*]: Can't stand it. Then I'd rather remain seated – where I am. In a twosome.

BRACK: Well, but then a third party might climb in with the couple.

HEDDA: Now – *that* is very different!

BRACK: A tried and tested, understanding friend –

HEDDA: – entertaining on a variety of lively topics –

BRACK: – and with no trace of the academic!

HEDDA [*with an audible breath*]: Yes, that *is* certainly a relief.

BRACK [*hears the entrance door open and looks in that direction*]: The triangle is closed.

HEDDA [*in a lowered voice*]: And the train moves on.

> JØRGEN TESMAN, *in grey walking attire and a soft felt hat, enters from the hallway. He has a number of unbound books under his arm and in his pockets.*

TESMAN [*walks up to the table by the corner sofa*]: Phew – that was really hot work – lugging all this about. [*Puts the books down*] I'm positively sweating, Hedda. Ah look, look – you're already here, my dear judge. What? Berta didn't say anything.

BRACK [*rises*]: I came up through the garden.

HEDDA: What sort of books have you got there?

TESMAN [*stands leafing through them*]: Some new academic works I had to have.

HEDDA: Academic works?

BRACK: Aha, those are academic works, Mrs Tesman.

> BRACK *and* HEDDA *exchange a knowing glance.*

HEDDA: Do you need yet more academic works?

TESMAN: Yes, my dear Hedda, one can never have enough. One has to keep up with what's being written and published.

HEDDA: Yes, I suppose one must.

TESMAN [*rummages amongst the books*]: And look here – I've managed to get hold of Eilert Løvborg's new book too. [*Holds it out*] Perhaps you'd like to look at it, Hedda? What?

HEDDA: No, thank you. Or – yes, later perhaps.

TESMAN: I leafed through it briefly on the way.

BRACK: Well, so what did you think – as an academic?

TESMAN: I find its sustained and measured tone remarkable. He never used to write like that before. [*Gathers up the books*] But I want to take this lot in now. It'll be a joy to cut the pages –! And then I'll get changed. [*To* BRACK] We don't need to leave straight away, do we? What?

BRACK: Good gracious – there's no hurry for a long time yet.

TESMAN: Right, I'll take my time, then. [*Walks away with the books, but stops in the doorway and turns*] Oh, by the way, Hedda – Auntie Ju won't be coming out to see you this evening.

HEDDA: Really? Is it that business with the hat that's stopping her?

TESMAN: Oh, not at all. How can you believe that of Auntie Ju? To think –! But Auntie Rina is terribly ill, you see.

HEDDA: She always is.

TESMAN: Yes, but she's in a really bad way today, poor thing.

HEDDA: Well, then it's only reasonable that the other should stay with her. I'll just have to put up with it.

TESMAN: And you can't begin to think, my dear, how overjoyed Auntie Ju was – at your having got so nice and plump on the trip.

HEDDA [*in a lowered voice, gets up*]: Oh – these eternal aunts!

TESMAN: Pardon me?

HEDDA [*walks over to the glass door*]: Nothing.

TESMAN: Well, well.

He walks through the back room off to the right.

BRACK: What was this hat you were talking about?

HEDDA: Oh, it was something with Miss Tesman this morning. She'd put her hat there on that chair. [*Looks at him and smiles*] And then I pretended to think it was the maid's.

BRACK [*shakes his head*]: But, my dear sweet Mrs Hedda, how could you do that? To that respectable old lady!

HEDDA [*nervous, walks across the floor*]: Well, you know – these things come over me every so often. And then I *can't* stop myself. [*Throws herself down in the armchair by the stove*] Oh, I don't know myself how to explain it.

BRACK [*behind the armchair*]: You're not really happy – that's probably it.

HEDDA [*stares straight ahead*]: Nor do I know why I should be – happy. Or perhaps you can tell me?

BRACK: Well – among other things, because you've just got the home you wished for.

HEDDA [*looks up at him and laughs*]: Do you believe in that wishing-story too?

BRACK: Is there nothing in it then?

HEDDA: Oh, heavens, yes – something.

BRACK: Well?

HEDDA: There is *this* much – that I used Tesman last summer to accompany me home[33] from evening events –

BRACK: Unfortunately – I was taking another route entirely.

HEDDA: True. You did indeed pursue other routes last summer.

BRACK [*laughs*]: Shame on you, Mrs Hedda! But – you and Tesman –?

HEDDA: Yes, so one evening we passed by here. And Tesman, poor thing, he was squirming about, not knowing what to talk about. So I took pity on the learned man –

BRACK [*smiles sceptically*]: You did, did you? Hmm –

HEDDA: Yes, I did indeed. And so, to help him out of his agony – I happened to say, quite frivolously, that I would love to live in this villa.

BRACK: Nothing more?

HEDDA: Not *that* evening.

BRACK: But later?

HEDDA: Yes. My frivolity had consequences, my dear judge.

BRACK: As our frivolities all too frequently do, Mrs Hedda – sadly.

HEDDA: Thanks! But it was in fantasizing over Mrs Falk's villa that Jørgen Tesman and I found some mutual ground, you see! *That* led to the engagement, the wedding, the honeymoon and everything else. Well, well, judge – as you make your bed, you must lie in it – I almost said.

BRACK: That's priceless! And perhaps you didn't really care a jot for this place?

HEDDA: No, God knows I didn't.

BRACK: Yes, but now? Now that we've furnished it and made it homely for you?

HEDDA: Ugh – I think all the rooms smell of lavender and rose water. But perhaps Auntie Ju brought the smell in with her.

BRACK [*laughs*]: No, I think that's likely to be a legacy from the late Right Honourable Mrs Falk.

HEDDA: Yes, there is something deathlike about it. It reminds one of a posy – the day after the ball. [*Clasps her hands behind her neck, leans back in the chair and looks at him*] Oh, my dear judge – you can't imagine how atrociously bored I'm going to be out here.

BRACK: Mightn't life have some sort of task to offer you too, Mrs Hedda?

HEDDA: A task – that might have some allure?

BRACK: Preferably, of course.

HEDDA: God only knows what kind of task that might be. I often think – [*Breaking off*] But that's unlikely to come to anything either.

BRACK: Who knows? Let me hear.

HEDDA: If I could get Tesman to go into politics, I mean.

BRACK [*laughs*]: Tesman! No, you know what – something like politics is really – absolutely not for him.

HEDDA: No, you're probably right. But if I could get him into it anyway?

BRACK: Well – what satisfaction would there be in that for you? When he's not up to it. Why would you get him into that?

HEDDA: Because I am bored, you hear! [*A brief pause*] So you think it would be absolutely impossible for Tesman to be a government minister?

BRACK: Hm – well, you see, my dear Mrs Hedda – for *that* he would first have to be a reasonably wealthy man.

HEDDA [*gets up impatiently*]: Yes, there we have it! It's these frugal circumstances in which I find myself –! [*Walks across the floor*] *They* are what makes life so paltry! So utterly ludicrous! – Because that's what it is.

BRACK: I believe the fault may lie elsewhere.

HEDDA: Where, then?

BRACK: You've never experienced anything to truly awaken you.

HEDDA: You mean, something serious?

BRACK: Yes, you might indeed call it that. But it may well come now.

HEDDA [*tosses her head*]: Oh, you're thinking of the trouble and strife over that pathetic professorship! But that'll have to be Tesman's own affair. I won't waste a single thought on it.

BRACK: Well, that aside. But when you're faced with – what one might – in more elevated parlance – describe as a solemn duty – a demand that will bring you responsibility? [*Smiles*] New demands, my little Mrs Hedda.

HEDDA [*angry*]: Quiet now! You will never see such a thing!

BRACK [*gently*]: We'll talk about that in a year's time – at the most.

HEDDA [*curtly*]: I've no talent for such things, judge. Nothing that makes any demand upon me!

BRACK: Wouldn't you, like most other women, have some talent for a calling³⁴ as –?

HEDDA [*over by the glass door*]: Oh, be quiet, I say! I frequently think I have a talent for only one thing in this world.

BRACK [*comes closer*]: And what's that, if I may ask?

HEDDA [*stands looking out*]: For boring myself to death. Now you know it. [*Turns around, looks towards the back room and laughs*] Yes, indeed! Here's our professor!

BRACK [*quietly with a warning tone*]: Steady now, Mrs Hedda!
    JØRGEN TESMAN, *dressed in party clothes, with gloves and hat in his hand, arrives from the right through the back room.*

TESMAN: Hedda – there's been no message from Eilert Løvborg declining my invitation? What?

HEDDA: No.

TESMAN: Well then, he'll be here shortly, you'll see.

BRACK: You really think he'll come?

TESMAN: Yes, I'm almost certain of it. Since in all likelihood what you told us this morning is nothing but a loose rumour.

BRACK: Really?

TESMAN: Yes, Auntie Ju said, at least, that she didn't think for a second that he'd stand in my way again. Just think.

BRACK: Right, so everything's perfectly fine and dandy.

TESMAN [*puts his hat, with his gloves inside, on a chair to the right*]: Yes, but I really must be allowed to wait for him as long as possible.

BRACK: We've got ample time for that. Nobody's coming to my place before seven or half past.

TESMAN: Well, we can keep Hedda company in the meantime, then. And see how things go. What?

HEDDA [*moves* BRACK's *coat and hat over to the corner sofa*]: And if it comes to the worst, Mr Løvborg can settle down here with me.

BRACK [*reaching to take his things himself*]: Allow me, Mrs Tesman! – What do you mean by 'comes to the worst'?

HEDDA: If he doesn't want to go with you and Tesman.

TESMAN [*looks doubtfully at her*]: But, my dear Hedda – do you think it's quite the done thing for him to stay here with you? What? Remember Auntie Ju can't make it.

HEDDA: No, but Mrs Elvsted is coming. And so the three of us will take a cup of tea together.

TESMAN: Ah, that's all right then!³⁵

BRACK [*smiles*]: And that might just be the healthiest option for him.

HEDDA: Why's that?

BRACK: Good God, Mrs Tesman, you've ribbed me over my little bachelor parties often enough. Unsuitable for gentlemen of anything but the strongest principle, you said.

HEDDA: But Mr Løvborg is surely principled enough now. A reformed sinner –

BERTA *appears in the hallway door.*

BERTA: Madam, there's a gentleman wants to come in –

HEDDA: Yes, let him come.

TESMAN [*quietly*]: I'm sure that's him! Just think!

EILERT LØVBORG *comes in from the hallway. He is of slim build; the same age as* TESMAN *but looks older, with a wasted look about him. Very dark brown hair and beard, longish face, pale, only with a couple of red patches on his cheeks. He is dressed in an elegant, black, reasonably new visiting suit. Dark gloves and a top hat in his hand. He stops close to the door and bows quickly. Seems a little shy.*

TESMAN [*walks over to him and shakes his hand*]: Well, my dear Eilert – so we finally meet again!

EILERT LØVBORG [*speaks with a quiet voice*]: Thanks so much for the letter, old chap! [*Approaches* HEDDA] May I extend a hand to you too, Mrs Tesman?

HEDDA [*takes his hand*]: Welcome, Mr Løvborg. [*With a wave of her hand*] I'm not sure if you two gentlemen –?

LØVBORG [*bows lightly*]: Judge Brack, I think.

BRACK [*likewise*]: Goodness, yes. – Quite a few years –

TESMAN [*to* LØVBORG, *with his hands on his shoulders*]: And now you must make yourself at home, Eilert! Isn't that right, Hedda? – I hear you want to settle here in town again? What?

LØVBORG: I do, yes.

TESMAN: Well, that's only reasonable, of course. Listen here, old chap – I managed to get hold of your new book. But I honestly haven't had the time to read it yet.

LØVBORG: And you can spare yourself the trouble.

TESMAN: Why – what do you mean?

LØVBORG: Because there's really not much in it.

TESMAN: To think – how can you say that?

BRACK: But it's received such praise, I hear.

LØVBORG: That was exactly what I wanted. So I wrote a book that everybody could go along with.

BRACK: Very sensible.

TESMAN: Yes but, my dear Eilert –!

LØVBORG: Because I want to re-establish a position for myself. To start afresh.

TESMAN [*slightly awkward*]: Yes, I expect you do? What?

LØVBORG [*smiles, puts his hat down and pulls a packet wrapped in paper from his coat pocket*]: But when this arrives – Jørgen Tesman – then you'll have to read it. Because *this* will be the real thing. My true self is in this one.

TESMAN: Oh, really? So what is it?

LØVBORG: It's the sequel.

TESMAN: Sequel? To what?

LØVBORG: To the book.

TESMAN: To the latest?

LØVBORG: Naturally.

TESMAN: Yes but, my dear Eilert – that goes right up to the present day!

LØVBORG: It does indeed. And this one concerns the future.

TESMAN: The future! But, good Lord, we know nothing at all about that!

LØVBORG: No. But there are one or two things to say about it all the same. [*Opens the packet*] Here, I'll show you –

TESMAN: But that's not your handwriting.

LØVBORG: I dictated it. [*Leafs through the papers*] It's in two parts. The first is about the forces that will shape our civilization. And this second part here – [*leafs on further*] – this is about how that civilization will progress into the future.

TESMAN: Extraordinary! It would never cross my mind to write about anything like that.

HEDDA [*by the glass door, drumming on the pane*]: Hmm –. No, quite.

LØVBORG [*stuffs the papers back in their cover and puts the packet on the table*]: I brought it with me, thinking I'd read a bit for you this evening.

TESMAN: Well, that was extremely kind of you, my friend. But this evening –? [*Looks over at* BRACK] I'm not altogether sure how that could be arranged –

LØVBORG: Well, another time, then. There's no hurry after all.

BRACK: I should tell you, Mr Løvborg – there's a little event over at my place this evening. More or less in honour of Tesman, you understand –

LØVBORG [*looks for his hat*]: Ah – then I shan't stay –

BRACK: No, listen to me. Wouldn't you do me the pleasure of coming along?

LØVBORG [*quickly and resolutely*]: No, I can't. Thank you kindly.

BRACK: Oh, come on! Please do. We'll be a select little circle. And you can be sure we'll have a 'lively' time of it, as Mrs Hed – as Mrs Tesman puts it.

LØVBORG: I've no doubt. But still –

BRACK: You could bring your manuscript and read it to Tesman *there* at my place. I've enough rooms.

TESMAN: Yes, think, Eilert – you could do that! What?

HEDDA [*interjects*]: But darling, if Mr Løvborg doesn't *want* to! I'm sure Mr Løvborg would much prefer to settle down here and eat some supper with me.

LØVBORG [*looks over at her*]: With you, Mrs Tesman!?

HEDDA: And Mrs Elvsted.

LØVBORG: Ah – [*Casually*] I met her briefly around noon.

HEDDA: Did you now? Well, she's coming out here. So it's almost a necessity that you stay, Mr Løvborg. Otherwise she'll have nobody to walk her home.

LØVBORG: That's true. Yes, many thanks, madam – then I shall stay.

HEDDA: I'll just have a quick word with the maid then –
She walks over to the hallway door and rings. BERTA *arrives.* HEDDA *speaks quietly with her and points to the back room.* BERTA *nods and exits again.*

TESMAN [*at the same time, to* EILERT LØVBORG]: Tell me. Eilert, old chap – this new topic – the future and what-not – is that what you want to give a lecture about?

LØVBORG: Yes.

TESMAN: Because I heard down at the bookseller's that you want to give a series of lectures here this autumn.

LØVBORG: I do, indeed. You don't blame me for that surely, Tesman?

TESMAN: Good heavens no! But –?

LØVBORG: I can see it might be rather awkward for you.

TESMAN [*timidly*]: Oh, I can't expect, that for my sake, you'd –

LØVBORG: But I shall wait until you've got your appointment through.

TESMAN: You'll wait! Yes but – yes but – aren't you going to compete? What?

LØVBORG: No. I just want to gain a victory over you. In the public's opinion.

TESMAN: But, good Lord – so Auntie Ju had it right after all! Oh, yes – I was quite sure of it! Hedda! Think – Eilert Løvborg isn't going to stand in our way at all!

HEDDA [*curtly*]: *Our* way? Do keep me out of it.
She walks over to the back room, where BERTA *is putting a tray with decanters and glasses on the table.* HEDDA *nods approvingly and returns.* BERTA *leaves.*

TESMAN [*at the same time*]: But you, Judge Brack – what do you say to this? Eh?

BRACK: Well, I'd say glory and victory – hm – they can be things of exceeding beauty –

TESMAN: Absolutely, yes. But still –

HEDDA [*looks at* TESMAN *with a cold smile*]: You look as though you've been struck by lightning.

TESMAN: Yes – maybe – almost –

BRACK: It was indeed a thunderstorm that passed over us, Mrs Tesman.

HEDDA [*points to the back room*]: Won't you gentlemen go in and have a glass of cold punch?

BRACK [*looks at his watch*]: One for the road? Well, that wouldn't go amiss.

TESMAN: Splendid, Hedda. Quite splendid! Now that my spirits are lifted –

HEDDA: Do go ahead, Mr Løvborg, you too.

LØVBORG [*declining with a wave of his hand*]: No, thank you very much. Not for me.

BRACK: But, dear God – cold punch isn't poisonous, you know.

LØVBORG: Not for everyone perhaps.

HEDDA: I'll keep Mr Løvborg company for now.

TESMAN: All right, Hedda darling, you do that.

He and BRACK *go into the back room, sit down, drink punch, smoke cigarettes and speak animatedly together during the following.* EILERT LØVBORG *remains standing by the stove.* HEDDA *goes to the writing desk.*

HEDDA [*with a slightly raised voice*]: Now I'll show you some photographs, if you like. Since Tesman and I – we took a trip through the Tyrol on our way home.

She brings an album, which she places on the table by the sofa, and sits down in the furthest corner of it. EILERT LØVBORG *comes closer, stops and looks at her. Then he takes a chair and sits down by her left side with his back to the rear room.*

HEDDA [*opens the album*]: You see this mountain range here, Mr Løvborg? Those are the Ortler Alps. Tesman's written it underneath. Here it says: 'The Ortler Alps near Merano'.[36]

LØVBORG [*who has been watching her steadily, says quietly and slowly*]: Hedda – Gabler!

HEDDA [*glances quickly over at him*]: Shush!

LØVBORG [*repeats quietly*]: Hedda Gabler!

HEDDA [*looks in the album*]: Yes, that was my name before. Then – when we two knew each other.

LØVBORG: And from now on – for the rest of my life – I must get out of the habit of saying Hedda Gabler.

HEDDA [*still turning pages*]: Indeed, you must. And I think you ought to start practising. The sooner the better, I think.

LØVBORG [*with quiet anger*]: Hedda Gabler married? And to – Jørgen Tesman!

HEDDA: Yes – that's how it goes.

LØVBORG: Oh Hedda, Hedda, my dearest[37] – how could you throw yourself away like that!

HEDDA [*looks sharply at him*]: Stop! Not that!

LØVBORG: Not what?

TESMAN *comes in and walks over to the sofa.*

HEDDA [*hears him coming and says casually*]: And this, Mr Løvborg, is down in the Ampezzo Valley. Just look at these mountain peaks. [*Looks affectionately up at* TESMAN] What was the name of these weird-looking mountain peaks, darling?

TESMAN: Let me see. Ah, they are the Dolomites.

HEDDA: That's right! They are the Dolomites, Mr Løvborg.

TESMAN: Oh Hedda – I just wanted to ask if we ought to bring a little punch in here anyway? For you at least. What?

HEDDA: Oh yes, please. And a couple of cakes perhaps.

TESMAN: No cigarettes?

HEDDA: No.

TESMAN: Fine.

He goes into the rear room and over to the right. BRACK *is sitting there, keeping an occasional eye on* HEDDA *and* LØVBORG.

LØVBORG [*hushed, as before*]: Answer me then, Hedda, my dearest[38] – how could you go and do that?

HEDDA [*seemingly engrossed in the album*]: If you continue to address me that way, I shan't speak to you.

LØVBORG: Mightn't I do so even when we're alone?

HEDDA: No. You may be permitted to think it. But you mustn't say it.

LØVBORG: Ah, I understand. It offends your love – for Jørgen Tesman.

HEDDA [*glances over at him and smiles*]: Love? That's a good one!

LØVBORG: Not love, then!

HEDDA: Nonetheless no infidelity! I won't hear of it!

LØVBORG: Hedda – just answer me this one thing –

HEDDA: Sssh!

TESMAN, *with a serving tray, comes from the rear room.*

TESMAN: Here we are! Here come the goodies. [*He puts the tray on the table*]

HEDDA: Why are you serving it yourself?

TESMAN [*pours into the glasses*]: Well, because I think it's such fun to serve you, Hedda.

HEDDA: But now you've filled both glasses. And Mr Løvborg doesn't want any –

TESMAN: No, but doubtless Mrs Elvsted will come soon.

HEDDA: Oh yes, true – Mrs Elvsted –

TESMAN: Had you forgotten about her? What?

HEDDA: We're so engrossed in this. [*Shows him a picture*] Do you remember this little village?[39]

TESMAN: Oh, that was the one below the Brenner Pass! It was *there* we slept the night –

HEDDA: – and met those lively summer residents.

TESMAN: Oh yes, it was there. Just think – if only we could have had you with us, Eilert! Well now –!

He goes back in and sits down with BRACK.

LØVBORG: Just answer me one thing, Hedda –

HEDDA: What?

LØVBORG: Was there no love in your relationship with me either? Not a hint – not a glimmer of love in that either?

HEDDA: Yes, I wonder if there really was? To me it seems we were two good comrades. Two close confidants. [*Smiles*] *You*, in particular, were extremely open-hearted.

LØVBORG: You, Hedda, were the one who wanted it that way.

HEDDA: When I think back on it now, there was certainly something beautiful, something alluring – something daring about it, I suppose – about our secret sharing of confidences – the comradeship that no living person had the least suspicion of.

LØVBORG: That's right, Hedda! There was, wasn't there? – When I came up to your father in the afternoons –. And the general sat over by the window reading his newspaper – with his back turned –

HEDDA: And the two of us sat on the corner sofa –

LØVBORG: Always with the same illustrated magazine in front of us –

HEDDA: For want of an album, yes.

LØVBORG: Yes, Hedda – and when I confessed to you –! Told you things about myself that nobody else knew back then. Sat there and admitted that I'd been out on the rampage all day and night. For days on end. Oh, Hedda – what sort of power was it in you that drove me to confess such things?

HEDDA: You believe there was a power in me?

LØVBORG: Yes, what other explanation can I find? And all those – those oblique questions you asked me.

HEDDA: Which you understood so perfectly well –

LØVBORG: To think you could sit there and ask me such questions! So brazen, so bold!

HEDDA: Oblique, if you please.

LØVBORG: Yes, but brazen all the same. To question me about – about such things!

HEDDA: And – that you could answer me, Mr Løvborg.

LØVBORG: Yes, that's precisely what I can't grasp – looking back now. But tell me, Hedda – was there really no love at the core of this relationship? Wasn't it, from your side, as though you somehow wanted to wash me clean – when I turned to you for confession? Wasn't it?

HEDDA: No, not really.

LØVBORG: What drove you, then?

HEDDA: Do you find it so completely incomprehensible that a young girl – when the possibility presents itself – in secret –

LØVBORG: Well?

HEDDA: That she might want to take a little peep into a world
that –

LØVBORG: That –?

HEDDA: That she is not permitted to know anything about?

LØVBORG: So that's what it was?

HEDDA: In part. In part – I rather think.

LØVBORG: Comradeship in the lust for life.⁴⁰ But if so, why
couldn't *that* at least have endured?

HEDDA: You have yourself to blame for that.

LØVBORG: It was you who broke it off.

HEDDA: Yes, when there was the impending danger of reality
entering the relationship. Shame on you, Eilert Løvborg,
how could you want to take advantage of your – your brazen
comrade!

LØVBORG [*clenches his fist*]: Oh, why didn't you just have
done with it! Why didn't you shoot me down, as you
threatened!

HEDDA: *That* is how fearful I am of scandal.

LØVBORG: Yes, Hedda, you're a coward deep down.

HEDDA: An appalling coward. [*Changes tack*] But that was
fortunate for you, of course. And now you've found such
delightful solace up at the Elvsteds'.

LØVBORG: I know what Thea's confided to you.

HEDDA: And you've perhaps confided things about *us* to her?

LØVBORG: Not a word. She's too stupid to understand anything like that.

HEDDA: Stupid?

LØVBORG: In such matters she is stupid.

HEDDA: And I am cowardly. [*Leans closer to him, without
looking him in the eyes, and says more quietly*] But now *I*
want to confide something to *you*.

LØVBORG [*excited*]: Well?

HEDDA: My not daring to shoot you –

LØVBORG: Yes?!

HEDDA: – *that* wasn't my worst act of cowardice – that night.

LØVBORG [*looks at her for a moment, understands and whispers passionately*]: Oh, Hedda! Hedda Gabler, my dearest!⁴¹

Now I glimpse a hidden depth to this comradeship! You and I –! There *was* that demand for life[42] in you –

HEDDA [*quietly, with a sharp glance*]: Careful now! Don't you believe it!

It has started to grow dark. The hallway door is opened from the outside by BERTA.

HEDDA [*slams the album shut and, smiling, calls*]: There now, at last! Thea, dear – come right in!

MRS ELVSTED *arrives from the hallway. She is dressed for a social occasion. The door is closed after her.*

HEDDA [*on the sofa, stretches her arms towards her*]: Sweet Thea – you can't imagine how I've waited for you!

MRS ELVSTED *exchanges a passing greeting with the gentlemen in the rear room, then walks over to the table and gives* HEDDA *her hand.* EILERT LØVBORG *has got up. He and* MRS ELVSTED *greet each other with a silent nod.*

MRS ELVSTED: Perhaps I should go in and have a quick word with your husband?

HEDDA: Oh, don't worry. Let them get on with it. They'll be off soon.

MRS ELVSTED: Are they leaving?

HEDDA: Yes, they're going on a boozy night out.

MRS ELVSTED [*quickly to* LØVBORG]: But *not* you, I take it?

LØVBORG: No.

HEDDA: Mr Løvborg – he'll stay right here with us.

MRS ELVSTED [*takes a chair and is about to sit down next to him*]: Oh, it's so good to be here![43]

HEDDA: No, my little Thea! Not *there*! You'll come like a good girl and sit next to me here. I want to be in the middle.

MRS ELVSTED: Yes, whatever you prefer.

She walks around the table and sits down on the sofa to the right of HEDDA. LØVBORG *sits down on his chair again.*

LØVBORG [*after a short pause, to* HEDDA]: Isn't she lovely to look at?

HEDDA [*strokes her hair lightly*]: Just to look at?

LØVBORG: Yes. Because *we* two – she and I – *we* are two solid comrades. We believe in each other unconditionally. And so we can sit and talk together quite candidly, almost brazenly –

HEDDA: And not obliquely, Mr Løvborg?

LØVBORG: Well –

MRS ELVSTED [*quietly, clinging to* HEDDA]: Oh, I'm so happy, Hedda! Just think – he says I've inspired him.

HEDDA [*looks at her with a smile*]: No, does he really?

LØVBORG: And what courage she shows, Mrs Tesman!

MRS ELVSTED: Oh, Lord – *me* – courage?

LØVBORG: Immense courage – where it concerns your comrade.

HEDDA: Yes, *courage* – indeed! If one only had *that*!

LØVBORG: Then what?

HEDDA: Then one might even be able to live life. [*Quickly changes tone*] But now, my dear Thea – you're going to have a nice glass of cold punch.

MRS ELVSTED: No thanks – I don't drink anything like that.

HEDDA: Well, how about *you*, Mr Løvborg.

LØVBORG: I don't either, thank you.

MRS ELVSTED: He doesn't either!

HEDDA [*looks sharply at him*]: But what if I want you to?

LØVBORG: Makes no odds.

HEDDA [*laughs*]: Do I really have no power over you? Poor me!

LØVBORG: Not when it comes to *that*.

HEDDA: But seriously, I think perhaps you ought to. For your own sake.

MRS ELVSTED: Oh, but Hedda –!

LØVBORG: What do you mean?

HEDDA: Or, for other people's sakes, to be more precise.

LØVBORG: Oh?

HEDDA: Otherwise people might get the idea that – that deep down – you didn't feel so bold and brazen – so absolutely sure of yourself.

MRS ELVSTED [*quietly*]: Oh no, please, Hedda –!

LØVBORG: People can think what they want – for now at least.

MRS ELVSTED [*happy*]: Yes, isn't that right!

HEDDA: I saw it so clearly in Judge Brack, just now.

LØVBORG: What did you see?

HEDDA: He smiled so scornfully when you didn't dare join them at the table in there.

LØVBORG: I didn't dare? Naturally I preferred to stay here and to talk to *you*.

MRS ELVSTED: That was only reasonable, Hedda!

HEDDA: But the judge couldn't know that. And then I also saw him smile and glance at Tesman, when you didn't dare go along with them to this pathetic little party either.

LØVBORG: Dare! Are you saying I didn't dare?

HEDDA: Not me. But Mr Brack understood it that way.

LØVBORG: Well, let him.

HEDDA: So you won't join them?

LØVBORG: I'm staying here with you and Thea.

MRS ELVSTED: Yes, Hedda – as you'd expect!

HEDDA [*smiles and nods approvingly to* LØVBORG]: Indeed, steady as a rock. Staunch in his principles. Yes, that's how a man should be! [*Turns to* MRS ELVSTED *and pats her*] Well now, wasn't that exactly what I told you when you came here in such a panic this morning –

LØVBORG [*puzzled*]: Panic?

MRS ELVSTED [*in horror*]: Hedda – Hedda, please –!

HEDDA: Just see for yourself now! There's no need at all for you to go about in such deadly fear – [*Interrupts herself*] Anyway! Now the three of us can liven up!

LØVBORG [*shocked*]: Ah – what is all this, Mrs Tesman?

MRS ELVSTED: Oh God, oh God, Hedda! What are you saying? What are you doing?

HEDDA: Quiet! That nasty judge is sitting there watching you.

LØVBORG: In deadly fear, eh? On my behalf.

MRS ELVSTED [*quietly, wailing*]: Oh Hedda – you've made me so miserable now!

LØVBORG [*looks at her unflinchingly for a moment, his face contorted with pain*]: So much for my comrade's bold and brazen trust in me.

MRS ELVSTED [*implores*]: Oh, my dearest friend – let me explain –!

LØVBORG [*takes one of the full punch glasses, lifts it and says in a hoarse voice*]: Cheers, Thea!

   He drains the glass, puts it down and picks up the other.

MRS ELVSTED [*quietly*]: Oh Hedda, Hedda – how could you want to do this!

HEDDA: Want! Me? Are you mad?

LØVBORG: And cheers to you too, Mrs Tesman. Thanks for the truth. Long may it live!

He empties his glass and goes to fill it again.

HEDDA [*puts her hand on his arm*]: Now, now – no more for now. Remember you're going to the party.

MRS ELVSTED: No, no, no!

HEDDA: Shh! They're sitting in there looking at you.

LØVBORG [*puts the glass down*]: But Thea, dear – tell the truth now –

MRS ELVSTED: Yes?

LØVBORG: Did the bailiff know that you came after me?

MRS ELVSTED [*wringing her hands*]: Oh, Hedda – just listen to what he's asking!

LØVBORG: Was there some agreement between you and him, that you should come to town to watch over me? Was it the bailiff, perhaps, who put you up to it? Aha, I see – he probably needed me in the office again! Or was it at the card table he was missing me?

MRS ELVSTED [*quietly, painfully*]: Oh Løvborg, Løvborg –!

LØVBORG [*grabs a glass and is about to fill it*]: A toast to the old bailiff too!

HEDDA [*lifts a hand to stop him*]: That's enough now. Remember, you're going to read aloud for Tesman.

LØVBORG [*calm, puts the glass down*]: It was stupid of me, Thea, all this. To take it that way, I mean. Don't be angry with me, my dearest, dearest comrade. You shall see – you and the others both – that I may have fallen –. But I have lifted myself up again![44] With *your* help, my dearest Thea.

MRS ELVSTED [*overjoyed*]: Oh, thank heavens –!

BRACK *has, in the meantime, looked at his watch. He and* TESMAN *get up and come into the drawing room.*

BRACK [*takes his hat and overcoat*]: So, Mrs Tesman, our hour has struck.

HEDDA: Ah, I suppose it has.

LØVBORG [*gets up*]: And mine too, Judge Brack.

MRS ELVSTED [*quietly, imploring*]: Oh Løvborg – don't do it!

HEDDA [*pinches her arm*]: They can hear you!

MRS ELVSTED [*with a muffled squeal*]: Ouch!

LØVBORG [*to* BRACK]: You were generous enough to ask me to join you.

BRACK: So you'll come after all?

LØVBORG: I will. Thank you.

BRACK: Delighted to hear it –

LØVBORG [*picks up the paper packet and says to* TESMAN]: Since I want to show you one or two things before I submit this.

TESMAN: Just think – that'll be fun! – But Hedda darling, how will you get Mrs Elvsted home? What?

HEDDA: Oh, I'll find a way.

LØVBORG [*looks over at the ladies*]: Mrs Elvsted? Well naturally, I shall come back and collect her. [*Closer*] At about ten, Mrs Tesman? Is that all right?

HEDDA: Of course. Perfectly all right.

TESMAN: Good, so everything's sorted? But you mustn't expect *me* back *that* early, Hedda.

HEDDA: Darling, you must stay just as long – as long as you wish.

MRS ELVSTED [*with concealed anxiety*]: Mr Løvborg – I'll be here waiting for you until you come.

LØVBORG [*with his hat in his hand*]: But of course, madam.

BRACK: And now let the pleasure-parade commence, gentlemen! I hope we shall have a lively time of it, as a certain beautiful lady says.

HEDDA: Ah! If only that beautiful lady could be invisibly present –!

BRACK: Why invisibly?

HEDDA: So as to hear a little of the liveliness unexpurgated, judge.

BRACK [*laughs*]: I wouldn't advise the beautiful lady to do that.

TESMAN [*laughs too*]: You really are a one, Hedda! To think!

BRACK: Well. Farewell, ladies!

LØVBORG [*bows as he leaves*]: Around ten, then.

BRACK, LØVBORG *and* TESMAN *leave through the hallway. At the same time* BERTA *comes from the rear room with a lit lamp, which she places on the drawing-room table, and exits the same way.*

MRS ELVSTED [*has got up and is pacing uneasily around the room*]: Hedda – Hedda – how is this going to end!

HEDDA: Ten o'clock – he will come. I see him before me. Vine leaves[45] in his hair. Flushed and bold –

MRS ELVSTED: Yes, if only that were true.

HEDDA: And then, you see – he'll have reclaimed the power over himself. He will be a free man for the rest of his days.

MRS ELVSTED: Oh my God, yes – if he would only come back the way you picture him.

HEDDA: In that way, and no other, he will come! [*Gets up and moves closer*] Doubt him for as long as you like. I believe in him. And now we'll put it to the test –

MRS ELVSTED: There's something you haven't told me, Hedda!

HEDDA: There is, indeed. I want, just once in my life, to have power over a person's destiny.

MRS ELVSTED: But don't you already have that?

HEDDA: Haven't – and never have.

MRS ELVSTED: Over your husband's at least?

HEDDA: Oh yes, that was worth the trouble. Oh, if only you knew how poor I am. Whilst *you* are allowed to be so rich! [*Throws her arms passionately around her*] I think I'll burn your hair off after all.

MRS ELVSTED: Let go of me! Let go of me! I'm frightened of you, Hedda!

BERTA [*in the doorway*]: The table is laid for tea, ma'am.

HEDDA: Good. We're coming.

MRS ELVSTED: No, no, no! I'd rather go home alone! Straight away!

HEDDA: Nonsense! You'll have some tea first, you little idiot. And then – come ten o'clock – then Eilert Løvborg will come – with vine leaves in his hair.

She almost drags MRS ELVSTED *by force towards the doorway.*

ACT THREE

The room at the Tesmans'. The curtains are closed over the doorway and glass door. The lamp is on the table, with a shade over it and the flame turned low. The door of the stove is open; in it are the remains of a fire which has almost burned out.

MRS ELVSTED, *draped in a shawl and with her feet on a stool, sits close to the stove, slumped in the armchair.* HEDDA *lies fully dressed, sleeping, on the sofa with a blanket over her.*

MRS ELVSTED [*a moment passes, before she suddenly straightens up in her chair and listens intently. Then she sinks back exhausted, and quietly moans*]: Still not! – Oh, God – God – still not here!
    BERTA *comes tiptoeing in through the hallway door. She has a letter in her hand.*

MRS ELVSTED [*turns round and whispers anxiously*]: Well – has anyone been?

BERTA [*quietly*]: Yes, a maid came just now with this letter.

MRS ELVSTED [*quickly, stretches her hand out*]: A letter! Give it to me!

BERTA: No, ma'am, it's for the doctor.

MRS ELVSTED: Ah, I see.

BERTA: It were Miss Tesman's maid that brought it. I'll put it here on the table.

MRS ELVSTED: Yes, do.

BERTA [*puts the letter down*]: It's probably best I put out the lamp. It's getting smoky.

MRS ELVSTED: Yes, put it out. It'll probably be light soon.

BERTA [*extinguishes it*]: It already *is* light, ma'am.

MRS ELVSTED: Yes, daylight. And still not come home –!

BERTA: Oh, good Lord – I thought it might go this way.

MRS ELVSTED: You thought so?

BERTA: Well, when I saw that a certain fellow had come back
to town –. And traipsed off with them. Since we've heard
enough about that gentleman before.

MRS ELVSTED: Don't talk so loudly. You'll wake the mistress.

BERTA [*looks over at the sofa and sighs*]: No, heavens – let her
just sleep, poor thing. Shouldn't I put a bit more wood in the
stove?

MRS ELVSTED: Not for me, thanks.

BERTA: Well, well.
       She quietly leaves through the hallway door.

HEDDA [*is woken up by the closing of the door, and looks up*]:
What's that –?

MRS ELVSTED: It was just the maid –

HEDDA [*looks around*]: Ah, in here –! Yes, of course, I remember now – [*Sits up on the sofa, stretches and rubs her eyes*]
What's the time, Thea?

MRS ELVSTED [*looks at her watch*]: It's gone seven now.

HEDDA: When did Tesman come?

MRS ELVSTED: He hasn't come.

HEDDA: Hasn't come home yet?

MRS ELVSTED [*stands up*]: No one has come at all.

HEDDA: And there we were, sitting up waiting until four –

MRS ELVSTED [*wrings her hands*]: And *how* I waited for him!

HEDDA [*yawns and says with her hand in front of her mouth*]:
Yes, well – we could have spared ourselves that.

MRS ELVSTED: Did you get a little sleep?

HEDDA: Oh yes. I think I slept rather well. Didn't you?

MRS ELVSTED: Not one bit. I couldn't, Hedda! It was totally
impossible for me.

HEDDA [*gets up and walks towards her*]: Now, now, now!
There really is nothing to worry about. It's obvious to me
what's happened.

MRS ELVSTED: Yes, so what do you think? Tell me, please!

HEDDA: Well, naturally things have dragged on terribly at the judge's –

MRS ELVSTED: Oh, God yes – most probably. But still –

HEDDA: And then, you see, Tesman didn't want to come home, making a rumpus and ringing the doorbell in the middle of the night. [*Laughs*] And he may not have been too keen to show himself either – after such a pleasant party.

MRS ELVSTED: But then – where would he have gone?

HEDDA: He'll have gone up to his aunts, of course, and slept *there*. They still have his old room after all.

MRS ELVSTED: No, he can't be with *them*. A letter just came for him from Miss Tesman. It's there.

HEDDA: Really? [*Looks at the writing on it*] Yes, it's in Auntie Ju's handwriting. Well, so he's stayed on at Judge Brack's then. And Eilert Løvborg, he's sitting there – with vine leaves in his hair, reading aloud.

MRS ELVSTED: Oh Hedda, you're just saying things you don't believe yourself.

HEDDA: You are a little nitwit, Thea.

MRS ELVSTED: Oh yes, unfortunately, I probably am.

HEDDA: And you look so deathly tired.

MRS ELVSTED: Yes, I *am* deathly tired.

HEDDA: Right, that's why you'll do as I say. You'll go into my room and lie on the bed for a while.

MRS ELVSTED: Oh no, no – I shan't be able to sleep anyway.

HEDDA: Of course you shall.

MRS ELVSTED: Yes, but your husband's bound to come home soon surely. And then I must hear immediately –

HEDDA: I'll tell you when he comes.

MRS ELVSTED: Really, you promise me, Hedda?

HEDDA: Yes, you can rely on it. You just go in and sleep for now.

MRS ELVSTED: Thank you. I'll try to do that, then.

She goes in through the rear room.

HEDDA *walks over to the glass door and pulls the curtain open. Daylight floods into the room. Then she takes a little hand mirror from the writing desk, looks at herself and tidies her hair. Then goes to the hallway door and presses the bell.*

Shortly afterwards, BERTA *appears at the door.*

BERTA: Is there something ma'am requires?

HEDDA: Yes, put more wood in the stove. I'm freezing here.

BERTA: Oh, Lordie – it'll be warm here in a jiffy.

She rakes the embers together and puts in a log.

BERTA [*stops and listens*]: That was the front-door bell, ma'am.

HEDDA: Well, go out and open it. I'll take care of the fire myself.

BERTA: It'll soon be burning.

She exits through the hallway door.

HEDDA *kneels on the footstool and places more logs in the wood stove.*

JØRGEN TESMAN *arrives a short while after from the hall-way. He looks tired and a little sombre. Tiptoes towards the doorway, wanting to sneak in between the curtains.*

HEDDA [*by the wood stove, without looking up*]: Good morning.

TESMAN [*turns*]: Hedda! [*comes closer*] Heavens – are you up this early! What?

HEDDA: Yes, I was up very early today.

TESMAN: And there was I certain you'd still be asleep! Just think, Hedda.

HEDDA: Don't talk so loud. Mrs Elvsted is lying down in my room.

TESMAN: Did Mrs Elvsted stay the night here?

HEDDA: Yes, nobody came to fetch her.

TESMAN: No, I don't suppose they did.

HEDDA [*closes the wood-stove door and gets up*]: So, was it good fun at the judge's?

TESMAN: Have you been worried about me? What?

HEDDA: No, that would never occur to me. But I asked if you'd had fun.

TESMAN: Yes, indeed. For *once* –. Though mostly at the start, I'd say. Because then Eilert read aloud to me. We arrived an hour early – just think! And Brack had so much to get organized. But then Eilert read.

HEDDA [*sits down on the right-hand side of the table*]: Well? Go on, tell me –

TESMAN [*sits down on a stool by the wood stove*]: Oh, Hedda, you'll never believe what kind of a work it'll be! It must be some of the most extraordinary stuff ever written. Just think!

HEDDA: Yes, yes, that's of no interest to me –

TESMAN: I want to confess something to you, Hedda. When he'd finished reading – something awful came over me.

HEDDA: Something awful?

TESMAN: I sat there and I was jealous of Eilert for having the ability to write something like that. Just think, Hedda!

HEDDA: Yes, yes, I'm thinking!

TESMAN: And then to know that – with all his talents – he unfortunately remains absolutely beyond reform.

HEDDA: Don't you mean that he has more courage than the others?

TESMAN: Good God, no – he just can't take his pleasures in moderation, you understand.

HEDDA: So what happened – in the end?

TESMAN: Well, I think I'd almost have to call it a bacchanalia,[46] Hedda.

HEDDA: Did he have vine leaves in his hair?

TESMAN: Vine leaves? No, I saw nothing of that. But he did give a long, confused speech for the woman who had been an inspiration to him in his work. Yes, that's how he put it.

HEDDA: Did he name her?

TESMAN: No, he did not. But I can only think it must be Mrs Elvsted. You wait and see!

HEDDA: Right – so where did you part company with him?

TESMAN: On the way back into town. We broke up – the last of us – at the same time. And Brack came along to get a bit of fresh air. And then, you see, we all agreed we'd walk Eilert home. Since he was decidedly the worse for wear!

HEDDA: I expect he was.

TESMAN: But now comes the strangest thing, Hedda! Or the saddest, I suppose I should say. Oh – I'm almost ashamed – on Eilert's behalf – to tell it –

HEDDA: Really, well –?

TESMAN: Yes, as we were making our way back into town, you see, I just happened to fall a bit behind the others. Well, only by a minute or two – just think!

HEDDA: Yes, yes, God above, *and* –?

TESMAN: And as I'm hurrying to catch up with the rest – d'you know what I find at the roadside? What?

HEDDA: No, how could I know?

TESMAN: Please don't tell anyone, Hedda. You hear! Promise me that, for Eilert's sake. [*Pulls out a packet wrapped in paper from his coat pocket*] Just think, Hedda – I found this.

HEDDA: Isn't that the packet he had with him here yesterday?

TESMAN: Yes, it's his entire, precious, irreplaceable manuscript! And he'd just gone and dropped it – without noticing. Think, Hedda. How sad –

HEDDA: But why didn't you return the packet to him there and then?

TESMAN: Well, I didn't dare to – not in the state he was in –

HEDDA: Didn't you tell any of the others that you'd found it either?

TESMAN: Absolutely not. I didn't want to for Eilert's sake, you understand.

HEDDA: So nobody knows you have Eilert Løvborg's papers?

TESMAN: No. And nobody must find out either.

HEDDA: What did you talk about with him later?

TESMAN: I didn't get a chance to talk to him again. Because when we came into the city streets, he and two or three others disappeared without trace. Just think!

HEDDA: So? They probably walked him home then.

TESMAN: Yes, it appears they did. And Brack went on his way too.

HEDDA: And where have you been kicking about since?

TESMAN: Well, I and some of the others went along with one of the more jolly chaps and had morning coffee at his place. Or night coffee, I suppose I should say. What? But, when I've rested up a bit – and I think Eilert's had a chance to sleep things off, poor chap, I must go over to him with this.

HEDDA [*reaches out for the packet*]: No – don't give it back! Not straight away, I mean. Let me read it first.

TESMAN: No, my darling, sweet Hedda, I daren't do that, Lord no.

HEDDA: You daren't?

TESMAN: No – surely you can imagine how utterly distraught he'll be when he wakes up and finds his manuscript gone. Since he's got no copy of it, let me tell you! He said so himself.

HEDDA [*looks rather inquisitively at him*]: Can't a thing like that be rewritten then? I mean, over again.

TESMAN: No, I don't believe that would be possible. The inspiration – you see –

HEDDA: Well, well – that's how it is, I suppose – [*Casually*] – Oh, I nearly forgot – there's a letter for you here.

TESMAN: Well, to think –!

HEDDA [*gives it to him*]: It came early this morning.

TESMAN: But it's from Auntie Ju! What could it be? [*Puts the paper packet on the other stool, opens the letter, skims through it and starts*] Oh, Hedda – she writes that poor Auntie Rina is near the end!

HEDDA: That was to be expected.

TESMAN: And if I want to see her one last time, I must hurry. I'll sprint over there immediately.

HEDDA [*suppresses a smile*]: You'll sprint, will you?

TESMAN: Oh, dearest Hedda – if you could find it in you to join me! Just think!

HEDDA [*gets up and says wearily and dismissively*]: No, no, don't ask such a thing of me. I've no wish to look at sickness and death. Leave me free from everything that's ugly.

TESMAN: Ah well, then – [*Dashes about*] My hat –? My overcoat –? Oh yes, out in the hallway –. I do so sincerely hope I won't be too late, Hedda? What?

HEDDA: Oh, you just sprint, and –

BERTA *appears in the hallway door.*

BERTA: Mr Brack is outside and asks if he may come in.

TESMAN: At this moment! No, I can't possibly receive him now.

HEDDA: But I can. [*To* BERTA] Ask the judge to come in.

BERTA *leaves.*

HEDDA [*whispers quickly*]: The packet, Tesman!
She grabs it from the stool.

TESMAN: Yes, give it to me!

HEDDA: No, no, I'll hide it for you for now.

She walks over to the writing desk and puts it on the shelf. In his haste TESMAN *cannot get his gloves on.* JUDGE BRACK *comes in from the hallway.*

HEDDA [*nods to him*]: Well. You really are an early bird.

BRACK: Yes, wouldn't you say? [*To* TESMAN] Are you out and about too?

TESMAN: Yes, I need to go over to my aunts urgently. Just think – our invalid, she's close to death, poor thing.

BRACK: Oh good God, is she? Well then you certainly mustn't let me detain you. At such a serious moment –

TESMAN: Yes, I really must run. Goodbye! Goodbye!

He hurries out through the hallway door.

HEDDA [*comes closer*]: It seems to have been more than lively at your place last night, judge.

BRACK: I've not even got out of my clothes, Mrs Hedda.

HEDDA: You too?

BRACK: Well, as you see. But what's Tesman said about the night's events?

HEDDA: Oh, boring stuff. Just that they stayed up and drank coffee somewhere.

BRACK: I know all about the coffee party. Eilert Løvborg wasn't with them, I don't think?

HEDDA: No, they'd walked him home beforehand.

BRACK: Tesman too?

HEDDA: No, but a couple of the others, he said.

BRACK [*smiles*]: Jørgen Tesman really is a naive soul, Mrs Hedda.

HEDDA: Yes, that's for certain. So is there more to it then?

BRACK: Yes, one might say that.

HEDDA: Really! Let's sit down, dear judge. So you can tell me properly.

She sits down on the left side of the table. BRACK *by the long side, close to her.*

HEDDA: Well, now?

BRACK: I had specific reasons to track the movements of my guests – or to be more precise, certain of my guests, last night.

HEDDA: And among them perhaps was Eilert Løvborg?

BRACK: I must confess – he was.

HEDDA: Now you really are piquing my interest –

BRACK: Do you know where he and one or two of the others spent the rest of the night, Mrs Hedda?

HEDDA: If it bears the telling, then please do.

BRACK: Heavens – it can be told all right. They turned up at an extremely animated soirée.

HEDDA: Of the lively sort?

BRACK: The absolute liveliest.

HEDDA: Tell me a little more, judge –

BRACK: Løvborg had received an invitation beforehand, as others had. I knew all about that. But at the time he had declined. Because he's recently assumed the garb of a new man,[47] as you know.

HEDDA: Up at the Elvsteds', yes. But he went nevertheless?

BRACK: Yes, you see, Mrs Hedda – I'm afraid the spirit came over him[48] earlier at my place –

HEDDA: Yes, he was truly inspired, I hear.

BRACK: Inspired to rather a violent degree. Anyway, I imagine he must have got other ideas in his head. Since we men are sadly not always as principled as we should be.

HEDDA: Oh, I'm sure *you* count as an exception in that, Judge Brack. But, Løvborg –?

BRACK: Well, to be brief – he finally ended up at Miss Diana's[49] salon.

HEDDA: Miss Diana?

BRACK: It was Miss Diana who gave the soirée. For a select circle of female friends and admirers.

HEDDA: A redheaded woman?

BRACK: Quite.

HEDDA: Some sort of – singer?

BRACK: Oh, yes – that too. And also a formidable huntress – of gentlemen – Mrs Hedda. You've probably heard talk of her. Eilert Løvborg was one of her warmest patrons – when he was at the top of his game.

HEDDA: And how did all this end?

BRACK: Not altogether cordially, it seems. Apparently, from the tenderest of welcomes, Miss Diana turned to physical assault –

HEDDA: Against Løvborg?

BRACK: Yes. He accused her or her lady friends of having robbed him. He claimed his wallet had gone missing. And some other items too. In short, he appears to have made an outrageous scene.

HEDDA: Which led to what?

BRACK: Which led to a common cockfight between the ladies and gentlemen both. Luckily the police arrived in the end.

HEDDA: The police arrived too?

BRACK: Yes. But it'll be a costly bit of fun for Eilert Løvborg, lunatic that he is.

HEDDA: I see!

BRACK: He put up a violent resistance, it seems. Hit one of the constables across the ear and ripped his coat apparently. So he had to go down to the station too.

HEDDA: Where did you get all this from?

BRACK: From the police themselves.

HEDDA [*looks straight ahead*]: So that's how it went. Then he didn't have vine leaves in his hair.

BRACK: Vine leaves, Mrs Hedda?

HEDDA [*changes tone*]: But tell me now, judge – why exactly are you going around tracking and spying on Eilert Løvborg?

BRACK: First, because it would not be of total indifference to me if it were revealed at the hearing that he went there straight from my place.

HEDDA: Will there be a hearing, then?

BRACK: Naturally. Although, as regards that, whatever happens happens. However, I do feel duty bound as a friend in this house, to give you and Tesman a full briefing on his night-time exploits.

HEDDA: Why exactly, Mr Brack?

BRACK: Well, I have a lively suspicion that he intends to use you here as a kind of screen,[50] Mrs Hedda.

HEDDA: But whatever gives you that idea?

BRACK: Good God – we're not blind, Mrs Hedda. Be careful! This Mrs Elvsted, she's certainly not about to leave town any time soon.

HEDDA: Well, if there's something between those two there must be countless places where they could meet.

BRACK: No home. From now on every decent household will be closed again to Eilert Løvborg.

HEDDA: And you're suggesting mine should be too?

BRACK: Well, yes. I confess it would be more than a little awkward if this gentleman were allowed access here. If he, as an outsider – an irrelevance – should force his way into –

HEDDA: – into the triangle?

BRACK: Quite. That would be tantamount to my being made homeless.

HEDDA [*looks at him and smiles*]: I see – the only rooster in the coop[51] – that's your goal.

BRACK [*nods slowly and lowers his voice*]: Yes, that's my goal. And it's a goal I will fight for – with every means at my disposal.

HEDDA [*as her smile fades*]: You're a dangerous person – when it comes to it.

BRACK: Do you think so?

HEDDA: Yes, I'm starting to think so. And I'm thrilled – so long as I'm never at your mercy in any way.

BRACK [*with an ambiguous laugh*]: Well, well, Mrs Hedda – perhaps you're right. Who can tell if I may not be a man capable of any number of things?

HEDDA: Listen here, Mr Brack! It almost sounds as though you were threatening me.

BRACK [*gets up*]: Oh, far from it! The triangle, you see – should preferably be secured and defended through mutual free will.

HEDDA: My sentiments entirely.

BRACK: Yes, well, now I've said what I came for. So I really must be getting back to town. Goodbye, Mrs Hedda!

He walks towards the glass door.

HEDDA [*gets up*]: You're going through the garden?

BRACK: Yes, it's quicker for me.

HEDDA: Yes, and it's a back way too, of course.

BRACK: Very true. I've nothing against back ways. At times they can be rather piquant.

HEDDA: When there's shooting with live ammunition, you mean?

BRACK [*in the doorway, laughing*]: Oh, one surely doesn't shoot one's tame cockerels!

HEDDA [*laughs too*]: Oh no. When one only has the one, then – *They nod goodbye as they laugh. He leaves. She closes the door after him.*

HEDDA stands there for a while, looking out with a serious expression. Afterwards she walks across the room and looks through the curtains at the back. Then she walks to the writing desk, takes LØVBORG's packet out from the bookcase and is about to leaf through the pages. BERTA's voice can be heard clearly out in the hallway. HEDDA turns and listens. She quickly locks the packet away in the drawer and puts the key on her writing stand. EILERT LØVBORG wearing an overcoat and with his hat in his hand flings the hallway door open. He looks rather confused and worked up.

LØVBORG [*turning towards the hallway*]: And I tell you, I must and I shall go in! You hear!

He closes the door, turns, sees HEDDA, immediately controls himself and greets her.

HEDDA [*by her writing desk*]: Well, Mr Løvborg, it's rather late to be coming for Thea.

LØVBORG: Or rather early to come in to you. My sincere apologies.

HEDDA: How do you know she's still here?

LØVBORG: They told me at her lodgings that she'd been out the whole night.

HEDDA [*walks over to the salon table*]: Did you notice anything in particular when they said that?

LØVBORG [*looks inquisitively at her*]: Notice anything in particular?

HEDDA: I mean, did they seem to be thinking anything about it?

LØVBORG [*suddenly understands*]: Ah yes, that's true, of course! I'm dragging her down with me! But no, I didn't notice anything. I don't suppose Tesman's up yet?

HEDDA: No – I don't think –

LØVBORG: When did he get home?

HEDDA: Very late.

LØVBORG: Did he tell you anything?

HEDDA: Yes, I heard that it got very jolly at Judge Brack's.

LØVBORG: Nothing else?

HEDDA: No, I don't think so. But then, I was awfully sleepy –
    MRS ELVSTED *comes in through the curtains at the back.*

MRS ELVSTED [*towards him*]: Ah, Løvborg! Finally –!

LØVBORG: Yes, finally. And too late.

MRS ELVSTED [*looks anxiously at him*]: What's too late?

LØVBORG: Everything's too late now. I'm done for.

MRS ELVSTED: Oh no, no – don't say that!

LØVBORG: You'll say the same when you've heard –

MRS ELVSTED: I don't want to hear anything!

HEDDA: You'd prefer to speak with her alone perhaps? In which
    case I'll go.

LØVBORG: No, stay – you too. I beg you to stay.

MRS ELVSTED: Yes, but I don't want to hear anything, I tell you!

LØVBORG: It isn't the night's adventures I want to talk about.

MRS ELVSTED: What is it then –?

LØVBORG: It's that our ways must now part.

MRS ELVSTED: Part!

HEDDA [*involuntarily*]: I knew it!

LØVBORG: Since I have no more use for you, Thea.

MRS ELVSTED: And you can stand there and say that! No
    more use for me! But surely I'll help you now as before?
    Surely we'll continue working together?

LØVBORG: I don't intend to work from now on.

MRS ELVSTED [*dejected*]: But what shall I use my life for then?

LØVBORG: You'll have to try to live your life as if you'd never
    known me.

MRS ELVSTED: But I can't do that!

LØVBORG: Try if you can, Thea. You'll have to go back home –

MRS ELVSTED [*in turmoil*]: Never in this world! Wherever
    you are, I want to be too! I won't let myself be chased off like
    this! I want to be right here! Here with you when the book
    comes out.

HEDDA [*just audible, in suspense*]: Ah, the book – yes!

LØVBORG [*looks at her*]: Mine and Thea's book. For *that's* what it is.

MRS ELVSTED: Yes, that's what I feel it is. Which is why I also have a right to be with you when it comes out! I want to be there to see it when respect and honour are showered upon you once again. And the joy – the joy, I want to share that with you.

LØVBORG: Thea – our book will never come out.

HEDDA: Ah!

MRS ELVSTED: It'll never come out?

LØVBORG: Can never come out.

MRS ELVSTED [*with foreboding*]: Løvborg – what have you done with the notebooks!

HEDDA [*looks expectantly at him*]: Yes, the notebooks –?

MRS ELVSTED: Where are they?

LØVBORG: Oh, Thea – please don't ask me about that.

MRS ELVSTED: Yes, yes, I want to know. I have a right to know this instant.

LØVBORG: The notebooks –. Well now – I've torn them into a thousand pieces.

MRS ELVSTED [*shrieks*]: Oh no, no –!

HEDDA [*involuntarily*]: But that's not –!

LØVBORG [*looks at her*]: Not true, you think?

HEDDA [*composes herself*]: Well yes. Naturally. If you say it yourself. But it sounded so improbable –

LØVBORG: True nonetheless.

MRS ELVSTED [*wrings her hands*]: Oh God – oh God, Hedda – torn his own work into pieces!

LØVBORG: I have torn my own life into pieces. So why shouldn't I tear my life's work into pieces too –

MRS ELVSTED: And that's what you did last night!

LØVBORG: Yes, you hear. Into a thousand pieces. And scattered them into the fjord. Far out. There, at least, there's fresh salty water. Let them drift upon it. Drift with the current and the wind. And in a moment they will sink. Deeper and deeper. Just like me, Thea.

MRS ELVSTED: You must know, Løvborg, that what you've done to this book –. For the rest of my days, it'll be for me as though you'd killed a small child.

LØVBORG: You're right. It is like a kind of child-murder.

MRS ELVSTED: But how could you go and –! I too had a share in that child.

HEDDA [*almost inaudibly*]: Ah, the child –

MRS ELVSTED [*sighing heavily*]: So it's over, then. Well, well, I shall go now, Hedda.

HEDDA: But you won't leave, surely?

MRS ELVSTED: Oh, I don't know myself what I'm doing. Everything before me is dark now.

She leaves through the hallway door.

HEDDA [*stands waiting a little*]: You won't walk her home, Mr Løvborg?

LØVBORG: Me? Through the streets? Should people perhaps see her walking together with me?

HEDDA: I don't know what else happened last night, of course. But is it really so irreparable?

LØVBORG: It won't be this one night alone. I'm convinced of that. But what's more, I can't be bothered to live that sort of life. Not over again. It's life's courage and fighting spirit that she's crushed in me.

HEDDA [*staring straight ahead*]: That sweet little fool has had her fingers in a human destiny. [*Looks at him*] But still, how could you be so heartless towards her?

LØVBORG: Oh, don't say it was heartless!

HEDDA: To go and destroy the very thing that has filled her mind for such a long, long time! You don't call that heartless!

LØVBORG: To you I can tell the truth, Hedda.

HEDDA: The truth?

LØVBORG: Promise me first – give me your word, that what I confide in you now Thea will never know.

HEDDA: You have my word on it.

LØVBORG: Good. Then let me tell you that what I stood here and said wasn't the truth.

HEDDA: About the notebooks?

LØVBORG: Yes. I haven't torn them to pieces. Nor thrown them into the fjord.

HEDDA: Right. But – then, where are they?

LØVBORG: I have destroyed them all the same. As good as, Hedda!

HEDDA: I don't understand.

LØVBORG: Thea said that what I'd done seemed to her like murdering a child.

HEDDA: Yes – she did.

LØVBORG: But to kill his child – that isn't the worst thing a father can do to it.

HEDDA: *That* isn't the worst?

LØVBORG: No. The worst is what I wanted to spare Thea from hearing.

HEDDA: So what is this 'worst' then?

LØVBORG: Imagine, Hedda, that a man – you know, in the early hours – after a confused, liquor-soaked night came home to the mother of his child and said: listen now – I've been here and there. To this place and that. And I had our child with me. At this place and that. The child has gone missing. Completely gone. Damned if I know whose hands it's fallen into. Who's laid their fingers on it.

HEDDA: Ah – but when it comes to it – it's still just a book –

LØVBORG: Thea's pure soul was in that book.

HEDDA: Yes, I understand that.

LØVBORG: Then you'll also understand that there's no future for her and me.

HEDDA: So what path will you take now?

LØVBORG: None. Except to ensure I put an end to it all. The sooner the better.

HEDDA [*takes a step closer*]: Eilert Løvborg – listen now –. Couldn't you ensure that – that it happened in beauty?

LØVBORG: In beauty? [*Smiles*] With vine leaves in my hair, as you used to imagine before –

HEDDA: Oh no. The vine leaves – I no longer believe in those. But in beauty just the same! For once! – Farewell! You must go now. And never, ever come back.

LØVBORG: Farewell, madam. And give Tesman my regards.
    He is about to leave.

HEDDA: No wait! You shall take one memento from me.
    She walks over to the writing desk and opens the drawer

and the pistol case. Then returns to LØVBORG *carrying one of the pistols.*

LØVBORG [*looks at her*]: That? Is *that* the memento?

HEDDA [*nods slowly*]: Do you recognize it? It was once raised against you.

LØVBORG: You should have used it back then.

HEDDA: There! *You* use it now.

LØVBORG [*puts the gun in his breast pocket*]: Thank you!

HEDDA: And in beauty, then, Eilert Løvborg. Just promise me that!

LØVBORG: Farewell, Hedda Gabler.

He leaves through the hallway door.

HEDDA *listens for a while at the door. Then she walks over to the writing desk and takes out the packet containing the manuscript, peers into the wrapping, pulls some of the pages halfway out and looks at them. Then she takes everything with her and sits down in the armchair by the stove. The packet rests in her lap. After a while she opens the door to the stove and then opens the packet too.*

HEDDA [*throws one of the notebooks into the fire and whispers to herself*]: Now I am burning your child, Thea! – You and your curly hair! [*Throws a couple more notebooks into the fire*] Your and Eilert Løvborg's child. [*Throws in the rest*] Now I am burning – now I am burning the child.

ACT FOUR

The same rooms in the Tesman house. It is evening. The draw-
ing room is in darkness. The rear room is lit by a ceiling light
hanging over the table. The curtains in front of the glass door
are closed.

HEDDA, *dressed in black, paces around the darkened room.*
Then goes into the rear room and walks off to the left. A few
chords on the piano are heard from within. She then comes
back out into the drawing room.

BERTA *enters from the right through the rear room with a lit*
lamp, which she places on the table in front of the corner sofa.
Her eyes are red from crying, and she wears a black ribbon on
her apron. She walks softly and quietly out to the right. HEDDA
goes over to the glass door, moves the curtains a little to the
side and looks out into the darkness.

Shortly afterwards MISS TESMAN, *in mourning clothes,*[52]
with a hat and veil, enters from the hallway. HEDDA *goes to*
meet her and extends her hand.

MISS TESMAN: Well, Hedda, I come in the colours of mourning. For my poor sister has finally ended her struggle.

HEDDA: Yes, I know that already, as you can see. Tesman sent
a card out to me.

MISS TESMAN: Yes, he promised me he would. But I thought
nonetheless that for Hedda – here in this house of life – I
ought to report the death in person.

HEDDA: That's most sweet of you.

MISS TESMAN: Oh, Rina should not have passed away *now*. Grief has no place in Hedda's house at this moment.[53]

HEDDA [*avoiding the subject*]: She died quietly, I understand, Miss Tesman?

MISS TESMAN: Oh, so beautifully – everything resolved itself so peacefully for her. And then the unutterable joy she got from seeing Jørgen one last time. And from being able to say a proper goodbye to him. He's not home yet perhaps?

HEDDA: No. His note said I shouldn't expect him home too soon. But do sit down.

MISS TESMAN: No thank you, my dear – my blessed Hedda. I would have loved to. But I've so little time. She must be tended to and dressed nicely now, as best I can. She'll be so pretty when she is laid in her grave.

HEDDA: Can't I help with anything?

MISS TESMAN: Oh, don't even think about it! This is not a thing for Hedda Tesman's hands. Nor for her thoughts to be fixed upon. Not at this time. No.

HEDDA: Oh, thoughts – they can't be controlled like that –

MISS TESMAN [*continuing unaffected*]: Yes, good heavens, that's the way of the world. Now, back at home we'll sew the linen for Rina. And then very soon, I shouldn't wonder, there'll be sewing to be done here too. But that will be of a very different sort – by God's grace!

JØRGEN TESMAN *enters through the hallway door.*

HEDDA: Well, a good thing you've come at last.

TESMAN: Are you here, Auntie Ju? With Hedda? Just think!

MISS TESMAN: I was about to leave again, my dear boy. But did you manage to get everything done that you promised me?

TESMAN: No, I'm awfully worried I've forgotten half of it. I'll have to sprint down to you again tomorrow. My head is in such a muddle today. I can't keep my thoughts together.

MISS TESMAN: But, my dear, sweet Jørgen, you really mustn't take it that way.

TESMAN: Oh? How do you mean?

MISS TESMAN: You should be happy in your grief. Happy about what has happened. Just as I am.

TESMAN: Oh, yes, yes. You're thinking about Rina, Auntie dear.

HEDDA: It'll be lonely for you now, Miss Tesman.

MISS TESMAN: In the first days, yes. But that won't last too long I hope. Our dearly departed Rina's little room will not stand empty, I'm sure!

TESMAN: Oh? Who do you want to move into it then? What?

MISS TESMAN: Oh, there's always some poor sick creature who needs care and succour, sadly.

HEDDA: Would you take such a cross⁵⁴ upon you again?

MISS TESMAN: Cross! God bless you, my child – it's certainly not been a cross for me.

HEDDA: But if a stranger were to come now, then –

MISS TESMAN: Oh, we soon become friends with the sick. Besides, I sorely need to have someone to live for, even I. Well, God willing – there may also be something or other for an old aunt to lend a hand with here in this house.

HEDDA: Oh, just don't talk about us.

TESMAN: Yes, just think, what a lovely time the three of us could have together, if –

HEDDA: If –?

TESMAN [uneasy]: Oh, nothing. It'll all work out. Let's hope. What?

MISS TESMAN: Well, well, the two of you have something to talk about together, I expect. [Smiles] And Hedda may also have something to tell you, Jørgen. Goodbye! I must get home to Rina now. [Turns in the doorway] Good Lord, it's so strange to think! Now Rina is both with me and with our dearly departed Jochum.

TESMAN: Yes, imagine, Auntie Ju! What?

MISS TESMAN leaves through the hallway door.

HEDDA [observing TESMAN with a cold, analytical gaze]: I almost think your heart is more troubled by this death than hers.

TESMAN: Oh, it isn't just this death. It's Eilert that I'm deeply uneasy about.

HEDDA [quickly]: Is there more news of him?

TESMAN: I wanted to run up to him this afternoon and tell him his manuscript was in safe keeping.

HEDDA: So? Didn't you see him then?

TESMAN: No. He wasn't at home. But then I met Mrs Elvsted, and she said he'd been here early this morning.

HEDDA: Yes, soon after you'd left.

TESMAN: And apparently he said that he'd torn the manuscript to pieces. What?

HEDDA: Yes, that's what he claimed.

TESMAN: But dear God, then he must have been completely deranged! And then I presume you didn't dare give it back to him either, Hedda?

HEDDA: No, he didn't get it.

TESMAN: But you told him we had it, surely?

HEDDA: No. [*Quickly*] Did you tell Mrs Elvsted perhaps?

TESMAN: No, I didn't want to. But you should have told him at least. Just think, if in his despair he goes and does himself an injury! Let me have the manuscript, Hedda! I want to sprint over to him with it right away. Where have you put the packet?

HEDDA [*cold and motionless, leaning on the armchair*]: I haven't got it any more.

TESMAN: You haven't got it? What on earth do you mean by that!

HEDDA: I've burned it – all of it.

TESMAN [*leaps up in fright*]: Burned! Burned Eilert's manuscript!

HEDDA: Don't scream like that! The maid will hear you.

TESMAN: Burned! But merciful God –! No, no, no – this is completely impossible!

HEDDA: Well, that's how it is.

TESMAN: But have you any idea what you've done, Hedda! This is the illegal appropriation of lost property. To think! Yes, just ask Judge Brack, he'll tell you.

HEDDA: It's probably advisable you don't talk about it – to the judge or anyone else.

TESMAN: But how could you go and do something so extraordinary! How could it even enter your mind? What came over you? Answer me that.

HEDDA [*suppresses an almost imperceptible smile*]: I did it for your sake, Jørgen.

TESMAN: For my sake!

HEDDA: When you came home this morning and said he'd read to you –

TESMAN: Yes, yes, what then?

HEDDA: Then you confessed that you envied him his book.

TESMAN: Oh, good God, I didn't mean it that literally.

HEDDA: Still. I couldn't bear the idea that someone else might put you in the shade.

TESMAN [*bursting out, between doubt and joy*]: Oh Hedda! Is this really true? Yes, but – but I've never seen your love in *that* way before. To think!

HEDDA: Well, I suppose you ought to know then – that just recently[55] –. [*Forcefully, breaking off*] No, no – you can ask Auntie Ju about it. She'll tell you, I'm sure.

TESMAN: Oh, I think perhaps I understand you, Hedda! [*Claps his hands*] My God, darling – could *that* be possible! What?

HEDDA: Don't shout like that. The maid might hear you.

TESMAN [*laughing in excessive happiness*]: The maid! No, but you're priceless, Hedda! The maid – that's Berta we're talking about! I'll go out and tell Berta myself.

HEDDA [*clenches her hands as though in despair*]: Oh, it's killing me – all this is killing me!

TESMAN: What is, Hedda? What?

HEDDA [*coldly, controlled*]: This – it's all too absurd – Jørgen.

TESMAN: Absurd? The fact I'm so overjoyed? But anyway –. Perhaps it's not worth me saying anything to Berta.

HEDDA: Oh, go ahead – why not that too?

TESMAN: No, no, not yet. But obviously Auntie Ju must be told. And that you've started calling me Jørgen[56] too! Just think! Oh, Auntie Ju will be so happy – so happy!

HEDDA: When she hears I've burned Eilert Løvborg's papers – for your sake?

TESMAN: No, that's true! The thing with the papers – naturally nobody must get to know about that. But that you're burning for me, Hedda – well, that really is something I must share with Auntie Ju! Incidentally, I wonder if such things are perhaps common among young wives, Hedda. What?

HEDDA: I suggest you ask Auntie Ju about *that* too.

TESMAN: Yes, I certainly shall when the occasion allows. [*Looks uneasy and thoughtful again*] No, but – but the manuscript! Good God, it's dreadful nonetheless to think about that poor Eilert.

MRS ELVSTED, *dressed in the same way as on her previous visit, with a hat and overcoat, enters through the hallway door.*

MRS ELVSTED [*gives a quick greeting and says emotionally*]: Oh, Hedda dearest, don't be cross with me for coming back.

HEDDA: What's happened to you, Thea?

TESMAN: Is it about Eilert Løvborg again? What?

MRS ELVSTED: Yes – I'm terribly worried that an accident's befallen him.

HEDDA [*grabs her by the arm*]: Ah – you think so?

TESMAN: No, but good God – what gives you that idea, Mrs Elvsted!

MRS ELVSTED: Well, I heard them talking about him at my guesthouse as I went in. Oh, there are the most unbelievable rumours going around town about him today.

TESMAN: Yes, just think, I heard that too! But I can testify to his going straight home to bed. Just think!

HEDDA: Well – what did they say at your guesthouse?

MRS ELVSTED: Oh, I didn't find anything out. Either they didn't know anything more, or –. They went quiet when they saw me. And I didn't dare ask.

TESMAN [*uneasy, pacing about*]: We must hope – we must hope you've misheard, Mrs Elvsted!

MRS ELVSTED: No, no, I'm sure it was him they were talking about. And then I heard mention of something or other about the hospital or –

TESMAN: The hospital!

HEDDA: No – that's utterly impossible!

MRS ELVSTED: I got so deadly frightened for him. So I went up to his lodgings and asked for him there.

HEDDA: You could bring yourself to do *that*, Thea?

MRS ELVSTED: Well, what else could I do? I didn't think I could take the uncertainty any more.

TESMAN: But you didn't find him there? What?

MRS ELVSTED: No, and nobody knew his whereabouts. They said he hadn't been home since yesterday afternoon.

TESMAN: Yesterday! To think they could say that!

MRS ELVSTED: Oh, I can only imagine that something bad has happened to him!

TESMAN: Look, Hedda – how about I go into town, darling, and make some enquiries at various places –?

HEDDA: No, no – don't get mixed up in all this.

JUDGE BRACK, *hat in his hand, comes in through the hallway door, which* BERTA *opens and closes for him. He looks serious and greets them in silence.*

TESMAN: Oh, are you here, my dear judge? What?

BRACK: Yes, I felt obliged to come out to you this evening.

TESMAN: I can see by your face that you've received Auntie Ju's message.

BRACK: Well, yes, that too.

TESMAN: It's awfully sad, isn't it? What?

BRACK: Well, Tesman, that depends on how one takes it.

TESMAN [*looks at him uncertainly*]: Has something else happened perhaps?

BRACK: Yes, it has.

HEDDA [*expectantly*]: Something sad, Mr Brack?

BRACK: That too depends on how one takes it, madam.

MRS ELVSTED [*bursting out involuntarily*]: Oh, it's something about Eilert Løvborg!

BRACK [*glances at her*]: What makes madam think *that*? Does madam already know something –?

MRS ELVSTED [*confused*]: No, no, I don't know anything whatever, but –

TESMAN: But, God help us, then, say it!

BRACK [*shrugs his shoulders*]: Well – unfortunately – Eilert Løvborg has been taken to hospital. He's probably already close to death.

MRS ELVSTED [*screams*]: Oh God, oh God –!

TESMAN: In hospital! And close to death too!

HEDDA [*involuntarily*]: That quickly –!

MRS ELVSTED [*wailing*]: And we parted without being reconciled, Hedda!

HEDDA [*whispers*]: But Thea – Thea now!

MRS ELVSTED [*paying no attention to her*]: I must go to him! I must see him alive!

BRACK: That will be of no use, madam. Nobody is allowed in to him.

MRS ELVSTED: Oh, but just tell me what's happened to him! What is it?

TESMAN: Surely he hasn't – not – himself –! What?

HEDDA: Oh yes, I'm convinced he has.

TESMAN: Hedda – how can you –!

BRACK [*who is following her with his gaze*]: Sadly, you've guessed quite correctly, Mrs Tesman.

MRS ELVSTED: Oh, how dreadful!

TESMAN: Himself! To think!

HEDDA: Shot himself!

BRACK: Also correctly guessed, madam.

MRS ELVSTED [*trying to compose herself*]: When did this happen, Judge Brack?

BRACK: This afternoon. Between three and four.

TESMAN: But good God – where did he do it, then? What?

BRACK [*a little uneasy*]: Where? Well, my friend – he presumably did it in his lodgings.

MRS ELVSTED: No, that can't be right. Because I passed by between six and seven.

BRACK: Right, well some other place then. I don't know the details. I only know that he was found –. He had shot himself – through the chest.

MRS ELVSTED: Oh, what a dreadful thought! That he should finish up like that!

HEDDA [*to* BRACK]: Was it through the chest?

BRACK: Yes – as I said.

HEDDA: So not through the temple?

BRACK: Through the chest, Mrs Tesman.

HEDDA: Yes, well – the chest is good too.

BRACK: What do you mean, madam?

HEDDA [*dismissively*]: Oh, no – nothing.

TESMAN: And the wound is life-threatening, you say? What?

BRACK: The wound is absolutely fatal. In all likelihood it's already over for him.

MRS ELVSTED: Yes, yes, I feel it! It is over! Over! Oh, Hedda –!

TESMAN: But tell me then – where did you learn all this?

BRACK [*cursorily*]: Through somebody in the police. Somebody I was going to talk to.

HEDDA [*loudly*]: At last, a real deed!

TESMAN [*shocked*]: God help us – what are you saying, Hedda!

HEDDA: I am saying, there is beauty in this.

BRACK: Hm, Mrs Tesman –

TESMAN: Beauty! Well, to think!

MRS ELVSTED: Oh Hedda, how can you speak of beauty in something like this!

HEDDA: Eilert Løvborg has settled his account with himself. He has had the courage to do what – what had to be done.

MRS ELVSTED: No, don't ever think it happened in *that* way! What he has done, he has done in a state of delirium.

TESMAN: He has done it in despair!

HEDDA: He has not. I am certain of it.

MRS ELVSTED: Yes, he has! In delirium! Just as when he tore our notebooks to pieces.

BRACK [*puzzled*]: The notebooks? You mean the manuscript? He tore it to pieces?

MRS ELVSTED: Yes, he did it last night.

TESMAN [*whispers quietly*]: Oh Hedda, we'll never get away from this.

BRACK: Hm, that's very odd.

TESMAN [*crossing the room*]: To think Eilert should exit the world in this way! And without leaving the very thing behind which would have secured his name for posterity –

MRS ELVSTED: Oh, if it could be put together again!

TESMAN: Yes, just think, if it could! I don't know what I would give –

MRS ELVSTED: Perhaps it could, Mr Tesman.

TESMAN: What do you mean?

MRS ELVSTED [*searches in her dress pocket*]: Look at this. I've kept the loose notes he used when he dictated it.

HEDDA [*one step closer*]: Ah –!

TESMAN: You've kept them, Mrs Elvsted! What?

MRS ELVSTED: Yes, I've got them here. I took them with me when I left. And they've been in my pocket –

TESMAN: Oh, let me just take a look!

MRS ELVSTED [*hands him a pile of loose pages*]: But it's so confused. Such a muddle.

TESMAN: What if we could make sense of it anyway! Perhaps if you and I help each other –

MRS ELVSTED: Oh yes, let's try at least –

TESMAN: It *will* work! It *must* work! I'll put my life into it!

HEDDA: You, Jørgen? Your life?

TESMAN: Yes, or rather all the time I can afford. My own collections, they must wait for now. Hedda – you do understand? What? I owe this to Eilert's memory.

HEDDA: Perhaps.

TESMAN: And now, Mrs Elvsted, we will collect ourselves. Heaven knows, there's no purpose in brooding over that which is past. We must find sufficient calm within ourselves, to –

MRS ELVSTED: Yes, yes, Mr Tesman, I'll try the best I can.

TESMAN: Right, come here then. We must look at those notes immediately. Where should we sit? Here? No, there in the back room. Apologies, my dear judge! Come along then, Mrs Elvsted.

MRS ELVSTED: Oh God – if only it can be done!

> TESMAN *and* MRS ELVSTED *go into the rear room. She takes off her hat and outdoor clothes. Both sit down at the table under the ceiling light and engross themselves in investigating the papers.* HEDDA *walks over to the wood stove and sits down in the armchair. After a while* BRACK *goes over to her.*

HEDDA [*in a lowered voice*]: Oh, judge – there's such release in this affair with Eilert Løvborg.

BRACK: Release, Mrs Hedda? Well, for him this is indeed release, I suppose –

HEDDA: I mean, for me. A release in knowing that there can be acts of courage born of free will in this world after all. Something imbued with a glow of impulsive beauty.

BRACK [*smiles*]: Hm – my dear Mrs Hedda –

HEDDA: Oh, I know what you'll say. After all, you're practically an academic too, of sorts – well, go on!

BRACK [*looks at her steadily*]: Eilert Løvborg was more to you than you perhaps want to admit to yourself. Or might I be mistaken?

HEDDA: I'll not answer you on such matters. All I know is that Eilert Løvborg has had the courage to live life in accordance with his own self. And then now – this great act! Imbued with beauty. And that he had the strength and the will to break away from life's party[57] – so early.

BRACK: It pains me, Mrs Hedda – but I am obliged to shake you out of a pretty illusion.

HEDDA: An illusion?

BRACK: Which, incidentally, you'd soon come out of anyway.

HEDDA: And what would that be?

BRACK: He didn't shoot himself – of his own free will.

HEDDA: Not of his own free will?

BRACK: No, this business with Eilert Løvborg isn't quite as I told it.

HEDDA [*in anticipation*]: Is there something you've kept quiet? What is it?

BRACK: For poor Mrs Elvsted's sake, I revised a few little details.

HEDDA: Which?

BRACK: Firstly, that he is in fact already dead.

HEDDA: In the hospital.

BRACK: Yes. And without regaining consciousness.

HEDDA: What more have you kept quiet?

BRACK: The fact that the incident did not take place in his room.

HEDDA: Well, I suppose that may also be fairly immaterial.

BRACK: Not entirely. Since I must tell you – Eilert Løvborg was found shot in – in Miss Diana's boudoir.

HEDDA [*is about to get to her feet, but sinks back*]: That's impossible, Mr Brack! He can't have been *there* again today!

BRACK: He was there this afternoon. He went to demand something, which he said they'd taken from him. Spoke confusedly about a child that had disappeared –

HEDDA: Ah – so that's why –

BRACK: I thought it might be his manuscript. But he's laid waste to that himself, I hear. So I assume it must have been his wallet.

HEDDA: It must have been. And so it was there – there that he was found.

BRACK: Yes, there. With a discharged pistol in his breast pocket. The shot had hit him fatally.

HEDDA: In the chest – yes.

BRACK: No – it hit him in the groin.

HEDDA [*looks up at him with an expression of disgust*]: That too! Oh, something ludicrous and base settles like a curse over everything I touch.

BRACK: There's another thing, Mrs Hedda. Something that might also be classified as base.

HEDDA: And what is that?

BRACK: The pistol he had on him –

HEDDA [*breathless*]: Well! What about it?

BRACK: He must have stolen it.

HEDDA [*leaps to her feet*]: Stolen! That's not true! He didn't!

BRACK: Anything else is impossible. He *must* have stolen it –. Shh!

> TESMAN *and* MRS ELVSTED *have got up from the table in the rear room and come into the drawing room.*

TESMAN [*with papers in both hands*]: Oh Hedda – it's almost impossible for me to see under that ceiling light in there. Just think!

HEDDA: Yes, I am thinking.

TESMAN: Might we be permitted to sit for a while at your writing desk? What?

HEDDA: Yes, that's fine by me. [*Quickly*] No, wait! Let me clear it first.

TESMAN: Oh you really don't need to, Hedda. There's plenty of space.

HEDDA: No, no, just let me get it cleared, I say. I'll carry this over to the piano for now. There we go!

> *She has pulled out from the shelf in the writing desk an object hidden under sheet music, she then adds a few more sheets and carries everything to the left in the rear*

room. TESMAN *puts the notes on the desk and then brings the lamp over to it from the corner table. He and* MRS ELVSTED *sit down and continue with their work.* HEDDA *returns.*

HEDDA [*behind* MRS ELVSTED'*s chair, ruffles her hair gently*]: Now, my sweet Thea – is Eilert Løvborg's memorial coming along?

MRS ELVSTED [*looks up at her dispiritedly*]: Oh, God – it's going to be terribly hard to sort out.

TESMAN: It *has* to work. There's nothing else for it. And bringing order to other people's papers – that's precisely my line of work.

HEDDA *walks over to the wood stove and sits down on one of the stools.* BRACK *stands over her, leaning on the armchair.*

HEDDA [*whispers*]: What was it you said about the pistol?

BRACK [*quietly*]: That he must have stolen it.

HEDDA: Why stolen?

BRACK: Because any other explanation ought to be impossible, Mrs Hedda.

HEDDA: Oh?

BRACK [*looks at her for a moment*]: Eilert Løvborg was, of course, here this morning. Right?

HEDDA: Yes.

BRACK: Were you alone with him?

HEDDA: Yes, for a while.

BRACK: You didn't leave the room while he was here?

HEDDA: No.

BRACK: Think carefully now. Weren't you gone, even for a moment?

HEDDA: Yes, maybe a brief moment – out in the hallway.

BRACK: And where was your pistol case at the time?

HEDDA: I had it down in –

BRACK: Well, Mrs Hedda?

HEDDA: The case was over there on the writing desk.

BRACK: Have you checked since whether both pistols are there?

HEDDA: No.

BRACK: Nor do you need to. I saw the pistol Løvborg had on him. And I recognized it straight away from yesterday. And, of course, from before.

HEDDA: Do you have it perhaps?

BRACK: No, the police have it.

HEDDA: What would the police want the pistol for?

BRACK: To track down whoever owns it.

HEDDA: You think that can be discovered?

BRACK [*bends down over her and whispers*]: No, Hedda Gabler – not as long as I keep quiet.

HEDDA [*looks timidly at him*]: And if you *don't* keep quiet – what then?

BRACK [*shrugs his shoulders*]: There's always the other way out – that the pistol was stolen.

HEDDA: I'd rather die!

BRACK [*smiles*]: That's what people *say*. But they don't *do* it.

HEDDA [*without answering*]: And suppose the pistol wasn't stolen. And the owner is discovered. Then what?

BRACK: Well, Hedda – then comes the scandal.

HEDDA: The scandal!

BRACK: The scandal, yes – of which you have such a deadly fear. You, of course, must appear in court. Both you and Miss Diana. Naturally she must explain the course of events. If it was an accident or a murder. Does he try to pull the pistol from his pocket in order to threaten her? And is that when the shot goes off? Or does she grab the pistol from his hand, shoot him, and stick the gun back in his pocket again? That would certainly seem in character. After all, she's a handy sort of girl, that Miss Diana.

HEDDA: But these sordid details have nothing to do with *me*.

BRACK: Indeed. But you'll have to answer this question: why did you give Eilert Løvborg the pistol? And what conclusion will people draw from the fact that you gave it to him?

HEDDA [*lowers her head*]: True. I've not thought about that.

BRACK: Well, fortunately there's no danger as long as I keep quiet.

HEDDA [*looks up at him*]: So I am in your power, Judge Brack. You have me at your mercy[58] from now on.

BRACK [*whispers more quietly*]: Dearest Hedda – believe me –
I won't abuse my position.

HEDDA: In your power all the same. Dependent on your
demands and your will. Unfree. Yes, unfree! [*Gets up violently*] No – I can't bear the thought! Never!

BRACK [*looks almost mockingly at her*]: People generally
accept the inevitable.

HEDDA [*returns his gaze*]: Yes, perhaps so.
She walks over towards the writing desk.

HEDDA [*suppresses an involuntary smile and mimics* TES-
MAN'*s tone*]: Well? Any success, Jørgen? What?

TESMAN: Oh, God only knows. There's months of work in all
this.

HEDDA [*as before*]: No, just think! [*Runs her fingers lightly
through* MRS ELVSTED'*s hair*] Isn't it strange for you, Thea?
You're sitting here with Tesman now – just as you used to sit
with Eilert Løvborg.

MRS ELVSTED: Oh God, if only I could inspire your husband
too.

HEDDA: Oh, that will come – with time.

TESMAN: Yes, you know what, Hedda – I do believe I'm starting to sense something of the sort. But you go back and sit
over there with the judge again.

HEDDA: Is there nothing the two of you can use me for here?

TESMAN: No, nothing at all. [*Turns his head*] *You* will have to
be kind and keep Hedda company hereafter, my dear judge!

BRACK [*glancing towards* HEDDA]: It'll be an inordinately
great pleasure.

HEDDA: Thank you. But I'm tired this evening. I want to take
a little lie down in there on the sofa.

TESMAN: Yes, you do that, darling. What?
HEDDA *walks into the rear room and pulls the curtains
behind her. Short pause. Suddenly she is heard playing a
wild dance tune on the piano.*

MRS ELVSTED [*leaps up from her chair*]: Ugh – what's that!

TESMAN [*runs to the doorway*]: But, dearest Hedda – don't
strike up a dance tune – not tonight! Think about Auntie
Rina! And Eilert too!

HEDDA [*pops her head through the curtains*]: And about Auntie Ju. And about all of them. – Hereafter I shall be silent.

She closes the curtain again.

TESMAN [*by the writing desk*]: I don't think it's good for her to see us at this mournful work. You know what, Mrs Elvsted – you should move in with Auntie Ju. Then I'll come up in the evenings. And we can sit and work *there*. What?

MRS ELVSTED: Yes, that might be best –

HEDDA [*in the rear room*]: I can hear what you're saying, Tesman. But what will I spend my evenings on out here then?

TESMAN [*leafs through the papers*]: Oh, I'm sure Mr Brack will still be kind enough to look in on you.

BRACK [*in his armchair, calls out cheerfully*]: Every evening, with pleasure, Mrs Tesman! We'll most certainly have some fun here together, the two of us!

HEDDA [*loud and clear*]: Yes, don't you just cherish that hope, judge? You, the only rooster in the coop –

A shot is heard from within. TESMAN, MRS ELVSTED *and* BRACK *jump up.*

TESMAN: Oh, now she's fiddling with those pistols again.

He parts the curtains and runs in. As does MRS ELVSTED. HEDDA *lies lifeless across the sofa. Confusion and shouting.* BERTA *enters in distress from the right.*

TESMAN [*shouts to* BRACK]: Shot herself! Shot herself in the temple! Just think!

BRACK [*almost paralysed in the armchair*]: But God have mercy – people don't actually *do* such things!

Acknowledgements

'The strongest man in the world,' Dr Stockmann famously pronounces in *An Enemy of the People*, 'is he who stands most alone.' Those involved in this new Penguin Classics edition of Henrik Ibsen's modern prose plays have, with all due modesty, begged to disagree. This project is very much the result of a collective effort.

Many therefore deserve thanks, not least at the very end of this more than decade-long project. The idea first came from Alexis Kirschbaum, then editor of Penguin Classics. As we moved into first draft stage it was taken over by a new Penguin editor, Jessica Harrison, who has shown patience, flexibility and good cheer all along, as well as being an admirably alert reader.

On behalf of all involved, I would like to extend a special thanks to the Norwegian Ministry of Foreign Affairs. Without their generous support it would have been impossible to stick to our original ambitions. Along the way workshops have twice been hosted by the Norwegian Embassy in London, where I would like to thank Eva Moksnes Vincent and Anne Ulset in particular, and once by the Centre for Ibsen Studies at the University of Oslo, where Frode Helland and Laila Yvonne Henriksen deserve thanks. We are also very grateful to the Faculty of Humanities at the University of Oslo for letting us base this edition on *Henrik Ibsens Skrifter (HIS)*. It makes this the first English-language edition based on the most comprehensive critical edition of Ibsen available. The extensive critical apparatus which only became available with *HIS* has also been a most valuable resource in our work and in composing our own endnotes.

A special group of expert readers have been invaluable during the many rounds of feedback and revisions: Paul Binding, Colin Burrow, Terence Cave, Janet Garton and Toril Moi. A number of other people have participated in seminars and discussions or offered their help or advice on various points, and I would like to mention Carsten Carlsen, Bart van Es, Narve Fulsås, Christian

Janss, Peter D. McDonald, Martin Puchner and Signe Ihlen Tønsberg, in addition, of course, to the four translators involved in the project, Deborah Dawkin, Barbara Haveland, Erik Skuggevik and Anne-Marie Stanton-Ife. Many thanks also go to my employer, the Department of Literature, Area Studies and European Languages, University of Oslo, and to my head of department, Karen Gammelgaard, as well as to the governing body of St Catherine's College, Oxford, for hosting me as Christensen Visiting Fellow during the spring of 2013. I will always remember the generosity of the late Master of St Catz, Roger Ainsworth.

A very particular debt of gratitude is owed to Professor Terence Cave, who has ended up acting as the main reader and my main support throughout the project. It is difficult to conceive where we would have been without his sensitive readings, extraordinary attentiveness to detail and stubborn commitment to the cause, the re-creation of Ibsen's storyworld. I would also like to thank Janet Garton for her many contributions, and to extend my warmest thanks to my family, Norunn, Anne Magdalene and Johannes Sakarias Bru Rem, for their love and patience. Transferring Ibsen into English has been an exceptionally challenging task, a work that has inspired in us all an even greater respect for this towering artist. For those of us who have acted as readers and re-readers of various versions of these translations, it has also demonstrated how exceptionally difficult the art of translation can be. Finally, I would therefore like to thank the translators, without whom these new texts would not exist, for their stubbornness, persistence and commitment, and, not least, for their competence and gift for mediation.

Tore Rem
Oslo, August 2019

Notes

THE WILD DUCK

1. *photographer*: Photography became a profession in Norway during the 1860s. During the next decades there were discussions about whether to categorize it as an artistic activity or an industry. For the census of 1891 it was moved to the category of 'industry'.

2. *fourteen years of age*: Age at this time could be given according to either the last or the next birthday. As the latter is confirmed later in the play, Hedvig is still thirteen.

3. MRS: The term in the original is 'fru', indicating that the woman in question is married and has a relatively high social standing (belonging to the bourgeoisie or the higher levels of the rural community).

4. *Høidal Works*: Ibsen simply has 'Højdal', which literally means 'high valley', a mountain valley. The 'j' has been changed to 'i' in order to facilitate pronunciation.

5. *a schnapps and a bottle of stout*: The original has 'bitter', a liquor with added bitter ingredients, and 'bajersk', a semi-dark type of beer.

6. *Madam*: The term 'madam' was at this time used for married women from lower social strata.

7. *fortress*: Fortresses in which criminals were imprisoned seem to have been associated with more serious crimes.

8. *chamberlain*: A title which could be a mere honorary title granted by a royal person, as in this case. It was not as exclusive as, for example, the title of the British Lord Chamberlain, and these chamberlains did not serve at court.

9. *maraschino*: Liqueur made of sour cherries.

10. *learn photography*: Learning photography was thought of as being relatively quick and easy.

11. *hour of need*: The expression in the original ('i trængselens dage', literally 'in the days of tribulation') has clear biblical or religious connotations.

12. *struggle for existence*: The expression alludes to Charles Darwin's *On the Origin of Species by Means of Natural Selection* (1859). It had been translated into Danish by the novelist J. P. Jacobsen in 1872. One of the chapter titles was 'The Struggle for Existence' ('Kampen for tilværelsen').

13. *denied knowing him*: An allusion to St Peter's denial of Jesus; see Luke 22:57.

14. *dive to the bottom*: An allusion to the poem 'Søfuglen' ('The Seabird') by the Romantic poet Johan Sebastian Welhaven (1807–73) and more specifically the line 'En Vildand svømmer stille' ('A wild duck swims quietly').

15. *neurotic*: Ibsen has 'overspændt'. It refers to a state of mind in which one experiences a weakened sense of reality.

16. *floozy*: 'Fruentimmer', which is the word in the original, at first meant 'a woman's room'. It became a joking or pejorative way of referring to a woman.

17. *Madam Eriksen's establishment*: The original uses the word 'restauration', meaning restaurant. The fact that it is run by a madam indicates that it is a low establishment.

18. *muddy porridge*: Many kinds of ink contained materials which created a sediment when left for a while.

19. *Ekdal*: It was not uncommon for a wife to address her husband by his surname, as a polite form.

20. *pottrits*: One of Gina's several malapropisms. The original has 'potrætterne' instead of 'portrætterne'. Gina's malapropisms are generally a matter of small mispronunciations or misunderstandings of foreign loan words.

21. *rich man's table*: Biblical connotations, most likely to the story of poor Lazarus and the rich man; see Luke 16:21.

22. *you mustn't*: Hjalmar here employs the informal form of address in the plural ('I'). He is thus addressing both Gina and Hedvig.

23. *Bohemian folk dance*: Bohemian folk music was popular at the time. Many Bohemian musicians toured Europe during the nineteenth century.

24. *into the street*: Having been convicted of crimes, Ekdal has lost his right to wear his uniform in public.

25. *Really – you, Mr Werle*: Gina uses 'du' (the informal 'you'). She corrects herself in her next line and continues to use 'De' (the formal 'you') for the rest of the scene.

26. *doctor*: The original has 'dokter' for 'doktor'. This is hardly audible in speech, but signals a lower-class sociolect. Gina gets the word right when she shouts for Dr Relling in Act V, however.

27. *soon be ripe*: Ibsen uses the expression 'tidens fylde' (literally 'the fullness of time'), deriving from Galatians 4:4.

28. *breakfast*: The original 'frokost' means two different things in Danish and Norwegian. In Danish it means 'lunch', in Norwegian 'breakfast'. Here it must mean 'breakfast', since it is clearly the first meal of the day, but the next reference to the meal is 'formiddagsfrokost', an old word for lunch, translated here as 'early lunchtime bite'.

29. *without a hat*: It was unusual for adults to go outdoors without some kind of head covering.

30. *You*: Gregers here employs the polite form for 'you' ('De') rather than the informal 'du', thus indicating that he is not speaking to Hedvig as a child.

31. *Harryson's History of London*: Hedvig refers to Walter Harrison's *A New and Universal History, Description and Survey of the Cities of London and Westminster, the Borough of Southwark, and Their Adjacent Parts* (London, 1776).

32. *Death with an hourglass*: An allegorical book illustration, typical of the seventeenth and eighteenth centuries.

33. *flying Dutchman*: A nautical legend about a Dutch sailor cursed to sail on until Doomsday. Richard Wagner popularized the story with the opera *Der fliegende Holländer*, first performed in 1843. In this version the Dutchman is finally saved from his sufferings through the self-sacrificing love of a woman, the Norwegian fisher girl Senta.

34. *basket-weaving and straw-plaiting*: This was common handiwork for the blind and weak-sighted.

35. *she*: At this point Hedvig begins to refer to the wild duck as 'hun' ('she') instead of 'den' ('it').

36. *diversify*: In the original Gina mixes up the word 'dividere' ('divide') with 'divertere' ('entertain').

37. *bone oil*: A dark, foul-smelling oil made by carbonizing bones, or the liquid portion of bone fat, primarily used to soften and preserve leather.

38. *grey garb*: In 1835 dark grey had been made the colour for prisoners' outfits in Norway.

39. *eat, drink and be merry*: Biblical allusion; see Luke 12:19: 'eat, drink, and be merry.'

40. *pontrificating*: Gina uses the word 'ressensér', meaning to 'speak critically of' or 'in pejorative terms'. By using this word in the wrong way, she involuntarily implies that she thinks of the compliment as criticism.

41. *wet glass plate*: In 1851 Frederick Scott Archer discovered that the use of wet glass plates (the wet-collodion process) outdid earlier techniques of photography. It improved both detail and clarity. Towards the end of the 1870s the wet glass plates were replaced by more sensitive dry plates.

42. *sustaining injury to his soul*: This is a biblical allusion; see Matthew 16:26: 'For what is a man profited, if he shall gain the whole world, and lose his own soul?'

43. *delusion*: Ibsen's 'vildfarelse' (more literally 'going astray') clearly belongs to a religious vocabulary.

44. *a light of transfiguration*: The original phrase 'forklarelsens lys' came into Danish via King Christian III's Bible translation of 1550. See Matthew 17:2: 'And was transfigured before them: and his face did shine as the sun, and his raiment was white as the light.'

45. *bitter cup*: Jesus was offered vinegar to drink during his crucifixion; see e.g., Matthew 27:48: 'And straightway one of them ran, and took a spunge, and filled it with vinegar, and put it on a reed, and gave him to drink.'

46. *royal assent*: The word 'kongebrev' (literally 'royal letter') was originally used for all kinds of royal decrees in written form. At this time the expression referred to a licence given by the county governor ('amtmand') for a marriage without Church blessing.

47. *womenfolk*: The word used in the original is 'fruentimmer'. See above, note 16.

48. *own eyes*: A biblical allusion; see Matthew 5:38: 'An eye for an eye, and a tooth for a tooth'.

49. *Miss*: Ibsen uses the word 'frøken'. It was used in contrast to the older 'jomfru' (meaning both 'maiden' and 'virgin'), with gradually reduced connotations of nobility or higher social standing. Young girls were called 'frøken' after having been confirmed. It is here used as a polite form of address in the third person.

50. *anything evil*: The expression 'og alt det, som ondt er' (literally 'and all that is evil') comes from the litany prayer used by the Lutheran Church in Norway during Lent and on the Repentance and Prayer Day (at this time celebrated on the fourth Friday after Easter).

51. *intricate demands*: Gina's misunderstanding of 'den ideale fordring' ('the ideal demand').

52. *shooting stars*: The original has 'vidunderfluerne' (literally 'wonder flies'). This expression refers to the first stage of delirium.

53. *life-lie*: Ibsen's neologism 'livsløgnen' is reminiscent of certain statements by the German philosopher Friedrich Nietzsche (1844–1900). There are examples of Nietzsche stressing the need for illusions, as Relling does here, but there is no evidence that Ibsen had read him.

54. *incision*: 'Fontanellen' in the original refers to a small wound made in the skin in connection with epilepsy and some other diseases, in order to distract the patient.

55. *not done*: The phrase 'er fuldbragt' can also be translated as 'is finished', a possible allusion to Jesus' words on the cross; see John 19:30: 'It is finished.'

56. *firm foundation*: Ibsen's 'fast grund' (literally 'firm ground') has biblical connotations. See the parable in Matthew 7:24–7 about building one's house on rock and not on sand.

57. *reparation*: The original's 'oprettelsen' can also mean 'restoration'. It has religious connotations.

58. *The child is not dead, but sleepeth*: The original phrasing is almost identical to Jesus' words in Mark 5:39 when he heals Jairus' daughter.

59. *lie on parade*: Gina is misusing the French expression 'lit de parade' (lying in state), also used in Norwegian. 'Lit de parade' is the tradition in which the body of a dead official is placed in an open coffin or on a platform to allow the public to pay their respects.

60. *to dust thou shalt return*: This is part of the phrasing in the Lutheran funeral ritual, taken from Genesis 3:19: 'for dust thou art, and unto dust shalt thou return'. The ritual ends with 'and from dust shalt thou rise again'.

ROSMERSHOLM

1. *clergyman*: The original gives the more precise title 'sogneprest'. The 'sogneprest' was the leading vicar in a congregation. He was a civil servant, appointed by the government cabinet and bound by oath.

2. MRS: The term in the original is 'madam'. It was at this time used for married women from lower social strata.

3. *manor house*: At a time when aristocracy in Norway had been abolished (formally in 1821), the term 'herregården' generally

meant a big farm with a certain history of having played a significant social, economic and cultural role in the local area.

4. *old-fashioned*: If the living room had been furnished a generation before, it would most likely be in a post-Romantic Biedermeier style. The style was originally German and developed between 1815 and 1848, and was extremely influential in Scandinavia. It is classicizing, with elegant, clean lines and simple ornaments. After the middle of the century Biedermeier style was replaced by heavier Victorian interiors.

5. *wood stove*: The word 'kakkelovn' generally refers to a stove with the sides and top made of square tiles of burnt clay, used for burning wood. There are, however, examples of Ibsen associating the word with the new iron stoves first introduced at the beginning of the century.

6. *miss*: Ibsen uses the word 'frøken'. It was used in contrast to the older 'jomfru' (meaning both 'maiden' and 'virgin'), with gradually reduced connotations of nobility or higher social standing. Young girls were called 'frøken' after having been confirmed.

7. *white horse*: None of the native Norwegian breeds of horse are white, but white horses did play a role in folk mythology.

8. *Rosmer*: The use of address was strictly regulated by social convention. Kroll is Rosmer's brother-in-law and is therefore allowed to address him by his first name. He must not, however, use Rosmer's first name in conversation with Rebekka, a person whom he addresses in the third person. In the original, both Kroll and Rebekka use both first and last name in contexts where they have a particular emphasis. Rosmer's former teacher Ulrik Brendel can use both the first name and 'du' (the informal 'you'), while Rosmer uses 'De' (the formal 'you').

9. *as a woman*: The original word is 'fruentimmer'. It at first meant 'a woman's room' and later became a joking or pejorative reference to a woman.

10. *Finnmark*: The northernmost province of Norway.

11. *twenty-nine*: The great majority of women in the middle and upper classes married before the age of thirty.

12. *Mr Rosmer*: Normal courtesy meant that one could only say 'du' (the informal 'you') to people one would address by their first name, generally only closest family. People outside the closest family circle were addressed by their civil and professional titles and, in direct address, the polite form 'De' (the formal 'you'). When a wife spoke about her husband to someone with whom she was not on intimate terms, it was considered correct

for her to use his surname. Even if two people knew each other well, they would not use the informal 'du' or first names in formal settings. If others were present with whom each of the two was not on intimate terms ('Dus'), it was normal that they used the polite 'De' also to each other.

13. *Rebekk – both Miss West*: See note on polite forms of address above, note 12.

14. *professional life*: The word in the original is 'embedsgerning', a somewhat more solemn term. Kroll is headmaster at a higher school in which the teaching staff are civil servants. He speaks of his professional duties, which are guided by an oath to God and the King.

15. *leaders of the masses*: Kroll probably alludes to the politicians of the Liberal Party, called 'Venstre' ('The Left').

16. *a calling*: The term 'kald' ('calling') has biblical and religious connotations. But here it primarily refers to the position of priest in this particular parish.

17. *prodigal*: Ibsen's use of the word 'forlorne' is a direct allusion to the parable of the prodigal son; see Luke 15:11–32. The original's 'forlorne' means 'lost' or 'wayward' and is thus starker than in the English.

18. *whom I have loved more than any*: An allusion to John 19:26. The apostle's name in Norwegian is Johannes, so the allusion is a more direct one than it can be in English.

19. *Donnerwetter!*: A German word, used as a swearword. It literally means 'thunderstorm'.

20. *knew you*: Brendel here changes from addressing Kroll with the formal 'De' ('you') in his last line to the informal and more intimate 'dig' ('you'). It is a consequence of his recognition of their shared past. Kroll reacts against this claim to intimacy.

21. *halberdiers*: The original has the word 'drabanter' ('drabants'). This was a medieval term used for the life guards of kings and lords, but would be obscure in English. 'Halberdiers' similarly signals Brendel's love of the archaic.

22. *Debating Society*: During the first half of the nineteenth century there were a number of similar societies for the bourgeoisie.

23. *Nach Belieben*: A German expression meaning 'as you wish'.

24. *enfin*: French for 'finally'.

25. *die is cast*: When Caesar in the year 49 BC crossed the River Rubicon and thus started a civil war, he is supposed to have exclaimed: 'The die is cast' ('Alea jacta est' in Latin). In the original Brendel mistranslates the expression by introducing the plural 'dice'.

26. *unter uns*: German for 'between us'.

27. *Working Men's Association Hall*: This probably refers to the workers' societies which were first established in Norway during the 1860s. They were initially an expression of bourgeois philanthropy and often had conservative boards. From the late 1870s they became a part of the struggle between the conservatives and the liberals ('the Right' and 'the Left') and were gradually taken over by 'the Left'.

28. *Dozent*: The devaluation of Kroll from 'Professor' to the less prestigious 'Dozent' (both are wrong, he is a headmaster) contributes to the comedy.

29. *the new man*: Biblical allusion to the phenomenon of being born again; see Ephesians 4:24.

30. *solstice*: The original 'solhverv' is a term that covers both summer and winter solstice. Brendel is talking about an age of change.

31. *sybarite*: Person who is self-indulgent, with an inclination for pleasure and luxury.

32. *Ein Feinschmecker*: German for 'a connoisseur'.

33. *crown of laurels*: Laurels represented Apollo, the sun god. Poets and artists were honoured by receiving a laurel wreath.

34. *Temperance Society*: Revivalist movements had initiated the foundation of temperance societies. The first was established in 1859, and many were to follow all over Norway.

35. *A la bonheur*: Brendel uses this French expression in the wrong way. It should be 'à la bonne heure' ('all in good time').

36. *ten-kroner notes*: Average pay for a day's work for labourers in Kristiania (now Oslo) in 1875 was 2.33 kroner.

37. *miss*: Mrs Helseth switches, in addressing Rebekka, from the second person ('frøken') to the third person ('frøkenen').

38. *so long, Johannes*: In the original Rebekka actually calls Rosmer by his surname here and later when they are on their own. But since English cannot capture the transition between 'du' and 'De' (the informal versus the formal 'you'), which signals their intimacy in the original, 'Johannes' is used to indicate this here. Later in the original, Kroll will be shocked by their use of the 'wrong', informal form of address; in this translation he is shocked by hearing them use first names to each other.

39. *the lady*: The original 'frøkenen' means that Kroll is using the polite form of address in the third person.

40. *purpose of marriage*: A 'progressive' view at this time meant viewing reproduction as the overall goal of marriage, and regular sexual intercourse as a prerequisite for good health.

41. *must marry*: 'Having to marry' was a standard expression for marrying because the woman was pregnant.

42. *fray of life*: Ibsen uses the composite word 'livsstriden' (literally 'life's struggle'). The 'struggle for existence' was a topical notion. Darwin had used it as the title of the third chapter of his *On the Origin of Species* (1859).

43. *war to the knife*: Originally a rallying cry ('War to the knife and knife to the hilt') related to the issue of slavery. It first seems to have appeared in the Kansas *Atchison Squatter Sovereign* (*c*.1854). Ibsen also uses the expression in *An Enemy of the People*.

44. *we mustn't bear false witness*: In the Danish King Christian III's Bible (1550), 'Thou shalt not bear false witness' was the eighth commandment.

45. *seventh*: He is referring to what is in fact the sixth commandment in Danish and Norwegian Bible translations: 'Thou shalt not commit adultery.'

46. *our party's*: Mortensgård is referring to the Liberal Party, but possibly more precisely to its conservative wing.

47. *miss*: Mrs Helseth uses 'frøkenen' as a polite form of address in the third person.

48. *sort of infection*: At this time it was commonly believed that infection spread through the air, or rather through a particular form of 'bad air'. This was called the 'miasma theory'.

49. *conscience is troubled*: Ibsen uses the now dated 'brøde' ('crime', 'guilt', 'feeling guilty'). It is potentially both an action and a state of mind. Here it is closer to 'having committed an offence'. The choice has been made in order to retain the repetition of this word above, where it is closer to 'conscience'.

50. *district physician*: The original 'distriktslægen' was the publicly appointed doctor of a rural district. After a royal resolution of 1836 there were sixty-three such positions in Norway, all part of the civil service. These doctors were charged with providing ordinary medical services and with preventing the outbreak of infectious diseases in their districts.

51. *marriageable age*: The great majority of women in the middle and upper classes married before the age of thirty.

52. *first names*: The original has the phrase 'vi siger du til hinanden' (literally 'we say you to each other', with the informal 'you' ('du')). The transition from the formal to the informal mode of address, especially with a third person present, marks a change in the relationship between the two, from one between employer and employee to one of equality and greater intimacy.

53. *new era*: During the 1870s and 1880s Norwegian society went through radical changes, both politically and in its business and cultural life. In the countryside there was a transition from a rural to a money economy, industrialization and urbanization picked up speed, and the cultural life experienced liberalization.

54. *woman*: The original uses the word 'fruentimmer'. It has negative connotations.

55. *nichts*: German for 'nothing'.

56. *Le Président*: The French term has been chosen in order to compensate for the loss of other foreignisms in this passage. The original simply has 'Præsidenten' ('the president').

57. *Ganz nach Belieben*: German for 'as you wish'.

58. *Beispiel*: German for 'example'.

59. *shifting sand*: An allusion to Jesus' parable about the importance of building one's house on rock; see Matthew 7:26.

60. *rosy-white little finger*: Fingers and ears were central concerns during the prosecutions for witchcraft during the Middle Ages. This was based on a belief that the devil marked witches on their little finger and bit them in the ear. In Norwegian mythology cutting one's little finger was believed to have magical effects.

61. *like a sea-troll*: Trolls generally inhabit forests and mountains, but in the Norse tradition, for example in the thirteenth-century *Kongsspegelen* (*The King's Mirror*), there are also female sea-trolls. In the Danish folk ballad 'Rosmer', Rosmer Havmand ('Rosmer Ocean Man') is an undersea troll.

62. *hand upon your head*: Danish and Norwegian wedding ceremonies had long involved the laying on of hands after the vows.

63. *Man and wife must go together*: See Genesis 2:24: 'Therefore shall a man leave his father and his mother, and shall cleave unto his wife: and they shall be one flesh.'

THE LADY FROM THE SEA

1. *local doctor*: The 'distriktslæge' was the publicly appointed doctor of a rural district. After a royal resolution of 1836 there were sixty-three such positions in Norway, all part of the civil service. These doctors were charged with providing ordinary medical services and with preventing the outbreak of infectious diseases in their districts.

2. *MRS*: The original's 'fru' indicated that the woman in question was married and had a relatively high social standing (belonging to the bourgeoisie or the higher levels of the rural community).

3. *schoolmaster*: The original has 'overlærer'. The term refers to a senior teacher with a university education.

4. *fjord town*: Several factors, among them the fact that the place has no midnight sun, indicate that this is not a town in what from the end of the nineteenth century was called Northern Norway. Rather, it is reminiscent of Molde and the Romsdal fjord in the northwest of the southern part of the country, where Ibsen had spent time during his visit to Norway in 1885.

5. *the left*: Ibsen always pictures the stage from the perspective of the audience.

6. *Miss*: Ibsen uses the word 'frøken'. It was used in contrast to the older 'jomfru' (meaning both 'maiden' and 'virgin'), with gradually reduced connotations of nobility or higher social standing. Young girls were called 'frøken' after having been confirmed.

7. *steamboat*: There was a strong growth in tourist traffic in the western fjords during the 1880s. Large steamships were still quite a new phenomenon.

8. *stage décor*: The original has the word 'dekorationsfaget' (literally 'the profession of decoration'), referring to the professional task of painting the scenery in a theatre.

9. *a call*: Ibsen uses the borrowed term 'visit'. This referred to a short and formal visit, made in order to have a brief conversation or to honour a particular occasion.

10. *Brass Band Association*: Brass bands were common in Ibsen's time. They could be quite small, consisting of five or six musicians.

11. *lunch*: Ibsen uses the word 'frokost', which here seems to have its Danish meaning, i.e. 'lunch', rather than its Norwegian meaning, 'breakfast'.

12. *Old Ma Jensen*: This is a literary allusion lost in translation. In the plays of Ludvig Holberg (1684–1754) the original 'Hils mor Jensen fra mig' ('Greet mother Jensen from me') were used as parting words expressing ridicule, disgust or superiority.

13. *summerhouse*: The summerhouse and the arbour are one and the same thing.

14. *ship's name*: The female name Ellida comes from the name of the saga hero Frithiof's ship (cf. *Frithiof's Saga*, c.1300).

15. *birthday*: The word for birthday, 'fødselsdag', had gradually taken over for 'geburtsdag' after the middle of the century.

Lyngstrand has just said 'geburtsdag', but when Ellida responds by saying 'fødselsdag', he follows suit after a momentary hesitation ('fruens ge – fruens fødselsdag').

16. *gestalt*: From the German, referring to a figure, a form, something appearing. It is more commonly used in Danish and Norwegian than in English. The motif of the drowned man coming back to fetch his girlfriend has a number of sources.

17. *four-part harmony*: Probably refers to a men's choir. Men's choirs were very popular in Norway in the latter half of the nineteenth century. The songs were almost always in four-part harmonies.

18. *meine Damen und Herren*: Ballested's language indicates that the tourists are German- and English-speaking. For 'meine Damen und Herren' the original has 'meine Herrschaften'.

19. *dort*: German for 'there'.

20. *Das willen wir . . . then herunter*: This mix of German and English means something like 'We will also climb that (hill) and then come back down.'

21. *switches to English*: In the original Ballested presumably moves from mangled German-Norwegian to mangled English-Norwegian.

22. *name is Hans*: Hans was a very common name.

23. *horrible name*: 'Bolette' was rare and somewhat old-fashioned.

24. *Lodskollen*: The name refers to a 'knoll' ('kolle') from which the local 'ship's pilot' ('lods') looks for ships that need help in navigating towards land. The quotation marks in the original indicate a reservation about referring to it as a proper place name.

25. *northbound*: Ibsen uses the word 'nordfarer' (literally 'someone travelling north'). It referred to a ship sailing to and from Northern Norway.

26. *Friman*: This word is pronounced exactly like 'Free man' ('frimann') in Norwegian.

27. *emigrated*: There were several waves of Finnish emigration to Northern Norway from *c*.1720 until the end of the nineteenth century. In the two northernmost counties, Troms and Finnmark, 9,300 'kvener' (see below) were registered in 1875. As many as 25 per cent of the population of Finnmark were of Finnish descent.

28. *Kven*: Finnish immigrant or descendant of such immigrants, particularly in Finnmark. The word was often used in a pejorative way.

29. *his kin*: After the dissemination of Charles Darwin's theories, there was much debate about the relationship between animals and humans.

30. *goldmines*: The mining of gold increased drastically after the discovery of gold in California in 1848 and in Australia in 1851.

31. *allowed to study*: Women received the right to sit the 'examen artium', the entrance exam to the university in Kristiania (now Oslo), in 1882. In 1887, 9 out of 361 students sitting this exam were women.

32. *employment*: Women from the middle classes did not have many professional opportunities. City schools and the telegraph system recruited the most women from these classes. Other public institutions followed, but very slowly.

33. *no hat*: When outdoors, it was common for both men and women to wear a hat.

34. *in the sea*: In the 1880s theories circulated claiming that humanity's origins were in the sea. Among these were those of the German biologist and philosopher Ernst Haeckel (1834–1919).

35. *my dearest*: In the original Ellida uses 'du' (the informal 'you'), meaning that she thinks that the person arriving is her husband.

36. *you*: Ellida here changes to 'De' (the polite form of 'you'), showing that she now recognizes that the newcomer is a stranger.

37. *You know*: The Stranger does not respect polite conventions and uses 'du' (the intimate 'you'). The 'dear' has been introduced in order to compensate for the loss of this distinction in English.

38. *a stranger hereabouts*: In the original Wangel says that he has heard that a stranger has been asking for Ellida 'inde i gården'. The word 'gården' may refer to many things including an area, farm or other large building. Here it is usually translated as 'at the house'. This, however, implies at the doctor's own house, but since according to the text there would have been nobody there to meet the Stranger or spread such a rumour, this cannot be the case.

39. *not to her*: Legally married women were minors, under the guardianship of their fathers and husbands. In 1888, the year of the publication of *The Lady from the Sea*, Norwegian married women were given majority status, but the man still retained ownership of their common property.

40. *Ellida*: The use of the first name reveals a close relationship.

41. *vocation*: Ibsen uses the word 'kald' ('calling'). It has biblical and religious connotations and can be associated with a particular profession or service.

42. *south of Europe*: In the first part of the nineteenth century, Nordic artists who could afford it often travelled to Italy; later they also went to France and Germany.

43. *'Soon shall each and every strait be closed'*: An allusion to the tragedy *Hakon Jarl* (1807) by the Danish playwright Adam Oehlenschläger (1779–1850).

44. *no keys*: Nothing has connected her to the role of housewife.

45. *carry you*: Biblical allusion; see Matthew 4:6: 'He shall give his angels charge concerning thee: and in their hands they shall bear thee up, lest at any time thou dash thy foot against a stone.'

46. *vocation*: Ibsen uses the compound word 'livskald' (literally 'life calling'). For 'calling', see above, note 41.

47. *Like a thief in the night*: Biblical allusion; see 1 Thessalonians 5:2: 'For yourselves know perfectly that the day of the Lord so cometh as a thief in the night.'

48. *the hour has come*: Biblical allusion; see John 12:23: 'And Jesus answered them, saying, The hour is come, that the Son of man should be glorified.'

49. *first bell*: The first of three signals with the ship's bell warning the passengers to get on board.

50. *you*: Having used 'du' (the informal 'you') up till now, the Stranger changes to the polite form 'De'. This indicates that he has now adopted a formal relation to Ellida.

51. *The last voyage*: The expression in the original is an allusion to Henrik Wergeland's poem 'Sidste Reis' ('The Last Voyage', 1845), about the journey to heaven.

HEDDA GABLER

1. *scholar*: Ibsen uses the term 'stipendiat', someone who has been given a stipend of some duration. The only university in Norway at this time, Det Kongelige Frederiks Universitet (The Royal Frederik's University) in Kristiania (now Oslo), could hand out stipends to 'needy' academic citizens. Stipends were also available to graduates who wanted to remain at the university for some time after having completed their studies.

2. MRS: The term used in the original is 'fru', indicating that the woman in question is married and has a relatively high social standing (belonging to the bourgeoisie or the higher levels of the rural community).

3. MISS: The word in the original is 'frøken'. It was used in contrast to the older term 'jomfru' (meaning both 'maiden' and 'virgin'), with a gradually reduced connotation of nobility or higher social class. Young girls were called 'frøken' after having been confirmed.

4. *JUDGE*: The Norwegian 'assessor' is a particular kind of judge, a member of a court with several judges, where the leader was generally called 'justitiarius' or 'president'.

5. *EILERT*: The spelling has been changed from 'Ejlert' to 'Eilert' in order to facilitate pronunciation.

6. *BERTA*: The spelling has been changed from 'Berte' to 'Berta' in order to facilitate pronunciation.

7. *west side*: In many towns of a certain size the western part was (and remains) the most fashionable one. This was also the case with Kristiania (now Oslo).

8. *porcelain wood stove*: Tiled stove made of porcelain tiles. These tiles were often white or light in colour, but darker colours also became fashionable during the latter half of the nineteenth century, such as deep green or brown.

9. *grey walking attire*: Feminine fashion at this time was colourful. Grey was unusual.

10. *General Gabler's*: German family name. Many Norwegian military families had a German background.

11. *master*: The original uses the title 'kandidaten' ('the candidate'), an informal title referring to someone who has studied for a higher degree.

12. *from the right*: Ibsen always sees the stage from the position of the audience.

13. *Ju*: The original has 'Julle', a family nickname for this old aunt who is really called Juliane.

14. *Right Honourable*: The title used in the original is 'statsrådinde', the feminine form for a minister of government, in this case meaning such a minister's wife.

15. *Brabantine*: Belonging to Brabant, a landscape partly in Holland, partly in Belgium.

16. *Tesman darling*: Hedda is using her husband's surname ('kjære Tesman', literally 'dear Tesman'), thereby communicating a distance both from him and from 'Auntie Ju'.

17. *Slippers*: Slippers were a symbol of womanhood, since women were supposed to belong at home and used slippers indoors.

18. *Auntie Ju*: In the original Tesman asks Hedda to use 'du' (the informal 'you') to his aunt. Polite convention meant that one could not say 'du' to anyone but those with whom one was on first-name terms, most often only immediate family.

19. *Mrs Elvsted*: The original has 'Fru foged Elvsted' (literally 'Mrs Chief Bailiff Elvsted'). The term 'foged' ('chief bailiff') had been used in Norway since the fourteenth century. It was one of the

most important positions within the civil service. The 'foged' was a civil servant with both legal and administrative duties and with responsibility for a large district. Norway had fifty-five such districts, 'fogderier', in 1866.

20. *visit*: The borrowed word 'visit' in the original specifically denotes a short and formal visit, made in order to have a brief conversation or to honour a particular occasion.

21. *high school*: Around the middle of the nineteenth century the word 'institut' (literally 'institute') referred most often to a girls' high school, but also to other kinds of more advanced schools.

22. *cultural development*: Cultural history was not established as a subject at the university in Kristiania at this time. The German philosopher Friedrich Nietzsche (1844–1900) had, however, made the development of Western culture a central concern.

23. *first names*: In the original Hedda says that they used the intimate form of 'you' ('du') *and* called each other by first names.

24. *call me Hedda*: In the original Hedda asks Mrs Elvsted both to address her by the intimate form ('du') and to call her by her first name.

25. *Mrs*: Mrs Elvsted here makes the mistake of switching back to 'De' (the formal 'you').

26. *restored him*: Hedda uses the word 'genoprejst' (literally 'raised up again') here and again later. She means that Mrs Elvsted has once more made Løvborg a morally respectable man.

27. *cut short*: Fashion in the 1880s and 1890s prescribed short hair for men. Around 1890 the fashion was for very short hair and a side parting. Men with longer hair would be assumed to be aspiring poets or musicians.

28. *petit bourgeois*: As the daughter of a high-ranking officer and civil servant, Hedda originally belonged to a higher social class than the Tesmans. The petty bourgeoisie included shopkeepers and trades-men, as well as artisans and other small-scale producers.

29. *sport*: A relatively new word, borrowed from English, first used in Danish around the middle of the nineteenth century.

30. *lunch*: Ibsen uses the word 'middag', now best translated with 'dinner'. But at this time it referred to a hot meal in the middle of the day, around the time of today's lunch.

31. *calling*: The term 'kald' ('calling') has biblical and religious connotations. It can be associated with a particular profession or service.

32. *ankles*: Feminine fashion required floor-length skirts. It was not regarded as suitable for women to show their ankles.

33. *accompany me home*: No respectable woman would go out on her own after dark. She was dependent on a man, who would accompany her home to her gate. In the early British reception of the play the fact that the supposedly upper-middle-class Hedda was not taken home in a carriage was seen as a mark of provincialism.

34. *calling*: The word is 'kald'; see above, note 31.

35. *that's all right then*: According to the conventions for polite and seemly behaviour, it would be unsuitable for Hedda and a male guest to be in the house together without others present. The presence of servants was not sufficient.

36. *The Ortler Alps near Merano*: The Ortler Alps are in the borderlands between what are now the north Italian provinces of South Tyrol, Trentino and Sondrio. Merano is a town in South Tyrol, at this time in Austria-Hungary, but now in Italy. It was known for its spa resorts.

37. *my dearest*: The original has 'du' (the informal 'you'). Løvborg clearly goes too far here and again later in communicating intimacy in this situation.

38. *my dearest*: In the original, Løvborg again uses the intimate form of address ('du'), and Hedda reacts against his breach of etiquette by asking him not to.

39. *village*: Most likely a reference to Gossensass, where Ibsen spent his summer holidays between 1876 and 1889. The Brenner Pass is the lowest mountain pass across the Alps and one of the most important routes for traffic between Italy and northern Europe. In 1890 the pass belonged to Austria-Hungary.

40. *lust for life*: Ibsen uses the compound word 'livsbegæret' (literally 'life desire/lust/craving'). This is one of Ibsen's memorable coinages. Compound nouns are common in Norwegian, but in Ibsen's plays they are often – as in this case – used to represent distinctive thematic motifs.

41. *my dearest*: In the original Løvborg uses 'du' (the informal 'you').

42. *demand for life*: The original has the compound word 'livskravet' (literally 'the life demand'). This is another of the distinctive compound nouns referred to above, note 40.

43. *good to be here*: The slightly more formal phrasing in the original contains an allusion to the story of Jesus' transfiguration; see Matthew 17:4: 'Then answered Peter, and said unto Jesus, Lord, it is good for us to be here.'

44. *lifted ... up again*: Biblical language. The original's 'rejst mig igen' ('stood up again') is related to 'genoprejst' ('raised up again').

45. *Vine leaves*: The expression should be understood as an allusion to Dionysos, Greek god of wine, fertility and ritual ecstasy.
In Ibsen's time vine leaves were associated with festivities. When
there were parties at the Scandinavian Society in Rome, guests
would appear with laurels. With the publication and first production of *Hedda Gabler* in London in 1891, 'vine leaves in his
hair' seems to have become something of a catchphrase among
the Aesthetes and Decadents.

46. *bacchanalia*: The use of this word, meaning 'a wild party, with
dance, revelry and song', but also evoking the cult of the Roman
wine god Bacchus, is consistent with Hedda's recurrent vision
of Løvborg with 'vine leaves in his hair'.

47. *new man*: A biblical allusion, referring to the notion of rebirth.

48. *spirit came over him*: A phrase with biblical resonances.

49. *Miss Diana's*: In Roman mythology Diana is the goddess of the
moon and of hunting, as well as a helper during birth.

50. *screen*: The original, 'skærmbret', is closer to a boudoir vanity
screen, but as such hardly works as a metaphor in English.

51. *rooster in the coop*: The expression 'hane i kurven' (literally
'cock in the basket') is a set idiom in Norwegian, meaning the
only man in a group of women. It derives from the country
practice of taking hens and cocks to market in a basket.

52. *mourning clothes*: Feminine attire for mourning consisted of a
black dress and a bonnet with a veil.

53. *at this moment*: This is the first of Miss Tesman's hints that
Hedda may be pregnant.

54. *cross*: Biblical allusion; see, e.g., Matthew 10:38: 'And he that
taketh not his cross, and followeth after me, is not worthy of me.'

55. *just recently*: Hedda hints at her possible pregnancy, as well as
the notion that pregnant women might behave irrationally or
even hysterically.

56. *calling me Jørgen*: It was not unusual for married women to call
their husbands by the polite form 'De' (formal 'you') and surname, thus expressing respect. Using the first name was a sign
of intimacy and rarely happened in the company of others.

57. *life's party*: The original has a compound word, 'livsgildet',
referring to a notion of life as a feast.

58. *at your mercy*: Ibsen uses the idiom 'har hals og hånd over' (literally 'having neck and hand over'), meaning that someone has
one's destiny in his or her hand.

A DOLL'S HOUSE AND OTHER PLAYS

Henrik Ibsen

'Our home has never been anything other than a play-house. I've been
your doll-wife here, just as at home I was Daddy's doll-child'

With her assertion that she is 'first and foremost a human being'
rather than a wife, mother or fragile doll, Nora Helmer sent shock-
waves throughout Europe when she appeared in Ibsen's greatest
and most famous play, *A Doll's House*. Ibsen's follow-up *Ghosts*
was no less radical, with its unrelenting investigation into religious
hypocrisy, family secrets and sexual double-dealing. These two
masterpieces are accompanied here by *The Pillars of the Community* and *An Enemy of the People*, both exploring the tensions
and dark compromises at the heart of society.

Translated by Deborah Dawkin and Erik Skuggevik
Introduced by Tore Rem
General Editor Tore Rem

ISBN: 978 0 141 19456 1

PEER GYNT AND BRAND

Henrik Ibsen

'Stories of princes and trolls, the strangest of tales, of brides who were stolen still in their wedding-veils, not to be seen again in this world of ills'

These two masterly and contrasting verse dramas by Ibsen made his reputation as a playwright. The fantastical adventures of the irrepressible Peer Gynt – poet, idler, procrastinator, seducer – draw on Norwegian folklore to conjure up mountains, kidnappings, shipwrecks and trolls in an exuberant celebration of life; while *Brand*, an unsparing vision of an idealistic priest who lives by his steely faith, explores free will, sacrifice and the self. This volume brings together the poet Geoffrey Hill's acclaimed stage version of *Brand* with a new poetic rendering of *Peer Gynt*, published for the first time.

Verse translations by Geoffrey Hill
Introduced by Janet Garton
General Editor Tore Rem

ISBN: 978 0 141 19758 6

THE MASTER BUILDER
AND OTHER PLAYS

Henrik Ibsen

'Castles in the air – they're so easy to retreat into. And easy to
build, too – especially for those master builders with – with dizzy
consciences'

Ibsen's last four plays – *The Master Builder, Little Eyolf, John
Gabriel Borkman* and *When We Dead Awaken* – were sensational
bestsellers, performed in theatres across Europe. These final works,
exploring sexuality and death, the conflict between generations,
the drive for creativity and the fraility of the body, cemented Ibsen's
dramatic reputation, and continue to fuel debate today on whether
they celebrate freedom and love or are instead savagely ironic
studies of our shared human flaws. These new translations, the
first to be based on the latest critical edition of Ibsen's works, offer
the best versions available in English.

.Translated by Barbara Haveland and Anne-Marie Stanton-Ife
Introduced by Toril Moi
General Editor Tore Rem

ISBN: 978 0 141 19459 2

FEAR AND TREMBLING

Søren Kierkegaard

'He who loved himself became great in himself, and he who loved
others became great through his devotion, but he who loved God
became greater than all'

In *Fear and Trembling* Kierkegaard, writing under the pseudonym
Johannes de silentio, expounds his personal view of religion
through a discussion of the scene in Genesis in which Abraham
prepares to sacrifice his son at God's command. Believing Abraham's unreserved obedience to be the essential leap of faith needed
to make a full commitment to his religion. Kierkegaard himself
made great sacrifices in order to dedicate his life entirely to his
philosophy and to God. The conviction shown in this religious
polemic – that a man can have an exceptional mission in his life
– informed all Kierkegaard's later writings, and was also hugely
influential for both Protestant theology and the existentialist
movement.

Translated with an Introduction by Alastair Hannay

ISBN: 978 0 14 044 449 0

THE COMPLETE ENGLISH POEMS

John Donne

'The heavens rejoice in motion, why should I Abjure my so much
loved variety?'

No poet has been more wilfully contradictory than John Donne,
whose works forge unforgettable connections between extremes
of passion and mental energy. From satire to tender elegy, from
sacred devotion to lust, he conveys an astonishing range of emotions and poetic moods. Constant in his work, however, is an
intensity of feeling and expression and complexity of argument
that is as evident in religious meditations such as 'Good Friday
1613. Riding Westward' as it is in secular love poems such as 'The
Sun Rising' or 'The Flea'. 'The intricacy and subtlety of his imagination are the length and depth of the furrow made by his passion,'
wrote Yeats, pinpointing the unique genius of a poet who combined
ardour and intellect in equal measure.

Edited by A. J. Smith

ISBN: 978 0 14 042 209 2

A ROOM OF ONE'S OWN /
THREE GUINEAS

Virginia Woolf

'A woman must have money and a room of her own if she is to
write fiction'

Ranging from the silent fate of Shakespeare's gifted (imaginary)
sister to Jane Austen, Charlotte Brontë and the effects of poverty
and sexual constraint on female creativity, *A Room of One's Own*,
based on a lecture given at Girton College, Cambridge, is one of
the great feminist polemics. Published almost a decade later, *Three
Guineas* breaks new ground in its discussion of men, militarism
and women's attitudes towards war. These two pieces reveal
Virginia Woolf's fiery spirit, sophisticated wit and genius as an
essayist.

Edited with an Introduction and Notes by Michèle Barrett

ISBN: 978 0 24 137 197 8

THE PICTURE OF DORIAN GRAY

Oscar Wilde

'The horror, whatever it was, had not yet entirely spoiled that
marvellous beauty'

Enthralled by his own exquisite portrait, Dorian Gray exchanges
his soul for eternal youth and beauty. Influenced by his friend
Lord Henry Wotton, he is drawn into a corrupt double life, indulg-
ing his desires in secret while remaining a gentleman in the eyes
of polite society. Only his portrait bears the traces of his decadence.
The Picture of Dorian Gray was a *succès de scandale*. Early readers were shocked by its hints at unspeakable sins, and the book
was later used as evidence against Wilde at his trial at the Old
Bailey in 1895.

Edited with an introduction and notes by Robert Mighall

ISBN: 978 0 14 143 957 0